MANUAL
OF
HOUSING LAW

AUSTRALIA
The Law Book Company
Brisbane ● Sydney ● Melbourne ● Perth

CANADA
Carswell
Ottawa ● Toronto ● Calgary ● Montreal ● Vancouver

Agents:
Steimatzky's Agency Ltd., Tel Aviv;
N.M. Tripathi (Private) Ltd., Bombay;
Eastern Law House (Private) Ltd., Calcutta;
M.P.P. House, Bangalore;
Universal Book Traders, Delhi;
Aditya Books, Delhi;
MacMillan Shuppan KK, Tokyo;
Pakistan Law House, Karachi, Lahore

Manual

of

Housing Law

By

ANDREW ARDEN Q.C.
and
CAROLINE HUNTER
Barrister, Senior Lecturer in Law,
Sheffield Polytechnic

Fifth Edition

London
Sweet & Maxwell
1992

First Edition 1978 (HOUSING: Security and Rent Control)
Second Edition 1983
Reprinted 1983
Reprinted 1984
Third Edition 1986
Reprinted 1987
Reprinted 1988
Fourth Edition 1989
Fifth Edition 1992

Published in 1992 by
Sweet & Maxwell Limited
183 Marsh Wall, London E14

British Library Cataloguing in Publication Data

A catalogue record
for this book is
available from
The British Library

ISBN 0–421–461004

Preface

My continuing work on the practitioners' works, *Encyclopedia of Housing Law and Practice* and *Housing Law Reports*, with Caroline Hunter, and on the textbook, *Housing Law*, with Professor Martin Partington and Caroline Hunter, means that I owe a continuing debt to both of them for the material reflected in this book.

Andrew Arden
July 1992

Introduction

This is the fifth edition of the Manual (including the first edition under the title Housing: Security and Rent Control) and I am pleased to be joined as co-author by Caroline Hunter with whom I have worked closely over a number of years, including on the *Encyclopaedia of Housing Law and Practice* and the *Housing Law Reports*: she is also working with myself and Professor Martin Partington on the forthcoming, second edition of our textbook, *Housing Law*. The main purpose of this work is - of course - to update the fourth edition, although the only substantive (*cf.* below, Chap. 13) legislative changes that have occurred since its publication have been those brought about by the Local Government and Housing Act 1989 (see, in particular, below Chap. 12), and case-law has wrought somewhat fewer changes than usual.

Instead, discharging the undertaking in the Introduction to the last edition, the opportunity has been taken to restructure the book to reflect more closely what has emerged as the current range of issues as they confront pracititioners and advisers, *i.e.* with the emphasis no longer on the Rent Acts, followed by the (two) Housing Acts (secure tenancies under the 1985 Act and assured tenancies under that of 1988), but on secure, assured and protected tenancies in that order. The range of designations is now so wide that, cumbersome though it may be to the eye and ear, all references to these three principal classes of security are spelled out in full, as Housing Act secure, Housing Act asseured and Rent Act protected or statutory, for both the risk and consequences of error are considerable. In addition, individual paragraph headings have been inserted, for ease of reference and clarity of direction.

The term "housing law" is one which has seen much revision over the last few years. Until some years ago, the term was used exclusively in relation to public housing law, *i.e.* that law contained in statutes, as judicially considered, which was specifically called housing law and affected the housing responsibilities of local authorities. Gradually, the term came to apply also to the quasi-public sector, housing associations and the like. Private sector housing was considered part of the law of landlord and tenant. Other subjects which affected housing included public (now commonly called environmental) health law, planning law, compulsory purchase, domestic legislation, contract, tort and judicial review of administrative action, all considered under their own heads.

Today, the term "housing law" is most commonly used to cover all that law affecting the way in which people occupy property residentially. At its broadest it includes conveyancing, house construction, and all of the subjects mentioned in the last paragraph. Clearly, a book of this size cannot even outline all the topics which could and do qualify in relation to or as housing. It follows that this Manual is selective in approach. Some subjects have gone entire by-the-board; conveyancing and house construction, planning law, most compulsory purchase, and mobile homes are not even touched upon. Other subjects are treated briefly, *e.g.*, owner-occupation (including the right to buy) and domestic breakdown will almost invariably require an occupier to secure the assistance of a solicitor, and these are topics conventionally covered extensively in law courses.

Financial assistance, by way of housing benefit, is merely mentioned because the provisions and details change so frequently that anything written here would be out-of-date by the time of publication and there are other, annual publications easily available and which (as this work) seek to address all those with an interest, not merely lawyers.

The principal approach of this Manual, however, remains the same as in earlier editions, and is to identify the principal housing rights of tenants and other occupiers, above all those whose access to the most qualified legal advice may be restricted. The underlying thesis is that in almost every case it will be impossible to determine what are the respective rights and liabilities of a party to a housing arrangement without first determining what is the status of the occupier in law. The first chapter is the child of the common law. Only once common law status has been determined is it possible to turn to the work of Parliament, and consider the many different categories of occupier which now exist by statute. The reader is accordingly urged, then, to bear with the first chapter, devoid as it may be of substantive rights and duties, for without it the remainder of the book will be of little practical value at all.

The law is stated as at May 31, 1992. The relatively brief period until actual publication reflects the fact that we have been able to produce this book with the assistance of the advanced information and communications technology provided by our publishers, to whom we express our gratitude.

Andrew Arden Q.C.,
Gray's Inn Chambers,
Gray's Inn.   May 1992

Table of Contents

Table of Cases

[All references are to paragraph numbers]

Table of Statutes

Table of Statutory Instruments

Rules of the Supreme Court

1 The Classes of Occupation

Occupation at Common Law.   At common law, there are only four   1.01
ways in which a person can come to use premises as a residence:
1. *Owner-occupation;*
2. *Trespass;*
3. *Licence;* and
4. *Tenancy.*
In addition, however, there are combinations of circumstances, some
of which must also be considered:
5. *Tied accommodation;*
6. *Sub-tenants;*
7. *Joint tenants;*
8. *Tenants of mortgagors;*
9. *Assignees;* and
10. *Change of landlord.*

Common Law and Statutory Protection.   These are, however, only   1.02
the classes of occupation known to common law without the
intervention of Parliament. They have less contemporary relevance than
do the classes of *protection,* afforded by statute, described in the
following chapters. None the less, the classes of protection are based on
the common law classes of occupation, and it is impossible to understand the former without an understanding of the latter. There is, further,
a number of arrangements which do not fit comfortably or easily within
either the common law classes of occupation, or the specific classes of
protection considered in the following chapters. For example, a relatively novel concept is that of equity-sharing or "shared ownership," where
a person pays "rent" which is partly for use and occupation, and partly
towards purchase. There are also "co-ownership" schemes, where
member-tenants pay rent, but have an interest in the capital value of,
usually, a block of flats. The complexity of such schemes, and the
relatively few people affected, put the details of them beyond the scope
of this book.

1. *Owner-Occupation*

1.03   **Unmortgaged Freehold.** A person who owns the freehold of the house in which he lives, untrammelled by any mortgage, is, of course, the principal "model" for owner-occupation. Such a person has the fullest rights of occupation and protection of all. The right to occupy the house can only be interfered with in limited circumstances. For example, if a local authority or some other public body should purchase the house compulsorily, perhaps for some new development; or else, if the property falls into considerable disrepair, the local authority might put a closing order or demolition order on the house, as a result of which it will become illegal to live in it. Another way in which such an owner-occupier might lose the right of occupation is if he goes into bankruptcy and the trustee in bankruptcy forces the sale of his home. Some of these incidents are outside the scope of this book: closing and demolition orders, and clearance by a local authority, are dealt with in Chapter 12. We shall consider one further way in which a freehold owner might come to lose the right to occupy his home, and that is as a result of a court order made in the course of a domestic break-up. This is dealt with in Chapter 9.

1.04   **Mortgaged Freehold.** Many people who have a freehold interest in their homes, however, do so under mortgage. A mortgage is a loan against the security of property, *i.e.* a house or a flat. The money is usually borrowed in order to buy the property, although sometimes it may be needed for carrying out repairs or improvements. Sometimes people raise money by way of mortgage simply because they are in other financial difficulties. This should only be done as a last resort. If a person falls into arrears with his mortgage repayments, eviction may follow: see Chapter 2.

1.05   **Long Leaseholders.** The term "owner-occupier" is also used, artificially, to describe those who do not have a freehold interest in their homes, but who have a long leasehold interest. A freehold interest is one which is unlimited in time: there is no "superior" interest or landlord who can claim the property in the future. A leasehold interest is one where there is a superior interest, a landlord to whom what is usually a small, annual ground rent is paid and who, in theory at least, is entitled to reclaim the property at the end of the lease. The term "owner-occupier" is usually only applied to a leaseholder with a long lease, *i.e.* one for more than 21 years. In practice, on the termination of the lease, most such occupiers have rights of occupation similar to those enjoyed by other tenants and, in some circumstances, a leasehold occupier may have the yet greater protection afforded by a right to compel the landlord to sell him the freehold. These rights will also be considered in Chapter 2.

Mortgaged Leasehold. Leasehold interests may be held under mortgage, although it will usually not be possible to obtain a mortgage on a leasehold property unless there is at least a 30-year period to run on the lease. This is because mortgage companies want to have security for their loan, and must calculate what they can recover by resale of the property if the occupier falls into arrears on the mortgage at any given point in time. If the occupier falls into arrears in the last few years, the mortgage company will not have much to resell: but, then, there will not be much of a debt left on the property. If the occupier falls into arrears soon after the mortgage is granted, there will be time enough on the lease for the mortgage company to recoup its loan.   1.06

Leasehold by Assignment. Many people do not purchase a leasehold interest from the freeholder. They take it instead from an existing leaseholder, commonly the existing occupier who is selling his interest. During the course of such a transaction, the freeholder will have little or nothing to do with the arrangements, save perhaps to give his consent to them. Where a would-be occupier under leasehold purchases from an outgoing leaseholder, the transaction is called an assignment, but it is in all other respects much like a straightforward purchase. It does not matter how much time there is to run on the lease: the incoming occupier steps into the shoes of the outgoing occupier. It is the length of the interest itself, *i.e.* the lease, not the length of occupation left under it, which will determine the quality of the class of occupation.   1.07

2. *Trespass*

Absolute Trespass. From those with the greatest rights of occupation, to those with the least. A trespasser is one who occupies premises without any permission at all to do so. Such permission may be given by anyone in a position to grant the authority. For example, an owner may obviously give permission to occupy property, but so may his agent, or a director of a company which owns property, or even someone who is himself no more than a tenant. A tenant is in a position to give permission because so long as his tenancy lasts, it is the tenant, rather than the landlord or the owner, who has possession of the premises. It follows, therefore, that an owner or a landlord could not give someone else permission to occupy premises if he has already let them to a tenant.   1.08

1.09   Squatting. Because of the housing shortages which exist in most areas
        of the country, trespass is far from uncommon. Many are forced to
        trespass simply in order to find somewhere to live. This is the phenom-
        enon, by no means recent, of squatting. In fact, the squatting movement
        has created so much pressure upon public authorities, and others who
        are publicly accountable for the use of their properties, that many local
        authorities and housing associations now consent to properties being
        "squatted" for some specific time, or else until they are ready to be
        redeveloped.

1.10   Legal and Illegal Squatting. There is little *popular* distinction between
        those who squat without permission, and those who use short-life
        property with permission. But there is considerable difference in law:
        those without permission are trespassers, those who have permission are
        "licensees" (*G.L.C.* v. *Jenkins*, 1975). The term "squatter" is not
        therefore one which it is appropriate to use in discussion of housing law,
        although in one case in which it was used (*McPhail* v. *Persons
        Unknown*, 1973) the description given was consistent with trespass,
        rather than licence. This does not mean that all squatters are trespassers,
        but simply that if the term is to be used in law, it must be confined to
        those who squat without permission. As far as possible, the term
        "squatter" will not be used further in this book.

1.11   Criminal Law. Because of the growth of this sort of trespass,
        legislation was introduced to deal with the situation. This is contained
        in the Criminal Law Act 1977 and will be considered further in Chapter
        7.

3. *Licence*

1.12   Permission. While the normal arrangement whereby one person rents
        as a home property belonging to another is that of tenancy (1.38-1.62),
        there are a number of arrangements of less formality which are known
        as licences. The term "licence" means "permission," whether used in
        connection with housing, driving a car, or selling alcohol (*Thomas* v.
        Sorrell, 1673). In the housing context, it is used to describe one who is
        not a trespasser (because he has permission to occupy) but who is
        neither an owner-occupier nor a tenant. Were it not for "licences,"
        there would be no term appropriate for such people as family, friends or
        casual guests.

1.13   Family. The most common example of licence is a person living in property which is either owned or rented by a member of the family, *e.g.* a parent. The non-owner, or non-tenant, is in this circumstance in law a licensee. Similarly, a cohabitant is a licensee of his partner, if it is the partner who owns or who is the tenant of the accommodation in which they live. Technically, if one spouse is the owner or tenant of the matrimonial home, the other spouse is only his licensee, but it has been held that, as a matter of practice and as a matter of good taste, it is inappropriate to consider one spouse as the licensee of another (*National Provincial Bank* v. *Ainsworth*, 1965): the special position of both spouses and cohabitants will be considered in the context of break-up of a relationship in Chapter 9.

Friends. Some people are quite obviously no more than licensees of another. Common sense dictates that a friend who comes to stay for a while is not to be considered a tenant, while at the same time he cannot be a trespasser because, of course, he is there by the host's invitation. This position does not change simply because, for example, the guest is invited to stay for several weeks and even agrees to pay some sort of contribution towards the housekeeping expenses, or indeed, an amount of rent, although at this last stage the agreement is beginning to border on the sort of formal arrangement whereby common sense might lead as easily to one answer (friendly arrangement) as to another (tenancy). 1.14

Long-Stay Hotel Occupation. There are other arrangements, however, where it is less immediately obvious whether a person is to be considered a licensee or a tenant. If someone goes to stay in a hotel for a few days, for example, it would not be considered that he had become a tenant of the hotel. But what if he made his home over a number of years in the hotel? There are many who live for considerable periods of time in hotels, (more commonly cheaper, long-stay hotels), who have nowhere else to live and who regard the hotel as a home. In *Luganda* v. *Service Hotels* (1969) the Court of Appeal considered that, none the less, such an occupier was only a licensee and did not become a tenant. 1.15

Hostels. In the same way, the occupier of a hostel is usually considered a mere licensee: *e.g.* a Y.W.C.A. hostel, as in *R.* v. *South Middlesex Rent Tribunal, ex p. Beswick* (1976) or one of the many hostels which exist not primarily to provide housing for people, but principally to help those who have had some sort of difficulty, such as drug addicts, mental patients, ex-prisoners, and only secondarily, in order to assist people to reach the point at which they can manage on their own, provide housing for some period or other: *Trustees of the Alcoholic Recovery Project* v. 1.16

Farrell (1977). The distinction which may be drawn between hostels and houses of bedsitting-rooms is that in the hostel there is normally a resident housekeeper or manager, and the occupier is bound to obey rules and regulations which interfere far more than normal housing management rules do with the occupier's way of life. See for example *Westminster City Council* v. *Clarke* (1992) where a hostel provided accommodation for vulnerable single homeless men.

1.17   **Old Person's Home.** Another example is provided by the case of *Abbeyfield (Harpenden) Society* v. *Woods* (1968). The society ran an old people's home, consisting of single rooms for which the old people paid a weekly rent. The project could only exist satisfactorily so long as each of the occupiers was self-sufficient. Once an elderly person required constant care and attention, it was no longer possible for him to go on living there. There were not the facilities for the provision of such assistance and, clearly, in a house containing nothing but the elderly, the consequences could be serious. It was held that the occupier was a lodger, *i.e.* a licensee, not a tenant.

1.18   **Acts of Kindness.** Acts of kindness or generosity are deemed not to be the acts from which tenancies spring. In *Booker* v. *Palmer* (1942), a city family were provided with accommodation in the country during the war. They later suggested that they had become tenants of the property but the Court of Appeal applied what it termed a ''golden rule'' of interpretation of such matters: that the courts will not impute intention to enter into legal relations (including tenancy), where the spirit of the arrangement is family or friendly.

1.19   **Staying On.** This attitude found some extension in the case of *Marcroft Wagons* v. *Smith* (1951). A woman had lived with her parents in a cottage for 50 years. Her father was the original tenant, and on his death, his wife was entitled by the law then in force to ''succeed'' to the tenancy. However, only one such ''succession'' was then permitted and, on the death of her mother, the daughter faced eviction. She asked for the tenancy to be granted to her but the landlords refused, though they permitted her to remain in occupation while she found somewhere else to live, during which they continued to charge her the same weekly rent as her mother had been paying. It was (with some hesitation) held, in effect, that there had similarly been no intention to create a new contract. The court emphasised that this could only be the result where the would-be tenant was already in occupation of the premises at the time at which the arrangement was made; if an arrangement on those lines was offered to someone not living in the premises, this could still constitute a tenancy.

New Tenancy v. Statutory Protection. The result of this case, and a 1.20
number of cases which followed it, has been that when a tenancy came to an end, but the occupier stayed on for a period of time paying a weekly sum of money, the courts have not necessarily assumed a new tenancy agreement. If the reason why the occupier had gone on paying, and the landlord accepting, rent was because there was a statutory right to remain in occupation, *i.e.* "protection," the courts would assume that what was intended by the payment and acceptance of rent was the exercise of the statutory right to remain, rather than a new contractual tenancy (*Clarke* v. *Grant*, 1950), with whatever statutory consequences the particular legislation has in mind (see Chapters 3-5).

Disputed Right to Remain. Even if there was a dispute between the 1.21
parties as to whether or not the occupier was entitled to remain in occupation, then even if the occupier continued to pay the rent, and the landlord to accept it, the courts might not assume a new tenancy (*Longrigg, Burrough and Trounson* v. *Smith*, 1979). The position today is that while it is true that the *normal* inference to be drawn from payment and acceptance of tent is that there is a tenancy (*Lewis* v. *M.T.C. (Cars)*, 1975; see also *Street* v. *Mountford*, 1986), if there is some *particular* or *peculiar* explanation or "special circumstance" why the landlord is leaving an occupier in his premises, and on that account accepting money, other than an *agreement* to enter into a new contract, the courts are likely to uphold a finding that there is no tenancy, and consequently only a licence. The operative word is "agreement." When a person stays on after the termination of a tenancy without a new tenancy, "rent" is properly called "mesne profits," and landlords frequently declare that money will only be accepted as such, although such a declaration is not decisive as to whether or not a new tenancy has been created. The fact that the payment is called "rent" will also not be decisive (*Westminster City Council* v. *Basson*, 1990).

Bedsitting Rooms. Returning to cases where there has been no prior 1.22
tenancy, in *Marchant* v. *Charters* (1977), there was a house of bedsitting-rooms: each of the occupiers had cooking facilities and equipment in his own room, the rooms were furnished and the occupiers lived wholly separate lives, that is to say there were no communal facilities. The house was expressed to be let, and was actually let, "to single men only," and there was a resident housekeeper with whom an

arrangement could be made for the provision of evening meals, although this was not an obligatory part of the accommodation arrangement and was not something agreed to by the occupier in question. None of these circumstances would individually cause the arrangement to be considered only a licence. Indeed, many would have thought that even taken together there was nothing to distinguish the arrangement from a conventional bedsitting-room letting; such lettings have always been considered to constitute tenancies, rather than licences, and there is nothing exceptionable in the idea of a tenancy of a single room (*A.G. Securities* v. *Vaughan*, 1988). None the less, it was held that, in the individual circumstances of the case, the occupier was no more than a licensee.

1.23   **The End Of "Intention".** *At the time*, it was said that this was because the parties to the agreement would not have *intended* a tenancy, with all the formal consequences as to grant of separate possession (below) that this implied. The intention in question was not that of one or other of the parties, but the intention that the law would impute to the parties on the basis of the arrangement as a whole. But this "intention" test has been roundly rejected by the House of Lords in the important decision of *Street* v. *Mountford*, 1986, in which the House of Lords declared a return to a more traditional approach to the distinction between tenancy and licence, described as lying "in the grant of land" - including housing - "for a term at a rent with exclusive possession."

1.24   **Lodger or Tenant? Attendance or Services.** "In the case of residential accommodation there is no difficulty in deciding whether the grant confers exclusive possession. An occupier of residential accommodation at a rent for a term is either a lodger or a tenant. The occupier is a lodger if the landlord provides attendance or services which require the landlord or his servants to exercise unrestricted access to and use of the premises. A lodger is entitled to live in the premises but cannot call the place his own..." Such attendances or services (see also 5.43-5.44, below) might include daily room-cleaning, emptying of rubbish, changing sheets periodically, the provision of meals (see also 5.46) or other "housekeeping-type" activities.

1.25   **A Term, A Rent, Exclusive Possession.** "If on the other hand residential accommodation is granted for a term at a rent with exclusive possession, the landlord providing neither attendance nor services, the grant is a tenancy; any express reservation to the landlord of limited rights to enter and view the state of the premises and to repair and maintain the premises only serves to emphasise the fact that the grantee is entitled to exclusive possession and is a tenant... There can be no tenancy unless the occupier enjoys exclusive possession; but an occupier who enjoys exclusive possession is not necessarily a tenant. He may be owner in fee simple, a trespasser, a mortgagee in possession, an object of charity or a service occupier. To constitute a tenancy the occupier must be granted exclusive possession for a fixed or periodic term certain in consideration of a premium or periodical payments. The grant may be express, or may be inferred where the owner accepts weekly or other periodical payments from the occupier.''

Review of Earlier Decisions. The House of Lords analysed a number   1.26
of the cases in which licence had been upheld, notwithstanding the grant of exclusive possession, describing *Booker* v. *Palmer* (above) as a case only concerned with intention to create legal relations, and *Marcroft Wagons Ltd.* v. *Smith* (above) as of similar quality. *Abbeyfield (Harpenden) Society* v. *Woods* and *Marchant* v. *Charters* (above) were considered cases of ''lodging.'' ''...In order to ascertain the nature and quality of the occupancy and to see whether the occupier has or has not a stake in the room or only permission for himself personally to occupy, the court must decide whether upon its true construction the agreement confers on the occupier exclusive possession. If exclusive possession at a rent for a term does not constitute a tenancy then the distinction between a contractual tenancy and a contractual licence of land becomes wholly unidentifiable...''

The Three Hallmarks of Tenancy. The House of Lords considered the   1.27
three hallmarks of tenancy to be exclusive occupation of residential accommodation, payment and term (*i.e.* periods or length of tenancy): ''Unless these three hallmarks are decisive, it really becomes impossible to distinguish a contractual tenancy from a contractual licence save by the professed intention of the parties or by the judge awarding marks for drafting ... The only intention which is relevant is the intention demonstrated by the agreement to grant exclusive possession for a term at a rent. Sometimes it may be difficult to discover whether, on the true construction of an agreement, exclusive possession is conferred. Sometimes it may appear from the surrounding circumstances that there was no intention to create legal relationships. Sometimes it may appear from the surrounding circumstances that the right to exclusive possession is referable to a legal relationship other than a tenancy. Legal relationships to which the grant of exclusive possession might be referable and which would or might negate the grant of an estate or

interest in the land include occupancy under a contract for the sale of the land, occupancy pursuant to a contract of employment or occupancy referable to the holding of an office. But where as in the present case the only circumstances are that residential accommodation is offered and accepted with exclusive possession for a term at a rent, the result is a tenancy ..."

1.28   **A Fork By Any Other Name.** The question is determined not by what name the parties put on the agreement, but by what the agreement is considered to amount to in law: "It does not necessarily follow that a document described as a licence is, merely on that account, to be regarded as amounting only to a licence in law. The whole of the document must be looked at and if, after it has been examined, the right conclusion appears to be that, whatever label has been attached to it, it in fact conferred and imposed on the grantee in substance the rights and obligation of a landlord, then it must be given the appropriate effect, that is to say, it must be treated as a tenancy agreement as distinct from a mere licence ... The important statement of principle is that the relationship is determined by the law, and not by the label the parties choose to put on it ... It is simply a matter of ascertaining the true relationship of the parties ..." (Jenkins, L.J., *Addiscombe Garden Estates* v. *Crabbe*, 1958). Or, as it was put graphically in *Street*: "The manufacture of a five-pronged implement for manual digging results in a fork even if the manufacturer, unfamiliar with the English language, insists that he intended to make and has made a spade."

1.29   **Paying Arrangement.** In every case, one should ask whether the arrangement is the normal arrangement by which one person comes to occupy premises belonging to another for use as a home, customarily paying rent in money for the right. If it is, then this is likely to be a tenancy, however the parties have described it and whatever they may have said that their intentions were ("the courts must pay attention to the facts and surrounding circumstances and to what people do as well as to what people say" - *A.G. Securities* v. *Vaughan*, 1988). Once the occupier is paying for the accommodation, then there must be some overriding reason, such as those illustrated or referred to above or those considered below, which reduces the occupation to that of licence. Strictly, it is not even necessary to pay rent in order to establish that there is a tenancy (see most recently *Ashburn Anstalt* v. *Arnold*, 1989), but the courts tend to look sceptically in this day and age at any arrangement purporting to be tenancy under which no rent is paid (*Heslop* v. *Burns*, 1974) and will only be prepared to do so if they can find some other consideration.

Evasion of Protection. In addition to these questions, however, a per- 1.30
son will only be a licensee if the rights which he has been given are not
enough in law to amount to tenancy (*A. G. Securities* v. *Vaughan,* 1988).
The necessary elements of tenancy are considered below (1.54-1.62) and
include the grant to the occupier of "exclusive possession" of the
premises (1.58-1.62). One device by which landlords seek to avoid the
impact of Rent Act (and Housing Act) protection is the agreement which
has come to be known as the "non-exclusive occupation agreement."
This, too, is considered further below (1.89-1.93). Another device is
"rental purchase," whereby a person is allowed into occupation as a
licensee, paying money towards purchase, but not enjoying the status of
owner until the whole of the purchase price has been paid. These rental
purchases are also considered further, below (7.32-7.33). There is high
authority (*A. G. Securities* v. *Vaughan,* 1988, H.L.) for the proposition
that the courts should lean against "pretences" designed to defeat
statutory protection.

Trespassers, Licensees and Eviction. A person who is a trespasser 1.31
but who is subsequently given permission, not amounting to tenancy, to
remain on the premises becomes a licensee. A person whose licence is
brought to an end becomes, technically, a trespasser. However, most of
the recent laws relating to trespass do not affect those who entered as
licensees but subsequently became trespassers. Some licensees whose
licences began before the commencement of Part I, Housing Act 1988
(January 15, 1989) are entitled to refer their contracts to the Rent
Tribunal which has power to register a reasonable rent for the premises,
and which means that a court, and in the case of some now
long-standing licences, the Tribunal, has power to allow more time to
leave premises occupied under licence. This is considered in greater
detail in Chapter 6.

Eviction of Licensees. Licensees may be termed "bare licensees," or 1.32
may be termed "contractual licensees." One who is, by arrangement,
paying a fixed sum of money for the right of occupation will be a
contractual licensee. A friend, member of the family or cohabitant, even
although he may be paying some amount by way of contribution to
household expenses, will normally be considered a bare licensee. The
distinction may be relevant when the question of bringing a licence to
an end arises. So long as the licence remains in existence, the licensee
not only commits no offence by remaining on the premises but cannot

be turned off them without the person who does so himself committing an offence: see Chapter 7. Once the licence comes to an end, however, the person who is immediately entitled to possession of the premises in question, which may be the owner of the premises, or may be a landlord, or may even be only a tenant of the premises, can reclaim possession from the former licensee, save in the case of a licence which attracts security of tenure under the Housing Act 1985 (3.08). In most circumstances, it is necessary to obtain a court order before evicting the former licensee, and an offence is committed if this is not done; in other circumstances, it may not be necessary to obtain a court order: see Chapters 7 and 8. But unless the licence has been duly brought to an end, the person who seeks possession is not entitled to reclaim it, with or without court proceedings.

1.33 **Fixed Term Licences.** There are a few arrangements which may be described as "fixed-term" licences. That is to say, the period for which the right of occupation has been granted is fixed in advance. These arrangements require no notice to be given to bring them to an end because, in effect, the notice has been given at the outset of the arrangement. Most licences, however, are not for a fixed period but exist from week to week, even from day to day, or perhaps as much as from month to month. In such cases, it is necessary to give notice in order to bring the arrangement to an end. It may be that some agreement about the length or form of notice has been reached while arranging the licence in the first place, *e.g.* one month's notice in writing. This is not a necessary element of a licence. If there is such an agreement, it would indicate that the licence was a contractual, not a bare licence. If there is such an agreement in force, then the licence cannot be determined except in accordance with it, for the law will not support a breach of contract (*Winter Garden Theatre (London)* v. *Millenium Productions*, 1947).

1.34 **Reasonable Notice.** Whether or not there is such agreement, however, the law additionally implies into every licence, whether bare or contractual, a term that it will not be brought to an end without "reasonable notice" being given. This means that a licence agreement which contractually provided for, *e.g.* one day's notice, would not be brought to an end in one day, unless the law considered one day a reasonable time (*Minister of Health* v. *Belotti*, 1944). In the case of a periodic licence, the law now requires written notice of a minimum period of four weeks, and which contains specified information, *other than* in the case of what is called an "excluded licence" (for the definition of which, see 8.10). The information is the same as for a notice to quit for tenancies (see 1.50).

Reasonable Time. What is a reasonable time is a question of fact. It 1.35
will depend upon many circumstances: how long the licensee has been
in occupation, how much furniture or property he has in the premises,
size of family, what alternative arrangements have been or could be
made, even the time of day or night could affect it. In addition, behaviour may affect what the law views as a reasonable time for determination of a licence. A violent licensee will not be given much time at all,
e.g. a violent man who is cohabiting with the woman who is the tenant
or owner-occupier cannot expect a matter of weeks in which to leave,
even if he has lived in the property for years.

Alternative Requirements. The rule may be shortly stated in this way: 1.36
a licensee is entitled to a reasonable period of notice *or* a contractually
agreed period of notice, or in the case of a periodic licence which is not
an "excluded licence" (8.10) four weeks' notice, whichever is the
longest. In most cases (other than excluded licences), court proceedings
for eviction are required: see Chapter 8.

Alternative Procedures.   Court proceedings may be brought by or- 1.37
dinary possession action, or by a special, speedy form of procedure
originally intended for trespassers, but also applicable to former
licensees. This is a short application to the court known as Order 24 in
the county court, and Order 113 in the High Court. If these speedy
proceedings are used, then the person seeking to evict the former
licensee must establish that the licence came to an end *before* the
application was issued at the court (*G.L.C.* v. *Jenkins*, 1975). If normal
proceedings are used, however, it is enough to show that the licence has
expired by the time of the court hearing.

4. *Tenancy*

The Normal Arrangement. This is the normal arrangement by which 1.38
one person comes to occupy premises which are owned by another. It
is, of course, customarily granted in exchange for a monetary payment,
rent. It has been said (1.29) that this is not an essential element of
tenancy but, except in the context of service tenancy (1.63-1.69), it is so
likely that an arrangement under which no rent is paid will be
considered a mere licence that this point will not be considered further
here.

1.39 Termination of Periodic and Fixed Term Tenancy. There are two common forms of tenancy: periodic tenancies and fixed-term tenancies. A periodic tenancy is one which is granted to run from period to period, *e.g.* week to week or month to month. The normal way it can be brought to an end is by service of a valid notice to quit. A fixed-term tenancy is one which is granted for a specific period of time, *e.g.* three months, six months, or a year, and this normally comes to an end simply because the time runs out. Neither sort of tenancy needs to be in writing, except for fixed-term tenancies in excess of three years (Law of Property Act 1925, s.53).

1.40 Identity of Landlord. A landlord under a *weekly* tenancy (but no other) is obliged to provide a rent book or similar document, and commits a criminal offence if he does not do so (Landlord and Tenant Act 1985, ss.4, 7). Under that Act, any tenant can ask, in writing, the person who last received rent under the tenancy for the full name and address of the landlord. If the person to whom the demand is made fails to reply, also in writing, within 21 days, he commits an offence. This may be important information if, for example, the tenant wants to commence proceedings against an absentee landlord and cannot do so without first establishing his identity. Both of these offences should be reported to the council's Tenancy Relations Officer: see Chapter 8.

1.41 Surrender. As well as the two ways mentioned above, there are two other common ways of bringing a tenancy to an end. One is by way of surrender. It occurs, commonly, when a tenant wants to leave accommodation before the end of a fixed term. Strictly, a surrender happens by drawing up a formal declaration of surrender. However, it can also happen by operation of law, if the tenant performs some unequivocal act of surrender, such as returning the keys to the landlord, or removing from the premises all signs of occupation, including furniture, belongings and any family or friends who were living with him, and the landlord accepts these acts as acts of surrender. The landlord is not obliged to do so and can continue to consider the tenant liable for rent and other responsibilities in the premises. Abandonment of occupation may be considered a surrender (*R.* v. *London Borough of Croydon, ex p. Toth*, 1988). There can even be surrender, by clear agreement, without quitting occupation (*Dibbs* v. *Campbell*, 1988).

1.42 Forfeiture. The other common way of bringing a tenancy to an end, and one which is also normally only used in connection with fixed-term tenancies, is forfeiture. In order for there to be a forfeiture, there must be a provision in the agreement that forfeiture can occur. Commonly, forfeiture is something which the landlord can claim to have occurred automatically once rent has been in arrears for a stated period of time, *e.g.* 14 days. It can also be a part of an agreement that forfeiture will occur if some other breach of the tenancy takes place. When there is a forfeiture in this way, the landlord claims to "re-enter" the premises, but cannot in practice do this because of the rules governing eviction of tenants. A court has power to order "relief" from forfeiture, if the breach of the tenancy has been remedied, *e.g.* arrears of rent have been paid off.

Relief from Forfeiture. All forfeitures of residential premises in which 1.43 anyone is living must be by way of court proceedings (Protection from Eviction Act 1977). It is normally in the course of these proceedings that relief is sought. Where the forfeiture is for a reason *other* than arrears of rent, a preliminary notice must be served, identifying the breach, calling for remedy (if the breach is remediable), and demanding compensation (where applicable) (Law of Property Act 1925, s.146). There will be no entitlement to forfeit if the breach has been *waived*, *e.g.* waiver of illegal sub-letting (1.78). The courts are chary of laying down general principles governing relief (*Hyman* v. *Rose*, 1912), although remedying the breach will usually be necessary, and will invariably be so if the breach is non-payment of rent (*Barton, Thompson & Co.* v. *Stapling Machines Co.*, 1966), though time will be allowed in which to do this. Relief may be granted in the High Court, if that is where the proceedings (which will be proceedings for possession) are brought, but may also be granted in the county court. There can be no relief from forfeiture for breach of a covenant not to use premises for an immoral purpose (*British Petroleum Pension Trust Ltd.* v. *Behrendt*, 1986). It is thought that relief from forfeiture is not available to a Housing Act assured tenant (4.25).

Arrears and Automatic Relief. Where proceedings are brought in the 1.44 county court, and the breach is non-payment of rent, there is *automatic* relief if all the arrears and the costs of the action are paid into court at least five days before the hearing; otherwise, the order for possession must give at least four weeks, in which case again there will be relief if all the rent and costs are paid into court; these provisions do not apply if the forfeiture is for, or also for, any other breach (County Courts Act 1984, ss.138-140). Relief for non-payment of rent in the High Court is now governed by Supreme Court Act 1981, s.38. There is additional power to apply for relief from a section 146 notice concerned with internal decorative repairs (Law of Property Act 1925, s.147). In the case of a lease of at least seven years, with at least three years left to run, the Leasehold Property (Repairs) Act 1938 prevents forfeiture without the prior leave of the court (11.58). Relief may be granted in relation to part only of the premises the subject of the lease (*G.M.S. Syndicate* v. *Elliott (Gary) Ltd.*, 1982). The effect of relief is to reinstate the lease as if there had been no forfeiture.

1.45   **Notice to Quit and Periodic Tenancies.** Forfeiture is not commonly used in connection with periodic tenancies because of the comparative ease with which these can be determined by notice to quit. Notice to quit a tenancy is a formal and technical document, to which old common law rules apply, as well as modern regulations introduced by legislation. Notice to quit can be given by either landlord or tenant, although it is uncommon for a tenant to give notice to quit with sufficient degree of accuracy for it to qualify as such. An invalid notice to quit may be treated as valid by the party who receives it, at least insofar as the technicalities of the common law are concerned, and a landlord who receives an invalid notice from the tenant may treat this as a surrender. If the tenant subsequently changes his mind about departing, whether after notice to quit or surrender, the landlord will still have to take court proceedings to evict him and might not be able to do so (5.81).

1.46   **Requirements of Notice to Quit.** All notices to quit residential tenancies, *other than* "excluded tenancies" which began on or after the commencement of Part I, Housing Act 1988 (January 15, 1989) must be in writing, must be of a minimum length of four weeks (Protection from Eviction Act 1977, s.5) and must expire on either the last day of the first day of a period of the tenancy. The meaning of "excluded tenancy" is considered in Chapter 8 (8.09). The final condition - expiry on last or first day of tenancy - is derived from the common law, as is the provision that the notice must also be of at least one full period's length of tenancy, so that a four-week notice to quit a monthly tenancy would be invalid, as a month is longer than four weeks. However, only six months' notice is required to terminate a yearly periodic tenancy. The four weeks include day of service or day of expiry (*Schnabel* v. *Allard*, 1967).

1.47   **Saving Clauses.** A notice to quit which is of insufficient length will not become valid at a later, correct time, but will be wholly invalid. Because of this need for accuracy, many notices to quit, especially those from landlords to tenants, add a saving clause, which will read something like this: "... on the 13th day of December 1992 or at the end of the period of your tenancy expiring next four weeks after service of this notice upon you." Such a saving clause is valid and if December 13, 1992 was neither the first nor the last day of a period of the tenancy, the notice to quit would take effect on the next of those two possible days, four weeks after service. The rent day is normally the first day of the tenancy, in the absence of evidence that it is another day.

Service of Notice to Quit. Service of a notice to quit has to be personal. Most service is effected by post, although some service is carried out by leaving it at the premises. It is not validly served until the tenant himself receives it, or it is left with a tenant's spouse or some other person who may be treated as the tenant's agent for this purpose, *i.e.* someone left by the tenant in possession or control of the premises (*Harrowby* v. *Snelson*, 1951).

1.48

Contents of Notice to Quit. A notice to quit must identify the premises which are the subject of the tenancy, so that a notice given for the wrong address will be invalid. But minor defects in description, such as specifying a back garden that does not exist, are unlikely to invalidate the notice; and if a notice to quit identifies the wrong address, it may be validated by a covering letter sent to the right one. In one case, a notice to quit *two* rooms was held invalid where the tenant was tenant of only one (*Jankovitch* v. *Petrovitch*, 1977). The notice must be addressed to the tenant, although if only the first name is wrong this will not be enough to invalidate it. It may be enough to specify only one of two or more joint tenants (1.84–1.95) and it is certainly enough to *serve* one only of the joint tenants. The notice must also state that it is given by or on behalf of the landlord, unless it is given by an agent acting in normal course of his business on the landlord's behalf when serving the notice.

1.49

Prescribed Information. In addition, a notice to quit from a landlord to a tenant must contain certain specified information, also in writing. Without this information the notice is invalid. The information is as follows (by virtue of the Notices to Quit etc. (Prescribed Information) Regulations 1988), although it does not have to be in the same form of words and will not be invalid if the different wording from earlier regulations is used (*Beckerman* v. *Durling*, 1981, *Swansea City Council* v. *Hearn*, 1990):

1.50

(*a*) If the tenant or licensee does not leave the dwelling, the landlord or licensor must get an order for possession from the court before the tenant or licensee can lawfully be evicted. The landlord or licensor cannot apply for such an order before the notice to quit or notice to determine has run out.

(*b*) A tenant or licensee who does not know if he has any right to remain in possession after a notice to quit or a notice to determine runs out or is otherwise unsure of his rights, can obtain advice from a solicitor. Help with all or part of the cost of legal advice and assistance may be available under the Legal Aid Scheme. He should also be able to obtain information from a Citizen's Advice Bureau, a Housing Aid Centre, a rent officer or a Rent Tribunal Office.

1.51   **Special Procedures for Housing Act Secure and Assured Tenancies.** Note that the termination of a Housing Act secure (public sector) tenancy (Chapter 3), and of a Housing Act assured tenancy (Chapter 4) are by a special, and different, procedure. Termination is by the court, and only on specified grounds.

1.52   **Tenants and Eviction.** Although at the end of a tenancy a tenant becomes in strict common law a trespasser, this is so untrue in practice as to be deceptive. A tenant who is a Rent Act protected tenant (Chapter 5) becomes a statutory tenant and, in effect, can remain on in the premises indefinitely, or subject only to proof of one of a limited number of sets of circumstances, until a court orders him to leave.

1.53   **Rent Act Restricted and Wholly Unprotected Tenants.** A Rent Act restricted tenant is one who can refer his tenancy to the Rent Tribunal, in respect of rent registration, and who may also be able to secure some temporary relief from eviction, either from a court or from the Tribunal (6.23-6.35). *All* tenants, other than "excluded tenants" (8.09) whose tenancies began on or after the commencement (January 15, 1989) of Part I, Housing Act 1988, are protected from eviction without due process of law, *i.e.* without a court decision which orders them to leave (Protection from Eviction Act 1977, ss.1-3, as amended): see Chapter 8. The position of tenants who are neither Housing Act secure, Housing Act assured, Rent Act protected, nor Rent Act restricted, is considered in Chapter 7.

1.54   **The Four Essential Qualities of Tenancy.** In order to establish, however, that there is a tenancy at all, to which these provisions apply, then it is necessary to establish that what are known as the four essential qualities of tenancy are present. If one or more of them is missing, then the arrangement cannot be tenancy and for this reason will be that of licence (*A.G. Securities* v. *Vaughan*, 1988). The four qualities are:

(i) *Identifiable parties*

A Landlord and A Tenant. There must be a landlord and a tenant. This 1.55
does not mean that the tenant must know the identity of the landlord, for
this is frequently unknown, where, for example, agents have granted the
tenancy on behalf of the landlord. It means that a person cannot be a
tenant either of himself, or of premises or land which have no owner
(*Rye* v. *Rye*, 1962). A person can, however, be a tenant of a company
of which he is a director, or an employee, or even the major shareholder,
and a person can be a tenant of a partnership of which he is one of the
partners. In such a situation, it would be wrong to refer to the tenant
alone as the owner: he is only the owner when taken together with the
other partners. The same applies to trustees or joint owners (*Rye*). A
person can also be a tenant of another who is himself no more than a
tenant in the premises. Such a tenancy is called sub-tenancy and is dealt
with below (1.70-1.83).

(ii) *Identifiable premises*

A Tenancy of Premises. There must be premises of which to consti- 1.56
tute a tenancy. These premises can be as little as a single room, or as
much as hundreds of acres of land. It is not, however, possible to be a
tenant of part only of some premises, *e.g.* a shared room. It is possible
to be a joint tenant with another of premises (1.84-1.95); but if genuinely separate agreements have been independently reached with the
landlord conferring on more than one person (not in themselves a group)
a right to occupy, *e.g.* a room, this cannot be tenancy because there is no
identifiable part of the premises of which to have a tenancy. Even if the
two - or more - individuals occupying were to divide up the room
between themselves, they would still have to have access to the door in
common. In this connection it is important, however, to bear in mind the
questions governing whether arrangements are evasive referred to below
(1.89-1.93).

(iii) *Period of tenancy*

Tenancy and Time. One cannot have a tenancy in respect of which 1.57
there is no period of time involved. For that is exactly what tenancy is:
a slice of time in the exclusive use of the premises belonging to another,
although this will be adequately fulfilled if the length of period is
unknown, but is capable of being brought to an end by one of the parties
(*Ashburn Anstalt* v. *Arnold*, 1989; *Canadian Imperial Bank of Com-*

merce v. *Bello*, 1991). The one exception to this is a form of tenancy known as tenancy at will, but this is rare and, in this day and age, an arrangement which might once have attracted the title of tenancy at will is more likely to be considered a licence (*Heslop* v. *Burns*, 1974). The need to indentify the period of the tenancy does not mean that a tenancy cannot in practice be granted for an indefinite time, for that is normally what happens when a periodic tenancy is granted. In these cases, the period for which the tenancy has been granted is the time of the periodic tenancy, *e.g.* one week, but the tenancy is automatically renewed from week to week until determined by notice to quit.

(iv) *Exclusive possession*

1.58   The Tenant's Use. Exclusive possession is the most important, and on occasion (albeit now only rarely) the hardest to establish of the four essential qualities of tenancy. It is hard to establish because even a licensee can have exclusive *occupation* of premises, and yet be considered no more than licensee, although only in the limited circumstances described above (1.12-1.30). Exclusive *possession* means that the arrangement in fact conveys to the tenant the use to the exclusion of all others of the premises in question.

1.59   Rights of Entry. This exclusive use is not destroyed because the landlord retains some right to visit, for example, to inspect for disrepair, or to collect the rent, nor, for example because under the terms of the tenancy the landlord provides cleaning of the premises and a cleaner has access to the premises to carry out his duties, unless in the latter case the extent of services is such that access has to be unrestricted, *i.e.* not limited to particular times or occasions, in which case the arrangement will be that of lodging (see 1.24). Such functions are visits to the premises, or services performed to or in the premises, but they are not use of them. The question is simply whether, as a result of the arrangement, the premises are effectively being turned over to the tenant for the period of the tenancy (1.55).

1.60   The Control Test. It may be that in the normal management of a hotel or hostel, the landlord reserves the right to shift occupiers from room to room, as the occasion may demand. It is for this reason that the occupier cannot be described as having exclusive possession of the premises, even though he may have exclusive use of whatever room he is occupying for the time being. This is the "control" test: because the landlord controls even the internal use of the premises, the tenant cannot be described as having exclusive possession.

Sham Rights. Difficulties arise because it is at this quality of tenancy 1.61
that landlords direct the most concerted attacks. The reservation of a
right for the landlord himself to use the premises, not merely to visit
them, or else a right to put in some other person to use them, would, if
upheld by the court as a genuine term of the arrangement, effectively
destroy the idea of exclusive possession (*Somma* v. *Hazelhurst*, 1978),
but it is today much more likely that the courts *would* find that the term
was a "sham" or "pretence" and not uphold it (see 1.27-1.30).

Possession Against All. Possession if exclusive is exclusive as against 1.62
the whole world, including the person who granted the tenancy, so that
even a landlord commits a wrong by contravening his tenant's exlusive
possession without permission. Such a wrong is a trespass and is dealt
with below (8.51-8.53).

5. *Tied Accommodation*

Job-Related Accommodation. Many people who live in premises they 1.63
do not own are occupying accommodation which "goes with the job."
Such people are not merely the obvious classes of service occupier or
tenant, such as resident housekeepers, porters, au pairs, live-in help,
caretakers, etc., but also people such as the managers of pubs and many
who work in off-licences, employees of some of the nationalised and
former nationalised industries, which together own considerable housing
stock, *e.g.* the railways, gas, and electricity companies and the coal
board, and even some teachers and social workers are provided with
accommodation by local authorities as an inducement to work in
particular areas. The accommodation is often job-related and the right
to it customarily ends when the job itself is brought to an end.

An Additional Test. The classes of tied accommodation pose partic- 1.64
ular problems in terms of housing law. Clearly, they do not constitute
trespass or owner-occupation, and so must, of definition, be either
tenancy or licence. But there are particular tests which apply in relation
to tied accommodation. These tests exist *in addition* to those which we
have already discussed (1.12-1.62). A person might appear to qualify as
a tenant by application of one of the particular, job-related tests, and yet
lack one of the four essential qualities of tenancy, or else be a licensee
for some other reason, *e.g.* because on taking up new employment in a
strange area, the employer offered to provide some temporary

accommodation as a favour. Unless, however, one of the prior tests applies, then the test which follows will determine whether occupation is by way of tenancy or licence. A service resident who is a licensee is called a "service occupier," and one who is a tenant is called a "service tenant."

1.65   **A Single Arrangement.** In all these circumstances, it is assumed that the employment and the housing arrangements were reached as part of an overall package. It is entirely possible that a tenant subsequently becomes his landlord's employee. The tenancy would not then normally become a service tenancy, any more than it would if someone subsequently rented accommodation from his employer. However, it is *possible* that the landlord who has become the employer will offer a new arrangement which, if accepted, becomes one of licence (*Scrimgeour* v. *Waller*, 1980). In deciding whether the new arrangement is valid, the courts will not take into account the inequality of bargaining power between the parties (*Mathew* v. *Bobbins*, 1980), although they will recognise that a mere statement of intention is not binding, and may have been signed by the occupier because he had little choice (*A.G. Securities* v. *Vaughan*, 1988).

1.66   **The Test of Necessity.** A person living in tied accommodation will be a service occupier if it is necessary for him to live in the premises in question in order to carry out the employment duties (*Smith* v. *Seghill Overseers*, 1875; *Street* v. *Mountford*, 1986), or *possibly* merely if it is a requirement of the contract of employment that he do so, and that requirement is imposed at the least for the better performance of employment duties (*Fox* v. *Dalby*, 1874; *Glasgow Corporation* v. *Johnstone*, 1965), not merely as an arbitrary regulation, or whim, on the part of the employer (*Gray* v. *Holmes*, 1949). The fact that it is merely convenient for the employee to reside in the premises in question is not sufficient to make it for the better performance of his duties (*Ford* v. *Langford*, 1949; *Chapman* v. *Freeman*, 1978). If neither of the factors above applies, then the occupier will normally be a service tenant.

1.67   **Agricultural and Forestry Workers.** Employees who occupy tied accmmodation in agriculture and forestry occupy a peculiar position of privilege. Shortly, given certain qualifications, including length of employment in agriculture or forestry (but not necessarily with the same employer), despite the fact that they would normally qualify as service occupiers, they may come to enjoy full Housing Act 1988 security as if they had Housing Act assured tenancies (Chapter 4), and Rent Act protection as if they had tenancies (Chapter 5).

Tied Accommodation and Rent. The problem which most commonly   1.68
occurs in connection with occupiers of tied accommodation lies in
establishing whether or not they are paying rent for their accommodation. Some will actually be doing so, *i.e.* they will be handing over
a sum of money which will normally be entered as received in a rent
book. This is likely to be the case where the nationalised industries are
involved. Others may have an agreement as to how much rent they are
paying for their accommodation, but this may be deducted from their
wages at source. They will be treated as paying rent if the rent, though
deducted at source, is quantified (*Montagu* v. *Browning*, 1954). Yet
others may not have any agreed quantification of rent, but receive lower
wages than they would normally get for the job in question on account
of the provision of accommodation. Whether rent is actually being paid
or not should not affect whether they are considered tenants or licensees,
contrary to the normal presumption that one who pays no rent is not a
tenant (*Heslop* v. *Burns*, 1974).

Tied Accommodation and Termination. A service licence which is   1.69
expressly terminable on the cessation of employment comes to an end
without any requirement of notice (*Ivory* v. *Palmer*, 1975). Notice in
accordance with the Protection from Eviction Act 1977 (1.34) is not,
therefore, required to terminate such a licence (*Norris* v. *Checksfield*,
1991).

6. *Sub-Tenants*

Mesne Tenants. It is of course entirely possible that a person's landlord   1.70
is himself no more than a tenant of another. In such a case, the
"middle" tenant is known as a "mesne" (pronounced "mean") tenant,
and the "lower" tenant as the sub-tenant. Many more people are
sub-tenants than realise it. In strict law, the owner who holds only on a
long lease is a tenant, although has been considered as owner-occupier
(1.05-1.07). There are major property holdings still in existence in
which the interests are all held on leasehold. Indeed, it is not only
possible but common for there to be many "intervening" interests by
way of superior leasehold between an actual occupier and the ultimate
freeholder.

Continuation of Mesne Tenancy. So long as the mesne tenancy con-   1.71
tinues to exist, the sub-tenant is in no different a position than any other

tenant. His landlord (the mesne tenant) must serve notice to quit in the normal way, and the sub-tenancy may fall into any of the classes of protection which will be discussed in Chapters 3-6. The position remains the same even when the mesne tenant is a Rent Act protected tenant (Chapter 5) and his contractual tenancy comes to an end. The mesne tenant becomes what is known as a statutory tenant, but the sub-tenant is in practice unaffected by this unless or until the mesne tenant's statutory tenancy is determined.

1.72   **Termination of Mesne Tenancy.** Difficulties arise once the mesne tenant's interest comes to an end. In such a case, the question to be decided is whether the sub-tenant has any right to remain in occupation as against the superior landlord.

This will depend upon two main factors:

(*a*) whether there is statutory protection afforded to the sub-tenant (Chapters 4 and 5); and

(*b*) whether or not the sub-tenancy is a legal or illegal sub-tenancy.

1.73   **Sub-Tenants and Statutory Protection - (1) Housing Act.** In the case of a Housing Act assured tenancy (Chapter 4), it is unlikely that both mesne and sub-tenant will be Housing Act assured because they both live in the same building (4.20-4.21); but otherwise a Housing Act assured sub-tenant will become the tenant of a superior landlord if the mesne tenancy is determined, *and* at the time the mesne tenancy comes to an end the sub-tenancy is legal, even if the mesne tenancy was not Housing Act assured, unless the landlord is one whose tenants are not normally Housing Act assured (Housing Act 1988, s.18; 4.19).

1.74   **Sub-Tenants and Statutory Protection - (2) Rent Act.** In the case of a Rent Act protected tenant (Chapter 5), it is similarly unlikely that a sub-tenant will be a Rent Act protected sub-tenant because the principal condition which excludes a tenancy from Rent Act protection is that the tenant lives in the same building as his landlord; most sub-tenants will indeed live in the same building as the mesne tenant who is, *vis-a-vis* the sub-tenant, the landlord. If both mesne tenant and sub-tenant are protected by the Rent Act, however, and at the time the mesne tenancy comes to an end the sub-tenancy is legal, the sub-tenant will become the tenant of the landlord directly (Rent Act 1977, s.137). The fact that the mesne tenant is himself not a Rent Act protected tenant but, *e.g.* a Housing Act secure tenant (Chapter 3), does not affect the position as between mesne and sub-tenant (*Lewis* v. *Morelli*, 1948; *Stratford* v. *Syrett*, 1958) but does mean that the Rent Act 1977, s.137 cannot apply.

Illegal Sub-Tenancy. What is meant by an illegal sub-tenancy is that 1.75 the terms of the mesne tenancy include a prohibition on sub-letting. Most written tenancies include such a term, and many weekly or monthly tenancies granted in the last few years and for which the terms are to be found in printed rent books provided by the landlord will also be subject to such a prohibition. Some prohibitions on sub-letting are absolute, *i.e.* they simply state that it is not permitted. Some are qualified, *i.e.* they state that it is not permitted without the consent of the landlord. The law implies into a qualified covenant a condition that such consent will not unreasonably be withheld and if a mesne tenant whose tenancy includes a qualified prohibition asks the landlord for consent and the landlord refuses without good reason, the law will override the refusal, and consent will be deemed to be given (*Balls Brothers Ltd.* v. *Sinclair*, 1931). This is not so where the covenant is implied by Housing Act 1988, s.15, into a Housing Act assured tenancy (4.56).

Withholding of Consent. There can only be an unreasonable with- 1.76 holding if there has been a request and a refusal *before* the sub-letting is granted (*Barrow* v. *Isaacs*, 1891; *Eastern Telegraph Co.* v. *Dent*, 1899), which is extremely rare. But it is withholding which is prohibited, so that if the tenant seeks consent, and the landlord fails to reply after a reasonable time, consent has been withheld (*Wilson* v. *Fynn*, 1948). The best tactic is to seek consent and, when it is withheld, seek a declaration from the court that the withholding is unreasonable (*Mills* v. *Cannon Brewery Co.*, 1920). Whether or not a withholding is reasonable will turn on the facts of each case (*Lee* v. *K. Carter (K.) Ltd.*, 1949) including the impact of statutory protection (*West Layton Ltd.* v. *Ford*, 1979). The reasonableness of withholding consent is not confined to questions about the proposed sub-tenant, but can include consideration of the landlord's own interests, provided they are interests which a reasonable landlord would have regard to (*Leeward Securities Ltd.* v. *Lilyheath Properties Ltd.*, 1983), *e.g.* questions of good estate management, rather than an attempt to extract some benefit outside of the tenancy, such as unanticipated surrender (*Rayburn* v. *Woolf*, 1985). The burden is on the tenant to show unreasonable withholding of consent (*Rayburn*).

Landlord and Tenant Act 1988. If the tenant seeks consent in writing, 1.77 then the position as set out in the last paragraph is affected by the Landlord and Tenant Act 1988. This Act applies only where the covenant is a qualified covenant (1.75). Where a written application is made, the landlord owes the tenant a duty to reply within a reasonable time, either consenting, or else giving written notice either of a refusal, in which case the reasons must be stated, or of a "conditional consent," in which case the conditions must be stated. An unreasonable condition is not permitted. Under this Act, the burden is on the landlord to show: (a) that he replied within a reasonable time; and, (b) that any condition attached is reasonable; and, (c) that a refusal is reasonable.

1.78 **Waiver of Illegality.** Even if an illegal sub-tenancy is created, it is possible that it will be subsequently "legalised." This can happen because the landlord learns of the illegal sub-letting and yet "waives" the breach of the term of the tenancy by continuing to accept rent from the mesne tenant as if nothing had happened. It must be shown that the landlord knew there had been an actual sub-letting, not, *e.g.*, merely that a friend had come to live with the mesne tenant, and waiver must be established, which normally means something more than a single rent payment accepted very shortly after the landlord found out when, perhaps, reaction to the subletting was still in process. The knowledge of the landlord's employees, agents or officers is imputed to the landlord, so that if one such person knows of the illegal sub-letting and the landlord continues to accept rent there will have waiver (*Metropolitan Properties Co.* v. *Cordery*, 1979).

1.79 **No Advantage of Own Wrong.** A mesne tenant who lets illegally cannot himself subsequently take advantage of it (*Critchley* v. *Clifford*, 1962) by claiming not to be bound by it. It is, after all, his wrong, or breach, not that of the sub-tenant. It is no ground for eviction of a sub-tenant by the mesne tenant that the letting was illegal. If there is nothing in the terms of the mesne tenancy which prohibits sub-letting, then by common law the mesne tenant is entitled to sub-let. Once waiver has happened, the sub-tenant becomes a legal sub-tenant as if in the first place he had been allowed in lawfully. A sub-tenant who is not a Rent Act protected sub-tenant (*Stanley* v. *Compton*, 1951), or one who is an illegal sub-tenant, whether or not Rent Act protected, cannot take advantage of Rent Act 1977, s.137 in order to become the tenant of the landlord direct. Similarly, it would seem that an illegal Housing Act assured sub-tenant will not be able to avail himself of Housing Act 1988, s.18.

1.80 **Surrender and Notice to Quit by Mesne Tenant.** However, if the mesne tenant himself surrenders (1.41) to the landlord, and the landlord accepts the surrender (*Parker* v. *Jones*, 1910), or if the mesne tenancy comes to an end because the mesne tenant gives *valid* notice to quit

(1.45-1.48) to the landlord (*Mellors* v. *Watkins*, 1874), then the sub-tenant becomes a tenant of the landlord regardless of whether or not the sub-tenancy is illegal, and regardless of class of protection. This is by operation of common law and operates also by way of waiver, *i.e.* of the illegality, although in this case it is a waiver that takes place even although the landlord does not know of the existence of the sub-tenant. By accepting the surrender or notice to quit, the landlord is deemed to have waived any breaches by the tenant and to have taken over the tenant's liabilities, which include the sub-tenancy. This cannot happen if the mesne tenancy was already a statutory tenancy (Chapter 5), however, because a statutory tenancy is not a tenancy at common law (*Solomon* v. *Orwell*, 1954).

Rent Act Subletting. A Rent Act protected tenant (Chapter 5) who   1.81
creates a lawful Rent Act protected sub-tenancy is obliged to notify the landlord of this in writing, within 14 days of creating the sub-tenancy, stating details of the sub-tenancy, including the name of the sub-tenant and the rent he is paying under the sub-tenancy (Rent Act 1977, s.139). Where the sub-tenant becomes tenant direct of the landlord by operation of section 137, but not by operation of common law, then the landlord is entitled to disclaim responsibility for the provision of furniture, if he does so in writing within six weeks of the sub-tenant becoming his tenant (s.138).

Sub-Tenants and Licencees. All of these provisions, however, are de-   1.82
pendent upon the sub-tenant being a tenant at all, not merely a licensee. Someone who is the licensee of a tenant will find that his licence comes to an end automatically, without the giving of any notice, on the determination of the tenancy, although it will still normally be necessary for court proceedings to be taken to evict him: see Chapter 8. Whether or not a person is the licensee or sub-tenant of another will be a question of fact based on the normal considerations, but it is true to say that where the parties are living in the same premises, the court will look closely at the arrangement and, unless there is clear evidence of separate living, is more likely to be inclined to view another occupier as a sharer, or as a lodger, and therefore in either event a licensee, even though rent is paid, rather than as a sub-tenant. Such clear evidence of separate living might be provided by a rent book, perhaps separate payment for gas and electricity, separate housekeeping, etc. This question, of whether a person is a licensee of for example, someone he is sharing, a flat with, is considered further under the next heading.

1.83   **Sub-Tenancy Terminating with Mesne Tenancy.** If the mesne and
          sub-tenancies are not both Rent Act protected, or if the sub-tenancy is
          not Housing Act assured, or if the sub-tenancy is illegal, so that neither
          Rent Act 1977, s.137, nor Housing Act 1988, s.18 appplies (1.73-1.74)
          and if there is no surrender or notice to quit by the tenant (1.80), the
          sub-tenancy automatically determines, *i.e.* without notice or forfeiture,
          on the determination of the mesne tenancy (*Moore Properties (Ilford)* v.
          McKeon, 1976). Note, though, that a sub-tenant, even an illegal
          sub-tenant, can apply for relief (1.42-1.44) from forfeiture (Law of
          Property Act 1925, s.146(4)).

7. *Joint Tenants*

1.84   **Shared Tenancy.** A joint tenancy occurs wherever more than one
          person shares the tenancy. Joint tenants do not each have a different part
          of, for example, a flat or a house: they are all equally entitled to share
          possession of the whole of it. Between them, they must establish the
          four essential qualities of tenancy (*A.G. Securities* v. *Vaughan,* 1988),
          but need not establish them (and, in particular, exclusive possession) as
          against each other. Joint tenants are, unless the agreement states to the
          contrary (*A.G. Securities* v. *Vaughan,* 1988, *Demuren* v. *Seal Estates,*
          1978), each liable for the whole rent of the premises, so that if a landlord
          can only trace one of them, that one will be obliged to pay any and all
          rent outstanding, even though he may subsequently be able to recover
          shares from any of the missing joint tenants. Where there is no joint
          liability for the rent this may prevent a joint tenancy arising, and the
          occupiers may only be licensees (*Mikeover Ltd.* v. *Brady,* 1989).

1.85   **Acting in Harmony.** Married or cohabiting couples are frequently joint
          tenants, but so also are groups of friends. So long as they all remain
          together, acting, at least in relation to the landlord, in harmony, their
          position is exactly the same as that of a sole tenant. If there is any
          application, *e.g.* for rent registration, then they must either all sign the
          application, or else one of them must sign as agent for the others (*Turley*
          v. *Panton,* 1975; *R.* v. *Rent Officer for Camden, ex p. Felix,* 1988).
          Service of a notice to quit on one is good service (*Doe d. Aslin* v.
          Summersett, 1830), although there is some doubt as to whether a notice
          to quit which identifies only one of the joint tenants as the tenant will be
          valid.

1.86   **Termination by One of Joint Tenants.** Problems arise when the joint
          tenants themselves wish to go their separate ways. If the tenancy is

periodic, then one joint tenant can serve notice to quit and bring the contractual tenancy to an end (*L.B. Greenwich* v. *McGrady*, 1983; *L.B. Hammersmith & Fulham* v. *Monk*, 1991), although if the tenancy is Rent Act protected (Chapter 5), this will not affect the right to security of tenure of the others (*Lloyd* v. *Sadler*, 1978). If it is fixed-term, however, one alone cannot surrender it without the consent of the others (*Leek and Moorlands Building Society* v. *Clark*, 1952). If one joint tenant simply departs, then the tenancy "devolves" on the remaining joint tenants (*Lloyd* v. *Sadler*, 1978).

Joint Tenancy v. Sole Tenancy. It is possible, however, that people who assume that they are joint tenants are not so considered in law. For example, a group of friends take a flat together, but only one of them is named in or signs the agreement, if any, or only one of them is named on the rent book. At first sight, the law would assume that the named occupier was the sole tenant, and that his sharers were either sub-tenants or licensees. It is possible to upset this first impression, with evidence that the entry of one name only was either an oversight or intentionally inaccurate, by showing that the landlord was contracting with the whole group, and that it was clearly intended, as between themselves and as between them and the landlord, that they should all have equal rights in the premises. This might be witnessed by the fact that they each pay the rent for the whole of the premises to the landlord in turn. Although not impossible, it is none the less hard to upset the first impression created by a written indication that the tenancy belongs to only one of them.   1.87

Sub-Tenancy v. Sharers (Licensees). Will the remaining occupiers then be licensees or sub-tenants? Again, the first impression that the law will receive is that if a group of sharers are not joint tenants, there will be a sole tenant with a group of licensees. There is some merit to this attitude, for as between the group of occupiers it is infrequently indeed that they will have intended the formality of landlord and tenant. More likely, they are all sharing the outgoings, perhaps even buying food together, and living as one household. This would all suggest licence, rather than sub-tenancy. Sub-tenancy could be established, however, if there was clear evidence of separate living, as suggested above, under the last heading (1.82).   1.88

Non-Exclusive Occupation. Another problem has been caused by the use of the evasive device of "non-exclusive occupation agreements." The technique of such arrangements is that the landlord enters into a series of separate contracts with each occupier, granting to the occupier   1.89

the right to use the premises in question in common with others, but not to use a particular part of the premises. In this way, the landlord seeks to avoid a finding of tenancy of some part of the premises as against him, and because the agreements are all separate, seeks also to avoid a finding of joint tenancy of the whole of the premises between himself and the group. Such evasive devices often purport to retain for the landlord a right to come and live in the premises himself, or else to select new occupiers as and when one or other of the original group departs. Such arrangements *could* be genuine, *e.g.* if the landlord was effectively running a small-scale "hostel," and choosing the occupiers himself. A genuine such arrangement would create a series of individual licences, or, if specific rooms were allocated to individual occupiers, could create separate tenancies of the individual, specific rooms (*A.G. Securities* v. *Vaughan*, 1988).

1.90   Sham Revisited. But these arrangements are rarely genuine. People wish to select with whom they share a home, and are usually the happier the less the landlord has to do with it. Landlords do not really want the trouble of finding new occupiers for these sharing arrangements, and do not want the loss of rental income which would follow if the remaining occupiers were not liable for the total rent of the premises as a whole. In *Street* v. *Mountford* (1986), three cases in which the courts had upheld non-exclusive occupation agreements as genuine were described as wrongly decided, and as obviously sham arrangements which the courts should have treated as tenancies. A "sham" (or "false label" as it is sometimes called) arises when a document claims one thing, but the reality or actuality is, and was intended to be, something quite different, as here, suggesting that the group of occupiers are not joint tenants.

1.91   Confusion in the Court of Appeal. Notwithstanding the decision in *Street*, in *Hadjiloucas* v. *Crean* (1987) the Court of Appeal appeared to consider that separate non-exclusive agreements for the same period of time, and which (unusually for such agreements) contained obligations to pay between the occupiers the whole of the rent for the premises, did not necessarily amount to joint tenancy. Conversely, in *A.G. Securities Ltd.* v. *Vaughan* (1988), the Court of Appeal held that there was a joint tenancy between occupiers who came into premises under such non-exclusive occupation agreements at different times, for different periods, and paying different rents, and therefore not enjoying (joint) exclusive possession for identical periods of time. The want of a single, identified rent for the whole of the premises was not considered fatal. Yet in *Antoniades* v. *Villiers* (1988), the Court of Appeal again upheld non-exclusive agreements against a cohabiting couple.

Pretences. This confusion was apparently brought to an end when the 1.92
decision in *Street* was followed, and strengthened, by the House of
Lords in *A.G. Securities* v. *Vaughan* (1988). Although so described, the
case was also the appeal on *Antoniades*. Save where the agreement was,
unusually, a genuine arrangement between the landlord on one hand and
separate individuals on the other, as in *Vaughan* itself, the House of
Lords held that "pretences" devised to get around statutory protection
would not be upheld. The courts should look at all the circumstances,
including the relationship between the occupiers, before they
approached the landlord, the negotiations and, so far as the written
agreement is alleged to be a pretence or sham, even after they have
taken up occupation. If the reality is that the occupiers are to use the
premises as a home, together, paying a rent for it, then the arrangement
will be construed as a (joint) tenancy no matter what documents have
been drawn up. The House of Lords also disapproved of the views of the
Court of Appeal in *Hadjiloucas*, and considered that a clear joint tenancy
had been created.

Subsequent Cases. The decision in *A.G. Securities* has not led to the 1.93
end of litigation in this area, and there has been a number of Court of
Appeal decisions which have sought to apply the principles laid down
by the House of Lords. In two of them (*Stribling* v. *Wickham*, 1989, and
Mikeover Ltd. v. *Brady*, 1989), the Court found that the arrangements
were genuine licences, while in three others (*Nicolaou* v. *Pitt*, 1989,
Aslan v. *Murphy*, 1989 and *Duke* v. *Wynne*, 1989), the agreements were
all found to be "pretences" and the occupiers held to be tenants.

Departing Joint Tenants. Once joint tenancy is established, there can 1.94
still be problems. Commonly, in the course of time, one or more of the
original occupiers will drift on to alternative accommodation. What,
then, is the position of new occupiers, assuming that they are selected
by the occupiers themselves and not by the landlord? If a new occupier
is selected by the landlord, this will afford the landlord evidence that he
is in overall possession of the premises and that there can therefore be
no tenancy at all.

New Occupiers. If the landlord consents, a new occupier may become 1.95
a joint tenant with the others. If he does not, then the existing occupiers
cannot impose a new party to the tenancy on the landlord against his
will. The new occupier must be either the sub-tenant or licensee of the

existing and remaining joint tenants and, given the remarks which have already been made, is likely to be no more than licensee. In the course of time, it may be that all the original occupiers will have left and there will only be such licensees in occupation. The only defence left is if the existing occupiers, or some of them, can show that by the acceptance of rent or by some other conduct, the landlord has accepted them as tenants, or as joint tenants (1.20-1.21).

8. *Tenants of Mortgagors*

1.96   **Normal Position.** A person is a tenant of a mortgagor when his landlord owns the property, whether freehold or leasehold, under a mortgage. If the landlord falls into arrears with mortgage repayments, the mortgage company may "foreclose" and, in effect, take the property over. It is in this situation that problems may arise for the tenant. As long as the mortgagor remains in possession, the tenant's position is wholly unaffected by the existence of a mortgage on the property, even if the tenancy is granted in contravention of the terms of the mortgage (*Church of England Building Society* v. *Piskor*, 1954).

1.97   **Prior Tenancy.** There are commonly prohibitions similar to those contained in tenancy agreements in the deeds of a mortgage. If a person owns property before taking a mortgage on it, then any tenancies existing at the date of the mortgage are unaffected by the deed (*Mornington Permanent Building Society* v. *Kenway*, 1953). In such a case, even if the deed prohibits the creation of tenancies, on foreclosure the tenant will become the tenant of the mortgage company.

1.98   **Illegal Tenants.** Almost all mortgage deeds prohibit the creation of tenancies, and the majority of tenancies from mortgagors are in fact created after the mortgage, so that there are many tenants of mortgagors who are "illegal" tenants. This does not avail the mortgagor, of course, or afford him any additional right to evict the tenant. But if the mortgage company forecloses, then no matter whether the tenant is statutorily protected or not, he has no right of occupation as against the mortgage company (*Dudley and District Benefit Building Society* v. *Emerson*, 1949; *Britannia Building Society* v. *Earl*, 1989).

1.99   **New Tenancy?** Even though the mortgage company knew of the illegal tenancy, but continued to accept repayments, there is no exact analogy with waiver of an illegal sub-tenancy (*Dudley and District Benefit Building Society*). The only possibility is that after foreclosure the mortgage company either actively agrees to accept the continued presence of the tenant and takes on the tenancy, or does so by implication, by taking rent from the tenant over such a long period that the only inference that can properly be drawn is that it is treating the tenancy as binding upon itself. (*Taylor* v. *Ellis*, 1960; *Stroud Building Society* v. *Delamount*, 1960.)

9. *Assignees*

Permitted or Prohibited? The term "assignment" has been used before, to describe the purchase of a long lease from the existing leaseholder (1.07). The same may occur in connection with lesser forms of tenancy, that is to say that one tenant may assign the tenancy to another. If there is nothing in the terms of the tenancy or the law (*e.g.* Housing Act 1988, s.15, prohibiting assignment of a Housing Act assured tenancy without the consent of the landlord; see 4.56) to prohibit this, then it is permissible. However, most tenancy agreements and rent books do include such prohibitions which, like sub-tenancies (1.75) may be absolute or qualified. Only a contractual tenancy can be assigned, *i.e.* not a Rent Act statutory tenancy (Chapter 5; *Jessamine Investment Co.* v. *Schwartz*, 1977).   1.100

Assignment by Deed. Strictly, like a surrender, assignment should be by formal deed, but it can also operate if the transaction is in writing, with a document that sets out all the express terms and which is signed (Law of Property (Miscellaneous Provisions) Act 1989, s.2). An assignee steps into the shoes of the outgoing tenant, and occupies on exactly the same terms. But an assignment not by deed will, though binding as between the two tenants, not bind the landlord unless he accepts the assignment, *e.g.* by payment and acceptance of rent, in much the same way and to the same extent as if he were to be deemed to have created a new tenancy (1.20-1.21) or at least to the extent that the law must consider that he is estopped from denying the validity of the assignment (*i.e.* that it would be inequitable to allow him to do so) (*Rodenhurst Estates* v. *Barnes*, 1936).   1.101

10. *New Landlords*

Purchase Subject to Existing Interests. When a person purchases property, he does so subject to existing interests in it. A tenancy is an interest in property as, indeed, is a sub-tenancy, and even an illegal sub-tenancy. Accordingly, a purchaser takes subject to existing   1.102

tenancies. A licence is not an interest in property, it is a personal right, and it would appear to be the case that a licence does not bind a new purchaser, although there is some contention about this (*National Provincial Bank* v. *Ainsworth*, 1965). The new landlord takes subject to all the old landlord's rights, liabilities and duties. He also takes liable to any knowledge the old landlord had, *e.g.* such knowledge as would found a claim for waiver of an illegal sub-tenancy or assignment. A tenancy dates from its original grant and there is no new tenancy on change of ownership. Before a tenant starts to pay rent to the new landlord, the old landlord should write to him, authorising the changeover, and will remain liable as landlord until either he or the new landlord does so (Landlord and Tenant Act 1985, s.3).

1.103   Change of Ownership: Special Issues. There are special provisions relating to change of ownership which apply to the question of whether or not a tenant has a resident landlord for the purposes of either the Housing Act 1988 (Chapter 4) or the Rent Act 1977 (Chapter 5). In addition, there are special provisions governing the transfer of ownership from local and other public authorities to Housing Action trusts, and in some cases into private ownership, which are considered in Chapter 3.

2 Owner-Occupation

Owner-occupiers. In this chapter, we shall examine in outline the rights of occupation of those who were described in Chapter 1 as owner-occupiers, *i.e.* freeholders and long leaseholders. As has already been remarked, the fullest status that anyone can enjoy is that of freehold owner-occupation, unencumbered by mortgage (1.03). He has to pay neither rent nor mortgage repayments and has an absolute right of occupation which can only be interfered with in the sorts of circumstances indicated (1.04). The position of the freeholder and the leaseholder as regards mortgage repayments is substantially the same, and will be considered under the general heading of mortgages (2.26-2.43). In addition, the position of the leaseholder, whether or not the property is mortgaged, at or before the end of the lease must be considered (2.02-2.10).

The questions with which this chapter is concerned, therefore, are:
1. *Leasehold rights*; and
2. *Mortgages.*

1. *Leasehold Rights*

(i) *Landlord and Tenant Act, 1954, Local Government and Housing Act 1989, Sched. 10.*

Long Leases. We are concerned here with "long leases," *i.e.* those for more than 21 years (Landlord and Tenant Act 1954 - "1954" - s.2(4), Leasehold Reform Act 1967 - "1967" - s.3(1), Landlord and Tenant Act 1987 - "1987" - s.59(3), Local Government and Housing Act 1989 - "1989" - Sched. 10, para. 2(3), although in this case the expression also includes a lease under the "right to buy" provisions of the Housing Act 1985, even if, as is occasionally the case, it is for less than 21 years). But though the lease must (normally) be for more than 21 years, that is not to say that the leaseholder must have been in occupation for that period, merely that the right under which he occupies is or was for that period, *i.e.* he may have taken an assignment (1.07). The time runs from when the lease was originally granted (*Roberts* v. *Church Commissioners for England*, 1972), and not from an earlier date if it is back-dated. But, similarly, if occupation is taken up under an enforceable claim to a lease for a shorter period, prior to its grant, if the period of lease *plus* such prior occupation amount to more than 21 years, that, too, is likely to be considered a long lease (*Brikom Investments* v. *Seaford*, 1981).

2.03   **Premature Termination.** So long as a leasehold interest has not expired, an occupier has as full a right of occupation as a freeholder and this can only be interfered with in the same ways referred to above (1.03). For this purpose, however, it is assumed that the lease runs its full length: leases can be terminated prematurely, *e.g.* because of breach of a term of the lease, or non-payment of charges. In such a case, the lease is susceptible to forfeiture proceedings, as any other fixed-term tenancy, with the possibility of relief discussed in Chapter 1 (see 1.42-1.44). If the lease is Housing Act secure (see Chapter 3), Housing Act assured (see Chapter 4) or Rent Act protected (see Chapter 5), the protection afforded to such tenants will also be available to the leaseholder whose lease has been forfeit, but the possibilities outlined in this chapter will be lost on forfeiture.

2.04   **Statutory Continuation.** Assuming continuation of the lease, so long as the occupier is using the premises, or part of them, as his home at the end of the lease, then unless his landlord is one of the public landlords whose tenants cannot be Housing Act assured (4.19) or Rent Act protected (5.52), the lease will not come to an end and the occupier can remain in occupation indefinitely because it is automatically continued by statute (Landlord and Tenant Act 1954, Part I, Local Government and Housing Act 1989, Sched. 10).

2.05   **Pre-April 1, 1990 Leases.** If the tenancy commenced before April 1, 1990, the landlord can, however, serve a notice proposing that a statutory tenancy should come into existence (1954, s.4). What this means is that he has brought the lease to an end, and that in its place there will be a statutory tenancy, exactly like that which a Rent Act protected tenant has at the end of his tenancy (5.12). The statutory tenancy is described here, for these purposes, as the right to remain indefinitely in the premises unless and until the landlord can establish one of a specified series of grounds for possession, with which he can obtain a court order for possession. Those grounds are by and large the same as those for a Rent Act protected statutory tenant (5.66-5.91), but in addition the landlord can seek possession if he can prove that he proposes to demolish or reconstruct the whole or a substantial part of the premises in question (1954, s.12).

Use As A Home. One essential element of protection under the 1954   2.06
Act, *i.e.* at the termination of the lease, is that the premises are being
used by the tenant as his home, to the same extent as is necessary to
sustain a Rent Act statutory tenancy (5.57-5.64); all the other qualifying
conditions (5.27-5.53) for Rent Act protection must similarly be fulfilled
(1954, s.2(1)) except the condition (5.47) that the tenancy must not be
at a low rent - this is disregarded for these purposes in relation to a long
lease (1954, s.2(1), (5)). During the last year of a long lease, the
landlord can seek to predetermine whether or not the tenant is going to
enjoy protection, by way of an application to the county court (1954,
s.2(2)).

Landlord's Notices (1). If there is no such predetermination, the ten-   2.07
ancy continues automatically, and contractually, at the old - and usually
low - rent, until brought to end by notice from the landlord (1954, s.3).
The protection may, however, extend to only part of the premises (1954,
s.3(2)), *e.g.* if the tenant occupies only one part, and does not intend to
resume possession of the remainder, *e.g.* a part which he has perhaps
sublet (*Regalian Securities* v. *Ramsden*, 1981). The landlord's notice
must either indicate that he intends to seek possession on one of the
available grounds (2.05), or propose a statutory tenancy to commence
at a specified date (1954, s.4). This notice must set out the proposed
terms of the statutory tenancy, and deal with the question of "initial
repairs" (1954, s.7). This issue is dealt with below (11.35-11.36). Once
the statutory tenancy has come into existence, it may later be determined
in exactly the same way as one which arises under the Rent Act 1977
(5.37-5.68).

Termination post-January 15, 1999. For tenancies which are termin-   2.08
ated under the 1954 Act after January 15, 1999, the tenancy will not be
become statutory, but will fall to be dealt with in the same manner as
those commencing after April 1, 1990, *i.e.* as assured tenancies under
the 1989 Act (1989, Sched. 10, para.3(2)).

Landlord's Notices (2). The 1989 Act continues the existing tenancy   2.09
until the landlord serves a notice either proposing a new assured
monthly periodic tenancy or giving notice of seeking possession (1989,
Sched. 10, para. 4(5)). A notice proposing a new tenancy must also
propose a new rent which must be sufficient to ensure that it is no longer
at a "low rent" and state that either it is to be on the same terms as the
long tenancy or propose new terms (1989, Sched. 10, para. 4(5), (6)).
Where a notice of seeking possession is served, it must state the

grounds. The landlord may rely on some of the grounds from the Housing Act 1988, *i.e.* ground 6 (4.35) and the discretionary grounds 9 to 15 (4.40–4.44). In addition, the landlord may also claim possession on the basis that he requires the premises for occupation for himself, any child over 18 or his parents or parents-in-law, provided his interest was not purchased after February 18, 1966, and that he can show that it is reasonable to grant possession. In addition to rely on this ground he must satisfy the "greater hardship" test (5.88: 1989, Sched. 10, para. 5).

2.10 **Tenant's Options.** The notice proposing a new tenancy or seeking possession, must give the tenant the option either to elect to remain or indicate a willingness to give up possession. Any application for possession must be made within two months of the tenant's election, or, if there is no reply, within four months of the landlord's notice (1989, Sched. 10, para. 13). The tenant may at any time, regardless of whether he has elected to remain, give one month's notice to terminate the tenancy (1989, Sched. 10, para. 13(4). An interim monthly rent may be proposed by the landlord, which the tenant may appeal to the rent assessment committee (1989, Sched. 10, para. 6). If the tenant wishes to dispute the proposed rent and terms of the new tenancy he must serve a notice on the landlord within two months proposing his own alternative. If no agreement can be reached the matter may be referred by either party to the rent assessment committee, which has similar powers as under the Housing Act 1988 (4.54: 1989, Sched. 10, paras. 11, 12).

(ii) *Leasehold Reform Act 1967*

2.11 **Enfranchisement and Extension of Long Leases.** Additionally, under the Leasehold Reform Act 1967, a person who is a long-leaseholder of a house, but not of a flat, can compel the landlord to extend the lease for a further 50 years beyond the date of its original termination, or may require the landlord to sell him the freehold. These rights only apply to those houses which are not horizontally divided from any other premises, *i.e.* they do not, to any extent, overlap or, as it were, underlap another property (1967, s.2). The house need not, however, be free-standing: it may be in a row of terraced houses. The house can be sub-divided, and even sub-let. Thus, a house which is also a shop can qualify (*Tandon* v. *Trustees of Spurgeons Homes*, 1982); the question is whether the building can reasonably be called a house (*Lake* v. *Bennett*, 1970). The Act only applies to tenancies at a low rent, *i.e.* a rent which is not more than two-thirds of the rateable value (1967, s.4);

it also applies only to long leases (2.02).

Occupation As A Residence. A leaseholder must exercise these rights 2.12
before the lease expires and within two months of the landlord serving
a notice proposing a statutory tenancy (2.05) but can only do so if, at the
time the right to purchase the freehold (known as enfranchisement) or
to extend the lease (extension) is claimed, the leaseholder has been
occupying the house as his only or main residence for a period of at least
three years or for three years out of the last 10 years (Leasehold Reform
Act 1967, s.1) It is enough to occupy only part of the premises, *e.g.* if
the occupier has the lease on a whole house, lives in part, and lets out
part, this will suffice (*Harris* v. *Swick Securities*, 1969), provided he
occupies at least part as his only or main, not just a residence (1967, s.1;
Poland v. *Earl Cadogan*, 1980). The purpose of the residential
qualification is to prevent speculation.

Purchase Price. The price of the purchase can be fixed, failing agree- 2.13
ment between the parties, by the leasehold valuation tribunal, and on
appeal therefrom by the Lands Tribunal, but the procedure is
complicated and anyone intending to use it should consult a lawyer or
surveyor. Unlike proceedings before most other tribunals, legal aid is
available to pay for the cost of a lawyer and a surveyor or a valuer
before the Lands Tribunal, though not before the leasehold valuation
tribunal. Extension does not cost anything, although a new ground rent
(*i.e.* low rent) which is appropriate to the value of the house at the date
when the new lease starts will be fixed to take effect from that date
(1967, s.15). Extension is provided mainly for those who cannot afford
to enfranchise or who, perhaps being elderly and with no relatives to
whom to leave any acquired interest, have no reason to do so. There are
special grounds of opposition to enfranchisement or extension available
to specified *public* landlords (1967, s.28).

Sooner is Cheaper. Enfranchisement can be extremely cheap. All that 2.14
is being bought back is the benefit of a very small ground rent and the
fairly remote possibility that the landlord will ever get the property back
at all. The longer there is to run on the lease at the time a notice
indicating an intention to purchase is served, the cheaper the price will
be because the landlord's expectations are the most remote. It follows
that once an occupier has fulfilled the residential qualification, he should
exercise the power to enfranchise as soon as possible. The price of
enfranchisement bears no *practical* relation to current property values or
even to the customarily lower than vacant possession value at which

many sitting tenants are permitted to buy from their landlords. It may be a figure of less than £100, or not much more. The advice of a surveyor will count for much more than that of a lawyer where prices in enfranchisement and extension are concerned.

(iii) *Landlord and Tenant Act 1987*

2.15   **Additional Rights.** Long leaseholders also benefit from a range of rights contained in the Landlord and Tenant Act 1987, Parts I, III and IV which may most conveniently be considered in this chapter; however, other tenants may also benefit from Part I. (Part II is considered in Chapter 11, below.)

2.16   **Right of First Refusal.** Part I contains provisions designed to give the tenants (including long leaseholders) of blocks of flats a "right of first refusal" should the freeholder or a superior landlord wish to sell his interest. The provisions apply only to flats, and there must be at least two flats in the building for them to operate, although the block need not be purpose-built. The provisions do not apply if the landlord is a resident landlord, or an exempt landlord, or if less than 50 per cent. of the flats are occupied by qualifying tenants, or if less than 50 per cent. of the floor area of the building (excluding common parts) is not in (or intended for) residential use (1987, s.1).

2.17   **Exempt Landlords.** "Exempt landlords" include local authorities, new town development corporations or the Commission for the New Towns, an urban development corporation, the Development Board for Rural Wales, the Housing Corporation and Housing for Wales, charitable housing trusts or registered housing associations and Housing Action Trusts (1987, s.58). "Resident landlord" is defined (1987, s.58) in terms very similar to the definition in the Housing Act 1988 (4.20-4.21), and accordingly the mere fact that the landlord lives in a *purpose-built* block of flats will not prevent the right of first refusal arising. Where the resident landlord exemption does apply, however, *e.g.* in a converted house, the landlord need not have been in residence since the commencement of the tenancy, but only for a period of at least one year before the prospective disposal; the residential test is not "a" residence (as under the Rent Act 1977: 5.30), but "only or principal residence" (as under the Housing Act 1985: 3.13).

2.18   **Qualifying Tenants.** All tenants, including Rent Act statutory tenants (5.12), are qualifying tenants, *except* shorthold tenants (6.38), assured tenants (Chapter 4), those to whom the business security of Part II, Landlord and Tenant Act 1954 (3.14) applies, and service tenants (1.63; 1987, s.3). However, if a person has a lease of three flats in the building, and if a person is a sub-tenant whose landlord is himself a qualifying tenant, he cannot be a qualifying tenant, (1987, s.3).

Relevant Disposal. The right of first refusal arises only in relation to a   2.19
"relevant disposal," which is the disposal of any interest in the whole or part of the building *other than* a schedule of specified classes of disposal which includes the grant of a tenancy of a single flat, a disposal of an interest by way of mortgage, disposal under Matrimonial Causes Act 1973, ss.24, 24A (9.12), a disposal related to compulsory purchase, a disposal by way of gift to a member of the landlord's family or to a charity, a disposal by will, a disposal to the Crown and a disposal to a company formally associated with the landlord company (1987, s.4). But a disposal *by* a mortgage company falls within the provisions, even if it has taken the property back from the landlord under the mortgage.

Requisite Majority. The provisions of Part I are highly technical and   2.20
can only be described here in outline. Where there is to be a relevant disposal, the landlord has to offer the tenants the right of first refusal, identifying what is on offer and its terms, including price; the offer can only be accepted by a "requisite majority" of the qualifying tenants, within a period of not less than two months (1987, s.5). The "requisite majority" means more than 50 per cent. of the "available votes," which latter term is defined to mean one vote for each flat involved. If the requisite majority accepts the offer, they have a further two months in which to identify a person to act on their behalf in the further transactions, and the landlord cannot sell to anyone else until the end of the "relevant period," which is defined to cover the designated procedure. If no one is nominated, then during the following 12 months the landlord can only dispose to someone else: (*a*) on the same terms; and, (*b*) at no less than the price at which the disposal was offered to the tenants (1987, s.6).

One Year Restriction on Disposal. Similarly, if the original offer is   2.21
not accepted, the landlord cannot dispose elsewhere for 12 months save on the same terms, unless there is a "counter-offer," in which case there are provisions as to how this is to be dealt with (1987, s.7); there are also provisions for a "counter-counter-offer" (1987, s.8). Unless the requisite majority is sustained throughout the process, the purchase possibility falls (1987, s.9). There are also provisions to deal with a

disposal which has not complied with the right of first refusal, which includes the possibility of forcing the purchaser to sell to the tenants (1987, ss.11, 12).

2.22   **Acquisition Order.** Part III of the 1987 Act permits a form of "compulsory purchase" by qualifying tenants, but for this purpose a qualifying tenant must have a long lease (2.02); a "business tenant" cannot be a qualifying tenant, nor can a tenant whose lease comprises more than two flats, nor if his own landlord is a qualifying tenant (1987, s.26). For the provisions to operate, a specified number of flats in a building must be occupied by qualifying tenants: if less than four flats, all of them; if four to 10, all or all but one; if 10 or more, at least 90 per cent. (1987, s.25). As under Part I (2.16), the provisions do not apply if more than 50 per cent. of the building (excluding the common parts) is non-residential, nor if there is an exempt or resident landlord (2.17).

2.23   **Preconditions.** The "acquisition order" can only be made by a court, which must be satisfied that the preconditions (above) apply *and* (*a*) that one of two sets of further conditions applies, *and* (*b*) that it is "appropriate" to make the order (1987, s.29). Before application can be made to the court, a "requisite majority" of tenants (defined in the same terms as for Part I: 2.20) must serve notice on the landlord of the intention to apply, identifying the grounds on which the application will be made, specifying what remedial steps might be taken to avert the application within a specified reasonable period, and containing other information such as might be prescribed by the Secretary of State (1987, s.27). The court can, however, waive the requirement of preliminary notice if it considers that it is not reasonably practicable to do so.

2.24   **Alternative Conditions.** Unless the prior notice is waived by the court, no application can be made until the period specified for remedial action has expired (1987, s.28). The alternative sets of conditions on which the court may make the acquisition order are: (*a*) that there is a breach of the terms of the lease concerning repair, maintenance, insurance or management, which is likely to continue, and which cannot adequately be remedied by the appointment of a manager under Part II (11.55); or, (*b*) a manager had formerly been appointed under Part II, and has been in charge of the premises for the last three years (1987, s.29). Further provisions govern the terms of the acquisition and if the landlord cannot be found (1987, ss.30-33), but a landlord can apply for discharge of the order if the tenants do not proceed within a reasonable time, or if the number of tenants wishing to proceed falls below the requisite majority

(1987, s.34).

Variation of Leases. Finally, attention may be drawn to the provisions   2.25
of Part IV of the Act, again confined to long leaseholders (2.02). These
provisions permit individual leaseholders to apply to court for a
variation of terms if a lease fails to make satisfactory provisions
governing repairs or maintenance of a flat or building, insurance, repairs
or maintenance of facilities necessary to ensure that occupiers enjoy a
reasonable standard of accommodation, the provision or maintenance or
services, or the way service charges are computed (1987, s.35). There
is also provision for the variation of other leases within a building to
ensure consistency (1987, s.36) and for ''block applications'' by a
specified number of leaseholders in a building: two to eight flats, all but
one; nine or more flats, 75 per cent. in support of the application, and
the application is not opposed by more than 10 per cent.

2. *Mortgages*

Repossession and Arrears. Both freehold and leasehold owner-occ-   2.26
upation can, and frequently will, be subject to a mortgage. Although all
mortgage deeds contain a variety of terms (*e.g.* not to create tenancies
in the property without permission (1.88-1.91)), it is usually only when
an occupier falls into arrears with the repayments that the company has
the right to take action to evict him.

Demand for Arrears. Before legal proceedings are started, the mort-   2.27
gage company will normally make a written demand for any arrears of
repayment. It is not obliged by law to do this, but in practice the court
(which has discretionary powers which are described below) will not
look kindly upon a mortgage company which has proceeded to exercise
its full legal rights without warning the occupier and giving him a
chance to redeem his position. If the arrears are paid off at that point,
nothing further will normally happen. If an occupier has a bad history
of arrears, however, the mortgage company may still decide to press on
with the full legal procedure.

Demand for Repayment. After any demand for the arrears, there will   2.28
be a formal demand for repayment of the whole of the outstanding debt.
This will be for all capital outstanding, and also any accumulated
interest. At this point, an occupier can, if he is in a position to do so, buy
off the mortgage company entirely, and retain possession of the
property. There has to be such a formal demand, even if it is quite

obvious that the occupier cannot comply with it.

2.29   **Possession Proceedings.** The next step is for the mortgage company
        to issue possession proceedings in the county court. The company
        cannot evict the occupier without court proceedings. The court is not
        obliged to grant the possession order immediately. It has power to grant
        an order suspended on condition that the occupier continues to pay
        current instalments under the mortgage, and a fixed amount per payment
        off the arrears.

2.30   **Suspended Orders.** The court will only exercise this discretion if it is
        of the view that the arrears can be cleared in a reasonable time
        (Administration of Justice Act 1970, s.36; *Town & Country Building
        Society* v. *Julien,* 1991). If it does not think this can be done, then the
        order will be final, but will usually be suspended for at least 28 days to
        give the occupier time to start making alternative arrangements: see
        Chapter 10.

2.31   **Reasonable Time to Clear Arrears.** There is no formal definition of
        reasonable time. The courts normally consider one year a reasonable
        time in which to clear the arrears. So far as a private mortgage company
        is concerned, if the arrears cannot be cleared in a year, or not much
        more, there is not much that can be done, unless the company itself is
        amenable to repayment over a longer period. The courts tend to regard
        mortgage companies as bound only by the normal rules of business
        ethics and private enterprise, and are therefore reluctant to impose upon
        them the effects of individual hardship.

2.32   **Public Authorities.** This is not necessarily the case where public
        authorities are concerned. Many mortgages are granted by local
        authorities. Local authorities may proceed more slowly. It is common
        for the first letter demanding arrears to arrive at a time when an occupier
        owes only a three-figure amount. But it may be a long time before the
        next letter arrives. This may be a further demand for the arrears, or it
        may be the final and formal demand for full repayment of the
        outstanding debt. In either event, the arrears will by then probably be a
        four-figure amount, and perhaps beyond what an occupier can hope to
        pay off within a year, at the same time as maintaining current
        instalments. While the courts will not regard this behaviour on the part
        of the local authority as "blameworthy," many will accept that public
        authorities have something of a duty to chase occupiers. They may be
        prepared to accept that such "contributory dilatoriness" should not

result in an outright order for possession and, therefore, that repayment of the arrears can take place over a longer period of time, even as long as two or three years.

Rearrangements. Many occupiers will have financial difficulties far too serious to be solved by a suspended order for possession and periodic repayment of arrears over a year or two. Indeed, such an obligation can often lead them further into financial difficulty. It may be that more drastic measures are desirable. Steps can be taken to avert arrears at an early stage and so avoid court proceedings altogether, if action is taken as soon as it appears that an occupier is running into financial difficulty. 2.33

Types of Mortgage. For example, rearrangement of a mortgage can increase the amount which an occupier who is in receipt of income support will receive by way of regular allowance. Similarly, it may be possible to approach a mortgage company with a proposal for rearrangement or for a temporary arrangement in order to tide an occupier over a period of particularly acute financial hardship. It may also be that the lending institution involved has an arrangement with a housing association which will purchase the property, and allow the occupier to remain in possession as a tenant. With these possibilities in mind, an outline knowledge of how mortgages work will be of some help. All mortgages are a form of loan against the security of the property in question. In all cases, the mortgage company wants back the capital sum loaned, and interest on it for the period for which it has been lent. Mortgages can be arranged for repayment over any period of time, although they are usually arranged for repayment over a period of 15 to 25 years. 2.34

There are two principal sorts of mortgage:

(i) *Capital repayment mortgage*

Capital Mortgage. A capital repayment mortgage is a loan which re-quires repayment in periodic amounts which are assessed in at least two and commonly three parts. Although it is not an essential part of a capital repayment mortgage, most reputable mortgage companies insist that there is included in the package an element of insurance, called the mortgage protection policy. This provides insurance against the death of the owner-occupier, in which case the insurance will pay off any outstanding mortgage and so leave the property unencumbered for the next-of-kin. 2.35

Capital and Interest. The two essential parts of the repayments are 2.36

capital repayment and interest. Monthly payments are assessed at an amount slightly larger than the interest due on the original capital loan. This means that at the beginning of a mortgage repayment period, an owner-occupier is not paying back much of the capital but is mostly paying interest on it. Gradually, however, the capital will decrease. The monthly payments remain the same, except for fluctuations in the rate of mortgage interest. In later years, therefore, when the amount of capital outstanding has been reduced, the monthly payment covers a smaller sum due by way of interest, and a correspondingly larger amount of capital repayment. In the final years of a mortgage, there is little interest due at all, and most of the payment is capital repayment.

(ii) *Endowment mortgage*

2.37   Endowment. The monthly payment under an endowment mortgage is a sum assessed in two parts only - interest repayment, and life assurance premium. Subject to fluctuations in the mortgage interest rate, both these amounts remain the same. There is no capital repayment. Instead, the life assurance premium guarantees that either at the end of the period for which the mortgage has been taken out, or on the death of the mortgagor, the insurance company will pay off the whole of the capital outstanding. There are other benefits which may be included in an endowment mortgage arrangement.

2.38   Tax Relief. It is generally well-known that there will be tax relief on mortgage interest. This, at least, is so provided that the purpose of the mortgage was principal home purchase or home improvement. It will not be available if the mortgage was taken out because of some other financial need, nor for a second home. Tax relief is available to the full amount of the interest payments, to the statutory capital limit, currently £30,000. It is allowed in addition to an individual's other personal tax allowances. In effect, it reduces the cost of the interest to the mortgagor by the amount of the current rate of income tax on it. Tax relief at the basic rate of tax is deducted at source.

2.39   Switching Types of Mortgage. There are several possible rearrangements of mortgage affairs which may be appropriate in different situations:
  (*a*) Capital repayment mortgages are usually slightly cheaper than endowment mortgages. At a time of financial hardship, therefore, it may be advisable to switch from one to the other.

2.40   Extending Term of Mortgage. (*b*) Another rearrangement of affairs which may reduce immediate costs applies only to capital repayment mortgages. In the later years, the interest element of a monthly repayment is fairly low. It may be possible to persuade a mortgage company to, as it were, re-grant the mortgage so that the capital outstanding is payable over a longer number of years than originally intended. This will not affect the interest payments, for the amount of capital outstanding is the same, but it will spread the capital repayments over that many more years. It follows that the capital portion of monthly repayments will be reduced and this will lead to an overall reduction, which may not, however, be very large, in the monthly payments.

Postponing Capital Payments. (*c*) It may be that a period of financial 2.41 hardship is, even at the outset, of an identifiably limited period. For example, when a relationship breaks up (see Chapter 9), there will often be a period during which a wife is not receiving any adequate maintenance from her husband, while at the same time she remains liable for all the normal household outgoings. A mortgage company is bound to accept repayments from a wife, even although the property is in the name of the husband (Matrimonial Homes Act 1983, s.1). A court may order the transfer of the property from one name into another. These questions are dealt with in Chapter 9, but while they are being sorted out, a wife may be able to persuade the mortgage company to accept payments of interest only, and nothing at all off the capital, to give her a financial breathing space.

Consolidation of Mortgages. (*d*) Some occupiers have not one but 2.42 two mortgages on their properties. This might have happened, for example, because an occupier needed money to improve an already mortgaged property and approached some other company to advance him the funds. The better procedure would be to approach a local authority for a maturity loan, which is an interest only loan subject to a charge on the property, which the authority realise on death of the borrower or on sale of the house. But an occupier may not have been aware of this possibility or may have been refused a loan by the authority. Second mortgages command higher rates of interest than do first mortgages because, if the property has to be sold to get the loan back, the first mortgage company will take priority out of the proceeds of sale. It is possible that at a time of financial hardship, the first mortgage company may be willing to take over the second mortgage and consolidate the whole of the loan into one, at the lower rate of interest.

Need for Consent. Most of these rearrangements cannot be imposed 2.43

on a mortgage company against its will. None the less, there is nothing to stop an occupier approaching the company with a request; and the clearer the proposals he can make, the greater are the chances of success. The larger, more reputable mortgage companies do not, as a matter of course, want to see occupiers evicted and the properties sold. Their money comes, after all, from keeping mortgages in existence and receiving interest on them.

3 Housing Act Secure Tenancies

Provision of Housing. Under the Housing Act 1985 ("1985"), s.8, local authorities are bound to consider the housing needs of their areas: Part II of the Act contains their powers to own, manage and dispose of their housing accommodation, although it should be noted that there is no *requirement* to have any accommodation at all (1985, s.9(5)). People who have registered with a local authority, by way of application for accommodation, are entitled to inspect the records of the authority to see whether the authority have correctly recorded the details they have provided to the authority, though not necessarily all the information the authority have recorded, *e.g.* from other sources (1985, s.106).   3.01

Allocation of Housing. The allocation of accommodation is, however, generally within the discretion of the authority although they are bound to afford a reasonable preference to those occupying insanitary or overcrowded houses, who have large families, or who are living in unsatisfactory housing conditions, and those towards whom they owe duties under Part III of the 1985 Act (see Chapter 10) (1985, s.22). They cannot adopt an allocations policy so rigid that it prevents them considering applications from those not within it (*R.* v. *Canterbury City Council, ex p. Gillespie*, 1987), nor apply requirements, such as payment of the community charge, which are irrelevant to housing need (*R.* v. *Forest Heath D.C., ex p. West*, 1991). Authorities are also bound to publish details of their allocation policies (1985, s.106).   3.02

Local Housing Authorities. Local authorities still remain the main providers of rented housing, although current government policy is to seek to reduce the amount of rented stock they hold (see below for provisions governing transfer out of the public sector). Local authorities for housing purposes are district councils, London borough councils and the Common Council of the City of London, although county councils may, with the consent of the Secretary of State for the Environment, exercise housing powers too. Until comparatively recently (1980), such public tenants were outside all forms of statutory regulation: it was   3.03

49

presumed that landlords who were not motivated by profit did not need legal protection. However, the absence of regulation produced many anomolies, and in response "secure tenancies" were introduced by the Housing Act 1980 ("1980"), although the provisions have subsequently been consolidated into the 1985 Act.

3.04 **Other Public Landlords.** Local authorities are not the only providers of public housing: new town commissions, the Development Board for Rural Wales, urban development corporations and the new Housing Action Trusts all fulfill functions similar to those of local authorities. Further, there is a so-called "quasi-public sector" comprised of housing associations, housing trusts and similar bodies who receive public funding for their activities. Most important of these are the housing associations, which are registered under the Housing Associations Act 1985, with the Housing Corporation or its Welsh counterpart, Housing for Wales. In 1980, all of these bodies were also brought within the concept of the "secure tenancy." From 1989, by Part I, Housing Act 1988, however, housing association tenants were taken out of the Housing Act 1985, and placed within the same framework as private sector tenants, as assured tenants: see Chapter 4, below.

3.05 **Pre- and Post-January 15, 1989 Housing Association Tenants.** In this chapter, accordingly, we are concerned with housing association tenancies *only* if they began before the commencement (January 15, 1989) of Part I, Housing Act 1988 ("1988"). A tenancy granted by a housing association on or after that date cannot be secure unless either:

(*a*) **Pre-Act Contract.** It was entered into pursuant to a contract for its grant which preceded that date; or

(*b*) **New Tenancy to Former Tenant.** It is the grant of a new tenancy (not necessarily of the same premises) to a person who was a former tenant of the same landlord, or one of a number of joint (1.77) such tenants; or

(*c*) **Suitable Alternative Accommodation.** It is the grant of a tenancy resulting from an order for possession against a secure tenant, on the gound of suitable alternative accommodation (3.28, 3.31), *and* (i) the premises in question are those which the court has found suitable, *and* (ii) the court directs that the new tenancy should be a secure tenancy on the ground that an assured tenancy will not provide sufficient security; or

(*d*) **New Town Corporation to Housing Association.** It falls within a small class of tenancy formerly held by a new town development corporation, and passed into housing association ownership before

March 31, 1996; or

(*e*) **Defective Premises.** The tenancy is one granted under special provisions (Housing Act 1985, Part XVI) dealing with buying back defective premises (not covered in this book): 1988, s.34. So far as this chapter concerns housing association tenancies, it therefore applies mainly to tenancies already granted. Tenancies granted on or after the commencement of Part I, 1988 Act are, subject to its own schedule of exclusions, likely to be assured tenancies, and are considered in Chapter 4.

Principal Issues. It is with these publicly-funded landlords that we are concerned in this chapter: most of their tenants now enjoy a security of tenure that is conceptually similar (but with important substantive differences) to that enjoyed by Housing Act assured (private sector) tenants (Chapter 4), and Rent Act protected tenants (Chapter 5), and a number of additional rights. The position of those public tenants who do not qualify as secure tenants under the Housing Act 1985 or assured tenants under the Housing Act 1988 will be considered in Chapter 7. In this chapter we shall, accordingly, consider: 3.06

1. *Secure tenants;*
2. *Security of tenure under the Housing Act 1985;*
3. *Additional rights of secure tenants;*
4. *Local authority rents;*
5. *Pre-1988 Act housing association rents;*
6. *Further financial protection and assistance;* and
7. *Transfer of public housing.*

1. *Secure Tenants*

Let As A Separate Dwelling. A secure tenant is one to whom residential accommodation is let as a separate dwelling under a tenancy *or licence* (1985, s.79), under which both the landlord conditions and the tenant conditions are fulfilled, and is not excluded from security under the schedule of exceptions (1985, Sched. 1). The term "let as a separate dwelling" is considered in relation to Housing Act assured tenancies (4.08) and Rent Act protected tenancies (5.26) as it is in connection with the private sector that the greatest attention has been paid to it (but see also 3.09).   3.07

Application to Licensees. The most important distinction between Housing Act 1988 (below, Chapter 4) or Rent Act 1977 (below, Chapter   3.08

5) and Housing Act 1985 security is therefore that the 1985 Act applies to licences, whether or not granted for a monetary payment (1985, s.79(3)), while licences are outside the full protection of the 1988 and 1977 Acts. It has been held, however, that security under the 1985 Act only applies to licenses which effectively grant the occupier exclusive possession (*cf.* 1.58), so that it will not apply, *e.g.* where the landlord retains the right to move tenants to other rooms (*Westminster City Council* v. *Clarke*, 1992). Furthermore, this extension to licensees does not include a licence granted as a temporary expedient to a person who entered the premises the subject of the licence, or other premises, as a trespasser (1985, s.79(4)): *i.e.* those who illegally entered unused public sector property awaiting demolition, who were allowed to remain or else offered somewhere else temporarily (1.10). Throughout this chapter, save where a distinction is drawn, a reference to a secure tenancy includes licences brought into security by section 79.

3.09   **Shared Living Accommodation.** Another important distinction is that, while the Housing Act 1988 and the Rent Act 1977 apply to those who share living accommodation (4.08, 5.42), but have a tenancy of their own room, the requirement of a separate dwelling under the 1985 Act means there cannot be a secure tenancy where living accommodation is shared *Central Y.M.C.A. H.A. Ltd.* v. *Saunders*, 1990; *Curl* v. *Angelo*, 1948). Living accommodation for these purposes is that where the essential activities of sleeping, cooking and eating are carried out, so that while it does not include the sharing of a bathroom or lavatory (*Cole* v. *Harris*, 1945), a shared kitchen will take the letting outside security (*Neale* v. *Del Soto*, 1945; *Central Y.M.C.A.*). While this requirement of a separate dwelling will be of little concern to most occupiers of public sector dwellings, it will affect those in hostels and other shared accommodation.

3.10   **Principal Considerations.** Under this heading, we must consider:
        (i) *the landlord condition*;
        (ii) *the tenant condition*;
        (iii) *exceptions*;
        (iv) *succession*;
        (v) *loss of security*.

        (i) *The Landlord condition*

3.11   **Secure Landlords.** The landlord condition is that the landlord under the tenancy is: a local authority; the Commission for the New Towns; a

New Town development corporation; the Housing Corporation or Housing for Wales; the Development Board for Rural Wales; in relation to a tenancy granted before the commencement of Part I, 1988 Act (January 15, 1989); a housing trust which is a charity within the meaning of the Charities Act 1960, or a housing association registered with the Housing Corporation/Housing for Wales, or whose application for registration with the Housing Corporation/Housing for Wales is pending, or one registered under the Industrial and Provident Societies Act 1965 whose rules restrict membership to persons who are tenants or prospective tenants of the association and prevent the grant or assignment of tenancies to non-members; a housing management co-operative (*i.e.* one to whom a local authority or New Town have leased land, or delegated their management powers, with the consent of the Secretary of State); or a county council exercising reserve housing powers with the consent of the Secretary of State (3.03) (1985, s.80).

Added and Excluded Landlords. In addition, the landlord condition is fulfilled if the landlord is an urban development corporation, designated under the Local Government, Planning and Land Act 1980, or a Housing Action Trust (3.78) established under Part III, Housing Act 1988 (1985, s.80). The list of landlords thus extended means that most public and publicly-funded landlords will be within the provisions of the 1985 Act. Excluded from the 1985 Act, is Crown property (including property held by government departments), although Crown property under the management of the Crown Estate Commissioners will qualify under the 1988 or the 1977 Act. The definition of a housing association registered under the Industrial Provident Societies Act 1965 (3.11) means that housing co-operatives popularly so-called (as distinct from housing management co-operatives, *cf.* 3.11), will qualify: these are bodies which, with the assistance of grant-aid secured under the Housing Associations Act 1985, and monitored and paid by the Housing Corporation, are both owned and managed by the tenants collectively, as the members of the co-operative. All of these landlords are exempt from the principal provisions of the Landlord and Tenant Act 1987 (Chapter 2). **3.12**

(ii) *The tenant condition*

Occupation by Individual as Only or Principal Home. The tenant condition is that the tenant is an individual, as opposed to a corporate body, *e.g.* a company, and that the tenant occupies the dwelling-house as his only or principal home (1985, s.81). This is a slightly different test **3.13**

(*Poland* v. *Earl Cadogan*, 1980) from that of statutory residence under the Rent Act 1977 (5.57-5.64), and is rather, closer to that to be found in relation to the Leasehold Reform Act 1967 (2.12). Whether premises are occupied as a home at all, is, however, to be adjudged in the same way as is the question whether they are occupied as a residence under the Rent Act 1977, so that actual physical occupation may not be necessary (*Crawley B.C.* v. *Sawyer*, 1987). If the tenancy is a joint tenancy, then at least one of the joint tenants must be an individual as opposed to a corporate body, and at least one of the joint tenants must be in occupation as an only or principal home (1985, s.81).

(iii) *Exceptions*

3.14   Exceptions from Security. The schedule of exceptions is lengthy (1985, Sched. 1). They are:

(*a*) Long Leases. Long leases, *i.e.* leases for a period in excess of 21 years (para. 1);

(*b*) Employee Accommodation. Premises occupied under a contract of employment which requires the tenant to occupy the dwelling-house for the better performance of his duties (1.62-1.66), and the tenant is an employee of the landlord, or of a local authority, a New Town development corporation, the Commission for the New Towns, a county council, the Development Board for Rural Wales, an urban development corporation or a Housing Action Trust; also, premises provided to policemen free of rent and rates under the Police Act 1964, and premises rented to firemen, in consequence of employment, and where their contract of employment requires the fireman to live close to a particular station (para. 2);

(*c*) Temporary Use of Employee Accommodation. Where premises have been occupied under a para. 2 exemption from security at any time in the last three years, the landlord can let them out in other circumstances, without the occupier becoming secure, provided: (i) the landlord gives the occupier notice that this exception will apply; and (ii) the tenancy, or tenancies, do not themselves extend more than three years beyond the last time when the premises were occupied under a para. 2 exemption (para. 2);

(*d*) Development Land. Premises on land acquired for development, being used pending development for temporary housing accommodation, *i.e.* short-life user (para. 3);

(*e*) Homeless Persons Accommodation. A tenancy granted to a person under section 63 (10.41), section 65(3) (10.44), or section 68(1) (10.34) of Part III of the 1985 Act (*i.e.* categories of homeless persons), for the first year following notification under section 64 (10.55), unless during that year the landlord notifies the tenant that he is to be a secure tenant (para. 4);

(*f*) **Job Mobility Accommodation.** Temporary accommodation granted to a person not hitherto resident in the same district or London borough as the premises, granted for the purposes of enabling the tenant to take up employment or an offer of employment within that district or London borough, or within an adjoining district or London borough, while looking for permanent accommodation. Before the grant of the tenancy, the landlord must notify the tenant that this exception applies; the exception only applies for one year, or less if during that year the landlord notifies the tenant that he is to be a secure tenant (para. 5);

(*g*) **Sub-Leasing Schemes.** Sub-leasing schemes under which the landlord takes a lease from a private sector landlord (*i.e.* one whose tenants would not be secure if granted a direct tenancy), which is either a fixed-term tenancy or one granted on terms that the lease will come to an end when required by the superior landlord. This scheme enables public landlords to take lettings of residential accommodation which would otherwise be left vacant by the private sector landlord, presumably for fear of Housing Act 1988 security, in order to lease it on to others (para. 6);

(*h*) **Accommodation Pending Works for Non-Secure Tenant.** Temporary accommodation provided to a tenant who is not a secure tenant, while works are executed to his usual home (para. 7);

(*i*) **Agricultural Holdings.** Agricultural holdings (para. 8);

(*j*) **Licensed Premises.** Licensed premises (para. 9);

(*k*) **Student Lettings.** Student lettings granted in order to enable the tenant to attend a designated course at an educational establishment, where the landlord has, before the grant of the tenancy, notified the student that the exception applies. This exception ceases at any time if the landlord notifies the tenant that he is to be a secure tenant. A designated course is one designated by the Secretary of State for this purpose. The tenant, unless otherwise notified, remains non-secure until six months after he ceases to attend the educational establishment, or if the tenant fails to take up his place on the course, six months after the grant of the tenancy (para. 10);

(*l*) **Business Lettings.** Business tenancies (see Chapter 6) (para. 11). Particular problems of definition may apply to those who occupy premises part of which consist of, for example, a shop or business. It is not possible for a tenancy which was originally let for a business purpose to become a letting within the 1985 Act, for it will not have been let "as a dwelling" (*Webb* v. *Barnet L.B.C.*, 1988) unless there is an agreed change to residential use (*Russell* v. *Booker,* 1982) but it is possible for a tenancy which was originally let as a dwelling under a secure tenancy to become a business letting and so "move" from 1985 Act protection into that of the Landlord and Tenant Act 1954, Part II (1985, Sched. 1, para.11), which is the main legislation concerned with business lettings. This will happen if the predominant use of the premises is, or becomes, business use (*Cheryl Investments Ltd.* v. *Saldanha,* 1978). Some business use, perhaps ancillary to offices elsewhere, will not necessarily achieve this effect (*Royal Life Saving Society* v. *Page,* 1978), and merely taking in lodgers will not do so either (*Lewis* v. *Weldcrest,* 1978). The business activity must be part of the reason for, and the aim and object in, occupying the house, not merely an incidental hobby which made some money (*Gurton* v. *Parrot,* 1990). It is always a question of fact and degree.

(*m*) **Almshouses.** Almshouses (para. 12).

(iv) *Succession*

3.15   **Solitary Succession.** Under the Housing Act 1985, there can be one statutory succession, to a surviving spouse or to a member of the deceased tenant's family (1985, s.87). Indeed, in some circumstances, there may be no succession at all. Thus, if the tenancy was originally a joint tenancy, but one of the joint tenants has died or otherwise surrendered his interest, there will be no further succession (1985, s.88).

3.16   **Qualifying Successor.** Only a qualifying person can succeed. A person qualifies if, at the time of the death of the secure tenant, the would-be successor was occupying the dwelling-house as his only or principal home (3.16) and he was either the deceased tenant's spouse, or another member of the deceased tenant's family (1985, s.87). In the case of anyone other than a spouse, it is necessary to show that the putative successor has been residing with the deceased tenant for at least 12 months before his death. "Residing with" means more than "living or staying at" the premises, although not necessarily so much as residing permanently or indefinitely: *Swanbrae* v. *Elliott* (1987); *Hildebrand* v. *Moon,* (1989). The twelve month residence with the deceased tenant does *not* have to have been at the property to which succession is being sought: *London Borough of Waltham Forest* v. *Thomas* (1992).

3.17   **Choice of Successors.** Where there is more than one qualifying person, the deceased tenant's spouse takes precedence, but otherwise the qualifying persons must agree amongst themselves who is to take over the tenancy: if they cannot so agree, the landlord is entitled to choose the successor. There is no obligation to notify the landlord who has decided or been agreed to succeed (*General Management* v. *Locke*, 1980). There can be no joint succession.

Members of Family. Members of the family are defined (1985, s.113)   3.18 as: spouses, parents, grandparents, children, grandchildren, siblings, uncles, aunts, nephews and nieces; including step-relation, half-relation and illegitimate children and persons living together as husband and wife. A homosexual couple cannot be considered to be living together as husband and wife: *Harrogate B.C.* v. *Simpson* (1984).

(v) *Loss of security*

Ways of Losing Security. There are several circumstances in which   3.19 security can be lost, leaving aside for the moment an order for possession made by the court (3.21-3.26). First of all, security will be lost if there is a change of landlord, and the new landlord does not fulfill the landlord condition (3.11-3.12; see also transfer of public housing, below). Secondly if the tenant ceases to occupy the premises as his only or principal home, the tenancy ceases to be secure (3.13). Thirdly, on the death of a fixed-term tenant during the term of the lease, the tenancy will only remain secure if the lease passes to someone who qualifies as a successor (3.15-3.16) (1985, s.90).

Loss of Security by Assignment. In addition, any assignment (1.100)   3.20 of a secure tenancy causes security to be lost, unless *either* the assignment is pursuant to an order of the court in the course of divorce (9.12), *or* it is to someone who qualifies as a successor (3.15-3.17), *or* it is pursuant to the "right to exchange" (1985, s.91) (below, 3.60). If the secure tenant sublets the whole of the premises, either at one go or piecemeal, security is also lost, even if the subletting is to a person who qualifies as a successor (1985, s.93). In any of the cases considered in this paragraph, once security is lost it cannot be regained (1985, ss.91, 93), *e.g.* by evicting a sub-tenant. Security will not now normally be lost by bankruptcy.

2. *Security under the Housing Act 1985*

Orders for Possession - (1) Immediate Orders. The most usual way   3.21 for a person who does not voluntarily give up possession of premises subject to a secure tenancy to leave the premises is because a court order for possession is made against him. There are three sorts of court order; the first sort is an immediate order which can be executed without any period of delay other than that resulting from the time it takes to get a bailiff to evict the occupier. The court will normally only make such an order against a trespasser (see Chapter 7).

3.22   **Orders for Possession - (2) Outright Orders.** Secondly, there is what is commonly called an outright order, which is to say that the court has power to grant some finite period of delay, usually two weeks but on occasion, in extreme hardship, sometimes stretched to a maximum of six weeks (1980, s.89). (The maximum only applies in the county court, and does not apply if proceedings are brought in the High Court: *Bain and Co* v. *Church Commissioners for England,* 1988.) Once the period of delay granted by the court has run out, then the landlord can issue a bailiff's warrant and there may be a further period of delay before any actual eviction. This sort of order will be granted against any former tenant who is not a Housing Act secure, Housing Act assured or Rent Act protected tenant, and in some circumstances it will be granted against former Housing Act secure, Housing Act assured or Rent Act protected tenants, where possession is made on mandatory grounds (3.42, 4.30, 5.68). It will also apply to former licensees (see Chapter 1).

3.23   **Orders for Possession - (3) Suspended Orders.** Finally, there is the suspended order for possession, which may either be an order suspended for a period longer than four or six weeks, or an order suspended indefinitely, but on conditions (1985, s.85).

3.24   **Statutory Security.** Under the Rent Act 1977, security of tenure is afforded first of all by a contract of tenancy, and secondly by the Act itself: the landlord is free to determine a periodic tenancy when he will, by notice to quit and a fixed-term tenancy may expire by effluxion of time, or by forfeiture (1.42-1.48). However, there then follows a statutory tenancy (5.12) and the landlord can only in practice evict by court order, which will only be available on specified grounds for possession (5.68-5.91).

3.25   **Contractual Security.** The procedure works differently under the Housing Act 1985 (and under the Housing Act 1988 - see Chapter 4). If a secure tenancy is a periodic tenancy, the landlord cannot bring the tenancy to an end at all: only the court can order the tenancy to come to an end, and this it can only do on specified grounds, and only after the landlord has followed the appropriate preliminary procedure. If the tenancy is a fixed-term tenancy, it can only be forfeit by court order, and even if it expires by effluxion of time, there will come into its place an automatic periodic tenancy, on the same terms as the preceding fixed-term tenancy, and of which the periods are the same as those for which rent was paid under the preceding fixed-term tenancy (1985, s.86). The only exceptions to this are: (*a*) if the landlord and the tenant agree a new fixed-term tenancy to follow the first fixed-term tenancy; and (*b*) if the court orders possession to be given up at the end of the fixed-term, *i.e.* in forfeiture proceedings. Thus, on proceedings to forfeit (1.42-1.44) a fixed-term secure tenancy, the court has a choice of orders: it may determine the fixed-term, but not order the tenant out, in which case the periodic (and Housing Act secure) tenancy will follow (1985, s.86(1)); or, it may grant a possession order.

Continuation Until Possession.   In the case of a periodic tenancy, 3.26 whether originally periodic or following a fixed-term, the tenancy itself continues until the date the court specifies for the tenant to give up possession (1985, s.82). The court can only make an order for possession on specified grounds, and only provided the landlord has followed the proper procedure (1985, s.83). This procedure is in place of notice to quit, and is commonly known as a "notice of seeking possession" or N.S.P.

Notice of Seeking Possession.   The N.S.P. must normally specify a 3.27 date after which legal proceedings may issue (1985, s.83(3)(*a*)). The N.S.P. then remains in force for only one year following that specified date (1985, s.83(3)(*b*)). The specified date must not be earlier than the date when the tenancy could have been brought to an end by notice to quit (1.45-1.47) (1985, s.83(3)).

Contents of Notice. The N.S.P. must be in the form prescribed by the 3.28 Secretary of State for the Environment, or substantially to the same effect, and it must specify the grounds on which the court will be asked to terminate the tenancy and make a possession order (1985, s.83(2)); the particulars must be sufficient to enable the tenant to know what he has to do in order to put matters right, *e.g.* must specify an amount of arrears (*Torridge D.C.* v. *Jones*, 1985). An error in the particulars will not invalidate the notice, provided it sets out what the landlord intends in good faith to prove (*Dudley M.B.C.* v. *Bailey*, 1990). The court cannot entertain proceedings for possession unless the proceedings are commenced after the specified date, and the N.S.P. is still in force at the time the proceedings are begun (1985, s.83(4)). A N.S.P. may be served on a fixed-term tenant, either in order to determine the fixed term (but not seek an actual order for possession, so that a periodic tenancy will follow - 3.25), or in order both to determine the fixed term and seek an order for possession. In either case, there is no need for a specified date, nor does the notice remain in force for only one year (1985, s.83(5)), although if no action is taken, it may well be that there has been waiver of any breach which has given rise to the attempt to bring the fixed term to an end (1.78).

3.29   **Grounds for Possession.** The crucial element of security is, of course, the grounds for possession. These fall into three classes:

(i) *ground plus reasonableness;*
(ii) *ground plus suitable alternative accommodation,* and
(iii) *ground plus suitable alternative accommodation plus reasonableness.*

(i) *Ground plus reasonableness*

3.30   **Reasonableness - Additional Requirement.** In relation to this class of ground for possession, the landlord must satisfy the court: (*a*) that the ground is itself made out; and (*b*) that it is reasonable to make the order sought (1985, s.84)). It is important always to bear in mind that this requirement is additional, and must be considered in every case (*Peachey Property Corporation* v. *Robinson,* 1967).

3.31   **Reasonableness - Examples.** The purpose of this overriding requirement of reasonableness is to ensure that a tenant does not lose his home because of some trivial breach, or perhaps because the landlord has written into the tenancy unduly onerous terms. The parties' conduct (*Yelland* v. *Taylor,* 1957), and other factors affecting the parties and the public generally (*Cresswell* v. *Hodgson,* 1951) may be taken into account under this heading. Thus, in *Lal* v. *Nakum* (1982), a tenant withheld rent on account of an alleged breach of repairing obligation by the landlord (Chapter 11), which allegation he did not manage to sustain in court. He had saved the withheld rent, and could have paid it all at once: none the less, the court made an outright order for possession. The Court of Appeal set this aside. Where, however, a tenant lost a counterclaim for disrepair and was unable to make any provision to pay off the arrears in *London Borough of Haringey* v. *Stewart* (1991) the Court of Appeal upheld the outright order for possession. In *Woodspring District Council* v. *Taylor* (1982), a couple had lived in their house for 24 years. The man lost his employment and suffered a heavy tax demand; the woman had diabetes and was attending a blood specialist. The Department of Health and Social Security took over their rent payments, and were paying £1 per week off the arrears. Until the recent difficulties, the Taylors had always been good tenants. The county court judge made an order for possession, but the Court of Appeal had ''difficulty in understanding how anyone could have made an order turning them out of their home.''

Conditions. The provision is an important protection for tenants. It is useful to bear in mind when a tenant confronts a claim for possession: the court has a generous discretion as to what it may do. Its powers may be exercised at any time before the order is actually executed, and include to adjourn a case, to suspend execution of the order, and to impose conditions; even if an order is made, it can be discharged or set aside. If conditions are complied with, *e.g.* to clear arrears, it is worthwhile applying for discharge, rather than leaving on the court file an order which might be activated erroneously and with inadequate warning to the tenant. In all cases, however, unless it will cause exceptional hardship to the tenant, or would otherwise be unreasonable, the court will order payments of rent and of any arrears that there may be (1985, s.85(3)). These powers may not only be exercised for the benefit of the tenant, but also for his spouse or ex-spouse (Chapter 9)(1985, s.85(5),(6)). If the court suspends an order indefinitely, the secure tenancy will continue; it will only come to an end if and when the court specifies a date for the tenant to give up possession (1985, s.82).   3.32

Rent Unpaid. The grounds for possession are to be found in Schedule 2 to the 1985 Act. Ground 1 is that rent due from the tenant has not been paid, or an obligation of the tenancy has been broken or not performed. There will be no arrears if the tenant has exercised his right to set-off an amount against the landlord's breach of his repairing obligations (11.50–11.52), although it has already been noted that if the tenant does so wrongly there will be a ground for possession but it is unlikely that it will be reasonable to make the order (3.31). It will usually be unreasonable to make the order if the tenant has paid off the arrears by the date of hearing (*Hayman* v. *Rowlands,* 1957), although in special circumstances, *e.g.* a long history of non-payment, it is still possible (*Bird* v. *Hildage,* 1948). A landlord can obtain an *ex parte* order requiring a tenant to pay to him any housing benefit (3.77) he is claiming, if, but only if, the tenant is still in occupation, and there is evidence that he will otherwise default (*Berg* v. *Markhill,* 1985).   3.33

3.34   **Breach of Term.** There will be no breach of a term of the tenancy if there has been a waiver (1.78) of the breach. It is only breach of a term of the tenancy which gives rise to the claim, not some additional, ancillary agreement, *e.g.* a personal undertaking (*R.M.R. Housing Society* v. *Combs*, 1951). In *Heglibiston Establishments* v. *Heyman* (1977), it was held that cohabitation did not amount to a breach of a covenant prohibiting immoral user.

3.35   **Nuisance and Annoyance.** Ground 2 is that the tenant or any person residing in the dwelling-house has been guilty of conduct which is a nuisance or annoyance to neighbours, or has been convicted of using the dwelling-house or allowing it to be used for immoral or illegal purposes. Nuisance or annoyance may have been committed by the tenant, or by anyone living with him, but the tenant cannot be subject to a claim if he has taken all reasonable steps to prevent the nuisance or annoyance (*Commercial General Administration Ltd.* v. *Thomsett*, 1979), including any such steps as may be open to him to evict any lodger or sub-tenant. The nuisance or annoyance must be to a neighbour but this does not mean that the occupier's property is necessarily physically contiguous (*Cobstone Investments Ltd.* v. *Maxim*, 1985), which concerned the Rent Act phrase "adjoining occupier" but held there is no real difference between "neighbours" and "adjoining occupiers" for this purpose.

3.36   **Illegal and Immoral User.** Immoral user will normally lead to an order for possession, though not invariably (*Yates* v. *Morris*, 1950). Illegal user only applies when the use of the premises has something to do with a criminal conviction, even if the offence was not one which as a matter of law necessarily involved use of premises, but the use of the premises must have been part of the facts leading to the conviction, rather than only incidentally the site of the commission of the offence (*S. Schneider and Sons* v. *Abrahams*, 1925). Thus, a conviction for possession of cannabis will be unlikely to lead to an order, especially as it will mean the imposition of a double penalty (*Abrahams* v. *Wilson*, 1971).

3.37   **Deterioration of Premises or Furniture.** Grounds 3 and 4 concern deterioration of the premises or common parts, or of any furniture provided by the landlord in the premises or common parts, which is attributable to the acts, neglect or default of the tenant, or of someone living with him. No order will be made on either of these grounds if the default was that of a sub-tenant or lodger and before the hearing the tenant has taken such steps as are open to him to evict the sub-tenant or lodger.

Deception. Grounds 5 and 6, have no counterpart in the private sector. 3.38
Ground 5 is that the tenant is the person, or one of the persons, to whom
the tenancy was granted, and the landlord was induced to grant the
tenancy by a false statement knowingly or recklessly made by the
tenant. Thus, obtaining a tenancy by deception. Note, first of all, that
such an allegation is of a quasi-criminal nature (and if the tenancy was
granted under Part III, an actually criminal nature, *cf.* 10.59), and will
accordingly require a high standard of proof; note, secondly, that if the
tenancy was granted to two persons, *e.g.* cohabitants, spouses, one of
whom has departed, the ground is only available against the remaining
tenant if the remaining tenant was guilty of the false statement.

Premium on Exchange. Ground 6 relates to the "right to exchange" 3.39
(3.60): it arises if the tenancy arose by exchange, to which either tenant
was a party, or a member of his family from whom he has taken over the
tenancy was a party (3.20), which member of his family is still living in
the property with him, and a premium (*i.e.* money or other pecuniary
consideration, *e.g.* goods) was paid in connection with the exchange
(whether to or by the tenant or member of his family still living in the
property).

Conflict with Non-Housing Purposes. Ground 7 governs employ- 3.40
ment-related accommodation (not excluded from security, *cf.* 3.14), and
arises where: (*a*) the premises are part of, or in the grounds of, a
building held by the landlord for non-housing purposes; and (*b*) the
letting was in consequence of employment; and, (*c*) the tenant or
someone residing in the property has been guilty of conduct such that -
having regard to the purposes for which the main building is held - it
would not be right for the tenant to remain in occupation.

Accommodation Pending Works. Ground 8 arises where the tenant of 3.41
one set of premises, under a secure tenancy, is asked to move to another
set of premises, while works are carried out to the first premises. The
ground may be compared to Schedule 1, para. 8 (1985) of the exceptions
to security (3.14(*h*)), excluding from security tenants who have similarly
been moved, but from an insecure tenancy. Ground 8 is only available
if the terms of the move included an undertaking that the tenant would
move back when works were completed, and the works are now
completed and the original property ready for re-occupation. The
requirement of reasonableness presumably allows the tenant to argue,
e.g. that the works have not been done as agreed, or that they have taken
so long that he has now set down new roots in the alternative property,

and ought not to have to move back again.

(ii) *Ground plus suitable alternative accommodation*

3.42   **Suitable Accommodation.** Under this class, it is not necessary to show in addition to the ground that it is reasonable to make the order, but it is necessary to show that suitable alternative accommodation is available. The court has, therefore, no discretion whether or not to make the order, once satisfied on both these points. Alternative accommodation will only be suitable if it is of premises to be let as a separate dwelling under a Housing Act secure tenancy, or under a Housing Act assured or a Rent Act protected tenancy, other than one subject to any of the mandatory grounds for possession (4.30-4.38; 5.68-5.76) including shorthold (Chapter 6; 1985, Sched. 2, Part IV, para. 1).

3.43   **Suitability for Tenant and Family.** The accommodation must be reasonably suitable to the needs of the tenant and his family, in the opinion of the court, in relation to which the court shall have regard to: the nature of the accommodation usually provided by the landlord to persons with similar needs; distance from the place of work or education of the tenant or members of his family; distance from the home of the family or any member of the tenant's own family (*e.g.* relatives who require or provide support), if proximity is necessary to the well-being of either relative or tenant; the needs (as regards extent of accommodation, which can in an appropriate case include a garden - *Enfield L.B.C.* v. *French,* 1984) and means of tenant and his family; the terms of the accommodation; and, if furniture has hitherto been provided, whether furniture is to be provided in the alternative accommodation, and its nature (1985, Sched. 2, Part IV, paras. 1 and 2). The schedule of matters to which regard is to be paid is not exhaustive; the weight to be given to each is a matter of degree in each case (*Enfield L.B.C.*). If the landlord is not the local authority, the certificate of the local authority that suitable accommodation will be provided by that authority will be conclusive evidence that alternative accommodation so provided is suitable (1985, Sched. 2, Part IV, para. 4).

3.44   **Overcrowded Accommodation.** The first ground under this class is Ground 9, and arises when the dwelling currently occupied is overcrowded within the meaning of Part X of the Housing Act 1985, in such circumstances as to render the occupier guilty of an offence (14.05-14.10). However, in relation to this ground only, it should be noted that alternative accommodation is not to be deemed unsuitable solely because it offends the space standard described in Chapter 14 (14.07(*b*); 1985, Sched. 2, Part IV, para. 3).

Redevelopment. Ground 10 is available when the landlord intends, 3.45 within a reasonable time of seeking possession, either: (*a*) to demolish or reconstruct the building, or part of the building which includes the dwelling in question; or (*b*) to carry out work on the building, or on land let together with the building, and in either case cannot reasonably do so without obtaining possession. The landlord has to be able to show an established, settled and clearly defined intention to do the works, and that it needs possession to do the works (*Wansbeck D.C.* v. *Marley*, 1987). Ground 10A was added in 1986, and applies when the landlord, within a reasonable period of obtaining possession, intends to sell with vacant possession, but it applies if, and only if, the property is in an "approved development area" (that is to say, approved by the Secretary of State or, in the case of a registered housing association, the Housing Corporation). There is provision for a dwelling which falls partly within, and partly outside of, such an area.

Conflict with Charitable Purposes. Ground 11 is available only to a 3.46 landlord which is a charity within the meaning of the Charities Act 1960, and the tenant's continued occupation of the dwelling would conflict with the objects of the charity, *i.e.* where the charity has a specific purpose, such as the assistance of single parents, or the disabled, and neither the tenant nor anyone living with him any longer qualifies for such a descripton.

(iii) *Ground plus suitable alternative accommodation plus reasonableness*

Suitable and Reasonable. In this class, the landlord must prove: (*a*) 3.47 that the ground is available and applicable; and (*b*) that suitable alternative accommodation (as defined, 3.42-13.43), is available; and (*c*) that it is reasonable to make the order sought, thus importing the court's discretion considered above (3.30-3.31).

Non-Housing Property Required for Employee, Disabled Persons 3.48 **Accommodation.** Ground 12 applies where: (*a*) the property forms part of, or is in the grounds of, a non-housing building, or in the grounds of a cemetery; and (*b*) was let in consequence of employment (3.14); and (*c*) the property is now reasonably required for a new employee. This is similar to Case 8 under the Rent Act 1977 (5.85). Ground 13 applies only to dwellings which have features which are substantially different from ordinary houses, designed to make the house suitable for the occupation of a physically disabled person. The ground is only available if there is no longer a physically disabled person of the class for whom it was provided (which need not be the tenant, but could be a member of his family), and the landlord requires it for occupation of one such disabled person.

3.49   **Required for Person with Special Needs.** Ground 14 is available only to housing associations or housing trusts, engaged in letting property to specific categories of persons who, for reasons other than poverty, have particular difficulty satisfying their housing needs, *e.g.* ethnic groups, battered women, young people, the mentally handicapped. This ground is only available when either there is no longer such a person in occupation (whether as tenant or not), or the local authority are offering the tenant a secure tenancy elsewhere, and in either case the landlord requires the dwelling for occupation by a person of the class they are engaged in assisting.

3.50   **Sheltered Accommodation.** Ground 15 applies to "sheltered accommodation," *i.e.* houses or flats in a group which are in practice let to people with special needs, and in close proximity to which a social service or other special facility is provided, *e.g.* for elderly people, or the disabled. As under the last two grounds, the ground is only available when there is no longer a person of the designated class in occupation, and the premises are required for occupation by such a person.

3.51   **Underoccupation.** Ground 16 is only available when the tenant has succeeded to the secure tenancy on the death of a previous tenant (3.15-3.18). It is, furthermore, never available when the tenant is the spouse of the deceased secure tenant. It is only available when the accommodation afforded by the dwelling is more extensive than is reasonably required by the successor, and notice of seeking possession (3.27) was served no earlier than six months after the death of the previous tenant, and no later than 12 months after his death.

3. *Additional Rights of Secure Tenants*

3.52   **Right to Buy.** The best-known additional right is the so-called "right to buy." The right to buy arises only after a tenant has acquired two years as a secure tenant, although not necessarily in the same premises, nor necessarily continuously (1985, s.119). The tenant has to be secure both when applying to buy, and at the end of the process, when it comes to the time actually to buy (*L.B. of Sutton* v. *Swann*, 1985). If the dwelling is a house, and the landlord owns the freehold, the right to buy is a right to the freehold (1.03); otherwise (*i.e.* if the property is a flat, or if the landlord only has a lease), the right is to a lease of, normally, 125 years, but will be less if the landlord's interest is itself not that long (1985, Sched.6). The right to buy is accompanied by an entitlement to a mortgage granted by the landlord, (or, in the case of a housing association, by the Housing Corporation or Housing for Wales) (1985, s.132).

Exemptions from Right to Buy. There are detailed provisions govern- 3.53 ing the definition of "house" and "flat" (1985, s.183), and the exercise of these rights by joint tenants (1985, s.118). Some property is exempt from the right to buy (1985, Sched. 5), including property belonging to a housing trust which is a charity, sheltered accommodation (*cf.* 3.49) and accommodation adapted for the physically disabled (*cf.* 3.48).

Discount. The right is to buy at a discount (1985, s.129), amounting to 3.54 (in the case of a house) 33 per cent. for up to three years as a secure tenant, plus 1 per cent. per year thereafter, to a maximum discount of 60 per cent., or (in the case of a flat), 44 per cent. for up to three years, plus 2 per cent. per year thereafter to a maximum of 70 per cent. However, the discount may have to be repaid if the house or flat is subsequently sold (1985, s.155).

Shared Ownership. Where the right to a mortgage is insufficient to 3.55 meet the full purchase price, the tenant has an alternative right, to a "shared ownership lease," under which he purchases a portion of the landlord's interest, and continues to pay a (proportionately reduced) rent on the remainder, subject to the right to purchase further "slices" of the landlord's interest as and when he can afford to do so (either out of savings, or because, *e.g.* increased earnings will increase his mortgage entitlement) (1985, ss.143-151). The procedure for exercising the right to buy or the right to a shared ownership lease is extremely detailed, and the provisions of Part V of the 1985 Act must be considered as a whole for a thorough understanding of this entitlement.

Non-Compliance with Time-Limits. It may be noted that tenants 3.56 whose landlords fail to comply with time-limits for handling the right to buy will be able to serve notices, the effect of which will be to "penalise" the landlord by treating rent payments during periods of delay as deductions from the purchase price (1985, s.153A, 153B).

3.57   **Improvements.** Secure tenants also enjoy the "right to improve" considered below (11.39). Rent is not to be increased on account of improvements carried out by the tenant (1985, s.101), and the landlord has power to reimburse the tenant for the cost of any improvements carried out, on the departure of the tenant (1985, s.100).

3.58   **Subletting and Lodgers.** Secure tenants have an absolute right to take in lodgers, and a qualified right to sublet part of their premises (1985, s.93). The right to sublet part is expressed as a negative obligation: that the secure tenant shall not sublet part without the written consent of the landlord (1985, s.93(1)(*a*)). However, this consent is not unreasonably to be withheld, and if unreasonably withheld is to be treated as given, so that it is in substance a positive entitlement to sublet with consent (1985, s.94). The exercise of a qualified right to sublet has been considered above (1.75-1.77) but it is worth restating that, no matter how well-founded may be anticipation of refusal, a tenant will not be able to claim unreasonable withholding without first making the request (*Barrow* v. *Isaacs*, 1891).

3.59   **Reasons and Conditions.** If the landlord fails to reply within a reasonable time, the consent is deemed to have been withheld (1985, s.94(6)), but if the landlord does refuse, then a written statement of reasons for refusal must be provided (1985, s.94(6)). Consent may, however, be sought after the subletting, and if then given will validate the subletting (1985, s.94(4)). No conditions may be attached to a consent (1985, s.94(5)). It will be relevant, when considering the reasonableness of a refusal, to take into account overcrowding (14.05-14.11) or any proposals for work which the landlord may have which would affect the accommodation likely to be used by the sub-tenant (1985, s.94(3)). The burden of proof lies always on the landlord to show that the withholding is reasonable (1985, s.94(2)), and the tenant may apply to the county court for a declaration that a withholding is unreasonable (1985, s.110).

3.60   **Right to Exchange.** Under this right, all secure tenants have the right to exchange their properties with another secure tenant, whether of the same landlord or not (1985, s.92(1)). The right has also been extended to include Housing Act assured tenants of the Housing Corporation,

Housing for Wales, a registered housing association, or housing trust which is a charity, *i.e.* those landlords formerly within the 1985 Act (3.05: 1985, s.92(2A)). There can even be three-way exchanges, provided all are Housing Act secure tenants or have a relevant assured tenancy, and the landlord of each has consented in writing (1985, s.92(2)). A landlord has 42 days in which to consent, and can only refuse consent on one of a specified schedule of grounds (1985, s.92(4), (5)). If the landlord refuses consent on another ground, consent is to be treated as given. The landlord loses the right to reply on any of the grounds unless he replies within 42 days.

Conditions. However, this does not mean that the exchange can nec-   3.61
essarily take place, for the landlord is entitled to attach one condition: that is, if there are rent arrears, or there is another breach of a term of the tenancy, the landlord can require the arrears to be cleared, or the breach to be remedied (1985, s.92(5)). Any other condition which a landlord seeks to attach may, however, be disregarded (1985, s.92(6)).

Grounds for Refusal.   The grounds for refusing consent are (1985,   3.62
Sched. 3): the tenant or proposed assignee already is under a court order to give up possession; proceedings for possession have commenced, or N.S.P. has been served (3.27), on any of the grounds for possession which require only that it is reasonable to make the order (3.33-3.41); the accommodation would be too large for the prospective assignee or otherwise not reasonably suitable to his needs; the premises were let in consequence of employment, and form part of, or are in the grounds of, a non-housing building or a cemetery (3.14, 3.48); the landlord is a charity and the proposed assignee's occupation would conflict with its objects (3.46); the property is designed for a physically disabled person, and if the proposed assignee moved in there would be no such person in occupation (3.48); the landlord is a special needs housing association or trust, and if the proposed assignee moved in there would be no one with the relevant need in occupation (3.49); the accommodation is sheltered and, as above, if the proposed assignee moved in there would be no one with the relevant needs in occupation (3.50).

Right to Repair. The "right to repair" (1985, s.96) gives the Gov-   3.63
ernment power to introduce regulations which in turn would permit secure tenants to carry out repairs, instead of waiting for their landlords to do so: the regulations are in the Secure Tenancies (Right to Repair Scheme) Regulations 1985 (S.I. 1985 No. 1493), which came into effect on January 1, 1986. Under this scheme the tenant is entitled to carry out

a *qualifying* repair, *i.e.* any repair the landlord is obliged to carry out under a repairing convenant (Chapter 11), *other* than a repair to the structure or exterior of a flat; the tenant can then recover a sum of money from the landlord for the works. The tenant must first serve a notice on the landlord describing the proposed works, why they are needed, and the materials to be used. Within 21 days the landlord must reply either refusing or accepting the claim.

3.64   **Grounds for Refusal.** Refusal may be on mandatory or discretionary grounds. The mandatory grounds are that the landlord's costs if the works were to be carried out would be less than £20, or that the works are not "qualifying repairs," or that the works would not be effective to remedy the disrepair. The discretionary grounds are that the landlord's costs would be more than £200, or that the landlord intends to carry out the works within 28 days, or that the works are within a planned maintenance programme which will be executed within one year and are not reasonably necessary for the personal comfort and safety of the tenant beforehand, or that the works would infringe a guarantee (*e.g.* given by a builder) of which the landlord has the benefit, or that the tenant has denied the landlord reasonable access to inspect the disrepair.

3.65   **Acceptance of Right.** The landlord's acceptance must state the date by which the payment claim must be made after execution of the works, the amount of its costs, the amount it is willing to contribute to the tenant's costs (which is to be 75-100 per cent. of its own costs) and any modifications to the works or to the materials which it considers necessary.

3.66   **Default Notice.** If the landlord does not respond, or fails to do works as promised in the refusal notice, the tenant may serve a default notice, which gives the landlord a further seven days to reply or carry out works, in default of which the tenant may proceed in accordance with his notice. After completion, the tenant may then claim payment. The landlord must again respond within 21 days, either accepting or refusing the claim. The landlord will refuse if the works have not been properly executed, or the tenant has not complied with a modification requirement, or the tenant did not comply with the default procedure.

3.67   **Refusal of Payment.** The landlord may also refuse if the authorised materials have not been used, access has not been granted for inspection, if the tenant did not do the works himself and they were not carried out by an approved person, or the claim was not made within the time allowed. If the ground for refusal of payment is unsatisfactory execution of works, the landlord must allow the tenant a further opportunity to do them properly. Once the claim has been accepted, the landlord must pay the money within 14 days, and can only do so by credit to the tenant's rent account if the tenant is in arrears.

Suspension of Repairing Obligation. Between commencement of works, and claim for repayment, the landlord's repairing obligation (Chapter 11) will be suspended in respect of the works to which the exercise relates. 3.68

Heating Charges. In addition, the Government have power to introduce special provisions which would entitle secure tenants to find out how their landlords have calculated heating charges, where such a charge is included in the rent (1985, s.108). However, the Government have not brought this power into use, and there is no indication as to whether or when they might do so, or how the provisions would operate. 3.69

Variation of Terms of Tenancy. There are provisions governing the rights of a landlord to vary the terms of a secure tenancy, which is to be by notice, warning of a variation to take effect no sooner than the landlord could have served notice to quit (1.45-1.47) before which date the tenant may respond with his own notice to quit, in which case the variation will not take effect before the tenant's departure (1985, ss.102, 103). Prior to notice of variation, there must be a preliminary notice, outlining the intended variation, and explaining its effect and inviting the tenant's comments. No such preliminary notice need be served in relation to variation of the rent payable, or of any amount in respect of rates, services or facilities provided by the landlord. A notice of variation cannot vary the extent of the premises let under the tenancy. 3.70

Consultation. Where general changes are intended, local authorities and some other landlords under secure tenancies are obliged to consult with their tenants (1985, s.105). All landlords bound by these consultation provisions (1985, s.114) must make and maintain consultation machinery or arrangements for notifying their tenants of proposed changes in matters of housing management, and ascertaining their views. "Housing management" is defined so as to exclude questions of rent, or payments for services or facilities provided by the 3.71

landlord (1985, s.105(2)). Otherwise, it includes such matters as new programmes of maintenance, improvement or demolition, and changes in practice or policy, likely to affect the secure tenants of the landlord as a whole or a group of them (1985, s.105(3)). Landlords affected must publish details of their consultation arrangements (1985, s.105(5)). When the landlord seeks approval of an area for the purposes of a "redevelopment scheme," in connection with Ground 10A (3.30), a different consultation provision applies instead; similarly, a disposal by a Housing Action Trust of a property subject to a secure tenancy (3.56) carries with it its own, alternative consultation provisions.

3.72   **Published Information.** Landlords under secure tenancies must publish information which explains the effect of the express terms of their secure tenancies, the security provisions of the 1985 Act and other provisions considered in this chapter, and the provisions of the Landlord and Tenant Act 1985, s.11, (11.21-11.33; 1985, s.104). Copies of this publication must be provided to secure tenants.

4. *Local Authority Rents*

3.73   **Reasonable Rents.** There is a long history of discretion in the determination of local authority rents. Local authorities are bound to charge reasonable rents, to review their rent levels from time to time and in setting their rent levels to have regard to the principle that rents of property of one class or description should bear broadly the same proportion to private sector rents as the rents of houses of any other class or description (1985, s.24). This last requirement of "relative desirability" was added by the Local Government and Housing Act 1989 ("1989").

3.74   **Challenging Local Authority Rents.** There have been many attempts to challenge local authority rent levels in the courts - both by those who think they are too high, and by those who think they are too low - but most of these attempts have failed. The provisions of the 1989 Act have severely limited the theoretical freedom which local authorities have over rent levels, by requiring the authority's Housing Revenue Account to be balanced (1989, s.76), and limiting what can be credited and debited to it (excluding any general fund subsidy: this is the policy known as "ring-fencing of the account"; see 1989, s.75 and Sched. 4). In *R.* v. *L.B.Ealing, ex p. Lewis* (1992), the Court of Appeal upheld a challenge to the authority's rent levels because there had been included contrary to 1989, Schedule 4, too much of the cost of the authority's homeless persons functions (see Chapter 10) and of the wardens in their sheltered accommodation (*cf.*, above, para. 3.50).

5. *Housing Association Rents*

Fair Rents. In relation to tenancies beginning before the commence-   3.75
ment (January 15, 1989) of Part I, 1988 Act (3.05), all housing
associations, housing trusts and the Housing Corporation, whose tenants
were excluded from Rent Act protection by sections 15 and 16 of the
Rent Act 1977 (5.52), are subject to the same fair rent structure as
private sector tenants (Rent Act 1977, Part. V1). The same is true of
those housing association tenancies which for one of the reasons set out
in 3.05, above, although granted after that date do not become Housing
Act assured tenancies (including, most importantly, those ordered by a
court to become housing association rather than Housing Act assured
tenancies).

Increase without Termination of Tenancy. Although there is a sep-   3.76
arate part of the register for housing associations and other such bodies
(1977, s.87), exactly the same general principles will apply (*Palmer* v.
Peabody Trust, 1975) on the determination of a fair rent for these
tenants, and for Rent Act protected tenants (5.93-5.102). Express
provision is made for housing associations to increase rent without the
need to determine a tenancy and grant a new one at the higher rent, by
notice of variation, similar to that already considered in relation to
Housing Act secure tenants generally (3.70) (1977, s.93). It is not
necessary to consider the operation of the fair rent system in relation to
housing association tenancies, for the system is largely the same as that
considered in relation to the private sector, and variations in detail are
relatively minor: it may, however, be noted that a registered rent forms
the rent limit for a housing association tenancy (5.118-5.124; 1977,
s.88). Housing association, etc., tenancies which are within the Housing
Act 1988 as Housing Act assured tenancies (Chapter 4) are subject to
the same rent provisions as there described for other Housing Act
assured tenants.

6. *Further Financial Protection and Assistance*

Miscellaneous Provisions. There are other forms of financial pro-   3.77
tection or assistance which may be applicable. The first of these,
premiums and deposits, are not specifically prohibited under the
Housing Act 1985: *cf.* 5.126-5.132. The second, accommodation agency

charges, and third, resale of utilities, *i.e.* gas and electricity, are unlikely
to be relevant as matters of practice, but the fourth, housing benefits,
will commonly apply. Under the Social Security Act 1986 rent rebates
and allowances, together with community charge rebates, are available
to assist those on income support and others with low incomes with their
housing costs. The details of these support schemes are so commonly
varied that it is impracticable to consider them here. There are a number
of annual publications which contain the contemporary provisions.

7. *Transfer of Public Housing*

3.78   **Housing Action Trusts.** As mentioned above (3.03), government
policy is to try to reduce the size of the housing stock held by local, and
other public authorities. Two mechanisms for achieving this were
introduced by the Housing Act 1988. Under Part III of the 1988 Act,
Housing Action Trusts were established, designed to take over housing
stock and, in a designated area, a number of other housing-related
powers and duties, either together with the local authority, or instead of
the local authority (many of which are referred to in Chapters 12-14,
below). The proposals are intended to deal with *parts* of a local
authority's area, not the whole of the area of each local authority. The
most important point of note is that the Secretary of State cannot
designate a Housing Action Trust without first carrying (or having
carried) out a ballot or poll, and if a majority of the tenants who respond
to the ballot or poll are opposed to it he must abandon the proposals
(1988, s.61).

3.79   **Criteria.** Presuming that the Secretary of State is entitled to proceed to
establish a Housing Action Trust, he appoints its committee members
(after consultation with the local authority for the area; 1988, Sched. 7,
para. 2): among the considerations which will influence the Secretary of
State when deciding whether or not (subject to ballot) to designate a
Housing Action Trust are the extent of local authority housing in an
area, its physical state and design and need for repair of accommodation
in the area generally, the way in which the local authority housing is
being managed, and living conditions generally in the area, and social
conditions and general environment (1988, s.60). The Secretary of State
also has to consult the local authority for the proposed area before
establishing a Housing Action Trust (1988, s.61). Housing Action Trusts
must in general terms comply with directions given to them by the
Secretary of State (1988, s.72), which renders his control over them
significantly greater than he has over a local authority.

Objects. The principal objects of the Housing Action Trust are to secure   3.80
repair or improvement of the accommodation it takes over, and its
proper and effective management and use, and to encourage diversity in
the ways in which people occupy accommodation (tenancy - public or
private, owner-occupation) and generally to secure or facilitate the
improvement of living conditions in the area, and social conditions and
the general environment (1988, s.63). Housing Action Trusts, like local
authorities, are under a specific duty to avoid racial discrimination, and
promote equality of opportunity in the exercise of their functions (1988,
s.63, applying Race Relations Act 1976, s.71). Once the Trust is
established, it must draw up its proposals, and publicise and consult on
them (1988, s.64).

Powers. The Secretary of State has power to transfer to the Housing   3.81
Action Trust: (*a*) certain housing powers under the Housing Act 1985
(1988, s.65), certain planning powers (1988, ss.66-67), certain public
health powers (1988, s.68), certain powers in respect of highways (1988,
s.69); and (*b*) land and housing belonging to a local authority in its area
(1988, ss.74-76). The purpose is not, however, for the Housing Action
Trust to replace the local authority indefinitely, for it is intended to
achieve its objects and wind itself up as soon as practicable (1988, s.88).
Its purpose, rather, is to transfer the housing to others, whether
owner-occupiers or landlords, (to both of whom a Trust may give
financial assistance: 1988, s.71). The first stage - transfer to Housing
Action Trust - will have some effect for tenants of the housing in
question, especially in relation to rents, but does not take them out of
being Housing Act secure tenants: *that* will follow when and if the
property is transferred to a private landlord, in which case the tenant will
become a Housing Act *assured* tenant (Chapter 4), *not* a Rent Act
protected or statutory tenant (Chapter 5), even though his tenancy will
have started before the commencement (January 15, 1989) of Part I,
1988 Act: 1988, s.38.

Approved Landlords. A prospective landlord only qualifies to take   3.82
Housing Action Trust property if he is a landlord approved for the
purpose by the Housing Corporation or Housing for Wales (the two
bodies whose principal duties are the regulation of housing associations:
3.04): 1988, s.79. The two Corporations cannot approve a public sector
landlord, or a county council, or any body who they think will be under
the control or influence of the public sector landlord or county council,
or its officers or members (1988, s.79). For this purpose, public sector
landlord means any local housing authority, a new town corporation or

the Development Board for Rural Wales. The Corporations can establish criteria for approval, and may seek undertakings from a prospective landlord, as a condition of approval, which may lead to revocation of approval if they are not complied with.

3.83 **Legal Assistance to Tenants.** Because of the role of the Corporations in approving landlords, there is a special provision which empowers them to provide legal assistance to a tenant who is transferrred from a Housing Action Trust to a private landlord (1988, s.82). The power applies only, however, to someone who was a Housing Act secure tenant at the time of the transfer, or his surviving spouse. There has to be consultation in writing with Housing Act secure tenants, before transfer of their homes, and the consultation documentation has to set out what the effect will be for the tenants (1988, s.84). This consultation replaces that which is normally required (3.71).

3.84 **Preserved Right to Buy.** On a transfer to the private sector, a Housing Act secure tenant's right to buy (3.52-3.56) is ''preserved'': 1985, ss.171A-171H. This provision is generally available on a disposal of public sector stock into the private sector. The preserved right to buy will be inapplicable if the right to buy as against the former landlord was unavailable because of paras. 1-3, Sched. 5, 1985 Act (charities and certain housing associations), or in such other cases as may be excepted by order of the Secretary of State: 1985, s.171A(3). The right to buy is only to be preserved so long as the tenant occupies the premises as his only or principal home (3.13): the right may be exercised by the tenant, or a qualifying successor, as defined, and may extend from the original premises to which the tenant has moved and which are rented from the same landlord (or if a company, a connected company): 1985, s.171B. By section 171F, a court is not to make an order for possession against a tenant or qualifying successor on the ground of suitable alternative accommodation without ensuring that the right to buy will be preserved (or that the tenant will be Housing Act secure as against the new landlord). Section 171C empowers the Secretary of State by regulation to modify Part V, 1985 Act for the purposes of the preserved right to buy, which he has done (S.I. 1989 No. 368, as amended), principally to exclude the right to a mortgage and a shared ownership lease.

3.85 **Termination of Preserved Right to Buy.** A subsequent disposal by the landlord does not terminate the preserved right to buy, unless either the new landlord is a landlord whose tenants are Housing Act secure, or the tenant has failed to register his right as a local land charge: s.171D.

The preserved right to buy may also be determined on the termination of the landlord's interest by a superior landlord, other than by merger, but where this occurs by reason of the landlord's act or omission, there is a right to compensation: s.171E.

Tenants' Choice. The preserved right to buy will also apply to the second mechanism introduced to encourage transfer from the public sector to the private sector: these are the provisions of Part IV, 1988 Act, and permit an approved (3.82) landlord to require a public sector landlord to sell him housing stock, with Housing Act secure tenants in it. For this purpose, public sector landlord means the local housing authority, a new town corporation, the Development Board for Rural Wales, or a Housing Act Trust itself (1988, s.93). It applies *only* to freehold property (*e.g.* house, or whole block of flats) occupied by at least one Housing Act secure tenant, *other than* one who is already occupying under a court order specifying a date to quit (3.25), or one who does not enjoy the right to buy because of the provisions of paras. 5-11, Sched. 5, 1985 Act (*i.e.* let in connection with employment, dwellings for the disabled and sheltered or adapted accommodation for the elderly). A landlord who takes a transfer under Part IV cannot subsequently sell the property without the consent of the Secretary of State, save under the "preserved right to buy" (3.84).

3.86

Transfer - Additional Provisions. The Corporations' power to approve a landlord (3.82) applies similarly under this Part (1988, s.94), and does their power to provide legal assistance (3.83), although is this case the assistance can be to a former Housing Act secure tenant, or to someone whose property is treatened with transfer (1988, s.107); the Corporations are also entitled to run an information and advice service, both for approved or would-be approved landlords, and for tenants who may be affected by a transfer under this Part (1988, s.106). The right to require transfer does not apply if less than 50 per cent. of the internal floor area (disregarding common parts) of a building is occupied for non-residential purposes; it also does not apply in the case of a building with flats in it, two or more of which are occupied by non-qualifying Housing Act secure tenants, and those non-qualifying Housing Act secure tenants occupy at least 50 per cent. of the total number of dwellings in the building (1988, s.95).

3.87

Consultation. There are extensive provisions detailing how the right to require transfer can be exercised, in which connection it is important to note that the Housing Act secure tenants must be consulted by the

3.88

prospective landlord, and there can be no transfer to him if more than 50 per cent. of the tenants affected express opposition to the proposal or a wish to contine as tenant of the current (public sector) landlord (1988, s.103): it is important to note that the result must show 50 percent. of the tenants *balloted* who are opposed, rather than 50 per cent. of those who reply. Failure to reply counts as a vote in favour. The Secretary of State may draw up regulations to exclude from the transfer housing occupied by tenants who object, or, in the case of a flat, to be the subject of a lease back to the public sector landlord from the new landlord (so that the tenant remains the direct tenant of his current landlord) (1988, s.100): see S.I. 1989 No. 367. There are time limits applicable to tenants' responses, and it is most important for tenants to comply with them.

4 Housing Act Assured Tenancies

New Class of Security. The Housing Act assured tenancy was devised   4.01
in 1988, by the Housing Act of that year ("1988"), to replace (*a*) the
Rent Acts in the private sector (Chapter 5), and (*b*) the secure tenancy
as it applied under the Housing Act 1985 (formerly, the Housing Act
1980) to housing association tenancies (Chapter 3): there are a small
number of circumstances in which a private sector letting commencing
on or after January 15, 1989 (when the 1988 Act came into force) may
still fall within the Rent Act 1977 (5.02), and a housing association
tenancy may still fall within the Housing Act 1985 (3.04); other public
sector lettings within the 1985 Act are unaffected by this part of the
Housing Act 1988. Housing Act assured *shorthold* tenancies are
considered in their own right in Chapter 6 and will not be referred to
again in this.

Old Assured Tenancies. The term "assured tenancy" was first used in   4.02
1980. Under the Housing Act of that year, two measures were enacted
designed to try to revive the flagging private sector: (Rent Act)
protected shorthold tenancies, and assured tenancies as then defined.
Neither of these measures was considered effective; hence, the further
measures in 1988. With the exception of a small number of 1980 Act
assured tenancies, "kept alive" pending application for a new tenancy,
all 1980 assured tenancies were converted into Housing Act 1988
assured tenancies, as from the commencement of Part I, 1988 Act
(January 15, 1989), subject only to minor qualifications (1988, ss.1, 37).

Assured Transitional Provisions. If there had been an agreement for   4.03
the grant of a 1980 Act assured tenancy prior to the commencement of
Part I, 1988 Act (January 15, 1989), but at that date the tenancy had not
been granted, then when granted it took effect as a Housing Act 1988
assured tenancy, subject to minor qualifications. The minor
qualifications are the same whether the 1988 assured tenancy arose for
this reason, or because of the automatic conversion of a 1980 assured
tenancy into a 1988 assured tenancy (4.02). The minor qualifications
operate in the tenant's favour, insofar as the tenant will not be excluded

from enjoying a Housing Act 1988 assured tenancy by reason of the
normal exclusions contained in the Housing Act 1988, Schedule 1
(4.09-4.23), other than on the grounds that the landlord is the Crown
(not including when the property is under the management of the Crown
Estates Commissioners), or another public body, *i.e.* only the exclusions
in the Housing Act 1988, Schedule 1, paras. 11 and 12 (4.19) will apply
(1988, ss.1, 37).

4.04   **Tenants Only.** In the remainder of this chapter, all references to
assured tenancies are to Housing Act 1988 assured tenancies. It is only
tenants who can enjoy assured protection, not trespassers or licensees
nor, except as described in Chapter 2, owner-occupiers; it should be
noted that assured tenants are excluded from being "qualifying" tenants
for the purposes of Part I, Landlord and Tenant Act 1987, *i.e.* the "right
of first refusal" (2.15-2.21). In the main, tenants whose landlords are
not public bodies, such as a local authority, will be assured tenants
provided that their landlords do not live in the same building as
themselves. This short description can, however, be misleading. In this
connection, it is important to bear in mind that landlords are likely still
to seek to avoid the effects of protection, by granting forms of letting
which are not within the ambit of the 1988 Act, as they have done under
the Rent Acts, *e.g.* by granting licences, holiday lettings or company
letting. The advent of the assured shorthold (6.51) has perhaps made this
less likely in relation to the 1988 Act, but the remarks made in Chapter
5 about such efforts at evasion will apply under the 1988 Act in the
same way (5.09).

4.05   **Succession.** Normally, an assured tenant will be the person to whom
the tenancy was granted. However, there is a limited right of "statutory
succession" to an assured tenancy, similar to (but not as extensive as)
that available to Housing Act secure tenants under the Housing Act 1985
(3.15-3.18) and to Rent Act protected and statutory tenants under the
Rent Act 1977 (5.14-5.18). On the death of an assured tenant, his spouse
can succeed, provided that immediately before his death, she was
occupying the dwelling-house as her only or principal home (4.09):
1988, s.17(1)(*a*). There can be no statutory succession if the deceased
was himself already a successor, whether by reason of this (or another:
5.15) statutory succession provision or because of inheritance (1988,
s.17(2)). If the tenancy was a joint tenancy (1.84), and the deceased
became the tenant on the death of his joint tenant, there can be no
statutory succession (1988, s.17 (2)). Statutory succession only applies
to a sole tenancy (1988, s.17(1)); on the death of one joint tenant, the

other or others become the sole tenant or remaining joint tenants, by right of survivorship. For these purposes, "spouse" is not limited to persons legally married, but includes persons who have been living together as husband and wife (see 3.18). Where there is no statutory succession, a tenancy can pass under a will or on intestacy, and if the inheritor occupies as an only or principal home, the tenancy will still be assured: but in this case there will be a mandatory ground for possession against the successor (4.37).

Agricultural and Forestry Workers. Under the Housing Act 1988, Part I, Chapter III there is protection for agricultural and forestry tied workers, whose occupation commenced on or after January 15, 1989. It is not possible in this book to consider these provisions in any detail, but the following points of distinction should be noted: Chapter III applies not only to service tenants but also to service occupiers (1988, s.24), *i.e.* licensees; the fact that such occupiers will not usually be paying rent does not take them out of protection (1988, s.24(2)); it is usually necessary to show that the employee has been an agricultural worker (though not necessarily with the same employer) for 91 out of the 104 weeks preceding the date when it is claimed that the Act applies (1988, Sched. 3). Additional provision is made for application by a landlord to the local authority, to provide rehousing "in the interests of efficient agriculture" for both assured agricultural occupiers and those protected by the Rent (Agriculture) Act 1976 (5.24) (1976, Part IV). Agricultural workers not within these provisions may get some temporary security for up to a year, under the Protection from Eviction Act 1977, by way of time granted by the court before a possession order takes effect. **4.06**

Principal Issues. The rest of this chapter will be taken up with the following issues: **4.07**

1. *Who is a Housing Act assured tenant?*
2. *What security of tenure do Housing Act assured tenants have?*
3. *Rent and other terms.*
4. *Further financial protection and assistance.*

1. *Who is a Housing Act Assured Tenant?*

Let As A Separate Dwelling. The Housing Act 1988 assumes that all tenants to whom property is let as a separate dwelling (on or after the commencement of 1988, Part I: January 15, 1989) are assured tenants *if* they fulfil the qualifying conditions, and *unless* there is some factor **4.08**

which takes them out of Housing Act assured protection (1988, s.1). The fact that a tenant may share living accommodation (3.09) with someone other than his own landlord will not prevent a tenancy qualifying as an assured tenancy (1988, s.3), even although, strictly, there is no letting as a separate dwelling (3.07).

4.09   Qualifications and Exclusion. There is also a small number of exclusions from protection which: (*a*) are rare enough in practice; and (*b*) are of sufficient particularity that they do not merit discussion: licensed premises, and lettings of agricultural and/or substantial land. The qualifying conditions for a Housing Act assured tenancy are: (i) that the tenant is an individual rather than a corporation, or if a joint tenancy that *all* the joint tenants are individuals; and, (ii) that the tenant, or if a joint tenancy at least one of them, occupies the dwelling as an "only or principal home" (3.13). The remaining factors which take a tenancy out of assured protection deal with:

(*a*) Homeless Persons. Housing for homeless persons, for first year (1988, s.1(6), (7));

(*b*) Prior Tenancy. Tenancies preceding commencement (1988, Sched. 1, para. 1);

(*c*) High Rateable Value. The rateable value or high rent of the premises (1988, Sched. 1, para. 2);

(*d*) No or Low Rent. Whether any or how much rent is paid (1988, Sched. 1, para. 3);

(*e*) Business Lettings. Whether it is a business letting (1988, Sched. 1, para. 4);

(*f*) Student Lettings. Whether it is a student letting (1988, Sched. 1, para. 8);

(*g*) Holiday Lettings. Whether it is a holiday letting (1988, Sched. 1, para. 9);

(*h*) Resident Landlord. Whether there is a resident landlord (1988, Sched. 1, para. 10);

(*i*) Exempt Landlords. The identity of the landlord (1988, Sched. 1, paras. 11, 12);

(*j*) Other Classes of Protection. A tenancy which remains a Rent Act protected, housing asociation, or Housing Act secure tenancy (1988, Sched. 1, para. 14).

4.10   Homeless Persons. Some of these exclusions from Housing Act assured tenancy can be dealt with by cross-reference. Tenancies provided to homeless people under the same provisions which prevent security under the Housing Act 1985, for a period of one year as defined

(3.14(*e*)) are also not assured for that time (unless notified to the contrary by the landlord); this applies when the authority with responsibility for homelessness (10.01) provide temporary accommodation through another landlord.

Prior Tenancy. A tenancy entered into before (or under a contract which pre-dates) the commencement of the Housing Act 1988 will be either Housing Act secure or Rent Act protected (3.05, 5.01). 4.11

High Rateable Value. Some premises have such a high rateable value that they are considered to be the sorts of accommodation which are beyond the scope of protection *i.e.* because they provide accommodation for the very wealthy. It is the part of the premises which the tenant occupies which must be valued, not the whole house in which the tenancy is situated. A block of flats will often, as a whole, have too high a rateable value for 1988 Housing Act purposes, but each individual flat will not. A tenancy will not be a Housing Act assured tenancy if the premises have a rateable value in excess of £1,500 (Greater London) or £750 (elsewhere) (1988, Sched. 1, para. 2A). Where a tenancy has been granted after April 1, 1990 and is for a property which had no rateable value on March 31, 1990 it will be excluded if the rent is greater than £25,000 a year (1988, Sched. 1, para. 2). 4.12

No or Low Rent. The 1988 Act is not designed to apply to those who purchase long leases and pay only a small, annual ground rent (1988, Sched. 1, para.3). These, of course, have been considered as owner-occupiers and were dealt with in Chapter 2. The annual ground rent will be less than two-thirds of the rateable value of the premises and as such the letting is excluded from protection by this "low rent" provision. A low rent is one which is less than two-thirds of the rateable value (1988, Sched. 1, para. 3B) or in the case of a tenancy which has been granted after April 1, 1990 and is for a property which had no rateable value on March 31, 1990, it is a rent £1000 or less a year in Greater London or £250 or less elsewhere (1988, Sched. 1, para. 3A). Tenancies at no rent are also excluded (1988, Sched. 1, para. 3). 4.13

Rent in Money. It has been decided that rent must mean payment of rent in money if the tenancy is to be brought within protection, *i.e.* not payment in goods, or services (*Hornsby* v. *Maynard*, 1925). However, there is some authority for the proposition that if the goods or services represent a quantified or agreed sum of money which would otherwise be payable by way of rent, the Act may apply, *i.e.* the tenancy may be 4.14

assured (*Barnes*v. *Barratt,* 1970). Certainly, where there is a true service tenancy (1.63) and an amount of rent between a landlord/employer and his tenant/employee has been agreed but is merely deducted at source, this will be considered sufficient payment of rent for the purposes of protection (*Montague* v. *Browning,* 1954). Specifically disregarded in ascertaining the rent is any part of the rent which is expressed to be payable in respect of rates, services, management, repairs maintenance or insurance, unless, even although so expressed, the rent could not have been regarded as so payable (1988, Sched. 1, para. 2(2)).

4.15   Business Lettings. Tenancies which are subject to the business protection of the Landlord and Tenant Act 1954, and are therefore outside of residential protection (under this Act, as under the Rent Act 1977 and the Housing Act 1985) have been described above (3.14(*l*)).

4.16   Student Lettings. A tenancy will not be a Housing Act assured tenancy if the landlord under the tenancy is a specified educational institution and the tenant is following or intends to follow a course of study at that or another specified educational institution (1988, Sched. 1, para. 8).

4.17   Holiday Lettings. If the purpose of the tenancy is use as a holiday home, then the tenancy will not be Housing Act assured (1988, Sched. 1, para. 9). This is another exemption which had already been widely used as a device to defeat the Rent Acts (see also 1.28, 5.09, 5.51). The mere fact that someone has been compelled to sign an agreement alleging falsely that the tenancy was for a holiday purpose does not make it so as a matter of law. The principles relating to sham will apply to determine whether the agreement was a mere device to exclude protection, although occupiers should be aware that once they have signed such an agreement, the courts will consider that the burden of proof is upon them to displace the inference that the tenancy is not protected: see *Buchmann* v. *May*(1976). It may, however, be enough to show that there is a "false label," which is a slightly less pejorative term and was applied in *R.* v. *Rent Officer for L.B. of Camden, ex p. Plant* (1981), in which the landlord was found to have known, either before the first or the second of two consecutive "holiday" lettings, that the occupers were students. What is a holiday is a question of fact and common sense. Following *A. G. Securities* v. *Vaughan* (1988, H.L.), it may now become easier to show "sham" - or "pretence" - than hitherto (5.11).

4.18   Other Classes of Protection. Those cases where a letting will be

Housing Act secure notwithstanding that the letting follows the commencement of Part I, 1988 Act, have also already been described and those which remain Rent Act protected are described below. (3.05, 5.01).

Exempt Landlords. The landlords whose tenants are not Housing Act 4.19 assured are: local authorities (including district and county councils, London Borough Councils, the Common Council of the City of London, the Council of the Isles of Scilly and the Inner London Education Authority); the Commission for the New Towns; the Development Board for Rural Wales; an urban development corporation, a new town development corporation, a waste disposal authority, a residuary body (under Local Government Act 1985, which took over the residual affairs of an abolished council, *i.e.* the Greater London Council and the metropolitan counties), a fully mutual association housing association and a Housing Action Trust. In addition, tenants of the Crown or a government department are not assured, unless the tenancy is under the management of the Crown Estate Commissioners.

Resident Landlords. The exclusion of the tenants of resident landlords 4.20 was developed, and operates similarly to its operation, under the Rent Acts (5.28-5.33). The exclusion operates only when the dwelling is part of a building and, save when the dwelling itself forms part only of a flat, that building is *not* a purpose-built block of flats (4.21). At the time of the grant of the tenancy, the landlord must have occupied as his only or principal home (3.13, 4.09) another dwelling forming part of the building (or, another part of the flat). For the landlord to take advantage of this exclusion he must establish that at all times since the commencement of the tenancy, he has used as an only or principal home the other part of the building or flat which he occupies.

The Building. Occupation must be within the same building. This will 4.21 not cover, *e.g.* a terrace of houses, but may include a house which has had an extension added, even if there is no interconnection between the house and extension (*Griffiths* v. *English*, 1981; *Lewis-Graham* v. *Conacher*, 1991). The term "purpose-built block of flats" means exactly what it says: a house converted into flats, no matter how long ago, or however separately the living units are now constructed (*Barnes* v. *Gorsuch*, 1982), will not be a purpose-built block (*Bardrick* v. *Haycock*, 1976; *Griffiths*), even if there are separate entrances. If the building is a purpose-built block, however, then it avails the landlord not at all that he lives in one and the tenant lives in another flat.

4.22   **Landlords and Residence.** A corporate landlord, *e.g.* a landlord which is a company, a trust, a partnership, cannot qualify as a resident landlord for these purposes, because it cannot occupy as a home. It is expressly provided that occupation by one of two or more joint owners/landlords is enough to keep the tenant from being a Housing Act assured tenant. Under 1988, Schedule 1, Part III, if the landlord sells the house, residence will none the less be treated as continuing for a further 28 days. If during that time the new owner serves notice that he intends to move into the premises for use as a home, then he has a total of six months in which to do so, during which period residence by the landlord will likewise be treated as continuing. If, by the end of the six months, the new owner has not taken up residence, the tenant will become a Housing Act assured tenant and will so remain, even when the owner moves in, for there will not have been continual residence since the start of the tenancy. During such a period, the landlord cannot evict other than as if the tenant was a Housing Act assured tenant.

4.23   **Death of Resident Landlord.** The position is somewhat different on the death of a resident landlord. In such circumstances, the executors, effectively have two years during which the fact that there is no resident landlord will be disregarded. The two periods (two years under this paragraph, six months under the last) may be added together (*Williams* v. *Mate,* 1982). However, during the period qualifying under this paragraph, the landlord's executors may freely evict, unlike the position on transfer between living landlords. There are also provisions in the Schedule to deal specifically with the position which arises when "the landlord" is a trustee, but the beneficiary is resident.

2. *What Security of Tenure do Assured Tenants have?*

4.24   **Continuation By Contract.** Security of tenure under the Housing Act 1988 operates closer to the Housing Act 1985 than under the Rent Act 1977, insofar as a *periodic* contractual tenancy cannot be brought to an end *by the landlord* other than by court order (1988, s.5), so that there is no division between a contractual and a "statutory" tenancy as in the case of a Rent Act protected tenancy (5.12). The periodic tenancy can still be brought to an end *by the tenant* in the normal way (1.45-1.48; *Greenwich L.B.C.* v. *McGrady,* 1983; *L.B. Hammersmith & Fulham* v. *Monk,* 1991). The court order will only be available on specified "grounds" (below).

4.25   **Fixed-Terms.** In the case of a *fixed-term* Housing Act assured tenancy which contains a forfeiture clause (1.42), the tenancy cannot be brought to an end by the landlord by the exercise of that power, from which it would seem that the power of a tenant to apply for relief from forfeiture (1.43-1.44) must also have been disapplied. Instead of forfeiture, the landlord has to obtain an order of the court to determine the tenancy, as if it was a periodic tenancy. If the fixed-term ends in any other way, *e.g.* because its time expires, then unless the tenant voluntarily quits there comes into being an automatic "statutory periodic tenancy," which will continue until determined, like an ordinary periodic tenancy, by a court, on specified grounds. There will be no statutory periodic tenancy, however, if the landlord and the tenant agree a new tenancy to start on the determination of the old.

Notice of Seeking Possession. Again as under the Housing Act 1985 (3.27), in place of notice to quit, the landlord has to serve a notice of seeking possession, specifying the ground he intends to rely on, before he can seek an order for possession (1988, s.8). The court can, however, dispense with such a notice if it considers it just and equitable to do so (other than when possession is sought on Ground 8: 4.38); unless the court dispenses with the notice, possession can only be ordered on a ground specified in the notice, but the court may give permission to alter or add to the grounds. Proceedings cannot commence before the later of the following: two weeks, or, if possession is sought on Grounds 1, 2, 5-7, 9 or 16, two months, or, if a periodic tenancy, the earliest date when a notice to quit could have expired. A notice of seeking possession can, however, be served during a fixed-term, to take effect in relation to the following statutory periodic tenancy.   4.26

Contents of Notice. The notice must be in the form prescribed, and must inform the tenant that the landlord intends to bring proceedings on the grounds specified, and that the proceedings will begin no earlier than a date specified in the notice, but no later than 12 months from service of the notice. Following *Torridge D.C.* v. *Jones* (1985), under the Housing Act 1985 (3.28), the particulars of the ground must be sufficient to allow the tenant to know what he has to do to avert eviction, although they need not be objectively accurate (*Dudley M.B.C.* v. *Bailey*, 1990).   4.27

Discretionary and Mandatory Grounds. As under both the 1985 and the 1977 Acts, grounds for possession (1988, s.7 and Sched. 2) are either discretionary or mandatory. The mandatory grounds are set out in Schedule 2, Part I; the discretionary grounds are set out in Schedule 2,   4.28

Part II. In the case of discretionary grounds, the court's powers to suspend or vary an order are the same as under the 1985 and 1977 Act (3.23; 1988, s.9), but the court's powers are otherwise as limited as under those two Acts where no security attaches or where a mandatory ground is available (1980, s.89: 3.22). The discretionary grounds for possession are those where the landlord has to prove that it is reasonable to make the order: the law on this subject, and the burden of proof, are the same as under the Housing Act 1985 (3.30-3.32).

4.29   **Termination of Housing Act Assured Tenancy.** Accordingly, a Housing Act assured tenant can continue living in the premises indefinitely, *until*:

(*a*) **Want of Residence.** The assured tenancy ceases to be Housing Act assured for want of continued use as an only or principal home, in which case the landlord can terminate the tenancy in the usual way (1.39-1.50); *or*

(*b*) **Ground for Possession.** The landlord establishes to a court, which will be the county court, that one of the stated sets of circumstances exists, as a result of which he is or may be entitled to an order of the court for possession; *or*

(*c*) **New Landlord.** The premises are bought by one of the public landlords described above whose tenants are not assured (4.19). The tenancy will usually then become a secure tenancy: see Chapter 3.

(i) *The mandatory grounds*

4.30   **Ministers of Religion.** There are eight mandatory grounds for possession, *i.e.* those which if proved, leave the court no alternative but to make an order for possession, to take effect within two to six weeks (depending on hardship, 3.22), regardless of whether or not it is reasonable to make the order (3.23). Ground 5 is a special ground, applicable to property occupied or formerly occupied by ministers of religion, and will not be considered further here.

4.31   **Absentee Owner-Occupiers.** Ground 1 concerns absentee owner-occupiers, although it may be noted that for these purposes the landlord may himself be a tenant, yet still qualify as an "owner-occupier." It is only available to a landlord who has served notice no later than the beginning of the tenancy, warning the tenant that the Ground might be used against him, though if the court thinks it just and equitable to do so it may waive this requirement. It is available to a landlord who has (or, if joint landlords, one of whom has) formerly occupied the property as his only or principal home. It is also available to a landlord who requires (or, in the case of joint landlords, one of whom requires) to occupy the property as his or his spouse's only or principal home; in this alternative circumstance, however, the Ground is not available if the would-be occupier bought the premises, with the tenant already in occupation, for money or money's worth.

Mortgaged Property. Ground 2 is available when the property is sub-   4.32
ject to a mortgage, which was granted before the beginning of the tenancy, and the mortgagee is entitled to exercise the power of sale under the mortgage (Chapter 2) and requires possession in order to sell with vacant possession. Again, there has to have been notice no later than the beginning of the tenancy that this Ground might apply, unless the court uses its power to waive notice on the basis that it is just and equitable to do so.

Out of Season Holiday Letting. An out-of-season fixed-term letting   4.33
for not more than eight months of premises occupied within the previous 12 months for a holiday (4.17) provides a mandatory ground for possession, provided notice was given no later than the beginning of the tenancy that the Ground would apply (Ground 3). There is no power for the court to waive the notice requirement.

Off-Season Student Letting. An off-season fixed-term letting for not   4.34
more than one year of premises occupied within the previous 12 months as a student letting (4.16) provides a mandatory ground for possession, provided notice was given no later than the beginning of the tenancy that the Ground would apply (Ground 4). There is no power for the court to waive the notice requirement.

Demolition. Possession can be ordered under Ground 6 in favour of a   4.35
landlord who intends to demolish or reconstruct the whole or a substantial part of the premises, or carry out substantial works on them, and the following conditions are fulfilled. The conditions are that the work cannot reasonably be carried out with the tenant in occupation either because the tenant will not agree to a variation in terms such as would allow sufficient access and facilities to permit the work to be carried out, or no such variation is practicable in the light of the intended works, or the tenant will not agree to accept a Housing Act assured tenancy of part only of the property, such as would permit the landlord to carry out the works, or no such "part-property" arrangement would be practicable. The Ground is similar to that available under the Housing

Act 1985; in particular, a landlord's plans have to be clear and certain before the Ground is available (3.45).

4.36   **Added and Limited Availability.** The Ground is also available in the case of a registered housing association or charitable housing trust (3.11) where the person intending to do the works is not the landlord under the tenancy, but a superior landlord. The Ground is *not* available, however, to a landlord who has bought the property for money or money's worth with the tenant in occupation, or when the assured tenant has become such by succession under the Rent Act 1977 (5.15).

4.37   **Inherited Tenancy.** Ground 7 is only available in the case of a periodic tenancy (including a statutory periodic tenancy: 4.25). It applies when the tenancy has devolved not on statutory succession (4.05) but under the will of the tenant, or on the tenant's intestacy, and proceedings for possession are commenced no later than one year after the death of the tenant (or, if the court so permits, one year after the court considers that the landlord - or in the case of joint landlords, one of them - became aware of the death of the tenant). It is expressly provided that if the landlord continues to accept rent from the successor, this will not amount to the creation of a new tenancy (1.21), unless there is a variation in the amount of rent, the terms of the tenancy, its periods or the property itself.

4.38   **Three Months' Rent Arrears.** Ground 8 concerns rent arrears (*cf.* 3.33, 5.78). This mandatory Ground is available if both at the date of service of the notice of seeking possession (4.26) and at the date of hearing of the action, there are at least 13 weeks' or one quarter of a year's rent arrears. There are also two discretionary Grounds concerning rent arrears (4.43).

(ii) *Discretionary grounds*

4.39   **Requirement of Reasonableness.** The discretionary grounds for possession are those in relation to which the court enjoys extensive powers, and in which the landlord must prove that it is reasonable to make the order, in addition to showing that the details of each ground are applicable (4.28).

4.40   **Suitable Alternative Accommodation.** Ground 9 applies when suitable alternative accommodation is available or will be available for the tenant when the order takes effect. Suitable alternative accommodation is defined in Part III of Schedule 2 to the 1988 Act. The landlord may be able to establish his claim by producing a certificate from the local authority that the tenant will be rehoused by them. In the alternative, a landlord can himself provide another private tenancy or obtain one for the tenant from another landlord. In this case, the Schedule regulates such details as suitability for the needs and means of the tenant and his family as regards extent and character; or its similarity to the existing accommodation; or its proximity to work (*Yewbright Properties Ltd.* v. *Stone*, 1980). The new tenancy must be Housing Act assured, excluding tenancies in respect of which notices under Grounds 1-5 have been given, and excluding a Housing Act assured shorthold tenancy (see Chapter 6), or else must give security equivalent to that enjoyed by a Housing Act assured tenant. Alternative accommodation will never be suitable if it will result in overcrowding, even if the tenant's present premises are overcrowded.

Part of Present Premises. Suitable alternative accommodation may consist of part only of a tenant's present premises, for example, if one room is sublet or disused (*Mykolyshyn* v. *Noah*, 1970). But if the part of the premises which the landlord is seeking to recover is used at all, for example, as a study or workroom, or a spare room for visiting family, it is extremely unlikely that the court will allow this ground for possession to be used to reduce the size of the tenancy (*MacDonnell* v. *Daly*, 1969).   4.41

Reasonableness, Terms, Character. The landlord must still establish that it is reasonable to make the order. A court will frequently refuse, even where the alternative premises are ostensibly eminently suitable, because of, for example, the age of the tenant. An order may well be made subject to undertakings from the landlord to do specific works to the new premises, or else to pay for various removal expenses, etc. If such undertakings are not fulfilled, the tenant can apply to the court to set aside or discharge the order, or sue for the amount owing. The character of the new premises can be a determining factor. In *Redspring* v. *Francis* (1973), it was held that premises on a busy road, next door to a fish and chip shop, were not suitable for a tenant who had hitherto been living in a quiet residential street. The extent of the facilities and amenities in an area, including shops, open space, transport, etc., will also influence a decision.   4.42

Arrears of Rent. Ground 10 is the first of the further grounds dealing with rent arrears, and applies when rent is in arrears *both* at the date   4.43

when the proceedings for possession are commenced, and at the date of service of the notice of seeking possession (4.26), unless such notice is waived by the court (4.26): it may be distinguished from the mandatory Ground 8 in that: (*a*) there may be no arrears at the date of *hearing*, and (*b*) there is no minimum amount. By Ground 11, regardless of whether there are current rent arrears, and whether there were arrears at date of service of notice of seeking possession, or issue of proceedings, or date of hearing, the tenant has persistently delayed paying rent.

4.44   **Remaining Discretionary Grounds.** The next series of grounds are familiar: Ground 12 concerns broken obligation of tenancy (3.34, 5.78); Ground 13 is deterioration of dwelling-house or common parts owing to acts of waste by, or the neglect or default of, the tenant or someone else residing in the property (whom no steps have been taken to remove) (3.37, 5.80); Ground 14 concerns nuisance, annoyance and illegal or immoral user (3.36, 5.79); Ground 15 concerns condition of furniture, with the same qualification in the case of default by someone residing in the premises other than the tenant (3.37, 5.80). Ground 16 concerns service tenancies (1.63-1.69): it is available when the property was let to the tenant in consequence of his employment, and he has ceased to be in that employment.

(iii) *Notes*

4.45   **Forfeiture.** In the case of a fixed-term tenancy which contains a forfeiture clause (4.25), the court can only make an order for possession on the discretionary grounds in Schedule 2, Part II, *other than* Grounds 9 or 16, or Grounds 2 or 8 of the mandatory grounds in Schedule 2, Part I (1988, s.7), and then only if the forfeiture clause itself permits the lease to be ended on that ground.

4.46   **Misrepresentation.** Where possession is ordered on any Ground, and it can later be shown to a court that the order was obtained by misrepresentation or concealment of a material fact, the landlord can be ordered to compensate the tenant (1988, s.12).

3. *Rent and Other Terms*

(i) *Varying rent and other terms*

4.47   **Starting Rents.** The starting-point of such rent control as is applicable to Housing Act assured tenancies is that what has been agreed i payable; there is no concept analogous to "registered rents" under the Rent Act 1977 (Chapter 5), by which an existing registration might override the rent agreed at the commencement of the tenancy. In the case of a fixed-term Housing Act assured tenancy, there is no means for varying the rent, other than as may be provided under the agreement, until such time as the agreement becomes a statutory periodic tenancy (4.25). Under a statutory perodic tenancy, the terms are prima facie the same as under the fixed-term, and its periods are the same as those for which rent was paid under the fixed-term (1988, s.5). Within one year of the termination of the fixed-term, however, either the landlord or the tenant may serve notice on the other, in prescribed form, proposing different terms and, if considered appropriate, a variation of rent to reflect the variation of terms (1988, s.6).

Initial Variation for Statutory Periodic Tenancy. When such a notice has been served, then the landlord or the tenant on whom it has been served has three months within which to refer it to a rent assessment committee (5.113; *n.b. not* the rent officer; rent officers have no role in relation to rent-fixing for assured tenancies) (1988, s.6). If the notice is *not* so referred, then the proposed terms, and rent, become the terms (and rent) of the statutory periodic tenancy (1988, s.6(3)). If there is a reference, the rent assessment committee has to consider the proposed terms, and determine whether they, or some other term (dealing only with the same subject-matter as the terms proposed) might reasonably be expected to be found in a Housing Act assured periodic tenancy of such a property, presuming: (*a*) that the tenancy began on the coming to the end of the former, fixed-term; and (*b*) that the tenancy was granted by a willing landlord on the terms (other than those now under review) that apply to that tenancy (1988, s.6(4)). 4.48

Additional Notes on Rent. When determining the rent, the committee have to disregard the fact that there is a sitting tenant (1988, s.6(6)). Even if the notice proposing the new terms did not include a proposal for the variation of rent to reflect them, the committee are entitled to adjust the rent to take account of the adjustment of the terms (1988, s.6(5)). Unless the landlord and tenant agree otherwise, the committee decide when the new terms and rent apply from, save that in the case of the rent, they cannot specify a date which is earlier than any proposed in the original notice (1988, s.6(7)). The committee are not bound to continue with the process, if the landlord and the tenant give notice in writing that they do not wish it it to do so; nor need they continue if the tenancy ends before they reach their determination (1988, s.6(8)). 4.49

4.50   **Other Variations and Increases.** In the case of a periodic Housing Act
            assured tenancy, or in the case of a statutory periodic tenancy to which
            the foregoing provisions do not apply, *e.g.* because no variation of terms
            is proposed, or because the one-year time-limit from the expiry of the
            previous fixed-term has passed, a similar procedure applies, but can only
            be initiated by a landlord seeking a rent increase (1988, s.13). Indeed,
            a landlord cannot even use this procedure - nor therefore can the tenant
            avail himself of his rights under it - if the periodic tenancy (not being a
            statutory periodic tenancy) following a fixed-term itself contains its own
            provisions for determining increases, *e.g.* an index-linked formula, or
            reference to arbitration (1988, s.13(1)).

4.51   **Statutory Process for Increase of Rent.** To obtain an increase by the
            statutory process when it is applicable (periodic tenancy without its own
            provisions, or statutory periodic following fixed-term), the landlord
            must serve notice on the tenant, in the prescribed form, proposing a new
            rent to take effect at the beginning of a period of the tenancy, which
            period must itself commence no earlier than: (*a*) the minimum period
            after service of the notice; *and* (*b*) other than in the case of a statutory
            period tenancy, the first anniversary of the date on which the tenancy
            began; *and* (*c*) if there has been a previous increase under the statutory
            process, the first anniversary of the date on which that increase took
            effect (1988, s.13(2)). The "minimum period" is six months in the case
            of a yearly tenancy, one month in the case of a tenancy the periods of
            which are less than a month, *e.g.* weekly or four-weekly, or in any other
            case (*e.g.* quarterly tenancy, six monthly tenancy) one period of the
            tenancy (1988, s.13(3)).

4.52   **Effect of Notice.** The new rent will take effect *unless* before the
            beginning of the (minimum) period specified, the tenant refers the notice
            to a rent assessment committee, by application in the prescribed form,
            or the landlord and the tenant agree a different rent (1988, s.13(4)). If
            the rent is referred to a rent assessment committee, the committee have
            to decide what rent the property concerned might reasonably be
            expected to obtain on the open market, by a willing landlord letting a
            Housing Act assured tenancy of the same periods, beginning at the
            period specified in the notice, the terms (other than rent) of which are
            the same, and in respect of which the same notices under Schedule 2,
            Grounds 1-5 (mandatory grounds for possession, 4.30-4.34) have been
            served (1988, s.14(1)). The committee have to disregard the fact that
            there is a sitting tenant, and any increase attributable to a "relevant
            improvement" by a person who at the time it was carried out was the

tenant (not necessarily the same as the current tenant), and any reduction in value attributable to the tenant's failure to comply with the terms of his tenancy (the tenant's failure only applies to the current tenant and not any predecessor: *N. & D. (London) Ltd.* v. *Gadson,* 1991) (1988, s.14(2)).

Relevant Improvement. An improvement is *not* to be disregarded - *i.e.* 4.53
is not "relevant" - if it was an improvement required under a term of the tenancy or any other "obligation" to the landlord (unless the obligation arose as a condition of consent given by the landlord on a request by the tenant to execute works) (1988, s.14(2)). A "relevant improvement" is otherwise one carried out during the current tenancy, or carried out no more than 21 years before the date of service of the notice proposing the rent increase, and during those 21 years the property has always been subject to a Housing Act assured tenancy on the termination of which the tenant (or if joint tenants, one of them) did not quit (1988, s.14(3)). Only such improvements are to be disregarded: the tenant will have to pay for others, by way of increased rent.

Powers of Committee. When determining rent, the rent assessment 4.54
committee are not concerned with a service charge within the Landlord and Tenant Act 1985 (1988, s.14(4)), as this can be referred to a court under that Act, and determine a rent exclusive of rates (1988, s.13(5)). If there is both a notice seeking an increase in rent, *and* a notice proposing a variation of terms (4.47-4.48) before the committee at the same time, and the notice proposing a variation of terms specifies a date no later than the proposed rent increase, the committee are entitled to hear the applications together, and when they do so are bound to decide the variation of terms before they decide the new rent (1988, s.14(6)). Unless the landlord and the tenant otherwise agree, the new rent takes effect from the date specified in the notice of increase unless it appears to the committee that this would cause undue hardship, in which case the committee may determine a later date (but no later than their decision): 1988, s.14(7). The committee are not bound to continue with the process if the landlord and the tenant give notice in writing that they do not wish them to do so; nor need they continue if the tenancy ends before they reach their determination (1988, s.14(8)).

(ii) *Implied Terms*

Access. It is an implied term of all Housing Act assured tenancies that 4.55
the tenant should afford to the landlord access to the property and all

reasonable facilities for executing repairs which the landlord is entitled
to execute (1988, s.16; 11.34).

4.56   **Assignment and Subletting.** With two exceptions, all Housing Act
assured *periodic* tenancies are subject to a prohibition on assignment of
the tenancy, in whole or part, and on subletting of the tenancy in whole
or part, without the consent of the landlord (1988, s.15(1)). In the case
of this implied prohibition, *there is no qualification that the landlord's
consent cannot unreasonably be withheld* (1988, s.15(2); 1.75). The first
exception is if the tenancy agreement itself contains a prohibition,
whether absolute or qualified (1.75, 1.100), in which case it is the
agreement which determines the rights, not the Act; the second is if a
premium is paid on the grant or renewal of the tenancy (1988, s.15(3)).
"Premium" has the same meaning as under the Rent Act 1977 (1988,
s.15(4); 5.126-5.129).

4. *Further Financial Protection and Assistance*

4.57   **Miscellaneous Provisions.** To avoid other forms of exploitation of
tenants, or ways of extracting more money from them than permitted,
there are other forms of financial protection and assistance which may
be applicable. We shall consider:
  (i) accommodation agency charges; and,
  (ii) resale of utilities, *i.e.* gas and electricity.
(Premiums and deposits are not prohibited under the Housing Act 1988:
cf. 5.126-5.131. Housing benefits are as available for Housing Act
assured tenants as for Housing Act secure tenants: see 3.77).

(i) *Accommodation agency charges*

4.58   **Prohibited Payments.** Under the Accommodation Agencies Act 1953,
it is a criminal offence to demand or to accept any payment either for
registering or undertaking to register the name and requirements of a
person seeking a tenancy of premises. It is also an offence under the
same Act to demand or accept a payment simply for supplying or
undertaking to supply addresses or other particulars of premises to let.
As well as constituting offences, such payments can be recovered as
civil debts within six years of the payment being made (Limitation Act
1980).

4.59   **Supplying Addresses.** The first provision, registration of requirements,
is comparatively straightforward. The second provision has been

considered in the case of *Saunders* v. *Soper* (1975). It was held that the purpose of the provision was to prohibit payments made simply for supplying addresses and particulars of property to let. It does not prohibit payment for actually finding somewhere for the prospective tenant to live. It follows that an illegal payment has been made, and is therefore recoverable by the tenant, if the payment is made simply for the provision of addresses, and also if the payment is made for the provision of addresses even though expressed to be returnable if the tenant does not accept a tenancy through the services of the agency. The payment is not illegal if made after a tenancy has been found and accepted.

(ii) *Resale of utilities*

Gas and Electricity. Another way in which rent control and the pro‐   4.60
hibition on premiums could be defeated would be if there was no maximum amount which a landlord could charge for such essential services as gas and electricity. The public electricity suppliers are entitled to publish a tariff, which may differ from area to area, indicating the maximum amounts which may be charged for the resale of electricity. This will usually be a figure that permits the landlord a small profit per unit, to cover, among other things, the cost of renting the electricity meter which monitors the occupier's use. The public gas suppliers are under a duty to fix such maximum prices. In either case, the amounts overcharged are recoverable by the occupier as a civil debt.

5 Rent Act Protected Tenancies

5.01   **No New Rent Act Protected Tenancies.** In this chapter, we shall examine the Rent Act protected tenancy, the rights of the protected tenant to security of tenure and to regulation of rent, and some further financial protection. No Rent Act protected tenancy can normally be created after the commencement of Part I, Housing Act 1988 ("1988"), (January 15, 1989).

5.02   **Exceptions.** There are exceptions to this general rule. There can be a new Rent Act protected tenancy created or or after January 15, 1989, if either:
   (*a*) **Pre-Act Contract.** It was entered into pursuant to a contract for its grant which preceded that date; or
   (*b*) **New Tenancy to Former Tenancy.** It is the grant of a new tenancy (not necessarily of the same premises) to a person who was a former protected or statutory (5.12) tenant of the same landlord, or one of a number of joint (1.84-1.95) protected or statutory tenants (not including a shorthold tenant (6.38)); or
   (*c*) **Suitable Alternative Accommodation.** It is the grant of a tenancy resulting from an order for possession on the ground of suitable alternative accommodation (5.91), and the premises in question are those which the court has found suitable, and the court directs that the new tenancy should be a protected tenancy because it considers that an assured tenancy (Chapter 4) would not afford sufficient security of tenure; or
   (*d*) **New Town Corporation to Private Ownership.** It falls within a small class of tenancy formerly held by a new town development corporation, and passed into the private sector prior to March 31, 1996: 1988, s.34.

5.03   **New Tenancies Normally Housing Act Assured.** This chapter accordingly applies mainly to tenancies already granted, but they remain, and for some time are likely to remain, a substantial proportion of private sector tenancies. Tenancies granted on or after the commencement of Part I of the 1988 Act are, subject to its own schedule of exclusions, likely to be assured tenancies, and are considered in Chapter 4.

Tenants Only. It is only tenants who can enjoy full Rent Act protect- 5.04 ion, not trespassers or licensees (see, *e.g. Marcroft Wagons* v. *Smith*, 1951), nor, except as described in Chapter 2, owner-occupiers.

Landlord and Tent Act 1987, Part I. It should be noted that Rent Act 5.05 protected tenants are included as "qualifying" tenants for the purposes of Part I, Landlord and Tenant Act 1987, *i.e.* the "right of first refusal" (2.16-2.21).

Private Tenants. In the main, tenants whose landlords are not public 5.06 bodies, such as local authorities, nor quasi-public bodies, such as housing trusts and registered housing associations, will be Rent Act protected tenants provided that their landlords do not live in the same building as themselves. This short description can, however, be misleading, as some who would appear to qualify will not be Rent Act protected tenants, and others who would appear to be excluded may, for one reason or another, in fact enjoy full Rent Act protection.

Notices and Mandatory Grounds. Of particular importance is the 5.07 class of Rent Act protected tenant on whom one of a number of notices has been served, which will preserve their landlords' rights later to reclaim possession, *e.g.* temporarily absent owner-occupiers, the purchasers of retirement homes, lettings by servicemen (5.69-5.71) and, most prominently, "shorthold lettings."

Shorthold Tenancies. Strictly, a Rent Act protected shorthold tenancy 5.08 is a Rent Act protected tenancy: it is, for example, subject to rent regulation (3.92-3.124). But a Rent Act protected tenancy without indefinite security of tenure is hardly security at all, and is certainly not "full security." For that reason, and because shorthold lettings are hedged about with their own particular technicalities, it has been decided to ignore them for the purposes of this chapter, and to consider them separately, in Chapter 6, along with: (*a*) the lesser form of security available under the Rent Act 1977 known as Rent Act restricted contracts; and (*b*) Housing Act assured shorthold tenancies, which have replaced Rent Act protected shorthold tenancies under the new regime. There will be no further reference to shortholds in this chapter.

Rent Acts and Evasion. Rent Act protection arises under the Rent Act 5.09

1977 ("1977"). It is called a "Rent" Act because formally its principal purpose is to regulate rents: but rent protection would be of no value at all if landlords could freely evict, so it also provides security of tenure. In this connection, it is important to bear in mind that landlords commonly seek to avoid the effects of protection, by granting forms of letting which are not within the ambit of the 1977 Act. The easiest class of letting, if it is available, is the licence: we have already considered one form of licence, the non-exclusive occupation agreement (1.89-1.93). We have also considered how the law approaches the task of interpreting an agreement as licence or tenancy (1.23-1.30).

5.10   **Substance and Reality.** In relation to the Rent Acts: "It has been said before, and it must be said again, that in the consideration of questions arising under the Rent Acts, the court must look at the substance and reality of a transaction, not its form ..." (Viscount Simonds, *Elmdene Estates* v. *White*, 1960). In an earlier case, *Samrose Properties* v. *Gibbard* (1958), Lord Evershed M.R., said that a court must always ask itself: "... Whether the transaction, viewed as a whole and according to the substance of it, is in truth one which ... is on that side of the line which frees the premises from the impact of the Acts, or whether, so regarded, the transaction is one which is of the mischief which the Acts were designed to avoid." More recently, it has been said that "the manufacture of a five pronged implement for manual digging results in a fork even if the manufacturer, unfamiliar with the English language, insists that he intended to make and has made a spade ... The court should ... be astute to detect and frustrate sham devices and artificial transactions whose only object is to disguise the grant of a tenancy and to evade the Rent Acts." (*Street* v. *Mountford*, 1986).

5.11   **General Principle.** These principles have been re-endorsed in *A.G. Securities* v. *Vaughan* (1988, H.L.). We will encounter two further classes of evasive device, to which the same general principle is applicable: look always to what the parties intended factually to be the arrangement (by which is meant what the law understands the parties to have intended), not how they have described the arrangement. The two further devices are: holiday lettings (5.51) and company lets (5.61).

5.12   **Protected and Statutory Tenancy.** Rent Act protected tenants are regulated tenants (1977, s.18). A former distinction within protection, between regulated and controlled tenants, has now been abolished (Housing Act 1980 - "1980" - s.64). The term Rent Act protected tenant technically refers to a tenant within Rent Act protection who is still a contractual tenant (1977, s.1), *i.e.* one whose contract of tenancy has not come to an end in one of the ways described (1.39-1.50). In this respect security operates rather differently than under the Housing Act 1985 ("1985", 3.25) and the Housing Act 1988 (4.24), where termination of the tenancy contract can only be effected by the courts. After the termination of the contractual, Rent Act protected tenancy, under the 1977 Act, security of tenure operates by providing a right to remain or status of irremovability which is known as a statutory tenancy (1977, s.2).

Terms of Statutory Tenancy. A statutory tenancy continues on exactly the same terms as the prior contractual tenancy save where such terms would be inconsistent with the idea of statutory tenancy (1977, s.3), for example a right to assign or sublet the whole of the premises (*Keeves* v. *Dean*, 1924; *Atyeo* v. *Fardoe*, 1978), and save as regards rent which, obviously, may be increased as the years pass (5.118-5.123).   5.13

Statutory Tenancy by Succession. Normally, a tenant will be first a contractual tenant and subsequently a statutory tenant. This may not be the case, however, when a protected tenant dies and his widow succeeds to the tenancy (1977, s.2). In such circumstances, the successor becomes a statutory tenant at once, and the terms are the same, save as already mentioned, as those of the contractual tenancy of the person to whom the new tenant has succeeded.   5.14

Rent Act Succession to Housing Act Assured Tenancy. Succession to a tenancy where the tenant has died on or after the commencement of Part I, 1988 Act is subject to the following rules. If the tenant who died was married, his spouse will have priority in the succession, provided she was living in the dwelling-house at the time of his death, but for this purpose the terms marriage and spouse include common law marriage, *i.e.* a couple living together as husband and wife (1977, Sched. 1, para. 2, as amended by 1988, s.37 and Sched. 4). Such a succession will be, as noted, as a statutory tenant. If there is no spouse to succeed, then any member of the family who was residing in the dwelling-house at the time of the tenant's death and for two years beforehand is entitled to succeed to the tenancy, but the tenancy will be a Housing Act *assured* tenancy (Chapter 4), not a Rent Act protected or statutory tenancy (1977, Sched. 1, para. 3, as amended). On the death of a successor spouse, a member of the family (of *both* the original tenant *and* the successor) residing in the dwelling-house at the time of the successor's death and for two years beforehand is entitled to a "second succession,"   5.15

but similarly only to a Housing Act assured tenancy (1977, Sched. 1, para. 6, as amended).

5.16   **Deemed Residence.** There are transitional provisions governing deaths within the first 18 months following the commencement of Part I, 1988 Act, under which a member of the family residing with the deceased for six months before the commencement date will be treated as having resided for two years. "Residing" means more than staying at an address, even if the quality of the residence is not permanent or indefinite (*Swanbrae Ltd.* v. *Elliott*, 1986, *Hildebrand* v. *Moon*, 1989).

5.17   **Cohabitation.** It is clear that a cohabitant of long standing may be treated as a spouse for the purpose of succession: *Dyson Holdings* v. *Fox* (1976), *Watson* v. *Lucas* (1980) (even though still legally married to someone else). A lengthy period of cohabitation may not be needed if there is additional supporting evidence of the nature of the relationship (*Chios Investment (Property) Co.* v. *Lopez*, 1987), but in *Helby* v. *Rafferty* (1979), a man failed in his claim to succeed to his cohabitant's tenancy - they had been together only five years, lived relatively independent lives, and she retained her own name. A couple of the same sex *cannot* be considered "husband and wife" (*Harrogate B.C.* v. *Simpson*, 1984).

5.18   **Member of the Family.** All of these cases, however, preceded the changes under the 1988 Act, and turned on whether or not the would-be successor had been "a member of the family" of the deceased, and by-and-large it will be easier to prove that two people have been living together "as husband and wife," than to prove that they have been cohabiting to such an extent that they are to be regarded as "family." Where a person claims to be a member of the family of another, *other* than as husband and wife, it is necessary to distinguish between merely "living as" a member of the family, and "being" a member of the family (*Sefton Holdings* v. *Cairns*, 1987).

5.19   **Expiry of Contractual Tenancy.** The distinction between a contractual tenancy and a statutory tenancy may not be without importance, as regards both security of tenure and rent regulation. This is especially so if the contractual tenancy is a fixed-term tenancy. Before any court proceedings to evict the tenant can be brought, on one or other of the grounds described below, the contractual tenancy must have been brought to an end (1.39-1.50). Even if a tenant is in arrears of rent, then it will be necessary for the landlord to forfeit a fixed-term agreement, or serve valid notice to quit. Unless he does so, then no matter how great the tenant's default, the proceedings will be wholly defective and no order will be made. The tenancy must have expired by the date proceedings are commenced, not just by the date of hearing.

Fixed Term and Rent. The tenant may be able to derive advantage as regards rent from a lengthy fixed-term tenancy. Although normally the registration of a fair rent early in the arrangement will result in a decrease in the amount the landlord is entitled to charge, later on it will increase beyond that which the landlord and the tenant have agreed between them. Under a fixed term tenancy, the landlord will still be limited by the contractual rent, until such time as he can bring the contractual tenancy to an end. The mere fact that there has been such an increase will not affect, for example, an agreement that the tenant shall occupy for three years at a particular, and lower, rent. For this reason, many fixed-term agreements now say that the contractual rent will be a particular sum or the registered rent, if that is higher. Such a clause is wholly valid. 5.20

Notice of Increase as Notice Terminating Tenancy. To bring the contractual tenancy to an end, a landlord must determine the tenancy in the normal way (5.19). In addition, however, a notice of increase of rent, in the proper form, and which specifies a date for the increase to take effect no earlier than a notice to quit could take effect (1.45-1.48), will be treated as a notice to quit for the purposes of converting the contractual tenancy into a statutory tenancy (1977, s.49). But only a notice of increase in the proper form will have this additional effect (*Aristocrat Property Investments* v. *Harounoff*, 1982). 5.21

Termination of Periodic Tenancy. Once the contractual tenancy has been brought to an end, howsoever this is done, there is no need to serve any further notice before bringing proceedings, even if there is a gap of several years between termination and commencement of proceedings. No new contractual tenancy comes into being, unless there is evidence that such was intended, *e.g.* because the landlord and the tenant agreed to vary some term of the tenancy other than rent and it is sufficiently substantial to warrant description as a new tenancy (1.20). The tenant simply occupies as a statutory tenant until such time as a court orders possession to be given up to the landlord. 5.22

Business Lettings. As with Housing Act secure tenancies, business tenancies are excluded from protection (1977, s.24) and this may lead 5.23

to the particular problems of definition outlined (3.14*l*).

5.24   **Agricultural and Forestry Workers.** Under the Rent (Agriculture) Act 1976 ("1976"), protection largely similar to that to be described in this chapter is available to agricultural and forestry tied workers whose rights of occupation precede the commencement of Part I, 1988 Act (January 15, 1989), *i.e.* those living in accommodation belonging to their employers (1.63-1.69). It is not possible in this book to consider the 1976 Act in any detail, but the same points made in relation to assured agricultural occupancies are relevant here (4.06).

5.25   **Principal Issues.** The rest of this chapter will be taken up with the following questions:

1. *Who is a Rent Act protected tenant?*
2. *What security of tenure do Rent Act protected tenants have?*
3. *What rent protection applies?*
4. *Other forms of financial protection.*

1. *The Rent Act Protected Tenant*

5.26   **Let As A Separate Dwelling.** The Rent Act assumes that all tenants to whom property was let as a separate dwelling before the commencement of Part I, 1988 Act (January 15, 1989) are Rent Act protected tenants unless there is some factor which takes them out of protection (1977, s.1). The phrase "as a separate dwelling" has been considered in relation to Housing Act secure tenancies (3.09) and Housing Act assured tenancies (4.08). Because of the provisions including sharers (5.42) it is of much less significance under the 1977 Act.

5.27   **Exclusions.** As under the 1988 Act there is also a small number of exclusions from protection which: (*a*) are rare enough in practice; and (*b*) of sufficient particularity that they do not merit discussion: licensed premises, lettings of agricultural and/or substantial land and "shared ownership leases." The other factors which take a tenancy out of protection deal with:
    (i) **Resident Landlord.** In respect of tenancies commencing on or after August 14, 1974, whether the landlord lives in the same building or not (Rent Act 1977, s.12);
    (ii) **Old Furnished Lettings and Resident Landlord.** In respect of tenancies commencing before August 14, 1974, whether the tenancy

was considered to be a furnished tenancy in law before that date, and whether the landlord has lived in the same building or not since August 14, 1974 (1977, Sched. 24);

(iii) **Sharing Living Accommodation with Landlord.** Regardless of when the tenancy commenced, whether the tenant shares living accommodation with the landlord or not (1977, s.21);

(iv) **Attendances.** Whether the tenant is provided with attendances (1977, s.7);

(v) **Board.** Whether the tenant is provided with board (1977, s.7);

(vi) **Low Rent.** Whether the rent is what the law knows as a "low rent" (1977, s.5);

(vii) **Student Lettings.** Whether it is a student letting (1977, s.8);

(viii) **No Rent.** Whether any rent is paid (1977, s.5);

(ix) **Holiday Lettings.** Whether it is a holiday letting (1977, s.9);

(x) **Identity of Landlord.** The identity of the landlord (1977, ss.13-16);

(xi) **High Rateable Value.** The rateable value of the premises (1977, s.4).

(i) *Tenancies commencing on or after August 14, 1974*

Resident Landlord. When the Rent Act 1974 came into operation on August 14, 1974, it brought with it two major changes. One was that it extended full Rent Act protection to the tenants of furnished accommodation. The other was that it created a new class of tenancy subject to the lesser jurisdiction of the Rent Tribunal: these are tenants whose landlords occupy another part of the same building (not being a purpose-built block of flats) as their residences.   5.28

Continuous Residence. For a landlord to take advantage of this exception to protection, he must establish that at all times since the commencement of the tenancy, he has used as a residence the other part of the building which he occupies (1977, s.12). Such occupation will also take a tenant out of protection if he and the landlord live in the same flat (even if that flat is in a purpose-built block). The law accepts that a person may have more than one residence at a time, but a purely token residence will not suffice: a landlord cannot simply keep one room in a house, or in several houses, in order to keep his tenants out of protection. The question that must be asked is not whether at all times the landlord has been in residence, or has resided in the part kept for himself, but whether the premises have been a legal residence of the landlord throughout the period in question, *i.e.* since the start of the   5.29

tenancy.

5.30   **Use As A Home.** Legal residence is discussed in greater detail below
(5.57-5.64), as the same test applies to the question of whether a
statutory tenant has sustained sufficient residence to maintain his right
to the statutory tenancy (1977, Sched. 2). Briefly, residence means that
premises are being used as a home, even if not the only home. However,
it is accepted that for short periods a person may cease to use premises
as a residence and still be treated as sustaining legal residence, provided
both that he fully intends to return to live in the premises, *and* that he
has left some physical sign of occupation in the premises, *e.g.* furniture,
belongings, family.

5.31   **Landlords and Residence.** A corporate landlord, *i.e.* a landlord which
is a company, a trust, a partnership, etc., cannot "reside" at all because
such a landlord has no natural life (*Hiller* v. *United Dairies (London)*,
1934). It is thought that residence by one of two or more joint
owners/landlords is enough to keep the tenant out of protection (*cf.*
4.22). The landlord must reside within the same building as the tenant.
For these purposes the question of what is a building and what is a
purpose-built block of flats is the same as under the Housing Act 1988
(4.21).

5.32   **Change of Resident Landlord.** If a landlord sells the house, residence
will nonetheless be treated as continuing for a further 28 days. If, during
that time, the new owner serves notice that he intends to move into the
premises for use as a home, then he has a total of six months in which
to do so, during which period also, residence by the landlord will be
treated as continuing (1977, Sched. 2). If, by the end of the six months,
the new owner has not taken up residence, the tenant will become a Rent
Act protected tenant and will so remain, even when the owner moves in,
for there will not have been continual residence since the start of the
tenancy. If, however, the contractual tenancy comes to an end within
this period, no statutory tenancy will arise, even though, during this
period, the landlord cannot evict other than as if the tenant was a
statutory tenant (1977, Sched. 2): at the end of the period, provided he
gets a court order (Chapter 8) the (new) landlord can simply evict
(*Landau* v. *Sloane*, 1981).

5.33   **Death of Resident Landlord.** The position is somewhat different on
the death of a resident landlord. In such circumstances, the executors
effectively have two years in which the fact that there is no resident

landlord will be disregarded (1977, Sched. 2). The two periods (two years under this paragraph, six months under the last) may be added together (*Williams* v. *Mate*, 1982). However, during the period qualifying under this paragraph, the landlord's executors may freely evict, unlike the position on transfer between living landlords (5.32).

Note

Former Tenancy In Same Building. In certain circumstances, a tenant 5.34 who would appear to have been excluded from protection because of (i), above, may in fact be protected: a landlord with good knowledge of the law might have been able to take protection away from a tenant, *e.g.* by moving into a house in which there is an existing protected tenant and offering him a new tenancy of the same or another part of the building, so as to claim that since the start of that tenancy, there has always been a resident landlord. The Rent Act 1977, s.12 provides that a tenant who was formerly a Rent Act protected tenant under a previous tenancy of the same or another part of the building remained a Rent Act protected tenant. This, however, is only so where the presence of the resident landlord was the only reason for exclusion from protection.

(ii) *Tenancies commencing before August 14, 1974*

Old Furnished Lettings and Resident Landlords. The general policy 5.35 of the legislature is to not remove protection from anyone who already has it (see also 5.34). It follows that questions may still arise, in connection with tenancies commencing before the Rent Act 1974 came into force, as to whether or not the tenant was protected before that date (*Mann* v. *Cornella*, 1980). If he was not, then the question arises as to whether there has been a resident landlord since that date (5.28–5.33). The test for this is exactly as described.

Furnished Lettings. Deciding whether or not premises were protected 5.36 prior to August 14, 1974 is no easy business. The class exempted from protection was that of furnished tenancies. But the law did not consider that any amount of furniture, however small, would take a tenant out of protection. The landlord had to provide enough furniture that the value *to the tenant* of the furniture formed a substantial proportion of the whole rent paid under the tenancy. For some years, it was considered that, notwithstanding the intricacy of this formula, a tenant would nonetheless be treated as a furnished tenant if a substantial amount of furniture was provided. It is, of course, perfectly possible to provide a substantial amount of furniture without any great expenditure or, indeed, without providing anything of much value to the tenant.

5.37   **Substantiality.** In the case of *Woodward* v. *Docherty*, however, decided only a matter of months before the 1974 Act came into force, the Court of Appeal accepted two important propositions: first of all, that it was correct to do a financial calculation of the value to the tenant of the furniture, so that even a substantial amount of furniture could leave the tenant protected; and secondly, that in calculating the value of the furniture to the tenant, regard may be had to the social conditions prevailing at the time. This meant that rather than acquiring some valuable and desirable asset by way of use of furniture, the tenant in fact lost the considerably more valuable asset of a protected tenancy, while the landlord gained being able to evict his tenant with little or no difficulty. In other words, the Court of Appeal recognised that the purpose of the provisions of furniture was not to benefit the tenant, but rather to benefit the landlord.

5.38   **Valuation of Furniture.** As this question can still occur, it is worthwhile being familiar with the correct approach to a furniture valuation. The first stage is to calculate the value to the tenant of the furniture, not the cost to the landlord. A second-hand dealer is the best person to do this and, as a rough-and-ready guide, what he values the furniture at will represent the value to the tenant; it is that amount which the tenant would have to pay to provide similar furniture of his own. The valuation is done as if it was being established as at the start of the tenancy.

5.39   **Proportion of Rent.** Having established this basic figure, a percentage is taken, which is customarily agreed at 20 per cent., which represents the fair return to the landlord on his notional investment in that valuation. It is this figure which is to be compared to the annual rent paid by the tenant at the outset of the tenancy and which must be considered from the point of view of substantiality. There is no legislative rule as to what does form a substantial proportion of the rent, but courts will normally view anything over 20 per cent. as substantial, anything between 15 per cent. and 20 per cent. as probably substantial, anything between 15 per cent. and 10 per cent. as possibly substantial, and anything below 10 per cent. as insubstantial (see *Nelson Developments Ltd.* v. *Toboada*, 1992). In the grey areas, such questions as how much furniture is provided may influence the court (*Palser* v. *Grinling*, 1948).

Furniture or Landlord's Residence. On the basis of this calculation, 5.40
it will be possible to decide whether the tenancy was Rent Act protected
or not at the start of the tenancy, *i.e.* whether or not it was furnished in
law. If it was protected, then the tenant remains a Rent Act protected
tenant, even though there has been a resident landlord in the building
since August 14, 1974; if it was not, then the question will be whether
he has been protected since that date. Neither the test contained under
this heading, nor that contained under the last, will, however, be
applicable if the conditions specified under (iii) below take the tenant
out of protection nor will they apply if the reason for the exclusion from
protection is one of those which follow.

(iii) *Sharing living accommodation with landlord*

Sharing Living Accommodation with Landlord. If the tenant shares 5.41
what the law recognises as living accommodation (3.09) with his
landlord, then regardless of when the tenancy commenced, it will not be
a protected tenancy (*Neale* v. *Del Soto*, 1945). This is so even if no
furniture at all was provided under the tenancy, and even if the degree
of residence by the landlord leaves in some doubt whether he qualifies
as a resident landlord in the normal way. However, a mere empty
retention of a right to share living accommodation, designed to defeat
protection, would probably not succeed because it would essentially be
a sham reservation (5.09).

Continuing Relevance. This issue is extremely unlikely to arise in 5.42
connection with a tenancy commencing after August 14, 1974, because
it could only apply to a situation in which, on the one hand, the landlord
used the premises, but, on the other, he did not establish sufficient
residence to qualify as a resident landlord. It may, however, be relevant
to an argument over whether or not the tenant was Rent Act protected
at the beginning of the tenancy if the landlord took up residence shortly
before August 14, 1974 and is trying to establish that the tenancy was
not Rent Act protected then. The fact that a tenant is sharing living
accommodation with other tenants only does not affect protection at all
(1977, s.22).

(iv) *Attendances*

Attendances. A tenancy will be a Rent Act protected tenancy unless the 5.43
tenant is, under the terms of the tenancy, provided with attendances, and
the value to the tenant of the attendance forms a substantial proportion

of the whole rent (1977. s.7). The substantiality test is identical to that applicable to the question of furniture and the same principles will apply, although attendances may be somewhat harder to value (5.36-5.37).

5.44 **Personal Services.** Attendance means some personal service performed in the premises in question, for the tenant, for example room cleaning, changing the sheets, doing the tenant's laundry, etc. (*Palser* v. *Grinling*, 1948). It does not include provision of gas or electricity, or hot water, nor does it include cleaning of the common parts of a house in multiple occupation, *e.g.* hallways, stairs, bathroom, lavatory, etc. (*King* v. *Millen*, 1922). The provision of a resident housekeeper does not mean that of definition the tenant is provided with attendances, but that is likely to be the case. The full amount of the wages of the resident housekeeper should not be attributed to the tenants, as a whole, even if apportioned between them, for the presence of a resident housekeeper is considered to be of value also to the landlord. Window-cleaning is another service which is considered to be partly of value to the landlord and partly an attendance upon the tenant (*Engvall* v. *Ideal Flats*, 1945).

5.45 **Within Jurisdiction of Rent Tribunal.** All tenants whose tenancies precede the commencement of Part I, 1988 Act (January 15, 1989) and who are excluded from protection for one of the reasons described above will be subject to the jurisdiction of the Rent Tribunal: Chapter 6.

(v) *Board*

5.46 **Board.** Any tenant who, under the terms of his tenancy, is provided with any amount of board cannot be a Rent Act protected tenant. Board means more than a mere morning cup of tea (*Wilkes* v. *Goodwin*, 1923), but no more than a continental breakfast has been upheld as the provision of board for this purpose, provided that at least some services are involved in preparing it and it includes the provision of crockery and cutlery with which to eat it (*Otter* v. *Norman*, 1988).

(vi) *Low rent*

5.47 **Low Rent.** As under the Housing Act 1988, the 1977 Act is not designed to catch those who purchase long leases and pay only a small, annual ground rent (1977, s.5). A low rent is defined in the same way as under the 1988 Act (4.13). There is one important exception to this:

people who used to have controlled tenancies (5.12) may still be paying a rent which is less than two-thirds of the rateable value of the premises they occupy. This provision, therefore, does not apply to former controlled tenancies at all (1980, Sched. 25, para. 75).

(vii) *Student lettings*

Student Lettings. A tenancy will not be a Rent Act protected tenancy 5.48
if the landlord under the tenancy is a specified educational institution and the tenant is following or intends to follow a course of study at that or another specified educational institution (1977, s.8).

Possible Jurisdiction of Rent Tribunal. Tenants whose tenancies 5.49
precede the commencement of Part I, 1988 Act (January 15, 1989) and who are excluded from protection for any one of the last three reasons described above may come within the jurisdiction of the Rent Tribunal: see Chapter 6.

(viii) *No rent*

No Rent. If no rent is paid under the terms of the tenancy, the tenancy 5.50
cannot be Rent Act protected (1977, s.5). This is because Rent Act jurisdiction over tenancies has always dealt primarily in the protection of rents, and only secondarily in the protection of rights of occupation (5.04). The same issues as to the meaning of rent apply here, as under the 1988 Act (4.14).

(ix) *Holiday lettings*

Holiday Lettings. If the purpose of the tenancy was use as a holiday 5.51
home, then the tenancy will not be Rent Act protected (1977, s.9). This is another exemption which has been widely used as a device to defeat the Rent Acts (see also 1.28, 3.04, 3.43), and is considered in relation to the same exemption which arises under the 1988 Act (4.17).

(x) *Identity of landlord*

Identity of Landlord. The tenants of the following landlords will not 5.52
be Rent Act protected: local authorities, New Town authorities, registered housing associations, housing trusts, the Housing Corporation (1977, ss.14-15). Most of these tenants will, however, if pre-Housing Act 1988, be secure tenants: see Chapter 3. Tenants of the Crown and

a government department will not be Rent Act protected unless the property is under the management of the Crown Estate Commissioners (1977, s.13). Tenants of a housing management co-operative, which is a body formed to manage or lease land belonging to, *e.g.* a local authority or housing association, will also not be Rent Act protected (1977, s.16). Other kinds of housing co-operative are usually housing associations and therefore exempt (1977, s.15).

(xi) *High Rateable value*

5.53   **High Rateable Value.** This exemption operates in the same way as under the 1988 Act (4.12). Under the 1977 Act this is presumed to be so unlikely to be the case that it is assumed not to apply unless the landlord shows the contrary (1977, s.4(6)).

5.54   **No Rent Tribunal Jurisdiction.** None of the tenancies excluded from protection by one of the last three reasons referred to above will fall within the jurisdiction of the Rent Tribunal. They are, therefore, considered in Chapter 7.

2. *Security of Tenure*

5.55   **Contractual Security.** As has already been remarked (5.09), no tenant can be evicted, whether lawfully in fact or by court proceedings, so long as the tenancy has not been brought to an end. In the case of a Rent Act protected tenant, this means the contractual tenancy (5.19). The contractual tenancy may have come to an end by expiry of a fixed-term, by notice to quit that complies with the conditions described, by forfeiture or by notice of increase. It is unlikely to have come to an end by surrender (1.41) if the tenant is still living in the premises.

5.56   **Statutory Tenancy.** Once the contractual tenancy has come to an end, the tenant has an absolute right to continue living in the premises indefinitely and as a statutory tenant on, by and large, the same terms as under the contractual tenancy (1977, s.3) *until*:
(i) the statutory tenancy itself terminates for want of continued residence; *or*
(ii) the premises become overcrowded in law, or are subject to a closing or demolition order because of their condition; *or*
(iii) the landlord establishes to a court, which will be the county court, that one of the stated sets of circumstances exists, as a result of which he is or may be entitled to an order of the court for possession; *or*

(iv) the premises are bought by one of the public or quasi-public landlords described above (5.52) and the tenant is removed from protection. The tenancy will usually then become a secure tenancy: see Chapter 3.

(i) *Statutory residence*

Statutory Residence. The purpose of the Rent Act is to protect homes (*Skinner* v. *Geary*, 1931). It is not designed to provide a sometime tenant with a source of income, through sub-letting or letting to a number of sharers, through as many tenancies as he can acquire. Once the contractual tenancy has come to an end, a statutory tenancy will only come into and remain in being so long as the tenant is in statutory residence. This is exactly the same degree of residence that a landlord must sustain in order to qualify as a resident landlord (5.29-5.36). During the contractual tenancy there is no obligation at all upon a tenant to do so much as set foot in the premises, although one who fails to do so may have a hard time later proving his residence during the statutory period.   5.57

Regular and Personal Use. Statutory residence, for these purposes as for the purposes of resident landlords, must be continual although, again, this does not mean that the tenant must constantly be living in the premises. It means that he must always be able to claim that the premises are still in his use as a home, even if not as an *only* home. If a tenant is absent from premises for a longish period of time, for example at least a few months, there may, on the face of it, be a claim that he has abandoned use of the premises as a home (*Brown* v. *Brash*, 1948). Use as a home means "a substantial degree of regular personal occupation by the tenant of an essentially personal nature" (*Herbert* v. *Byrne*, 1964). A person who is absent for long periods *may* still be using the premises as a home, even if he is also using somewhere else in the same way. The question is whether the tenant is keeping on the premises in question "as a mere convenience" (*Beck* v. *Sholz*, 1953) or whether it is in fact the case that he is actually using both places as homes, even if he only visits one or other of them infrequently (*Langford Property Co.* v. *Tureman*, 1949).   5.58

Intention to Return. Regardless of whether a person is laying claim to two homes or not, a person who absents himself from premises for a longish period of time can still claim to be a statutory tenant of them so long as he intends to return at some time in the future to use the   5.59

premises as a home, and leaves in the premises some visible signs of that intention (*Brown* v. *Brash*, 1948). This may be done by leaving belongings or furniture, or even by leaving a friend in occupation to, as it were, "keep the place warm." But simply leaving a friend in occupation without any intention to return himself to live there, will not be sufficient to maintain the claim to be statutory tenant of the premises. There must be both: intention to return, and some indication of it. A sufficiently prolonged absence may put the tenant to having to prove continued residence (*Roland House Gardens* v. *Cravitz*, 1974). A tenant who claims that he intends to return subject to a condition, *e.g.* works by the landlord, which he has no reasonable expectation of being fulfilled, will not be considered a statutory tenant (*Robert Thackray's Estate Ltd.* v. *Kaye*, 1988).

5.60   **Residence and Spouses.** A tenant can be treated as still in occupation, even though he has no intention to return, if he leaves his spouse living in the premises (*Wabe* v. *Taylor*, 1952). This is so only so long as the marriage lasts and will therefore cease to apply on decree absolute (*Metropolitan Properties Co.* v. *Cronan*, 1982; *Lewis* v. *Lewis*, 1985). A non-tenant abandoned spouse should take steps to have the tenancy transferred into his name before divorce proceedings are concluded: see Chapter 9. But there is no continued residence without intention to return, if the only sign of occupation is by a former cohabitant (*Colin Smith Music Ltd.* v. *Ridge*, 1974).

5.61   **Residence and Companies.** Neither a company nor any other "artificial" body can lay claim to residence (*Reidy* v. *Walker*, 1933), and one cannot claim to occupy through an agent. This requirement that the occupant should not be a corporate body has given rise to yet a further (1.28, 5.09), evasive device, which will only be defeated on the usual principles applicable to sham (5.09). The landlord lets not to the tenant, but to a limited company, as whose licensee the tenant occupies (*Firstcross Ltd.* v. *East West Ltd.*, 1980; *Tetragon Ltd.* v. *Shidash Construction Co. Ltd.*, 1981; *Hilton* v. *Plustitle Ltd.*, 1988). In such a case, the court will probably only allow the statutory tenancy to arise if it believes that the company took as agent or nominee for the tenant, and that was known to the landlord. The question to be asked in such a case is whether the company letting is genuine (*Kaye* v. *Massbetter*, 1990).

5.62   **Residence by Another.** In general, therefore, the courts will not permit abuse of the requirements of individual statutory residence by the Rent Act protected tenant by permitting the landlord to put the tenancy in one person's name for the real use of another (*Cove* v. *Flick*, 1954; *Dando* v. *Hitchcock*, 1954), but will only interfere to let the "true tenant" become the statutory tenant if the arrangement was a device (*Feather Supplies* v. *Ingham*, 1971). One person cannot suddenly step forward and say that he is the true tenant, and the named tenant no more than his agent unbeknownst to the landlord (*Hanstown Properties Ltd.* v. *Green*, 1977).

Former Contractual Tenant. As a general proposition, only the person   5.63
who was the actual former Rent Act protected tenant can become the statutory tenant. Thus, if a Rent Act protected (and therefore contractual) tenant goes bankrupt, his contract of tenancy may vest in his trustee in bankruptcy; when it is determined, the bankrupt does not become the statutory tenant because immediately before determination he was not the tenant (*i.e.* the trustee was) (*Smalley* v. *Quarrier*, 1975). But if the contractual tenancy determined *before* bankruptcy, the bankrupt can stay in possession as a statutory tenant (*Sutton* v. *Dorf*, 1932). This is because the statutory tenancy is not a true tenancy but only a "status of irremovability" (*Jessamine Investments Co.* v. *Schwartz*, 1977), so that it does not vest in the trustee. However, by a recent change in the law (1988, s.117), Rent Act protected tenancies will now not normally vest in the trustee in bankruptcy, unless the trustee elects to adopt it, and the bankrupt tenant will be permitted to retain the tenancy in his own name, so that the worst effects of this rule as here applicable have been averted; this does not, however, apply where the tenancy is one in respect of which a premium may lawfully be charged (5.126, *i.e.* because it has a value which the trustee can realise).

Cessation of Residence. Strictly, once the statutory residence ceases,   5.64
the statutory tenancy comes automatically to an end. However, the possibilities of a mistake being made, especially on the subject of abandonment, and especially by a landlord who may be a little too eager to reclaim the premises, are so high that most landlords will in fact commence proceedings for a court order for possession before taking the premises back over.

(ii) *Overcrowding and closing orders*

Housing Conditions. Even if statutory residence can be sustained, and   5.65
even if the contractual tenancy has not been brought to an end, the Rent Act will not apply to premises which are subject to a closing (12.24) or demolition (12.29) order because they are unfit (12.12-12.15) or to

premises which are being occupied by so many people that they are statutorily overcrowded (14.05-14.08). In order to obtain possession, however, the landlord must still terminate the contractual tenancy (1.39-1.50: *Aslan* v. *Murphy*, 1989)

(iii) *Grounds for possession*

5.66   **Orders for Possession.** The most usual way for a person who does not voluntarily give up possession of premises subject to a Rent Act protected tenancy to leave the premises is because a court order for possession is made against him. As under the Housing Act 1985 (3.26) and the Housing Act 1988 (4.28) the court may order possession only where either a mandatory ground for possession (1977, s.98 and Sched. 15, Part II) or a discretionary ground for possession (1977, s.98 and Sched. 15, Part I) is made out. In the case of discretionary grounds, the court's powers to suspend or vary an order are the same as under the 1985 and 1988 Acts (3.23; 1977, s.100), but the court's powers are otherwise as limited as under those two Acts where no security attaches or a mandatory ground is available (1980, s.89: 3.22). These powers may not only be exercised for the benefit of the tenant, but also for his spouse or ex-spouse (Chapter 9). Reasonableness has been considered in Chapter 3, in relation to the Housing Act 1985 (3.30-3.32).

5.67   **Voluntary Departure.** Not all tenants who are threatened with court proceedings remain in possession until an order is made. Courts are, after all, only there to resolve disputes. It may be that a tenant will agree that a breach is so serious that the court is going to make an outright order and so choose to depart, without running up liability to legal costs. Or else the tenant may be so seriously in arrears that he would rather leave before a court judgment for the amount in question is made and he becomes not only homeless but liable to a larger debt. When a tenant is confronted by the likelihood of action, it is as well to bear in mind the provisions of Part III of the Housing Act 1985 (Housing the Homeless), and in particular, the definition of intentional homelessness, which effectively removes the right to full rehousing by the local authority (see Chapter 10).

5.68   **Mandatory Grounds.** There are ten mandatory grounds for possession, *i.e.* those which if proved leave the court no alternative but to make an order for possession, to take effect within two to six weeks (depending on hardship, 3.22), regardless of whether or not it is reasonable to make the order (3.30). The grounds for possession are known as ''Cases'' (under the Rent Act 1977, but *cf.* Chapters 3 and 4, as "Grounds," under the Housing Act 1985 and 1988 Act). The mandatory grounds are Cases 11-20. Cases 15-18 are special grounds, applicable to property occupied or formerly occupied by ministers of religion, or people employed in agriculture, and we shall not consider them any further here. Case 19 is shorthold (6.38-6.50). Cases 11, 12 and 20 may be considered as one group, Cases 13 and 14 as another.

Owner-Occupiers. Case 11 concerns absentee owner-occupiers, al- 5.69
though it may be noted that for these purposes the landlord may himself be a tenant, yet still qualify as an "owner-occupier." It is only available to a landlord who has served notice at the commencement of the tenancy, warning the tenant that the Case might be used against him, though if the court thinks it just and equitable to do so it may waive this requirement. It is also only available if the landlord has not otherwise let the property out, other than on terms that include service of one such notice at commencement, although again this requirement may be waived by the court.

Retirement Homes. Case 12 is available to a landlord who has bought 5.70
property and intends to retire to it, when he ceases regular employment. Again, notice must have been served at the commencement of the tenancy warning the tenant that the Case might be used, and again the property must not have been let out even to another, without the service of such a warning notice, although in each case the court has power to waive the requiremets, if just and equitable to do so. The court should not exercise this power unless the tenant knew at the outset that he had only limited security, *i.e.* it should only be used where the failure was largely technical (*Bradshaw* v. *Baldwin-Wiseman*, 1985). The fact that the occupiers signed licence agreements, which the landlord later conceded amounted to the grant of a tenancy, is not sufficient on its own to make it just and equitable to dispense with notice (*Ibie* v. *Trubshaw*, 1990).

Member of Armed Forces. Case 20 is available to a landlord who, 5.71
both at date of purchase and of letting, is a member of the armed forces: the same requirements of notice, both to tenant and to anyone else to whom the property has been let other than the present tenant, are imposed, though may be waived by the court, again in limited circumstances.

Applicability of Additional Criteria. Assuming that a landlord falls 5.72

within one of these three Cases, he must go on to prove certain additional facts. There are seven such additional facts, but they are not all equally available. Under Case 11, the landlord must be able to show the second, fourth, fifth, sixth or seventh; under Case 12, the landlord must be able to show the third, fourth, fifth, sixth or seventh; under Case 20, the landlord must be able to show the first, fourth, fifth, sixth or seventh.

5.73   **The Additional Criteria.** These additional factual qualifications are: (1) the property is required as a residence for the owner; (2) the property is required as a residence for either the owner or for any member of his family who lived with him when last he occupied the property as a residence; (3) the owner has retired from regular employment and requires the property as a residence; (4) the owner has died, and the dwelling is required as a residence for a member of his family who was living with him at the time of his death; (5) the owner has died, and the dwelling is required by his successor in title, either to live in, or to sell with vacant possession; (6) the property is subject to a mortgage granted before the tenancy was granted, and the mortgagee requires vacant possession in order to sell the property under the power of sale, *i.e.* for default (by the landlord); (7) the dwelling is not reasonably suitable to the needs of the owner, having regard to his place of work, and he wants to sell it with vacant possession and use the proceeds of sale to buy somewhere more suitable for himself (1977, Sched. 15, Part V, added by 1980, Sched. 7).

5.74   **Requirement for Residence.** Where the landlord is in fact two people, *i.e.* joint owners, the necessary qualifications can be fulfilled by just one of them (*Tilling* v. *Whiteman*, 1980), so that, *e.g.* both do not need to show they want to come and live in the house. In each case, the landlord need only show that he requires the property, rather than "reasonably requires" the property: "requires" means no more than *bona fide* wanted and genuinely intended to be occupied as a residence at once, or at any rate within a reasonable time, but so wanted and intended whether reasonably or unreasonably, even from the landlord's point of view (*Kennealy* v. *Dunne*, 1977). But the requirement of *former* residence can be fulfilled by previous intermittent residence, or something less than permanent residence (*Naish* v. *Curzon*, 1984). Such residence does not have to be as a home (*cf.* 5.58; *Mistry* v. *Isidore*, 1990).

5.75   **Out of Season Holiday Lettings.** Case 13 only applies where the letting is for a fixed term of not more than eight months; the tenant must be given notice at the commencement of the letting that the Case may be used against him; and, within the 12 months preceding the commencement of the letting, the property was occupied under a holiday letting (5.51). It deals, in effect, with "out-of-season" holiday lettings.

Off-Season Student Lettings. Case 14, on the other hand, concerns   5.76
property normally used for student lettings (5.48). The letting in question must be for a fixed term of not more than 12 months; the tenant must be given notice at the commencement of the letting that the Case may be used against him; and, within the 12 months preceding the commencement of the letting, the property was occupied under a student letting.

Discretionary Grounds. The discretionary grounds for possession are   5.77
those in relation to which the court enjoys extensive powers (3.23), and in which the landlord must prove that it is reasonable to make the order, in addition to showing that the details of each Case are applicable (3.30). Most of the grounds imply some degree of fault on the part of the tenant, although they do not all have this quality, and many have been reproduced in the Housing Act 1985 or the 1988 Act.

Rent Arrears and Breach of Term of Tenancy. Case 1 is available   5.78
where either the tenant is in arrears with his rent, or the tenant has broken a term of the tenancy and is reproduced in the Housing Act 1985 (see 3.33-3.34). Breach of a condition attached to a grant of consent to improve (11.39) can constitute a breach of a term of the tenancy for these purposes (1980, s.83).

Nuisance, Annoyance, Illegal or Immoral User. Conviction for im-   5.79
moral, or illegal, user is also a ground for possession, as is nuisance and annoyance to adjoining occupiers (Case 2, see 3.36). The nuisance or annoyance must be to an adjoining occupier but this does not mean that the occupier's property is necessarily physically contiguous: it means the same as "neighbour" (*Cobstone Investments Ltd.* v. *Maxim,* 1985) (1.43).

Deterioration of Premises or Furniture. Cases 3 and 4 concern de-   5.80
terioration of the premises, or of any furniture provided by the landlord, attributable to the acts, neglect or default of the tenant, or someone living with him (3.37). Unlike the 1985 Act these Cases do not cover deterioration of common parts or funiture situated in common parts.

120 *Rent Act Protected Tenancies*

5.81 **Tenant's Notice to Quit.** Case 5 arises when the tenant has given notice to quit the premises, in consequence of which the landlord has contracted to sell the property, or to let it, or taken any other steps as a result of which he would be seriously prejudiced if the tenant were to remain. The Case is only available when the tenant gives a technically valid notice to quit (*De Vries* v. *Smallridge*, 1927), which is relatively uncommon (1.45).

5.82 **Assignment or Sub-Letting.** Case 6 arises when the tenant, without the consent of the landlord, has assigned (1.100) or sub-let (1.70-1.83) the whole of the premises, whether the sub-letting is in one go, or bit by bit. Commonly, though not inevitably, the tenant will in any event lose his statutory tenancy if he does this, for want of residence (5.57-5.64). The Case is available even if there was no prohibition in the tenancy agreement on sub-letting (*Regional Properties Co.* v. *Frankenschwerth*, 1951). But consent may be expressed or implied, and may be before or even after the assignment or sub-letting, at any time before hearing (*Hyde* v. *Pimley*, 1952), so that the analogy may be drawn with waiver of illegal sub-letting (1.78).

5.83 **Overcharging Sub-Tenant.** If the rent for the sub-tenancy has been registered (5.93-5.117), or if the Rent Tribunal has fixed a rent for the sub-tenancy (6.13-6.22), it is a ground for possession against the tenant that he has overcharged the sub-tenant, *i.e.* charged more than either class of rent (Case 10).

5.84 **Ground Against Tenant And Sub-Tenant.** It may be noted that in all cases, a ground for possession against tenant operates as a ground for possession against sub-tenant, although whether it is reasonable to make the order must be considered in relation to each of them separately: it will, of course, rarely if ever be reasonable to make an order against a sub-tenant for, as it were, permitting himself to be overcharged.

5.85 **Required For Employee.** Case 8 (Case 7 was repealed by the Housing Act 1980, Sched. 26) is available only in relation to a service tenant (1.63-1.69). The letting must have been in consequence of the employment, the tenant must have been in the landlord's employment, and the property must now be reasonably required (*cf.* 5.74), by the landlord for the occupation of someone else in his full-time employment, or someone with whom a contract of employment has been agreed, conditional upon the provision of accommodation (*cf.* 1985 Act, Ground 12, 3.48 and 1988 Act Ground 16, 4.44). In one case, the landlord was one person, but the employer was a partnership, of which the landlord was but one member: it was held that the case did not apply (*Grimond* v. *Duncan*, 1949).

Required by Landlord. Finally, Case 9: the property is reasonably 5.86
required (*cf.* 5.74), by the landlord for occupation as a residence by himself, any of his children over the age of 18, his parents, or his spouse's parents. This Case is not available if the landlord became the landlord by purchasing the property, with the tenant already in occupation (*Newton* v. *Biggs*, 1953). Purchase does not carry any technical meaning but covers what a reasonable person would consider a purchase (*Ammadio* v. *Dalton*, 1991). A landlord cannot use this Case if his true intention is to gain vacant possession in order to sell, no matter how reasonably he wishes to do this: he must want the property with a view to living in it for some reasonable period, definite or indefinite (*Rowe* v. *Truelove*, 1976).

Required for Residence. Under this Case (*cf.* 5.74), if the landlord is 5.87
comprised of two or more joint owners, they must all wish to live there before it can apply (*Macintyre* v. *Hardcastle*, 1948). It is not necessary, however, for any son or daughter for whom the property is required to be the child of both joint owners, it is sufficient if they are the child of any one of them (*Potsos* v. *Theodotou*, 1991).

Greater Hardship. This Case is often called "greater hardship" be- 5.88
cause the 1977 Act provides a particular defence to a claim under it - that, having regard to all the circumstances of the case, including the availability of other accommodation to either landlord or tenant, greater hardship would be caused by granting than by refusing the order (1977, Sched. 15, Part. III). The court must consider hardship long-term, so that even if a tenant who is to be rehoused by a local authority (Chapter 10) will suffer some short-term inconvenience, this is unlikely to amount to "greater hardship" (*Manaton* v. *Edwards*, 1985). This may none the less be a most useful defence: the landlord may have other property which he may be able to occupy; he has been drawing rent from the property for, perhaps, several years, and may be asked how he has applied it.

Burden of Defence. The burden of proving the defence lies, how- 5.89
ever, on the tenant (*Sims* v. *Wilson*, 1946), and he must produce evidence of attempts to find other accommodation in order to discharge it (*Alexander* v. *Mohamadzadeh*, 1985). Where there are joint tenants,

hardship to all of them has to be taken into account. The extent to which either landlord or tenant may be eligible for rehousing under Part III of the Housing Act 1985 (see Chapter 10), may well be decisive under this Case.

5.90   **Misrepresentation.** If an order for possession is made under either Case 8 (5.85), or Case 9 (5.86), and it is later made to appear to the court that the landlord obtained the order either by misrepresenting circumstances to the court, or by concealing some material fact, the court has power to order the landlord to pay damages to the tenant (1977, s.102). This can be a difficult claim, for a mere change of mind is not the same as a misrepresentation, and will not be enough.

5.91   **Suitable Alternative Accommodation.** The final "ground for possession," in relation to which reasonableness must still, and additionally, be shown, does not appear in the schedule of discretionary grounds (1977, Sched. 15). It is that the landlord can provide or obtain suitable alternative accommodation for the tenant (1977, s.98). The meaning of this phrase is defined in Schedule 15, Part IV, and is in similar terms to the 1988 Act (4.40). If the court seems likely to make an order on this ground, it will be in the tenant's interests to seek a ruling that the tenancy of the new premises should be Rent Act protected, rather than a Housing Act assured (Chapter 4) tenancy (5.02).

3. *Protection of Rents*

5.92   **Need for Protection of Rents.** All Rent Act protected tenants, whether statutory or contractual, are entitled to protection of their rents. Indeed, statutory tenancy itself would be valueless if landlords could increase rents beyond what tenants can afford to pay, and so force them speedily into arrears. The converse is equally true: protection of rents would be valueless if landlords could serve retaliatory notices to quit.
In this section we shall consider:
   (i) *what the fair rent is*;
   (ii) *how it applies to a tenancy*; and,
   (iii) *the rent limit for regulated tenancies.*

(i) *The fair rent*

5.93   **Rent Officers.** A fair rent is one that is considered fair for the premises and tenancy in question by a rent officer. He is a public official, employed by the Department of the Environment through a series of local rent offices throughout the country. Each rent office has jurisdiction over an area broadly corresponding to an area of local government.

Statutory Considerations. The Rent Act contains guidelines to rent officers as to what they should consider as a fair rent (1977, s.70). There are some things which they are obliged to take into account, and some which they are bound to disregard. Failure to obey these guidelines could result in an application to quash the decision of the rent officer. It is, however, hard to establish that a rent officer has either wrongly taken account of some factor, or else failed to apply some relevant consideration. The rent officer is obliged to take into account all the circumstances (other than personal circumstances) and in particular the age, character, and locality of the residential accommodation, its state of repair, and if any furniture is provided for use under the tenancy the quantity, quality and condition of the furniture (1977, s.70).

5.94

Personal Circumstances. The most common example of a personal circumstance is the tenant who is in straitened circumstances, or the landlord who claims that he cannot afford to keep the property in repair. Another example might be that of an elderly person who finds it more inconvenient to live at the top of a flight of stairs than would a hypothetical, average tenant; or a tenant with children who feels the lack of a garden. But the presence or otherwise of a garden, and the fact that a flat is at the top of, perhaps, a long flight of stairs, will affect the value of the premises themselves in any event, just not more so because of the particular characteristics or circumstances of the present tenant. The extent of a tenant's security of tenure (*e.g.* notice under mandatory ground (5.68-5.76) or housing association landlord, for in some circumstances these provisions also apply to such tenants, (3.75-3.76, 7.30), is a personal circumstance (*Palmer* v. *Peabody Trust,* 1975).

5.95

General Conditions in Locality. Although it is not permissible to take into account the tenant's financial circumstances, it is possible for a rent officer to consider the general level of wages throughout a particular locality (*Guppy's (Bridport) Ltd.* v. *Carpenter,* 1973). But it is up to the rent officer to determine just what he will consider the locality for the purposes of the determination (*Palmer* v. *Peabody Trust,* 1975). This could benefit a tenant of whatever income living in a working class district but, equally, could act to the detriment of a poor tenant living in an area that is, or that has become, predominantly middle class.

5.96

5.97   **Considerations in Practice.** Such matters as size and whether or not premises are on a noisy street are obviously relevant. Consideration of locality means more than just what part of town premises are in, but also whether they are near other amenities, such as parks and recreational facilities, public transport and good shopping centres. In other words, all the factors that would normally be considered as affecting the value of living in particular premises or that would tend to push rents up or down (*Metropolitan Property Holdings* v. *Finegold*, 1975). State of repair is very important indeed; if premises are in such a bad condition that they are not even habitable, or perhaps only in part habitable, then there is nothing to stop a rent officer determining a purely nominal rent for the premises as a whole, or attributing a purely nominal amount to the uninhabitable part (*McGee* v. *London Rent Assessment Panel Committee*, 1969) although, even if they are technically unfit for human habitation (12.11-12.14) he is not obliged to do so (*Williams* v. *Khan*, 1981).

5.98   **Disregard of Tenant's Improvements.** The rent officer will disregard, in addition to personal circumstances, any improvements done by the tenant, other than improvements which he is obliged to do under the terms of the tenancy, and any damage or disrepair attributable to the tenant's default.

5.99   **Scarcity Value.** The major element which the rent officer must disregard, that forms the cornerstone of the fair rent system, is the "scarcity value." It is scarcity, more than anything else, which pushes up the price of property and rents. It is easy to see how a landlord with considerable property holdings in a particular area could manipulate the supply of property and, accordingly, its relationship to demand, without difficulty. In order to avoid scarcity value, the rent officer is obliged to adopt the artificial assumption that there are not substantially more people seeking any particular sort of accommodation in one area, than there is such accommodation available.

5.100   **Rent Register.** Each rent office is obliged to maintain a rent register, which is open for public inspection. This contains details of all rent registrations in force. Normally these are rents which will have been registered by a rent officer since 1965, when the fair rent system was introduced (Rent Act 1965). There is one exception to this. Prior to August 14, 1974, furnished tenancies were subject to the Rent Tribunal (5.21) and rents may have been registered in respect of them with the Rent Tribunal (see Chapter 6). When the Rent Act 1974 came into force, such rent registrations were deemed to become fair rents and were included in the register (1977, Sched. 24).

Comparables. The rent register contains the documentary part of the experience which the rent officer will apply to any particular application. He will look at the register to see if there have been any previous registrations for properties of similar size, in similar areas, etc. These, the rent officer will treat as "comparables." Comparables are very important indeed and anyone considering an application for registration of a fair rent should take the trouble to go down to the rent office and inspect the register, which is open to the public. Comparables are considered the best evidence of what is a fair rent (*Mason* v. *Skilling*, 1974).

5.101

Use of Comparables. It is important to note the date of a comparable for, like everything else, rents increase with inflation and the cost of living generally. Rents are always registered exclusive of rates (1977, s.71) and many tenants will in fact be paying a rent that is inclusive, so that without bearing this in mind a comparable can be deceptively encouraging. They can be misleading for another reason; while the register gives details of any special facilities provided under the terms of the tenancy, such as services or furniture, and attributes how much of the rent is paid for them, and while the register also indicates the balance of repairing obligations as between landlord and tenant, the register will rarely include any or much information about the state of the property which is being considered comparable.

5.102

(ii) *Application of fair rents*

Old Registered Rents. A fair rent can apply to a tenancy in one of two ways; either there is a rent already registered, or there is an application for a registration after the tenancy starts. If there has been a registration before the tenancy starts, then this rent will apply to the new tenancy, even though the tenancy agreement is for a higher figure (1977, s.44). A fair rent applies to any subsequent Rent Act protected tenancy, unless and until such time as a new application is made. This is true even where the nature of the letting has changed, *e.g.* from unfurnished to furnished, unless the change is to the structure of the premises such that it can no longer be called the same dwelling-house (*Rakhit* v. *Carty*, 1990). Alternatively, in order to end the registration application may be made to cancel it (1977, s.73). The rent only applies, however, to exactly the same premises, *i.e.* not premises which have been enlarged

5.103

by the addition of a room, nor even premises reduced in size by letting them off less one of the rooms (*Gluchowska* v. *Tottenham B.C.*, 1954).

5.104 **Removal From Register By Agreement.** There is another way in which a fair rent can be removed from the register. This applies in very limited circumstances indeed. If a landlord and a tenant under a fixed term tenancy on which there is at least one year to run agree on a higher rent, they may jointly apply to the rent officer to remove the registration of a fair rent, which will be done provided that the rent officer approves the amount of the increase (1977, s.73).

5.105 **Recovery of Excess Rent.** If a tenant has been paying more than the registered rent, under a contract, then the excess is recoverable, for up to two years after it was paid, either by deducting it from future rent owing, or by a normal civil action (1977, s.57).

5.106 **Application for New Registration.** There can only be an application for a new registration, in normal circumstances, two years after the last (1977, s.67). This is so even if there is a new tenancy or, indeed, even if there is a new landlord, so that two completely different parties could find themselves bound by a registration secured by a former landlord and/or a former tenant. Either landlord, or tenant, or both jointly (1977, s.68) can apply for registration of rent.

5.107 **Joint Early Appplication.** There are three exceptions to the two-year bar. The first is where a landlord and a tenant apply jointly for a new rent to be registered, this may be done in less than two years.

5.108 **Landlord's Early Application.** A landlord may apply on his own, one year and nine months after the last registration, but the new rent cannot come into force until two years have elapsed.

5.109 **Change of Circumstances.** Finally, and most commonly, there can be an application before the expiry of two years, by either party, if there have been such substantial changes in the terms of the tenancy, the condition of the premises or furniture, that, in all the circumstances, the rent last registered is no longer fair.

5.110 **Approach to Rent on Change of Circumstances.** On such an application, the rent officer does not merely consider the changed circumstances and reduce or increase accordingly, but considers the whole rent anew (*London Housing and Commercial Properties* v.

Cowan, 1976). This provision is likely only to be of use to a landlord who has, for example, installed some facility such as a hot water system, since the last registration. A tenant who applies because of some deterioration may well find that the amount by which the rent ought to be decreased on account of the deterioration is not so great as the amount by which the rent has increased in respect of the rent of the tenancy, because of inflation. On the other hand, on a landlord's application for a higher rent because of an improvement, a tenant should not hesitate to point out any deterioration, so as to prevent the rent going up by too much.

Initial Applications. If there is no rent registration already in force, the tenant can apply at any time after the start of a tenancy. So can the landlord, though he is unlikely to want to do so in practice. The procedure is the same whether or not the application is a first application or a new application. The party making the application completes the appropriate forms, which are available from the rent office and from most aid or advice agencies. These forms will be sent to the other side, for example, the landlord on a tenant's application, who will have an opportunity to comment and to put the case from his point of view. If there are joint tenants or, indeed, joint landlords, then all must sign the application form or one must sign as agent for the others (*Turley* v. *Panton*, 1975; *R.* v. *Rent Officer for Camden L.B.C., ex p. Felix*, 1988). The applicant is obliged to state what is the fair rent that he wishes to have registered. 5.111

Inspection and Consultation. Although the rent officer is not obliged to do so, he will normally visit the premises. He will at that time hold a consultation, or else he may hold a consultation at a different time, and at his office. He will not necessarily hold a consultation if the rent has previously been registered, and there is no change other than the passage of time, but must do so in all cases (including this circumstance) if either party asks him to. The consultation is informal and it is not usual for parties to be represented, nor is legal aid available for such representation, although legal advice may be obtained beforehand. A lawyer may be of help if a question of jurisdiction arises, for example whether the tenancy is protected or not, or whether the time is correct for an application. A surveyor may be of more help if the only question is as to the amount of rent. Some rent officers give their decision at the hearing, others do so later. In either case, the decision will be in writing. 5.112

Rent Assessment Committee. If either party is dissatisfied with the 5.113

rent registration, he may appeal to the Rent Assessment Committee (1977, Sched. 11). This body has no power at all to decide an appeal on a point of law, *i.e.* as to jurisdiction (*London Housing and Commercial Properties* v. *Cowan*, 1976). Such a challenge can only be taken to the Divisional Court or to the county court (1977, s.141). The Rent Assessment Committee is a tribunal, not a court, and legal aid is not available for proceedings before it, although legal advice may be obtained beforehand. Again, representation by a surveyor may be helpful. There is a Surveyor's Aid Scheme operating in London for those who cannot afford a surveyor without help.

5.114   **Appeal De Novo.** When the Rent Assessment Committee hear an appeal, they do not start with the decision of the rent officer and decide whether he is right or wrong, but start all over again for themselves. They, too, will normally go to inspect the premises in question, and they will usually hold a consultation which will be slightly more formal than that before the rent officer and will always be at their office, not at the premises.

5.115   **Appeal from Rent Assessment Committee.** Rent Assessment Committee rents are customarily higher than those of the rent officer, by an average of about 10 per cent. There is no explanation for this but it tends to suggest that tenants are rarely well-advised to appeal, unless there is some general point at issue and a case is being laid by way of test-case, or the rent officer's decision is clearly unsupportable. There is no appeal from a Rent Assessment Committee decision, unless it can be shown to have acted wrongly in law, by wrongful inclusion or exclusion of some consideration. This would be made to the High Court. If asked to do so, the Rent Assessment Committee are bound to give their decision, and the reasons for it in writing (Tribunals and Inquiries Act 1971).

5.116   **Relevant Date.** The date when the registration is finally made, either by rent officer or Rent Assessment Committee, is known as the relevant date (1977, s.67(5)), and it affects the date when a new application can be made. The rent applies to the tenancy from the relevant date (1977, s.72).

5.117   **Effecting an Increase.** If an application is a first application, it will usually be made by a tenant and it will usually result in a decrease in the rent from that which was agreed contractually. If the rent registered is higher (taken together with rates if the contractual rent is inclusive) than the contractual rent, then the landlord cannot claim the increase until he has brought the contractual tenancy to an end, either by notice to quit or, in the case of a fixed term tenancy, by expiry of time (1.39), or by notice of increase specifying a date no earlier than the date when the contractual tenancy could have been brought to an end (1977, s.49).

(iii) *The rent limit*

Maximum Rent. The rent limit is the term used to describe the maximum amount which a landlord can claim from the tenant. It must be considered during the contractual period, after the contractual period, if or when no rent has been registered, and after the contractual period, once a fair rent has been registered.   5.118

Contractual Period. During the contractual period of a regulated tenancy, the rent limit is either the registered rent or the contractual rent, whichever is the lower (1977, s.44). If there is no registered rent, then the limit is the contractual rent. The contractual rent may be inclusive of rates, in which case it will be necessary to add to the registered rent the amount of rates attributable to the premises before determining how much rent is payable. Any increases up to the amount of the contractual limit can be imposed without notice of increase, and in order to exceed the contractual limit, the tenancy must be determined. The contractual rent may be increased by agreement, without registration, by way of a rent agreement (1977, s.51), which must comply with provisions for the protection of tenants considered below (5.96), and is otherwise invalid (1977, s.54), and may be recovered by the tenant if he pays the increase (1977, s.57). Recovery may be by way of deduction from future rent (1977, s.57).   5.119

Statutory Period - Pre-Registration. It may be that by the time the contractual tenancy comes to an end, there is still no registered rent in force. In that case, the landlord is confined by the former contractual rent limit until such time as he applies for registration of a fair rent (1977, s.45). In other words, the landlord cannot normally increase the rent payable without application. If the result of an application is an increase, then the landlord must first serve a notice of increase (1977, ss.45, 49).   5.120

Increase for Services or Furniture. The landlord can, however, increase the rent without applying for registration, on account of the costs of providing services or furniture (1977, s.47). The tenant may be able   5.121

to challenge the amount claimed in the county court (1977, s.49).

5.122   **Rent Agreement.** As an alternative to an increase other than on account of these items of expenditure and other than by way of application for registration, the landlord and the tenant may enter into a rent agreement for a new rent (1977, s.51). A rent agreement is only valid if it is in writing, and if at the head of the document there appears a statement in writing or print no less conspicuous than that used elsewhere in the agreement that the tenant is not obliged to enter into the agreement, and that his security of tenure will not be affected if he refuses (1977, s.51(4)). The statement must also advise the tenant of his right to apply to the rent officer at any time, then or even immediately after it has been signed, for registration of a fair rent. An agreement which does not comply with these terms is invalid (1977, s.54) and the excess can be reclaimed by the tenant for up to one year after it was paid, as an ordinary civil debt or by deduction from the rent (1977, s.57).

5.123   **Statutory Period - Post-Registration.** Once a rent is registered for the premises, then this becomes the rent limit and cannot be increased except by a new application, other than to pass on increases in the rates (1977, s.45). It is also possible to pass on increases in the cost of providing services without a new application, provided that the rent officer has agreed that the service element should be variable and has endorsed the landlord's proposed terms for any future variations, *i.e.* for how they are to be calculated. Other increases, which will be those by new application or, possibly, by appeal to the Rent Assessment Committee, can only be claimed by notice of increase.

5.124   **Rent in Advance.** With all regulated tenancies, whether contractual or statutory and whether or not a rent is registered in respect of the premises, it is illegal for a landlord to demand rent further in advance than the beginning of the period for which it is paid, *i.e.* the first day of a week for which a weekly rent is paid, or the first day of a month for which a monthly rent is paid (1977, s.26). If the tenancy is yearly, then the landlord cannot charge the year's rent earlier than half-way through the year for which it is due. A tenant can recover any money improperly demanded too far in advance, for up to two years after it was paid. This probably does not mean that the landlord is not entitled to the actual rent at the time when it would be lawful to ask for it, so that this would probably only be of any use to a tenant who has been charged a considerable amount in advance, or by way of defence to an action for arrears, or part of them, based on rent improperly charged in advance, *i.e.* because it is, in law, not yet due and therefore not in arrears.

4. *Further Financial Protection and Assistance*

Miscellaneous Provisions. To avoid other forms of exploitation of tenants, or ways of extracting more money from them than permitted, there are other forms of financial protection and assistance which may be applicable. We need only consider here premiums and deposits because the position so far as the availability of housing benefits is concerned is the same as for Housing Act secure tenants (and Housing Act assured tenants) - see 3.77 - and the position so far as accommodation agency charges and the resale of utilities, *i.e.* gas and electricity, is the same as for Housing Act assured tenants (4.58-4.60). 5.125

Premiums. It is illegal to charge a tenant a premium on the grant, continuance or renewal of a Rent Act protected tenancy (1977, s.119). A tenant who has paid one such premium can sue for its return (1977, s.125). Such a claim must be made within six years of the payment in the same way as for the recovery of a normal civil debt (Limitation Act 1980). It is also a criminal offence to require or to receive a premium and the matter should be reported to the Tenancy Relations Officer: see Chapter 8. However, in the case of certain long leases which come into protection on account of increases in rent (5.47), premiums may in some circumstances lawfully be charged (1977, s.127 and Sched. 18). 5.126

Premiums on Change of Tenant. A premium might be charged by a landlord, or by his agent, or by an outgoing tenant. An outgoing tenant might charge for an assignment, or else for arranging to surrender his own tenancy to the landlord, who contemporaneously consents to grant a new tenancy to the incoming tenant. In such a case, it may well be that there is no profit to the landlord. In all of these cases, however, the premium is an illegal payment (1977, s.120; *Farrell* v. *Alexander*, 1976). 5.127

Premiums Paid to or by Another. It is a premium whether a person demands that the money is paid to himself, or to someone else, perhaps, for example, in discharge of a debt that the person demanding the premium owes to the other (*Elmdene Estates Ltd.* v. *White*, 1960). Another example would be that of the outgoing tenant who agrees to assign the tenancy or arrange for a new tenancy to be granted to the incoming tenant, if the incoming tenant will pay arrears of rent that he owes. 5.128

5.129   **Premiums in Cash or Kind.** The most obvious form that a premium will take is cash. But an illegal premium might also be demanded or paid other than in cash, for otherwise this protection too could be circumvented without difficulty, *e.g.* by demanding payments in kind, such as goods, or else by demanding excessive prices for fixtures, fittings or furniture.

5.130   **Premiums for Fittings and Furniture.** It is lawful to make it a condition of the grant of a tenancy, whether by assignment or from the landlord, that an incoming tenant should have to purchase fittings, or even furniture (1977, s.123). After all, such items as fitted carpets may well be valueless to an outgoing tenant in his new home and it is considered only fair that he should be able to insist, before the assignment or an arrangement for surrender and new grant, that the incoming tenant, as it were, takes them off his hands. But only a fair price for fittings and furniture can be demanded and the excess constitutes an illegal premium (1977, s.123). Anyone seeking to make an incoming tenant pay for furniture is obliged to provide an inventory of it and of the price sought for each item, and failure to do so is a criminal offence (1977, s.124).

5.131   **Premiums for Fixtures, Alterations and Outgoings.** The position is slightly different where "fixtures" are concerned. These are items, such as fitted cupboards or double glazing, which effectively become a part of the premises and are valueless when removed. No tenant is allowed to remove fixtures in any event; as they attach to the premises, they become, eventually, the property of the landlord. But an outgoing tenant is permitted to charge an incoming tenant the amount it cost him to install the fixtures (1977, s.120). An outgoing tenant is also permitted to charge what it cost him to do any structural alterations to the premises, any amounts paid by way of outgoings on the premises, *e.g.* rates, telephone rental, which are attributable to the period after he has left, and any amount paid by the outgoing tenant to a former tenant which was payment for fixtures or alterations (1977, s.120).

5.132   **Deposits.** Landlords frequently require an incoming occupier to pay a deposit, either for furniture, for rent arrears or, for example, damage. Such a deposit will not, however be illegal if: (*a*) it is reasonable in relation to the purpose for which it is claimed; and (*b*) it does not exceed one-sixth of the annual rent (1977, s.128, as amended by 1980, s.79). By inference, a larger deposit will be likely to be considered a premium.

6 Limited Security

Pre-January 15, 1989 Restricted Contracts. In this chapter, we shall 6.01
consider two residual classes of occupier who enjoy a limited degree of
security of tenure. These are, first, people who come within the
jurisdiction of the Rent Tribunal, an official body (in fact composed of
the same people who constitute a Rent Assessment Committee: 5.113),
with power, where certain types of letting have been granted, to register
a reasonable rent for the letting, and in some cases (now very rare), to
defer for up to six months at a time a notice bringing the letting to an
end. These occupiers have what are known as "restricted contracts,"
which can be either tenancies or licences. No new restricted contracts
can be granted after the commencement of Part I, Housing Act 1988
("1988"; January 15, 1989), unless in pursuance of a contract made
before that date (1988, s.36). It follows that so far as we are concerned
with restricted contracts, we are *only* concerned with those beginning
before that date.

Pre-January 15, 1989 Protected Shortholds. The second class of 6.02
occupier with limited security, considered in this chapter, is the
"shorthold tenant." There are two kinds of shorthold tenancy. One kind
is the "protected shorthold tenant," who is a Rent Act protected tenant
(see Chapter 5) on whom was served a notice before the commencement
of his tenancy that he would be subject to the recovery of possession
under a mandatory ground. Although ostensibly otherwise a Rent Act
protected tenancy (Chapter 5), it is so easy for a landlord to get
possession that it is idle to consider the tenant as enjoying Rent Act
security of tenure. Because no new Rent Act protected tenancies can be
granted on or after the commencement of Part I, 1988 Act (January 15,
1989), it follows that no new protected shorthold tenancies can be
granted after that date, and, again, so far as we are concerned with
protected shorthold tenancies, we are *only* concerned with those
beginning before that date. Protected shorthold tenants are *not* within the
definition of "qualifying tenant" for the purposes of Part I, Landlord
and Tenant Act 1987, *i.e.* the "right of first refusal" (2.16-2.21).

January 15, 1989 (and *post*) Assured Shortholds. In place of the pro- 6.03
tected shorthold, the new class of Housing Act assured tenancies (Chap-

133

ter 4) carries with it a similar arrangement, for "assured shorthold tenancies" (1988, s.20), tenants under which are likewise persons who in all other respects qualify as Housing Act assured tenants, but on whom have been served, before the Housing Act assured tenancy was entered into, notices in a prescribed form, stating that the tenancy is to be shorthold, and which therefore entitles the landlord to recover possession on this ground alone (1988, s.21). There is provision for reference of rents to a Rent Assessment Committee additional to that enjoyed by an ordinary Housing Act assured tenant. As we are concerned in this chapter with assured shorthold tenancies, we can *only* be considering tenancies starting on or after January 15, 1989. As Housing Act assured tenants are not within the definition of "qualifying tenant" for the purposes of Part I, Landord and Tenant Act 1987 (4.04), *i.e.* the "right of first refusal" (2.16-2.21), so also are assured shorthold tenants excluded.

1. *Restricted Contracts*

6.04 **Tenants with Resident Landlords.** The largest class of occupiers with restricted contracts are tenants who have resident landlords (5.28-5.33). In addition, those who are provided with sufficient attendances to take them out of full Rent Act protection (5.43-5.44) or board, provided it is *not* substantial (5.46), have restricted contracts. Hostel-dwellers will frequently have restricted contracts, as will those in long-stay hotels. The class does not normally cover, lettings from landlords who are in some way publicly accountable (*e.g.* local authorities) nor family/friendly arrangements, nor those where no long-stay is involved.

(i) *Definition*

6.05 **Categorising Restricted Contracts.** There are two ways in which restricted contracts are defined: by general definition and by specific definition. However, lettings can be specifically *excluded* from the jurisdiction.

6.06 **General definition.** Restricted contracts are generally defined in Rent Act 1977, s.19. Restricted contracts are those "contracts...whereby one person grants to another person, in consideration of a rent which includes payment for the use of furniture or for services, the right to occupy a dwelling as a residence." In every case, it is the relationship between the occupier and the person who granted the right of occupation which is relevant: an occupier might be the restricted occupier of a protected tenant, or of a secure tenant, or of an owner-occupier or, indeed, even of a wholly unprotected tenant.

Tenancy and Licence. The use of the term "contracts" has been interpreted to include both tenancies and licences: *Luganda* v. *Service Hotels Ltd.* (1969). The arrangement must, however, be contractual, *i.e.* it has to be intended to be binding on the parties. 6.07

Services. "Services" *includes* attendances (5.43-5.44) and *also* the provision of heating or lighting, the supply of hot water and any other privilege or facility connected with the occupancy of a dwelling, other than a privilege or facility necessary for the purposes of access to the premises let, the supply of cold water or sanitary accommodation (1977, s.85). Furniture means any amount of furniture. 6.08

Student Lettings. Student lettings may be restricted contracts, even though they are excluded from full protection, provided that their lettings are furnished, or services are provided, as will commonly be the case. On the other hand, they may also be paying for board and this may be so substantial that they are excluded for this reason (6.12(*e*)). 6.09

Exclusive Occupation. The key element of a restricted contract is that of exclusive occupation. A hostel-dweller who is given a room to share with another will not have exclusive occupation, unless the occupiers approached the hostel together and took the room jointly. A hostel dweller with his own room will, however, usually have exclusive occupation sufficient to amount to a restricted contract (*R.* v. *South Middlesex Rent Tribunal, ex p. Beswick*, 1976). Any tenant will of definition have exclusive occupation (1.58). In every case, it will be a question of fact whether or not an occupier has exclusive occupation. It will not be missing just because, for example, a landlord retains a key to the room, or because one of the landlord's employees comes in to clean. There will still be enough exclusive occupation for these purposes if, in addition to the exclusive use of at least one room, there is shared use of other rooms (1977, s.19), even if those shared rooms constitute "living accommodation" (3.09). 6.10

Specific definition. Even if a tenant does not qualify under the general definition, above, the tenants of resident landlords who are excluded from full Rent Act protection for that reason (5.28-5.33), have restricted contracts, even if no furniture or services are provided (1977, s.20). Those who are excluded from full protection because they share living 6.11

accommodation with their landlords (5.41-5.42) are also included regardless of the provision of furniture or services (1977, s.21).

6.12   **Specific exclusion.** There are certain conditions which exclude an occupier from the definition of restricted contract, whether or not he qualifies under the general definition, or by specific inclusion (1977, s.19):

(*a*) **Rateable Values.** The rateable value of the (occupier's part of the) premises exceeds £1,500 (Greater London) or £750 (elsewhere). This is so unlikely to be the case that it may be assumed not to apply unless the landlord shows the contrary.

(*b*) **Regulated Tenancy.** The letting creates a regulated tenancy (5.12). This provision is inserted to ensure that there is no overlap between full Rent Act protection and Rent Tribunal restriction (*Baldock* v. *Murray*, 1980).

(*c*) **Public Landlords.** The landlord under the letting is the Crown, a government department or a local authority. However, if Crown property is under the management of the Crown Estate Commissioners, it is not so excluded.

(*d*) **Quasi-Public Landlords.** The landlord under the tenancy is a registered housing association, housing trust, the Housing Corporation or Housing for Wales, or a housing co-operative. Note that this only excludes the *tenants* of such landlords, and does not prevent their licensees from using the powers of the Rent Tribunal, if they otherwise qualify.

(*e*) **Board.** Under the terms of the letting, the occupier is provided with board and the value to the occupier of the board forms a substantial proportion of the whole rent paid. This is a similar application of the test applicable to whether or not premises were let furnished in law before August 14, 1974, and whether or not sufficient attendances are provided to keep a tenancy out of protection (5.36-5.39). Board may be hard to value and is almost certainly worth more than the mere cost of the food. What constitutes board has been considered (5.46). If *any* board is provided, a tenancy cannot be Rent Act protected: but if the value of the board forms an insubstantial proportion of the rent, then it will be restricted. Otherwise, it will be wholly outside of both protection and restriction.

(*f*) **Holiday Lettings.** If the letting is for the purposes of a holiday (4.17) the Rent Tribunal will not have jurisdiction over it.

(ii) *Rent Restriction*

Reasonable Rents. In respect of all the restricted contracts, the Rent   6.13
Tribunal can fix a *reasonable* rent (1977, s.78). That is to say, a rent
which it considers reasonable in all the circumstances. There are no
guidelines analogous to those to which the rent officer must pay heed,
but, under different legislation, it has been said that it would not be
reasonable to make a tenant pay for general shortages in the availability
of accommodation, *i.e.* scarcity value: *John Kay Ltd.* v. *Kay* (1952).

Rent Jurisdiction. In comparison with the systems of rent regulation   6.14
considered in Chapter 5, Rent Tribunal powers over rents are very easy
to describe indeed. An application may be made in respect of any letting
within its jurisdiction, so long as the letting lasts, and the Tribunal can
reduce, confirm or increase the existing rent. It can do this in respect of
a periodic letting, or a fixed-term letting, and irrespective of any
contractually agreed rent. The Rent Tribunal rent, if one exists in respect
of the letting, forms the only rent limit which binds the landlord (1977,
s.81), other than, of course, the actual terms of the agreement, *e.g.* for
a fixed-term at a specified rent.

Applications - Form. Application forms are available from the Rent   6.15
Tribunal office, or from a local aid or advice agency. A copy will be
sent to the other side, *e.g.* a landlord on a tenant's application, who will
have an opportunity to reply. If there are joint occupiers, or indeed joint
landlords, then they must all sign the application, or else one must sign
as agent for the others (*Turley* v. *Panton*, 1975). The application can be
made by the landlord, or occupier, or both, jointly (1977, s.77).

Applications - Time. An application to the Rent Tribunal *can* be made   6.16
at any time (1977, s.80). However, the Tribunal is not obliged to hear an
application made before two years have passed since the last time a rent
was registered, unless there has been such a change in the condition of
the dwelling, the furniture or services provided, the terms of the
contract, or any other circumstances taken into account when the rent
was last considered as to make the registered rent no longer reasonable
(1977, s.80(2)). The Tribunal must also hear an application before two
years have passed if the application is a joint application (1977, s.80(2)).

Rent Levels. Like the rent officer, a Rent Tribunal registers a rent ex-   6.17
clusive of rates, but will note that the actual rent payable is an inclusive
rent, as will almost invariably be the case (1977, s.79). If there is a fair

rent registered for the premises, even though it is now let out on a tenancy which is not protected, then the Tribunal may not register a lower rent for the restricted letting than the fair rent on the register (1977, s.78(3)). In practice, Rent Tribunal rents are noticeably higher than fair rents.

6.18   **Rent Limit.** Once a rent is registered with the Rent Tribunal then that too, like the fair rent, normally remains effective indefinitely, or until a new application is made, even on a subsequent letting and even between wholly different parties (1977, s.81). One exception to this is that the Rent Tribunal has power to order that the registration shall in fact lapse after a particular period of time (1977, s.78(4)). This is rarely exercised but when it is, then the registration lapses after that and the position is subsequently as if there had never been any registration. Like the fair rent, too, the registered rent only bites on exactly the same premises, *i.e.* neither larger nor smaller (5.103). A landlord can apply for cancellation of registration, if the premises are not at that time let out on a restricted contract (1977, s.81A): this forms the other exception to the normal rule about the lasting effect of registration.

6.19   **Recovery of Excess Rent.** If an occupier enters into a contract which is a restricted letting at a rent higher than a registered Rent Tribunal rent in force, then the excess rent paid is recoverable (1977, s.81(3)). This is recoverable for up to six years after it has been paid. There is, however, no provision for recovery of the overpaid rent by way of deduction from future rent (*cf.* 5.119). A major difference from the overcharging of a fair rent is that it is a criminal offence to overcharge a Rent Tribunal rent (1977, s.81(4)) and this should be reported to the tenancy relations or harassment officer: see Chapter 8.

6.20   **Procedure.** Rent tribunals, like rent officers, are not obliged to visit premises in question, but will usually do so. They are, however, obliged to hold a hearing. In the normal course of events, the Tribunal members will visit the premises in the morning, and hold a hearing in the afternoon. The hearing will not be as formal as a court hearing, but will be more formal than that before the rent officer. The Tribunal will consist of three people, and the chairman will normally be a lawyer. Legal aid is not available for proceedings before a Rent Tribunal, but legal advice may be sought beforehand. The Tribunal takes a fairly active part in the proceedings, asking questions and seeking out the information it is most interested in. The Tribunal does not normally permit, and always discourages, cross-examination. If there is a dispute as to exactly what services or furniture are provided, it prefers to ask each party separately than to allow any confrontation to develop.

No Need for Notice of Increase. There is no provision for any notice 6.21 of increase to be served, nor do any phasing provisions apply. The essence of Tribunal procedure is speed, informality, inexpensive arbitration, etc. The presence of laywers is not encouraged, save where a point as to jurisdiction is involved.

Need for Existing Letting. All applications must be made while the 6.22 letting is still in existence, *i.e.* before any notice or fixed period expires. Of particular relevance here are the remarks made about the time of expiry of a notice bringing a licence to an end (1.34-1.36). Such a notice will expire after any contractually agreed time or form of notice, *or* a reasonable period of time (or, in the case of a periodic licence which is not an excluded licence - 8.10 - four weeks), whichever is the *longer.* It follows that a shouted order to ''get out at once,'' or by the next day, will not expire as a notice bringing the licence to an end until a reasonable time has elapsed. It can, therefore, still be referred to the Tribunal although, for example, the day has passed.

(iii) *Security Provisions*

Lettings *Pre-* and *Post-*November 28, 1980. The security provisions 6.23 governing restricted contracts are completely different in relation to contracts starting before November 28, 1980 (the date when the relevant parts of the Housing Act 1980 came into force), and in relation to contracts starting on or after that date.

***Pre-*1980 Act Security.** Even if rent is not really a problem, security of 6.24 tenure is obtained by application to the Rent Tribunal for consideration of the rent, *plus* security. The Tribunal has no powers at all unless the application is made also for a rent registration. An occupier can only apply for security of tenure if a notice bringing the right of occupation to an end has been given and has not yet expired. This means that a fixed-term agreement cannot be referred to the Tribunal for security of tenure. It can, however, before the time runs out, be referred for consideration of rent.

Determination of Contract. A restricted contract - whether tenancy or 6.25 licence - requires notice to quit in writing, of a minimum period of four weeks, and containing the prescribed information described above

(1.50). Anything less will not be a valid notice to quit and the Tribunal neither can, nor need, bother to consider it. The contract continues as if nothing has happened. But in the case of a *licence* which is a restricted contract, this is only so if it is not an "excluded licence," for the definition of which see below, paragraph 8.10. To determine an excluded licence requires no formalities other than those already referred to (1.34-1.36).

6.26   **Automatic Suspension of Notice to Quit.** Once a rent has been referred to the Tribunal, *i.e.* an application has been made, then any notice served before the application is automatically suspended and will not take effect until at least seven days after the hearing and the Tribunal decision (1977, s.104), although customarily longer because of the security given by the Tribunal.

6.27   **Deferral of Notice to Quit.** If a notice has been served before application, then the Tribunal will not only decide what rent is payable under the letting, but also when the notice should take effect (1977, s.104). It can defer the notice for up to six months at a time. Before the six months run out, there is nothing to stop an occupier applying for more time. The Tribunal may order no security at all, or a period shorter than six months.

6.28   **Retaliatory Notice to Quit.** If no notice has been served by the time the application to the Tribunal is made, then different provisions apply in the event of a retaliatory notice following application. These apply whether notice is served between application and hearing, or after the hearing. Unless at the hearing for rent registration the Tribunal orders that a shorter period will be appropriate, any such notice will automatically be deferred, without any need to re-apply to the Tribunal, for six months from the date of the decision, *i.e.* usually, the date of the hearing (1977, s.103).

6.29   **Reduction of Security.** Whether security has been gained because an application was made after a notice was served, or because the notice has followed rent registration and been automatically deferred, a landlord can re-apply during the period for which the occupier has security of tenure for a reduction in that security (1977, s.106). The Tribunal will grant a reduction of such period of time as it thinks fit, if it appears to the Tribunal that:

(*a*) **Non-compliance with Terms.** The occupier has not complied with the terms of the contract (*cf.* 3.34);

(*b*) **Nuisance, Annoyance, Immoral or Illegal User.** The occupier or anyone living with the occupier has been guilty of conduct which is a nuisance or annoyance to adjoining occupiers (*cf.* 3.35), which will commonly include the landlord as most cases now involve resident landlords, or has been convicted of using the premises or allowing them to be used, for an immoral or illegal purpose (*cf.* 3.36); or

(*c*) **Deterioration of Premises or Furniture.** That the condition of the property or any furniture provided by the landlord has deteriorated because of the default of the occupier or anyone living with him (*cf.* 3.37).

No Further Application. If the Tribunal makes an order for reduced security, then no further application for security can be made to it (1977, s.106(3)).   6.30

Reduction by Court. No tenant or former tenant (other than an "excluded tenant" whose tenancy began on or after January 15, 1989: see 8.10) can be evicted without a court order. In normal circumstances, court proceedings cannot be commenced until notice has expired. However, where the letting is one which only continues in existence because of Tribunal security, then the landlord can commence proceedings even before that security runs out and the county court can make an order for possession, in effect reducing the Tribunal security, on - but only on - exactly the same grounds as those which will give the Tribunal power to reduce security (6.29). Like the Tribunal, it is not obliged to reduce security, and it can use the power by reducing security by such amount as it thinks fit.   6.31

Orders for Possession. In normal circumstances, a court making an order for possession against a *pre*-1980 Act restricted occupier will make what was described above as an outright order, that is to say one that will usually be suspended for 14 days and to maximum of six weeks (3.22). If the former restricted occupier was a licensee, then the landlord can use special speedy procedures, Orders 24 and 113, but this he cannot do in the case of a former restricted tenant.   6.32

Required for Landlord. None of the security provisions benefit an occupier on whom has been served, no later than at the beginning of the right of occupation, a notice in writing by the landlord that he has formerly occupied the premises himself *if*, at the time the notice to leave is to take effect, the landlord actually requires possession for use of the premises as a residence by himself or another member of his family who   6.33

lived with him when last the landlord used the premises as his own residence (*cf.* 5.74). This provision does not apply to a landlord who is already living in another part of the same building (1977, s.105).

6.34   *Post*-1980 Act Security. The position relating to these contracts is very different, and much easier to describe. Rent Tribunal jurisdiction over security was entirely abolished (1977, s.102A). In its place, the county court has a more limited power, to allow suspension of an order for possesion, to a maximum of three months from the date of its order (1977, s.106A). If the court grants less than three months initially, it can on a later application grant further suspension, to a maximum of three months from the date of the original order. These powers may be exercised not only for the benefit of the tenant or licensee, but also for the benefit of his spouse or ex-spouse (1977, s.106A(5), (6)). The court's power may be exercised on terms or conditions, which must include terms as to payment of rent and of any arrears, unless the court considers that to do this would cause exceptional hardship or would otherwise be unreasonable.

6.35   Need for Proceedings. Two points of further distinction emerge: first, the power is not limited to a former *periodic* restricted contract (6.24); secondly, although the obligation to take legal proceedings before evicting most licensees is less clear cut than former tenants (see Chapter 8), court proceedings must always be taken before evicting a former restricted licensee whose licence is a post-1980 Act contract (Protection from Eviction Act 1977, s.3(2A), added by 1980, s.69). If it were not for this amendment then the court's powers replacing the former security jurisdiction of the Rent Tribunal might well not have availed restricted licensees at all.

    (iv) *Further Provisions*

6.36   Premiums and Deposits. The prohibitions against premiums and excessive deposits described above (5.126-5.132), only applied to restricted contracts if there was an effective rent registration with the Rent Tribunal, *i.e.* one which applies to the letting in question (1977, s.122). If there was not, then there were no prohibitions on premiums. But if a rent registered with the Tribunal did apply to the letting, then all the remarks made under this heading in Chapter 5 will apply in the same way.

6.37   Change of Terms. If the rent under a restricted contract is varied after the commencement of Part I, 1988 Act (January 15, 1989), then a new contract is deemed to come into existence at the time of the variation, and accordingly, the contract will cease to be a restricted contract, *unless* the variation is one resulting from an application to the Rent Tribunal, or the variation is by agreement, but only in order to alter the rent to match one that is registered by the Rent Tribunal (1988, s.36). If other terms of the contract are varied, then it is a question of fact in each case whether it is a sufficiently substantial variation to amount to a new contract (which will not be a restricted contract if after January 15, 1989), or only a minor variation which leaves the old contract in existence.

2. *Protected Shorthold Tenancies*

Conditions. The protected shorthold tenancy was introduced by the Housing Act 1980, and abolished by the 1988 Act (when it was replaced by the assured shorthold). The protected shorthold tenancy (Housing Act 1980 - "1980" - s.51), is a tenancy which is in all other respects a fully Rent Act protected tenancy (5.26-5.54), granted after November 28, 1980 (when the provisions were brought into force), which fulfilled the following conditions:

6.38

(*a*) Fixed-Term. It had to be a fixed-term tenancy, as distinct from a periodic tenancy (1.39), granted for a minimum of one year, and a maximum of five (1980, s.52(1)). A tenancy granted on one date, but expressed to have commenced on an earlier date, would only be likely to be considered to fulfil the minimum/maximum time-limits if they were fulfilled from the date when the tenancy was actually granted, rather than any such earlier date (*Roberts*v. *Church Commissioners for England,* 1971; *Brikom Investments Ltd.* v. *Seaford,* 1981).

(*b*) No Break Clause. There had to be no provision in the agreement for bringing the tenancy to an end by the landlord, other than by way of forfeiture (1.42-1.44) for non-payment of rent or breach of some other term of the tenancy (1980, s.52(1)(*a*)). Thus, a "break-clause" allowing the landlord to give notice in the middle of, or any other time during, the term would defeat the shorthold. A clause which allowed a landlord to forfeit if the tenant went bankrupt was construed as creating an obligation on the part of the tenant not to go bankrupt, and therefore the forfeiture clause was one which only operated on breach of the tenant's obligation so that the tenancy was still a shorthold (*Paterson* v. *Aggio,* 1987).

(*c*) Prior Notice. Before the tenancy was granted, the landlord had given the tenant a valid shorthold notice (1980, s.52(1)(*b*)). This is described below (6.42).

(*d*) **Registered Rent.** In some cases, either there must have been a registered rent (5.93-5.102) at the commencement of the tenancy, or the landlord must have secured a certificate of fair rent (now no longer available), by the time the tenancy was granted (1980, s.52(1)(*c*)). This, too, is considered further below (6.43-6.44).

(*e*) **Previous Rent Act Protected or Statutory Tenant.** The tenancy was not granted to a person who, immediately before the grant, was a Rent Act protected or statutory (5.12) tenant of the same premises (1980, s.52(2)). This is designed to prevent landlords persuading existing tenants to sign shorthold agreements. However, it only protects the tenant if the new tenancy was of exactly the same premises as the pre-existing tenancy (*cf.* 5.34). Thus, another flat in the same building would not keep the tenant out of shorthold, nor even a new agreement in respect of, *e.g.* the same premises less or plus one room (*Gluchowska* v. *Tottenham Borough Council*, 1954).

6.39   **Notice by Tenant.** Although the landlord could not reserve the right to give notice during the life of the shorthold (6.38(*b*)), the shorthold tenant is absolutely entitled to give notice, even if the written agreement prohibits him from doing so (1980, s.53(1)). Further, any clause purporting to penalise the tenant for giving notice under the provision, *e.g.* imposing additional months' rent, is wholly void and of no effect (1980, s.53(2)). The notice may be given at any time during the fixed term: if the fixed term was for more than two years, the notice must be of three months; if for two years or less, it need only be of one month; in either event, it must be in writing (1980, s.53(1)).

6.40   **Continuation of Protected Shortholds.** A protected shorthold tenancy is only technically a shorthold during the initial fixed-term tenancy (1980, s.52(5)). But this is technical in the extreme, because the power of the landlord to recover possession under the shorthold ground continues indefinitely (6.45; *Gent* v. *De La Mare*, 1987) and references to "shorthold tenants" include those whose shorthold has ended, but who remain vulnerable to the shorthold ground. The shorthold tenant is also subject to the usual grounds for possession (5.68-5.91).

6.41   **Limited Assignability.** A protected shorthold tenancy cannot be assigned (1.100), other than by order of the court under Matrimonial Causes Act 1973, section 24 (9.12), at any time during the shorthold (6.40), or afterwards, *i.e.* so long as the tenant remains subject to the possibility (6.40) of use of the shorthold ground (1980, s.54(2)). It is unclear whether the Matrimonial Homes Act 1983 (9.23-9.26) could be used to order a transfer of tenancy between spouses, though this likely seems on balance as there is no express prohibition against it. While there is no restriction on subletting, a sub-tenant to whom some part of the premises, or even the whole of the premises, has been let at any time while the tenant is still subject to the possibility (6.40) of use of the shorthold ground cannot avail himself of Rent Act 1977, s.137 (1.74; 1980, s.54(1)), and so will only become the landlord's tenant directly if the circumstances would put him in that position at common law, *i.e.* if the tenant surrenders or gives notice to quit (1.80). It would seem likely that a notice under the special, shorthold power (6.46) would not qualify as notice to quit for this purpose, although the point is undecided.

(i) *Notice*

Valid Prior Notice. A valid notice must have been given by the land-   6.42
lord to the tenant before the tenancy was granted, that the tenancy is to be a shorthold tenancy (1980, s.52(1)(*b*); 6.38(*c*)). The notice must be in the prescribed form of notice. A notice given *after* the tenancy has begun will not suffice. However, on proceedings for possession under the shorthold ground, a court can waive the requirement for notice if it considers that it is just and equitable to do so (1980, s.55(2)). This would be an extremely severe decision: in effect, the court would be retrospectively deeming the tenancy to have been a shorthold; the court should only use this power when the omission to serve notice was known to the tenant, perhaps known to be an oversight or accident of which the tenant now seeks to take advantage in a way that the court considers unmeritorious, or the notice was in very slightly the wrong form. In *R.J. Dunnell Property Investments Ltd.* v. *Thorpe* (1991) a decision to dispense with notice, where the tenancy agreement had stated that the letting was a protected shorthold but no notice had in fact been served, was upheld by the Court of Appeal. It should not be used to take away from a tenant full security where the tenant had reason to believe that was what he enjoyed.

(ii) *Rent*

Need for Registered Rent. Under the Act, at the time the tenancy was   6.43
granted, either there must already have been a registered rent, or a certificate of fair rent, in relation to the premises (1980, s.52(2)(*c*); 6.38(*d*)). Registration of fair rents has already been considered (5.93-5.102). The certificate of fair rent was repealed with the

introduction of the Housing Act 1988. The certificate of fair rent was usually used by a landlord intending to let out premises on a fully Rent Act protected tenancy, after the execution of works, and who wanted to know what was likely to be his return on the property: in this case, the same procedure could be used by a landlord intending to let out on shorthold, even though no works were to be carried out by him beforehand. If the landlord let out the premises when there was only a certificate of fair rent: (*a*) prior to full registration, no more rent should have been charged than stated in the certificate; and (*b*) the landlord had to apply for full registration within 28 days of the beginning of the tenancy (1980, s.52(1)(*c*)).

6.44   **Waiver of Need for Registered Rent.** The Secretary of State reserved powers under the Act to waive the requirement for a registered rent or a certificate of fair rent (1980, s.52(4)). He used this power in 1981 to waive the requirement outside London (S.I. 1981 No. 1578) and from 1987 throught the whole of the country (S.I. 1987 No. 265). Further, the court may still order possession on the shorthold ground (6.45-6.49) even when there has been a failure to comply with the registered rent requirement, if it is just and equitable to do so (1980, s.55(2)). Again (*cf.* 6.42), this is likely only to be used when there has been a technical defect, or an application pursued a matter of days late. It is highly unlikely to be used if a very high rent has been charged, but where the failure was an honest mistake, and the rent set was fully acceptable to both parties, it may be (*R.J. Dunnell Property Investments Ltd.* v. *Thorpe*, 1991). Where there was no requirement for rent registration at commencement, or for a certificate of fair rent, the tenant may still apply for registration himself (5.111-5.117), and if the rent officer registers a rent lower than that stated in a certificate, it is the lower rent that will be payable from registration (5.119).

(iii) *The shorthold ground*

6.45   **Mandatory Ground for Possession.** The shorthold ground remains available for use as long as the original shorthold tenant remains the tenant of the premises (1980, s.54(3)). The ground itself is to be found, by way of amendment, in Rent Act 1977, Schedule 15, Case 19, as an added mandatory ground for possession, although it was originally contained in 1980, s.55(1). The landlord must show not only that the preliminary conditions were fulfilled (6.38), save insofar as he hopes to rely on the court's discretion (6.42, 6.44), but also that since the technical end of the shorthold tenancy, *i.e.* the termination of the original fixed-period (6.40), there has been no further grant of a tenancy of the premises to anyone other than the original shorthold tenancy. In addition, he *must* comply with the "warning" notice provisions (*Ridehalgh* v. *Horsefield*, 1992).

Warning Notices. The purpose of the warning notice provisions is to 6.46 ensure that the tenant is not kept constantly subject to the likelihood of proceedings. Accordingly, before applying for possession under Case 19, the landlord must serve the appropriate notice. He can only commence proceedings within three months after the expiry of the notice (1977, Sched. 15, Case 19(*b*)). The notice must be in writing, and must state that proceedings may be brought under Case 19 after it expires. The notice must give a minimum of three months: but it can be for an unlimited length, *i.e.* before it expires. It must be served during the last three months of the fixed term, or else during the same three months of any succeeding year. It must not be served earlier than three months after the expiry of the last notice.

Warning Provisions Exemplified. These provisions are very difficult 6.47 to untangle. They are best approached by way of illustration. A fixed term was granted on April 1, 1988 to expire on March 31, 1990. A warning notice may be served at any time between the beginning of January and the end of March during 1990, or any subsequent year in which the ground remains available to the landlord. It must give the tenant at least three months: if served on January 1, therefore, proceedings could commence on April 1: if not served until March 1, however, they could not commence before June 1. If the landlord gave longer than three months, the proceedings could not be commenced before the time allowed expires.

Commencement of Proceedings. Once the notice expires, the landlord 6.48 must bring his proceedings within three months, or else the notice lapses. He cannot serve a further notice during this three months. Thus, if the notice was for three months, and was served on January 1, proceedings must be commenced between April 1, and June 30, and during that time no further notice can be served. Accordingly, July 1 would be the earliest date when a new notice could be served, but as the notice can only be served during the January-March "season," he cannot serve a further notice until January 1 next. If, however, he gives nine months, from January 1, he can commence his proceedings at any time between October 1 and December 30; if he fails to do so, he can serve a new notice immediately after December 30, as: (*a*) he will be

back in the notice season; and (*b*) three months will have passed since
the notice lapsed.

6.49   **Eviction Season.** It follows that while it is true that a tenant cannot be
subject at any given moment to proceedings for possession under Case
19, the landlord has a generous discretion to select his eviction (as
opposed to notice) season, and may in practice, by careful choice of the
length of notice, keep the tenant in the position where proceedings are
always looming, or to be anticipated. These notice provisions do not,
however, dispense with the normal requirement to bring the tenancy to
an end, at common law, by notice to quit (1.45-1.50), or forfeiture
(1.42-1.44). Nor need the notice provisions be fulfilled once the tenancy
has become statutory (5.12) if *other* grounds for possession (5.68-5.91)
are used instead.

(iv) *Further Provisions*

6.50   **Premiums and Deposits.** The premium and deposit provisions
applicable to Rent Act protected tenants are also applicable to protected
shorthold tenancies in the same way.

3. *Assured Shorthold Tenancies*

6.51   **Notice of Assured Shorthold.** The assured shorthold tenant is in every
other respect a Housing Act assured tenant (Chapter 4), whose tenancy
is granted for a fixed term of not less than six months (which contains
no power for the landlord to determine the tenancy within that period,
other than by way of forfeiture - 1.42-1.44), and on whom, before the
tenancy began, a notice in the prescribed form has been served by the
person who is to be the landlord under the tenancy, on the person who
is to be the tenant, and which states that the tenancy is to be a shorthold
tenancy (1988, s.20). When the initial shorthold tenancy comes to an
end, a periodic tenancy comes into being, of the same or substantially
the same premises, which will also be an assured shorthold tenancy,
unless the landlord serves notice stating that it is no longer to be
considered a shorthold tenancy (1988, s.20). In each case "the
landlord," in the case of joint landlords, means at least one of them. To
prevent a landlord persuading a Housing Act assured tenant to enter into
a new arrangement which is shorthold, a tenancy will not be an assured
shorthold if immediately beforehand, the person to whom it is granted
(or if joint tenants, one of them) was a Housing Act assured tenant of the
same landlord (even if in different premises) (1988, s.20).

(i) *Security*

Mandatory Ground for Possession. The assured shorthold tenancy 6.52
works by the *addition* of a mandatory (4.28) ground for possession, so
that the landlord still enjoys all his usual grounds (Chapter 4). The
landlord cannot claim possession during the initial fixed term, unless he
can forfeit it in the normal way (1.42-1.44), but once it is over, a court
is obliged to make an order for possession provided the requisite notice
of seeking possession has been served. There are two kinds of notice.
One notice is served before the initial fixed term comes to an end, or on
its last day; such a notice merely has to be for a minimum of two
months. If no notice is served during the fixed term, however, the
landlord's notice must fulfil additional criteria: it must still be of at least
two months, but: (*a*) it must end on the last day of a period of the
tenancy; (*b*) that date must be no earlier than the tenancy could
otherwise have been brought to an end by notice to quit (1.45-1.50); and
(*c*) the notice must state that possession is required under these
provisions (1988, s.21).

(ii) *Rent*

Additional Protection. Assured shorthold tenants are subject to the 6.53
normal provisions governing rents which are applicable to Housing Act
assured tenants generally, with the following qualification, that there is
an additional method by which the tenant may refer the rent to the Rent
Assessment Committee (1988, s.22) even though the landlord is not
seeking an increase (4.50). This power is *only* available once, and it is
not available if the initial fixed-term tenancy has already expired, *i.e.* the
tenancy has become periodic.

Comparison with Other Rents. The basis of a decision to determine 6.54
the rent under this additional power is that the rent under the tenancy is
significantly higher than rents under other Housing Act assured
tenancies (whether or not shorthold). But merely because the rent is
referred does not mean that the Rent Assessment Committee are bound
to make a determination: they can *only* make a determination if satisfied
that there are sufficient other assured tenancies with which to make a
comparison (and that the rent payable is significantly higher than other
Housing Act assured tenancies). If they refuse to make a determination,
the tenant may accordingly re-apply in the future, if is seems that other
rents are now available with which to make a comparison, or much
lower.

6.55　　**Procedure.** Rent for this purpose excludes any service charges or rates (4.54). A reference may be withdrawn by written agreement between the landlord and the tenant (4.54). If the Rent Assessment Committee do proceed to a determination, they will decide from when it is to take effect, but no earlier than the date of the application to them, and any excess rent over their determination is irrecoverable from the tenant (1988, s.22(4)(*b*)). Once they have determined a rent, the landlord cannot serve a notice seeking an increase (4.51) for a year after the determination takes effect (1988, s.22(4)(*c*)). The Secretary of State for the Environment has power to dis-apply this additional means of referring a rent to the Rent Assessment Committee (1988, s.23).

4. *Further Protection and Assistance*

6.56　　(i) *Accommodation Agency Charges;*
　　　　(ii) *Resale of Utilities;* and
　　　　(iii) *Housing Benefit.*

These are all applicable to restricted contracts and to both classes of shorthold tenant, as to fully Rent Act protected or Housing Act assured tenants (4.57-4.60, 5.125-5.132).

7 Occupation without Security

Residual Classes of Occupation. In this chapter, we shall examine the   7.01
remaining classes of occupation:
1. *Trespassers;*
2. *Unrestricted licensees;*
3. *Non-secure public tenants;*
4. *Non-secure/assured quasi-public tenants;*
5. *Unrestricted tenants;* and
6. *Rental purchasers.*
In addition, we shall consider:
7. *Further financial protection and assistance.*

1. *Trespassers*

Least Security - Trespassers. Trespassers have no rights of occupa-   7.02
tion and, because they pay no rent, are subject to no rent control. They
have the least security of all. Court proceedings can be taken against
them at any time, without any warning, and special, speedy procedures
can, and in all probability will be used: Order 24 (county court) and
Order 113 (High Court).

Proceedings for Possession. These procedures do not even require the   7.03
landlord to identify the occupiers. A landlord can issue proceedings
against a named person on his own, or against persons unknown, or
against both a named person and persons unknown. A summons is
issued, stating the landlord's interest in the property, that the property
in question has been occupied without his consent and, if the summons
is also against persons unknown, that the landlord does not know the
names of some or all of the people on the property.

Orders for Possession. Once the summons is served, which can also be   7.04
by personal service but can also be, in the case of persons unknown, by
fixing the summons to the door of the premises, there need only be a
delay of five days, in the case of residential premises (two otherwise)
before a court hearing. If the court finds that the occupiers are, indeed,

trespassers, then it is obliged to make an immediate order for possession (*McPhail* v. *Persons Unknown*, 1973) not even subject to the normal 14-day delay to which, for example, a final order against a secure, or indeed any other tenant, will normally be subject (3.22). Landlords will still normally need to effect eviction by using court bailiffs, which may provide some slight delay of, perhaps, a week or 10 days. When bailiffs attend on an eviction, they must turn out of the premises all those people found there, whether or not they were parties to the proceedings, or even if they moved into the premises between the date of the court order and the actual eviction, unless the occupier can maintain a claim to have some separate right of occupation, *e.g.* a tenant who is on the premises (*R.* v. *Wandsworth County Court, ex p. Wandsworth London Borough Council*, 1975).

7.05   **Negotiated Suspension.** Although the court is obliged to make the immediate order, it is possible that the landlords will consent to a suspension of, for example, two or four weeks. This they may agree to before the actual hearing. If there is any prospect of a dispute, representatives of the landlord are likely to be amenable to granting such a delay in exchange for a decision by the occupier not to fight the case. Even if there is no prospect of dispute, more responsible landlords, such as public and quasi-public landlords, will usually be willing to agree to some time.

7.06   **Damages.** Although the court can order costs against an occupier during the course of proceedings brought under one of these speedy procedures, there is no provision for awarding any monetary compensation by way of damages to the landlord. If a landlord wants to seek such damages, he must use normal possession proceedings and claim damages for use and occupation.

7.07   **Criminal Offences.** The only protection that a trespasser has against eviction is such as is provided by the Criminal Law Act 1977, which creates certain offences in connection with squatting, and repeals the earlier Forcible Entry Acts. However, the Act also creates offences which a trespasser may commit in connection with squatting. Anyone who commits a criminal offence under the Criminal Law Act 1977 ("CLA 1977") in the course of evicting a trespasser who is using premises as a residence is likely also to commit an offence under the Protection from Eviction Act 1977 ("PEA 1977"): see Chapter 8.

7.08   **Offences against Trespassers.** The offence which serves to protect

trespassers is that of:
  (i) *violent eviction.*
Offences by Trespassers. The offences a trespasser must be careful not to commit are those of:
  (ii) *trespass with an offensive weapon;*
  (iii) *trespass on diplomatic or consular premises;*
  (iv) *resisting or obstructing an officer of a court in the course of an eviction;*
  (v) *refusing to leave premises when requested.*

(i) *Violent eviction*

Violent Entry. Any person, whether or not the landlord, who uses or threatens violence against either people or property in order to gain entry into premises, commits an offence if, but only if, the person seeking entry knows that there is someone present on the premises at the time of the attempted entry, and that that person is opposed to the entry (CLA 1977, s.6). The offence is, of course, not committed if the person seeking entry has lawful authority to do so, *i.e.* a court bailiff. It does not constitute lawful authority that the person trying to get in has some greater interest, *e.g.* licence, tenancy or ownership of the property.

7.09

Displaced Residential Occupier. There is an important exception to this offence. The offence is not committed by a person otherwise offending against its provisions if he or someone on whose behalf he is acting is a displaced residential occupier of the premises. A displaced residential occupier is any person, other than another trespasser, who was using the premises or part of them as a residence immediately before the trespasser entered (CLA 1977, s.12). This exception is designed to permit the owner-occupier, or tenant, who goes away on holiday and finds on his return that the premises have been "squatted," to evict the trespassers without any need to take court proceedings and without fear of committing an offence. In practice, such incidents of squatting in people's homes have been very rare, as it is no part of the ethos of the squatter to make another homeless. A displaced residential occupier must also take great care when using this privilege for he may still commit any of the ordinary, criminal offences of assault, actual or grievous bodily harm, etc.

7.10

(ii) *Trespass with an offensive weapon*

Offensive Weapon. It is a criminal offence for a person on the prem-

7.11

ises as a trespasser, having entered as such, to have with him any weapon of offence, *i.e.* anything which has been made or adapated for causing injury to another (CLA 1977, s.8). This, too, raises the spectre of "violent squatting" which has been virtually unknown in the recent history of the squatting movement. Because such a weapon can either be made or adapted for causing violence, a person can, in theory, be charged with causing violence on the basis of possession of virtually any common household implement, *e.g.* a kitchen knife or screwdriver. But for a person to have committed this offence, he must not only be a trespasser, but must have entered as such. This refers to the common law rule that a former licensee and, strictly, even a former tenant, remaining on premises after the end of the licence or tenancy, becomes a trespasser (1.31). Such people are not trespassers for the purposes of this provision.

(iii) *Trespass on diplomatic or consular premises*

7.12   **Diplomatic Premises.** This provision was designed to deal with "political squatting" (*Kamara* v. *D.P.P.*, 1974) and makes it an offence for a trespasser to enter diplomatic or consular buildings, unless he can show that he does not believe them to be diplomatic or consular premises (CLA 1977, s.9).

(iv) *Resisting or obstructing an officer of the court in the course of an eviction*

7.13   **Resisting Official Eviction.** It is an offence to resist or *intentionally* obstruct any person who is in fact an officer of a court executing a possession order issued by a county court or the High Court (CLA 1977, s.10). This offence is only committed by someone in premises in circumstances that are also defined in the Act. Briefly, the Act is intended to catch anyone resisting or intentionally obstructing an officer who is executing a possession order made under one of the speedy procedures referred to above, Orders 24 and 113. However, it is so worded that it applies to resistance or intentional obstruction of an officer executing any order which could have been brought under those procedures, but which have in fact been brought under normal proceedings, for example because he wishes to claim damages for use and occupation. The Orders can be used against any trespasser, which includes former licensees and has also been held to include illegal sub-tenants (*Moore Properties (Ilford) Ltd.* v. *McKeon*, 1976; 1.75-1.78). The orders do not catch illegal tenants of mortgagors

(*London Goldhawk Building Society* v. *Eminer*, 1977; 1.98-1.99).

(v) *Refusing the leave premises when requested*

Refusal to Leave. This was the major new offence introduced by the   7.14
Act (CLA 1977, s.7). It makes it an offence for any trespasser, who
enters as a trespasser, to fail to leave premises if asked to do so by a
displaced residential occupier or by a person who is, within the terms of
the Act, a protected intending occupier. Displaced residential occupier
has been described above (7.10). In general terms, protected intending
occupiers are those who have been designated to occupy, by a local
authority or housing association landlord, *i.e.* from their waiting lists,
and those who buy residential property only to find that it has been
occupied during the period it lay vacant while the sale was being
transacted.

Protected Intending Occupier. A person is a protected intending occ-   7.15
upier if he either has a freehold or a leasehold interest in the property,
and requires the premises for his own occupation (CLA 1977, s.7). The
leasehold interest must have not less than 21 years to run at the relevant
time. A person is also a protected intending occupier if he has been
given permission to occupy the premises as a residence by any of the
public or quasi-public landlords described below (7.24, 7.29). In either
case, the protected intending occupier must have been kept out of
occupation by reason of the trespass and, obviously, there can be no
offence of failing to leave when requested, until a request has been
made.

Request to Leave. The request does not need itself to be in writing but   7.16
protected intending occupiers have to produce statements which prove
their status as protected intending occupier. In the first case (would-be
owner-occupier), the statement has to specify the interest which the
would-be occupier has, to state the requirement for use of the premises
as a residence for himself, and must have been signed either in the
presence of a justice of the peace or commissioner of oaths who has also
signed the statement as a witness. In the second case (would-be tenant),
the statement must specify that the would-be occupier has been
authorised to occupy the premises and that the landlord is one of the
bodies referred to.

Defences. It is clear that a protected intending occupier could be a   7.17
licensee, *e.g.* for short-life use, of one of the public or quasi-public

landlords; and it is also clear that as it is necessary for a protected intending occupier to specify that the premises are to be used as a residence, it can only be used in connection with premises fit for use, *i.e.* not in connection with premises yet to be renewed or redeveloped. It is a defence for the trespasser to prove that he did not believe that the person asking him to leave was either a displaced residential occupier or a protected intending occupier, or that the premises in question are or form part of premises used mainly for a non-residential purpose and that he was only on that part. It is also a defence to prove that a protected intending occupier did not produce a statement of the class described in the last paragraph (7.16).

2. *Unrestricted Licensees*

7.18 **Resort to Common Law.** Most licensees do not enjoy any statutory protection at all and must therefore rely upon their common law rights of occupation. The exceptions are: a licensee within public sector security (3.08), a licensee whose licence pre-dates the commencement of the Housing Act 1988 ("1988"), and who has a restricted contract (6.07), and licensees who are service occupiers (1.63-1.69) who may either fall within the Housing Act 1988 (4.06) or the Rent (Agriculture) Act 1976 (5.24). Service tenants and occupiers who work in agriculture but are not protected by either the 1988 or 1976 Acts may enjoy a degree more protection against eviction than others, as the county court enjoys power to suspend the operation of a possession order against them for up to six months in certain circumstances (PEA 1977, s.4, as amended by the 1988 Act, to include service occupiers).

7.19 **Prescribed Information.** At common law, no licensee can be evicted until the licence has been brought to an end (1.33-1.36). A bare licence (1.32) can be brought to an end by reasonable notice, and a contractual licence by either reasonable notice or the contractually agreed period (and form), whichever is the longer (1.36). A fixed-term contractual licensee requires no notice and the licence terminates on the expiry of the term (1.33). An example of such an arrangement might be a letting for short-life use which is for a specific period only. If notice has to be given to determine a licence, then since the commencement of Part I, 1988 Act (January 15, 1989), such notice has to be in writing, of a minimum of four weeks, and contain such information as may be prescribed (PEA 1977, s.5(1A), added by 1988, s.32; 1.50), even if the licence began before the commencement of the 1988 Act. However, this is not so if the licence is within the class of "excluded licence" (s.5(1B)): excluded licences (and tenancies) are described in Chapter 8 (8.10), below.

Licensees and Rent Protection.   Only those contractual licensees whose licences pre-date the commencement of Part I, 1988 Act (January 15, 1989) and fall within Rent Tribunal jurisdiction (Chapter 6) enjoy any protection over the levels of rent they have to pay. Strictly, a licensee's rent cannot be increased without terminating the existing licence in the normal way and offering a new one. However, most licensees simply consent to a mutual variation of the terms as regards the rent unless they are actually prepared to leave because, lacking any legislative protection, they are in no bargaining position at all.   7.20

Status of Former Licensee. Once the licence has terminated, the former licensee is in strict law a trespasser. Indeed, both the former bare licensee and the former contractual licensee are in exactly the same position as a trespasser (7.02-7.06), save that they are not liable to be convicted for certain of the offences described. Court proceedings have to be taken to evict a former licensee, however, unless the licence is an "excluded licence" (PEA 1977, s.3(2B), (2C), added by 1988, s.30), even if the licence was granted before the commencement of the 1988 Act. It is also necessary to take legal proceedings to evict a former service occupier, who enjoys a special privilege of remaining in occupation until a court order is made, provided that he enjoyed exclusive occupation of the premises which he held with his job (PEA 1977, ss.3 and 8).   7.21

Use of Speedy Procedures. Proceedings may be brought against any former licensee under the speedy procedures provided by Orders 24 and 113. However, these proceedings should not be used where there is a triable issue (*Cooper* v. *Varzdari*, 1986), *e.g.* that the licence is a sham arrangement concealing a tenancy (*Crancour Ltd.* v. *Da Silvaesa*, 1986) or that the occupier is a tenant holding over (*Henderson* v. *Law*, 1984). Any licence must have determined before the issue of these proceedings (*G.L.C.* v. *Jenkins*, 1975), though where normal possession proceedings are used, the landlord need only show determination of the licence by the date of the hearing. In all cases, it is in any event practicable and advisable for the landlord to take court proceedings to evict a former licensee, because there is a risk that if he does not do so, he will commit a criminal offence, for example under CLA 1977, or of common law assault, etc. If a landlord commits a criminal offence in evicting a former licensee, then he will also commit an offence under PEA 1977   7.22

(Chapter 8).

7.23   **Offences.** Former licensees are not subject to proceedings for being on premises with an offensive weapon (7.09-7.10), nor are they required by law to leave when asked to go by a displaced residential occupier or a protected intending occupier (7.10-7.15). They can, however, commit the offence of resisting or intentionally obstructing an officer of the court in the execution of an order of the court for possession, because they are liable to Orders 24 and 113, even if those proceedings are not actually used against them, for example, because the landlord was claiming damages for use and occupation during or continuing after the licence and therefore chose to use normal possession proceedings (7.06), or because the proceedings are inappropriate on account of a dispute (7.22).

3. *Non-Secure Public Tenants*

7.24   **Public Landlords.** Those who are described as public tenants are the tenants of the Crown, a government department, or a local authority. Where the tenancy began before the commencement of 1988, Part I (January 15, 1989), a tenant of the Crown, in property under the management of the Crown Estates Commissioners, is Rent Act protected (5.52); later lettings, however, are within Housing Act assured protection (Chapter 4). Most tenants of local authorities are now secure tenants (3.06-3.12). In this section, we are concerned with tenants who are not secure (or protected or assured). All former tenants are entitled to remain in occupation until such time as a court order is obtained against them (PEA 1977, s.3), save for those who qualify as "excluded tenants" (for the definition of which, see 8.09) and it would be illegal eviction to regain possession in any other way: see Chapter 8.

7.25   **Eviction.** It is, of course, equally illegal to evict a tenant before the expiry of the tenancy. The rules relating to determination or expiry of a tenancy have been described above (1.39-1.50). Notices to quit must normally be in writing, contain prescribed information and be of a minimum period of four weeks, and are also subject to the other common law rules described: if the tenancy commenced on or after January 15, 1989, when Part I, 1988 Act came into force, however, the requirement for a minimum period and for writing, and for prescribed information, has been waived for "excluded tenants" (as to the definition of which, see 8.09), so that only compliance with common law is required.

No Rent Protection. There is no rent control for the public tenant. Nor- 7.26
mally, in order to increase the rent, the landlord must bring the tenancy
to an end in the usual way and, of course, in the case of a fixed-term
tenancy, he will not be able to do that simply in order to raise the rent.
A fixed-term tenant could consent to an increase during the period, but
it is fairly likely to be unenforceable should he subsequently change his
mind, because, in effect, the landlord will have given nothing in
exchange for the unplanned increase. A periodic tenant could likewise
consent to the increase without compelling the landlord to serve notice
to quit and offer a new tenancy, but this might be enforceable because
of the ease with which the landlord could otherwise bring the tenancy
to an end, *i.e.* there could be said to be some consideration from the
landlord, in that what the landlord has given is a failure to serve notice.
It is for this reason that many public periodic tenants would be inclined
to consent to an increase.

Local Authority Notices of Increase. Local authorities are under an 7.27
obligation to keep rents in their areas under review: however, they also
have a discretion to charge such rents as they consider reasonable. These
matters have been considered in Chapter 3 (3.73). Local authority
tenancies are almost invariably periodic. They have a particular
privilege, now to be found in the Housing Act 1985, s.25, to raise rents
without serving a notice to quit. They may, instead, serve a notice of
increase. This cannot take effect earlier than the authority could
otherwise have brought the tenancy to an end by notice to quit, *i.e.* not
less than four weeks, and the notice must warn the tenant of his right to
leave rather than pay the increase. In addition, the notice must tell the
tenant what he must do to bring the tenancy to an end if he chooses to
leave, and by what date the tenant must serve his own notice to quit to
the local authority, if he - as he rarely will in practice be able to do
(especially if he may wish to apply as homeless: see Chapter 10) -
chooses this course of action.

Reasonable Use of Powers. As regards security, although we are con- 7.28
sidering tenants without security of tenure as such, local authorities are
obliged by common law to act within their powers. Powers are so
defined at law as to preclude authorities acting in an unreasonable
fashion, and to require authorities to act reasonably. Where eviction is
concerned, this means that a local authority could not serve a notice to
quit, say, whimsically. Before making a decision to evict, the authority
must take into account all proper and relevant considerations, and must
exclude from consideration anything which it would be improper to take

into account. For example, a corrupt decision will always be outside their powers, as will a decision borne of malice. These principles are sometimes called the principles of administrative law (see further 10.61-10.62).

4. *Non-Secure/Non-Assured Quasi-Public Tenants*

7.29　　**Quasi-Public Landlords.** Non-secure and non-assured quasi-public tenants are the tenants of registered housing associations, housing trusts, the Housing Corporation or Housing for Wales, and housing co-operatives who for one reason or another do not qualify as Housing Act secure (3.06-3.12) or Housing Act assured (4.08-4.19) tenants.

7.30　　**Rents, Eviction.** Very little remains to be said of this class that cannot be achieved by cross-reference. If Housing Act secure, *i.e.* if preceding the commencement of 1988, Part I (January 15, 1989), their rents are governed by the fair rent system, subject to minor variations (3.75-3.76). They may increase rents without having to serve a notice to quit (Rent Act 1977, s.93). They cannot evict without determining the tenancy (1.39-1.50). If Housing Act assured, then their position is the same as other "private sector" tenants: Chapter 4. Housing Associations are not subject, as are local authorities (7.28), to the principles of administrative law (*Peabody Housing Association* v. *Green*, 1978).

5. *Unrestricted Tenants*

7.31　　**Minimal Rights.** This class will include the pre-Housing Act 1988 tenant who is provided with substantial board and the tenant occupying premises of very high rateable value. Unrestricted tenants enjoy the protection of their contracts against both eviction and rent increase but are in a weak bargaining position when it comes to increases, as the landlord can easily terminate the tenancy, *e.g.* if it is a periodic tenancy. Unless an "excluded tenancy" (as to the definition of which, see 8.09, below), the notice to quit must be in writing, contain the prescribed information, and be of a minimum of four weeks, and must otherwise comply with the common law (1.45-1.50). Unrestricted tenants benefit from no system of rent protection.

6. *Rental Purchasers*

7.32　　**Genuine and Sham.** A rental purchaser is a person who has entered into an agreement under the terms of which: (*a*) he makes payments towards the purchase of a freehold or leasehold interest (1.03-1.07): (*b*) the interest is not conveyed to him until he has completed all his payments under the agreement, in contrast to the normal mortgage arrangement; but (*c*) he is allowed into occupation, pending payment and completion, as a licensee. Of course, some such agreements are shams (5.09) and may be set aside as such. For example, in one case, the repayment period exceeded the length of the lease which the occupier was alleged to be in the process of buying (*Martin* v. *Davies*, 1952). In other cases, it may be possible to show that while some part of the payment is towards purchase, another part is for use and occupation, and should be construed as rent, *i.e.* as a tenancy (*Francis Jackson Developments Ltd.* v. *Stemp*, 1943).

Security Powers of Court. Nonetheless, many such agreements are   7.33
genuine, or cannot be set aside. Such a rental purchaser is a licensee, but when a possession order is sought against him, the court has generous powers to adjourn the proceedings, or stay or suspend or postpone an order (1980, s.88). The court may impose such conditions as it thinks fit on the exercise of such a power, including conditions as to payment, but in marked contrast to orders against other occupiers (3.23, 4.28, 5.66), there is no requirement to order payment of arrears. For the purpose of this power, a rental purchase agreement is defined as one for the purchase of a dwelling (freehold or leasehold), under which the whole or part of the purchase price is to be paid in three or more instalments, and completion is deferred until the whole or part of the price has been paid: this distinguishes and excludes the comparatively normal arrangement, whereby a purchaser pays a deposit on exchange of contract (payment one), an the balance on completion (payment two), but may have been allowed into occupation between exchange and completion. Such an arrangement will not qualify for the purposes of this power.

7. *Further Financial Protection and Assistance*

As trespassers do not pay for their occupation of premises, there is no   7.34
financial protection available to them. However, all of the other classes described in this chapter are subject to protection in respect of:
(*a*) *Accommodation Agency Charges* (4.58-4.59);
(*b*) *Resale of Utilities* (4.60); and
(*c*) *Housing Benefit* (3.77).
There are no restrictions on the charging of premiums which apply to these classes of occupation.

8 Harassment and Illegal Eviction

8.01   **Rachmanism.** In Chapters 1, 4, 5 and 7, we considered some of the ways used by landlords who seek to evade the effects of protective legislation. Such comparatively sophisticated devices are not used by all. Some landlords still resort to brute force and other crude devices in order to get rid of their occupiers when they want. In the early 1960s, these tactics grew to such a pitch that legislation had to be introduced to cope with what came to be known by the name of their most famous exponent, Rachmanism. The legislation was contained in the Rent Act 1965 and was subsequently consolidated into the Protection from Eviction Act 1977. It defines criminal offences of harassment and illegal eviction.

8.02   **Limits of Criminal Court Protection.** Individual occupiers may, however, in fact get much more help from the civil courts than the criminal, and recently their powers have been strengthened (Housing Act 1988 - "1988" - ss.27, 28). Thus, there are only limited circumstances in which the magistrates' courts can make an order for compensation, but they will rarely order damages for suffering or inconvenience. Similarly, the magistrates' court has no power to make an order compelling a landlord to readmit an evicted occupier, either immediately - which is when it will be most needed - or at all. Strictly, it cannot even order a landlord to cease harassing an occupier, although it can bind a landlord over to keep the peace, or they could discharge a landlord without punishment, conditional on no further offences being committed.

8.03   **Scope of Civil Court Protection.** The position is different in the civil courts - the county courts and the High Court - where remedies are pursued between the parties. These courts have power to order a landlord to re-admit an evicted occupier, and they can exercise this power so quickly that an occupier may be able to get back in the same day as the eviction, or, at least, the same day as he has sought advice. They can also make orders restraining further harassment or eviction. At the end of a case, civil courts can make permanent orders which remain in force indefinitely and breach of which would be contempt of court. They can also order the landlord to pay the occupier damages, for actual loss suffered, for distress, shock, suffering, and for the wrong that has been done him.

Different Approaches. The two approaches, civil and criminal, are wholly different. There are different procedures, in different courts, and the language and ideas of the two systems are also very different indeed. The approaches must, therefore, be described separately:
  1. *Criminal proceedings;* and
  2. *Civil proceedings.*

8.04

1. *Criminal Proceedings*

Principal Definitions. The definitions of the criminal offences of illegal eviction and harassment are contained in the Protection from Eviction Act 1977 ("PEA 1977"), s.1, as amended by the Housing Act 1988:

8.05

"(2) If any person unlawfully deprives the residential occupier of any premises of his occupation of the premises or any part thereof, or attempts to do so, he shall be guilty of an offence unless he proves that he believed, and had reasonable cause to believe, that the residential occupier had ceased to reside in the premises.

(3) If any person with intent to cause the residential occupier of any premises--

(*a*) to give up occupation of the premises or any part thereof; or

(*b*) to refrain from exercising any right or pursuing any remedy in respect of the premises or part thereof;

does acts calculated to interfere with the peace or comfort of the residential occupier or members of his household, or persistently withdraws or withholds services reasonably required for the occupation of the premises as a residence, he shall be guilty of an offence. (Note: in connection with acts from January 15, 1989, ie commencement of Part I, 1988 Act, for the word "calculated" is substituted the word "likely").

(3A) The landlord of a residential occupier or an agent of the landlord shall be guilty of an offence if--

(*a*) he does acts likely to interfere with the peace or comfort of the residential occupier or members of his household, or

(*b*) subject to subsection (3B) below, he persistently withdraws or withholds services reasonably required for the occupation of the premises in question as a residence, and (in either case) he knows, or has reasonable cause to believe, that that conduct is likely to cause the residential occupier to give up the occupation of the whole or part of the premises or to refrain from exercising any right or pursuing any remedy in respect of the whole or part of the premises.

(3B) A person shall not be guilty of an offence under subsection (3A) if he proves that he had reasonable grounds for doing the acts or withdrawing or withholding the services in question.''

(i) *Meaning of residential occupier*

8.06 **Application of Act.** The Act applies to ''residential occupiers.'' The term is also defined in section 1 of the Act:

''(1) In this section 'residential occupier,' in relation to any premises, means a person occupying the premises as a residence, whether under a contract or by virtue of any enactment or rule of law giving him the right to remain in occupation or restricting the right of any other person to recover possession of the premises.''

8.07 **Occupation as a Residence** Occupation as a residence is a question of fact, and common sense, not law. It is not necessary to show, for example, that the occupier had sufficient residence to sustain a claim to statutory tenancy (5.57-5.64). Obviously, someone who merely visits a friend is not residing in premises, not even if he stays overnight or, perhaps for a couple of nights. The same is no doubt true of a short-term hotel guest. But once a person begins to use premises to live in, in any normal sense of the expression, then the premises are being occupied as a residence. A person can have two residences, *e.g.* a student who lives away from home during the term-time will normally be considered resident both at home and at college. A person does not stop residing in premises just because, for example, he goes away for a holiday, or for some other reason is temporarily absent. The residence will continue during such breaks as if the occupier was actually present.

8.08 **Residential Occupation by Status.** *All* tenants and licensees (including service tenants and occupiers) whose tenancies and licences have not been brought to an end are residential occupiers because they are occupying under contract. It does not matter if the person harassing or evicting is not a party to the contract: what is in question is whether or not the occupier is a residential occupier. A leasehold owner-occupier does so by ''rule of law.'' Housing Act secure and Housing Act assured tenants occupy both under contract and by virtue of statute (Chapters 3,

4). Rent Act protected tenants whose contractual tenancies have been brought to an end and who occupy as statutory tenants (see Chapter 5) do so "by virtue of an enactment." The Housing Act 1980 applies PEA 1977, s.3, to those occupying under rental purchase agreements (7.32-7.33).

Excluded Tenancy. *All other* former tenants (together with those law- 8.09
fully living with them, even if the former tenant has himself departed) are residential occupiers because there is an enactment (PEA 1977, s.3) "restricting the right of any other person to recover possession of the premises," *unless* the tenancy was entered into on or after the commencement date of Part I, 1988 Act (January 15, 1989) *and* it qualifies as an "excluded tenancy." An excluded tenancy is one of the following:

(*a*) the tenant shares any accommodation (other than storage space, passages, corridors or other means of access, so that this includes a bathroom or lavatory, *cf.* above, 3.09) with the landlord who was in occupation of another part of the premises as an only or principal home (3.13) both before the tenancy was granted and at the time it comes to an end;

(*b*) the tenant shares any accommodation (other than storage space, passages, corridors or other means of access, so that this includes a bathroom or lavatory, *cf.* above, 3.09) with a member of the family of the landlord, who was in occupation of another part of the premises as an only or principal home (4.13) both before the tenancy was granted and at the time it comes to an end, and immediately before the tenancy was granted and at the time it comes to an end, the landlord occupies as his only or principal home (3.13) premises in the same building (not being a purpose-built block of flats: 4.21).

(*c*) the tenancy was granted as a temporary expedient to someone who originally entered premises as a trespasser, *i.e.* a former squatter who is granted a tenancy for a period of time;

(*d*) the tenancy was a holiday letting (4.17) or was granted other than for money or money's worth, *i.e.* was not a commercial arrangement;

(*e*) the tenancy is of part of a hostel provided by one of a specified number of public bodies, including local authorities, development corporations, Housing Action Trusts, and a housing trust which is a charity or a registered housing association.

Excluded Licence. Section 3 also protects former licensees who have 8.10
occupied under restricted contracts commencing on or after November 28, 1980 (see Chapter 6), former service occupiers who were granted

some exclusive occupation of their accommodation under the employment arrangement (PEA 1977, s.8), and all other former licensees *other than* those with "excluded licences," which carries the same meaning as "excluded tenancy" (last paragraph), in each case including anyone lawfully living with either such a licensee at the end of the occupancy. This will apply even if the former licensee or service occupier has himself left the premises.

8.11   **Spouses.** In addition, there are enactments restricting the right of another person to recover possession of premises which serve to protect deserted spouses and, in some cases, even trespassers. The Matrimonial Homes Act 1983 (Chapter 9) prohibits an owner or tenant-spouse from evicting a non-owner or non-tenant-spouse from the matrimonial home without an order of a court. Such an order will normally be made during the course of domestic proceedings and this subject is considered in the next chapter. However, because there is *an* enactment which restricts the right of *some* other person, the deserted spouse qualifies as a residential occupier for the purposes of the Protection from Eviction Act, even if it is not the other spouse who is attempting to get him out.

8.12   **Trespassers.** The criminal offence of violent entry for the purposes of eviction of a trespasser has been described in Chapter 7. Insofar as a trespasser is protected from eviction by that provision, so also will he be protected from eviction under this Act.

8.13   **Advisability of Proceedings.** The definition of residential occupier is, therefore, very wide indeed. It is possible to evict certain occupiers, *e.g.* trespassers, and some former licensees and tenants, without taking court proceedings, so long as the Criminal Law Act 1977 is not broken, so long as no other criminal offence is committed, so long as the licence or tenancy is already at an end (*R.* v. *Blankley*, 1979), etc. This list of reservations should deter any landlord from seeking to recover possession without taking court proceedings, for the risk of committing an offence when doing so will otherwise be very high. It is for this reason that landlords are invariably advised - and well - advised - by lawyers to take court proceedings before evicting an occupier.

(ii) *Acts of harassment*

8.14   **Intention and Knowledge.** Whatever is done must be done either with one of the two sorts of appropriate intention, or with the specified actual or deemed knowledge: the difference between section 1(3) and section

1(3A) is that the former creates an offence when the landlord does the specified acts with the *intention* of causing the occupier to quit or to refrain from exercising a right, while the latter creates an offence when the landlord does those acts *knowing or having reasonable cause to believe* that the *consequence* is likely to be to cause the occupier to quit or refrain from exercising a right. The most common intention is that of attempting to cause the occupier to give up possession of the premises or part of them, *e.g.* one room, and that is also the most common consequence. But harassment also occurs with the other objective in mind, *e.g.* to try and deter an occupier from applying to the rent officer, Rent Tribunal or Rent Assessment Committee, or to deter him from complaining to an environmental health officer (see Chapter 13), about the condition of the property.

Services, Peace and Comfort. The criminal action can also be committed in different ways: by persistently withholding or withdrawing services, such as gas and electricity, reasonably required for the occupation of the premises as a residence, *i.e.* more than just once or twice; or by doing an act (*R.* v. *Polycarpou,* 1983) or acts, which are likely to interfere with the peace or comfort of the residential occupier or members of his household. But withholding or withdrawal of services can be justified under section 1(3B) if the landlord proves there were reasonable grounds for the withdrawal or withholding, *e.g.* that services were dangerous to use. Mere non-payment of rent or other charges by the occupier is not sufficient justification, for the landlord has other remedies for this, *i.e.* to seek an order for possession. 8.15

Other Conduct. The breadth of the definition allows the law to catch odd actions which may not be obvious acts of harassment, such as hanging around a sensitive and perhaps elderly occupier, or coming into the premises so frequently that the occupier ceases to feel secure in his home. The act in question does not need also to be a civil wrong, so that a criminal offence may be committed by doing an act with the appropriate intention, even though the occupier has no other rights, *e.g.* refusing to supply a spare key when the occupier has lost his (*R.* v. *Yuthiwattana,* 1984) or deliberately disconnecting the door bell and preventing use of a particular bathroom and lavatory (*R.* v. *Burke,* 1990). 8.16

(iii) *Acts of eviction*

Core Issues. There are three points to note in connection with the 8.17

definition of eviction:

(*a*) eviction can be from the whole or part of the premises in question;

(*b*) an offence is committed either by a successful eviction or by an attempted eviction; and

(*c*) the defence which is available to an accused requires him to show that he believed and had reasonable cause to believe that the residential occupier had ceased to reside in the premises. This means that a subjective but unreasonable belief will not result in acquittal.

8.18   **The Typical Eviction.** Eviction normally takes place when an occupier is out of the premises, either away for a few days or even just out shopping. Quite often, the occupier, or perhaps a spouse with children, will return to find that all the family's belongings have been put out on the street, the locks changed, none of the other occupiers are willing to "get involved," and the landlord and perhaps some of his friends are inside to prevent any attempt to get back in by force. It must be recognised that the occupier who returns home to find this sort of situation is likely to suffer from some degree of shock. He will need immediate comfort but, most of all, guidance on what to do. The quicker the occupier can be restored to the premises, the less the suffering will be. An eviction which takes place while the occupier is at home is also likely to be an offence by the landlord against the provisions restricting violent entry (CLA 1977, s.6). Eviction means more than intending to lock the occupier out for only a short time, *e.g.* overnight, and such an action is more likely to be one of harassment (*R.* v. *Yuthiwattana*, 1984).

8.19   **Homelessness and Eviction.** An occupier who is evicted in this way will be homeless, and will qualify for assistance under Part III, Housing Act 1980 (see Chapter 10), although how much will depend on priority need (10.09-10.14).

(iv) *The accused*

8.20   **Who May Commit Harassment?** Anyone can be charged with either of these offences, not only a landlord or his friends or agents. It may, however, be difficult to establish the necessary intention for harassment unless the act is done by someone with connections to the landlord. On the face of it, no one else is likely to have the incentive to try and make the occupier get out. But where section 1(3A) is alleged, *i.e.* that the acts have been committed with the knowledge - actual or deemed - that it will cause the occupier to quit or to refrain from exercising a right or remedy, the definition of "landlord" is extended (PEA 1977, s.1(3C)) to include anyone who would have a right to occupation of the premises but for the occupier's protection and a superior landlord from whom such a person derives his right. A prospective future occupier may qualify in this way (*Jones* v. *Miah*, 1992). If the harassment or eviction is performed on behalf of a limited company, then a director or any officer of the company will also be guilty of an offence if he consented to or connived at the harassment, or it happened because of his negligence (PEA 1977, s.1(6)).

(v) *Criminal proceedings*

Magistrates' Court. Criminal proceedings are conducted in the magistrates' court. A prosecution may be initiated by an injured party, or, in cases of harassment and eviction, by a tenancy relations officer employed by most local authorities to deal with private sector tenancy disputes. Local authorities have express power to prosecute offences under the Act (PEA 1977, s.6). Unlike most other criminal matters, prosecutions are not brought by the police, but this is a matter of practice, not law.   8.21

Tenancy Relations Officer. The tenancy relations officer can also prosecute other landlord/tenant offences, *e.g.* failure to provide rent book, failure to provide landlord's name and address (1.40), demanding a premium or an illegal accommodation agency fee (4.58-4.59), overcharging a Rent Tribunal rent (6.19).   8.22

Role of Tenancy Relations Officer. In the event of any act of harassment or eviction, the tenancy relations officer should be contacted without delay. If it is urgent, he will normally call straight round to the premises and try to sort the problem out face to face with the landlord and the occupier. Some of them now have radio-linked cars. In addition or, if the matter is not urgent, in the alternative, he may write to the landlord, warning him of the possible offences and penalties, and inviting comment.   8.23

Negotiation v. Prosecution. The tenancy relations officer does not usually make prosecution the goal of his job. The officers work by way of conciliation, reinforced by the possibility of prosecution. A tenancy relations officer cannot normally decide on his own initiative to prosecute: the prosecution will be handled by the local authority's legal department. Some of these legal departments are ill-inclined to prosecute. The attitudes of individual tenancy relations officers can   8.24

range from those who consider they have failed in their work whenever they are forced into prosecuting, to those who cannot see why a landlord who has committed a criminal offence should not be prosecuted, like any other criminal.

8.25   **Private Prosecution.** If the tenancy relations officer will not prosecute, then it is still open to the individual occupier who has been harassed or illegally evicted to do so. Legal aid will not be available for a prosecution, although legal advice could be sought beforehand. Understandably, not many occupiers are prepared to shoulder the heavy responsibility of a private prosecution unassisted, and run the risk of having to pay the landlord's costs if he is acquitted.

8.26   **Penalties.** In theory, the court can order a fine of up to £2,000, or can impose six months' imprisonment, or both, although it rarely does more than force the landlord to pay a small fine. If the landlord elects trial in the Crown Court, then he could be fined up to an unlimited amount, or sent to prison for up to two years, or both.

8.27   **Compensation.** Either sort of court has power to award compensation for "personal injury, loss or damage resulting from [an] offence" (Powers of Criminal Courts Acts 1973, s.35). This power is not frequently used. This may be because when local authorities prosecute, they are not doing so strictly on behalf of or in the interests of the particular occupier, but in discharge of their public duties. The powers are usually only used in relation to ascertainable loss, such as damaged property, time off work through injury, cost of overnight accommodation or eating out, etc. They are not usually awarded for shock, distress, inconvenience or discomfort. Nor, in the case of legal eviction, will they be used for loss of the home itself as this does not have an easily identified value. But even though courts do not use these powers frequently, and may even be unfamiliar with them, they can and should be asked to order compensation where this would avoid the necessity to commence a wholly new set of proceedings, in the civil courts. A local authority lawyer who is prosecuting can be asked to apply on behalf of the occupier. Any documentary evidence of loss sustained by the occupier, such as bills, should be brought to court.

2. *Civil Proceedings*

8.28   **County Courts.** Civil proceedings are brought in either the county court, usually for the area in which the incident happens, or in the High

Court. Most cases of harassment and illegal eviction will be brought in the county courts, particularly since the extension of the county court jurisdiction allowing it to award damages (monetary compensation) up to £50,000.

Remedies. The civil remedies which may be awarded by either sort of court are: 8.29
  (i) *injunctions*; and
  (ii) *damages*.

(i) *Injunctions*

Injunctions. An injunction is an order of the court. It will always identify the person, or persons, who is or are to be bound by it. Failure to comply with the terms of an injunction is a contempt of court. Contempt can be punished by either a fine or imprisonment. It is uncommon for civil courts to send a landlord who is in breach of an injunction to prison, unless he persists in his refusal to obey it. 8.30

Final Orders. An injunction is normally awarded as part of the judgment at the end of the case. This is called a "final order." A civil case, even in the county court, can take many months to be heard. There are many stages of pre-trial procedure to be followed, there may be requests for adjournments because one side or the other is not ready for trial, and the court will have to find time to fit the case in. 8.31

***Ex Parte* Orders.** What an occupier who has been harassed or illegally evicted wants is an immediate order. Sometimes a matter is so urgent that it cannot even be left for the few days necessary to give the other side an opportunity to attend court. In cases of such urgency, the court will grant an *ex parte* order, *i.e.* one that is based upon the unchallenged evidence of the occupier only. This is normally produced in court by affidavit, *i.e.* a sworn statement. 8.32

No Delay. The courts will only use their powers to make *ex parte* orders if there has been little or no delay before they are asked to do so. A harassment must be quite serious, for example, disconnection of utilities, before a court will make an order either compelling the landlord to restore the utilities or restraining any further harassment, on an *ex parte* hearing. An illegal eviction will normally be considered sufficiently urgent, especially if the person evicted has nowhere else to stay, or nowhere else that is satisfactory, but the courts will not grant an *ex parte* 8.33

order if there has been any unnecessary delay before it is asked to do so. An *ex parte* order should always be sought immediately.

8.34   *Inter Partes* Hearing. If an order is granted *ex parte*, it will usually be for only a few days or a week, until a further hearing when the court will listen to the other side of the case and decide whether or not the order should be continued until the full trial of the matter. If a matter is not serious enough to merit an *ex parte* order, then the matter does not have to be left until the full trial: there can still be an application for a hearing within a few days or a week. This sort of hearing is called an *inter partes* hearing, *i.e.* between both parties. Orders made at either an *ex parte* or an *inter partes* hearing are called interim injunctions, or orders, to distinguish them from final injunctions, or orders, which are only made at the end of the case.

8.35   **Balance of Convenience.** When a judge is deciding whether or not to grant an interim injunction, he does not decide the full merits of the case. The judge does not decide which side is telling the truth, or which side is in the right. He only decides what order should be made, pending the full trial, on a *balance of convenience* (*American Cyanamid Co. Ltd.* v. *Ethicon*, 1975). Unless the premises have already been re-occupied by someone else, or by the landlord himself, the balance of convenience will almost always be in the occupier's favour, although it may be subject to an undertaking by the occupier to pay the rent pending the trial. The balance of convenience will also almost invariably be with the occupier where harassment is in issue.

8.36   **Strength of Claim.** Although the issue is one of balance of convenience, the strength of a case will still affect the decision of the court, for, otherwise, a complete stranger might wander into a court and allege that he has been evicted from an empty property, simply to gain a right of occupation for the few months pending trial. If the occupier's case is a strong one, on the face of it, then even if the landlord has re-let the premises, or if the landlord is himself in occupation, the court will be very reluctant indeed to allow the landlord to benefit from what appears to be both the commission of a criminal offence and a very serious breach of the civil law, by allowing him to remain in occupation until trial. The court will instead be inclined to grant the occupier's request for an immediate order. The strength of a case is measured not solely by reference to what evidence the occupier offers, but also by what sort of reply the landlord makes. At an *inter partes* hearing, the landlord is likely to file an answer, also by way of affidavit, to the occupier's claim. At this point, the court may allow either party to be cross-examined on his affidavit.

(ii) *Damages*

Types of Damages. Damages are not awarded until the end of the case. There are several different sorts of damages. A person claims *special* damages for specific sums of money, *e.g.* damage to furniture, cost of eating out or overnight accommodation, lost property, etc. These are the same sorts of damages which may be awarded in the magistrates' courts as compensation. *General* damages are unquantified sums which are claimed in respect of, for example, suffering, shock, distress, physical injury, inconvenience, the lost right of occupation itself or any other harm to which a specific value cannot be attached, *e.g.* additional electricity costs because gas is cut off. *Aggravated* damages are awarded where the manner of that which is being sued for was especially mean, unpleasant, brutal, etc. *Exemplary* damages are awarded where it would appear that the landlord has, for example, evicted a tenant, calculating to himself that any profit made, for example from sale of the property with vacant possession, will be more than any damages awarded against him. In other words, that he can make a profit, even out of doing something wrong.   8.37

Exemplary Damages - 1. In *Cassell & Co. Ltd.* v. *Broome* (1972), the House of Lords considered the question of exemplary damages and Lord Hailsham, L.C., said: 8.38

> "How, it may be asked, about the late Mr. Rachman, who is alleged to have used hired bullies to intimidate statutory tenants by violence or threats of violence into giving up vacant possession of their residences and so placing a valuable asset in the hands of the landlord? My answer must be that if this is not a cynical calculation of profit and cold-blooded disregard of a plaintiff's rights, I do not know what is ... "

Exemplary Damages - 2. In the case of *Drane* v. *Evangelou* (1977), Lawton L.J. said that to deprive a tenant of a roof over his head was one of the worst torts (wrongs) that could be committed. It brought the law into disrespect. He also expressed his surprise that the landlord had not been prosecuted under what is now section 1 of PEA 1977. Lord Denning, M.R. applied the words of an earlier case: "Exemplary damages can properly be awarded whenever it is necessary to teach a   8.39

wrongdoer that tort does not pay."

8.40 **Jurisdiction.** The High Court can award an injunction and/or damages to an unlimited amount in any civil action. The county court can normally only award an injunction if the plaintiff has made a claim for damages, at the same time. Once the claim has been made then, of course, it has the power to grant an interim injunction at an early stage in the proceedings, even though it will not finally decide whether to award a full injunction and/or damages, nor how much damages it will award, until the end of the trial.

8.41 **Special Jurisdiction in Land.** However, the county court has an additional and separate power, under the County Courts Act 1984, s.22, to grant an injunction even though no claim for damages has been made, in any case in which possession, occupation, use or enjoyment of land is in issue, *i.e.* harassment and illegal eviction. This claim may be made where the only real redress the occupier is seeking is the injunction, and a claim for damages would not be well founded, for example because the injunction was to prevent an eviction and no harm had yet occurred, or because an interim injunction would be awarded so quickly that no loss or suffering had yet taken place and the occupier was of a sufficiently robust character not really to have suffered shock or distress.

8.42 **Injunctions and Damages Distinguished.** Injunctions may be granted whenever whatever wrong has been done can be rectified by an order, or else in order to prevent a wrong being committed. Damages are awarded when there has been actual loss as a result of a wrong, even if only of the order of suffering, shock, distress, etc., although in some cases the law will assume that the act itself is injury enough to sustain a claim for damages in money, *e.g.* trespass.

8.43 **Need for Cause of Action.** Neither the county court nor the High Court can make any order at all, however, until an action has been commenced. Legal aid will be available for a civil action based on harassment or illegal eviction. In order to commence an action in a civil court, it is necessary to show that the plaintiff has what is known as a cause of action. A court does not have power to make an order because, for example, someone does not like the colour of his neighbour's hair, or because someone jumps in front of someone else in a bus queue, or because another person calls someone a silly idiot. On the other hand, there will be a cause of action if a neighbour plays music so loudly or at anti-social hours that he disturbs someone else's enjoyment of his own home, or if the queue-jumper used so much force that he assaulted someone, or if what was said was of a defamatory character.

Causes of Action Classified. All of these causes of action are known 8.44 as "torts," or civil wrongs. A tort is an action which the law recognises is wrongful for one person, who is the person complained about, to do to the person complaining. There are several torts which may be used in connection with harassment and illegal eviction. In addition, there is always a cause of action when one party breaks a contract with another, whether completely or in a material particular. Breach of contract will also often be appropriate to cases of harassment and illegal eviction.

(a) Breach of Contract. Both tenancy and licence are contracts. A li- 8.45 censee may sue for breach of contract or breach of a term of the contract (*Smith* v. *Nottinghamshire County Council*, 1981). A term of a contract may actually be stated, or it may be implied, if it is a term necessary for the contract to be effective, for example a contract for occupation as a residence would not be very effective if there was no term, at least implied, that during the subsistence of the contract the landlord would ensure that there was a supply of gas and electricity to the premises, for lighting and perhaps cooking. This does not mean that the licensee need not pay for the gas or electricity, even by way of coin meter, but that it is usually the landlord's responsibility to ensure that it is available for the occupier's use.

Quiet Enjoyment. A similar term will be implied, if not actually ex- 8.46 pressed, into a contract of tenancy. In addition, into every tenancy there is implied, again, unless it is actually expressed, a promise by the landlord that the tenant will have the "quiet enjoyment" of the premises so long as the tenancy shall last. In *Kenny* v. *Preen* (1962), it was said that the promise was broken by an act which was an invasion of the right of the tenant to remain in possession undisturbed. Clearly, this includes an actual or threatened eviction, and almost every act of harassment. In *McCall* v. *Abelesz* (1975), disconnection of utilities was described as both a breach of implied term, and as an interference wih quiet enjoyment. Any conduct by a landlord which interferes with the tenant's freedom of action in exercising his rights as tenant will be an interference with the convenant for quiet enjoyment. Only another party to a contract can be sued for breach of it.

Derogation from Grant. In addition, some actions by a landlord in 8.47 common parts, or in neighbouring property under his control, could amount to derogation fom his grant of the tenancy to the tenant (see further, 11.13).

8.48 **(b) Breach of Housing Act 1988, s.27.** In *McCall* v. *Abelesz* (1975) it was held that even though a landlord had committed an act or offence of illegal eviction or harassment, the occupier did not necessarily have a civil remedy, *i.e.* a right to sue. Accordingly, by section 27, 1988 Act, Parliament gave an express right to sue where *either* illegal eviction within PEA 1977, s.1(2) *or* such harassment within s.1(3), (3A) (8.07) that it leads to the occupier's departure has been committed (after June 9, 1988). This right is conferred on all residential occupiers, as defined (8.06-8.13), and carries an express right to damages; however much the damages may be, the claim may be brought in the county court. The action can be brought against the landlord, or anyone else who, but for the occupier's right to occupy, would be entitled to occupy, or any superior landlord from whom that person derives his right.

8.49 **Additional Cause.** The action is an action in tort (8.44) and is additional to any other rights, save that damages for loss of occupation are not to be awarded twice over. A landlord can defend the action by showing that he believed, *and* had reasonable cause to believe, that the residential occupier had already quit, or in the case of a departure based on withholding of services that there were reasonable grounds for withholding services. Furthermore, damages may be reduced if *either* the court considers that the occupier's conduct provoked the eviction or harassment, *or* (where eviction is concerned) that the landlord has offered to reinstate the occupier, before the proceedings under the 1988 Act were begun, and the offer was unreasonably refused. (There can be unreasonable refusal even if the occupier had found somewhere else before the offer). The offer of reinstatement must be genuine, and merely handing the tenant a key to a lock which does not work, and inviting her to resume occupation of a room which has been totally wrecked will not suffice (*Tagro* v. *Cafane*, 1991).

8.50 **Amount of Damages.** There are detailed provisions (1988, s.28) governing the amount of damages, essentially designed to deprive the landlord of the financial benefit of vacant possession, but no damages at all are payable if before the action is commenced, or at any time before it is finally over, the occupier is actually reinstated.

8.51 **(c) Trespass to Land.** Once there is a tenancy, the tenant has possession of the premises, to the exclusion of all others, including the landlord. A landlord can, therefore, trespass on the premises of his own tenant. There is some legal authority for the proposition that the sort of exclusive occupation which most licensees have is enough possession for the purposes of trespass. This is because it is possession in fact, rather than legally defined possession, which matters.

Trespass Illustrated. A person is a trespasser whenever he enters the 8.52 land or premises of another without permission. It is also a trespass to place anything on someone else's property without permission. In one case it was held to be a trespass to drive a nail into someone else's wall, which, by analogy, would apply to a landlord who nails up a door or blocks up a lock. A person is also a trespasser if he has permission to be on someone's premises for one purpose but uses it for another. For example, a landlord calling around to collect the rent or inspect for repairs will become a trespasser if he uses the occasion to abuse, threaten or harass the occupier. Similarly, a person given permission to enter must leave once he is asked to do so and, once a reasonable time has been given for the exit, becomes a trespasser. Reasonable time here, as with residential licence, is reasonable in all the circumstances and, where a person is just visiting, will be a matter of however long it would normally take to get to the door.

Liability for Trespass. Trespass is a tort and anyone who trespasses 8.53 can be sued for it. A landlord is liable for the torts of his agents, if the torts were committed with his approval or on his behalf. An evicted or harassed occupier can sue the landlord and, if the landlord got someone else to do the job for him, that person as well.

(d) Assault. Harassment and eviction will often be accompanied by 8.54 assaults. An assault is not necessarily a directly physical act. It may be no more than some gesture which suggests that the person to whom it is made is about to be attacked physically. Threatening words on their own are not an assault, and it is difficult to prove unless there has been some sort of physical attack, although this might be with a weapon, piece of furniture or merely by shoving an occupier around. An assault is a tort and the remarks in the past paragraph will, therefore, apply in the same way to assault.

(e) Nuisance. Like trespass, this is a cause of action which can be used 8.55 by someone in possession of land, which certainly includes a tenant and may include a licensee. A nuisance is anything which interferes with the reasonable use and enjoyment of property, *e.g.* noise, smells, even hanging about outside someone's home. Most acts of harassment will constitute a nuisance, although this may not be so if the act is negative, *e.g.* a withdrawal of services. Nuisance is also a tort.

8.56   **(f) Trespass to Goods.** Any direct interference with another person's belongings is a trespass to goods. If belongings are actually removed, this may also be conversion. Conversion is the act of dealing with someone else's property in any manner that is inconsistent with the right of the other person to possession of it. Trespass to goods and conversion are torts.

9 Break-up of Relationship

Outline. In this chapter, we shall consider in outline only (see Introduction) some of the law as it relates to housing in the event of the break-up of a relationship. This is an artificial study, because decisions cannot and will not be taken on the basis of housing law, or law itself, alone. There will be many other considerations to bring to bear, including that of the desirability of exercising particular rights and (always) the best interests of any children of the relationship. The law affecting domestic breakdown is substantial, and a study in its own right: the purpose of this chapter is merely to indicate some of the possibilities which it raises. 9.01

Relevant Provisions. In this chapter, we shall consider briefly: 9.02

1. *The common law;*
2. *The Matrimonial Causes Act 1973;*
3. *The Domestic Violence and Matrimonial Proceedings Act 1976;*
4. *The Domestic Proceedings and Magistrates' Courts Act 1978;*
5. *The Matrimonial Homes Act 1983;*
6. *The Matrimonial and Family Proceedings Act 1984;*
7. *The Children Act 1989;* and
8. *Further considerations.*

Cumulative Provisions. None of these Acts or laws is mutually exclusive: it will be common for provisions contained in more than one Act to apply in the same case. In addition, the courts have a fairly broad discretion to make such orders as are considered appropriate at any stage in proceedings: interim orders are commonplace. 9.03

1. *The Common Law*

Trust. The common law doctrine of trust applies in a cohabitation relationship, as much as it can apply to any other appropriate situation. This doctrine deals with the position which arises at law whenever property is held in the name of one person, but is intended for the bene- 9.04

179

fit of another. Such property is held on trust.

9.05 **Use for Purpose of Trust.** Property held on trust must be used for the purposes for which is was intended. Some people leave property on trust in their wills for example a large family estate may be left on trust so as to ensure that beneficiaries under the will can have the benefit and use of the property for their lifetimes, but cannot actually dispose of it.

9.06 **Beneficiaries.** Property can be held on trust for the benefit of a number of individuals including one of the trustees himself. A man, for example, could buy a house, and put it on trust for the use of himself and his wife and/or children. The man could not subsequently dispose of the property, unless all the beneficiaries consented to the proposed arrangements.

9.07 **Trust for Sale.** Property is automatically considered to be held on trust whenever two or more people own land or premises jointly. This is a particular type of trust: a trust for sale. The effect of a trust for sale is that any of the joint owners can actually force the property to be sold, even against the wishes of the other party. This is an obviously necessary provision, for the value of a half-share in a house will be non-existent if it is not possible to force a sale at will.

9.08 **Powers of High Court.** Whenever property is held on trust, or is alleged to be held on trust, the High Court has power to declare whether or not it is held on trust, and in what proportions or for whose benefit, and can also make orders which affect what should happen to the property in question.

9.09 **How Trusts Arise.** A trust sometimes arises under a formal deed. It may also arise if one person buys property, but for the benefit of another. It will also arise if one person buys property either wholly or in part with someone else's money. In the case of a house or flat, this might arise because, for example, a woman has put up all or part of the purchase price of the property, or all or part of the deposit on a property purchased under mortgage, or has simply contributed to the mortgage repayments, or even if she has contributed to maintenance or improvement of the property in such a way as to increase its value.

9.10 **Declaration of Trust.** It follows that if a woman living with a man, whether or not married to him, has made such a contribution, the law has power to intervene at a time of break-up, and make the appropriate declaration: for example, that the house is held for the benefit of the woman, or that she has a proportionate interest in it. These rights exist independently of the legislation described below and it will not normally be necessary for a wife to use them in relation to a husband. They may, however, be relevant in the case of a woman who has been cohabiting with a man without being married to him.

Trust and Owner-Occupation. These provisions will normally only be relevant in the case of owner-occupied property. In theory, a woman could claim that a man had taken a tenancy for her benefit and the courts would have power to declare that she was therefore entitled to the benefit of it, which would mean the right to occupy under it. In the absence of extremely strong evidence, however, that the man was only taking the tenancy for her benefit, it is unlikely that the courts would exercise this power, especially as it would affect the position of a third party, the landlord. 9.11

2. *Matrimonial Causes Act 1973*

Division of Property. It is this Act which contains the broad powers which a court now has to divide up matrimonial property when a marriage is in the course of breaking up or has broken up. These powers are only exercisable between married partners. These powers are exercised during the course of divorce or nullity proceedings. The court has power to apportion property between the parties and, if necessary, to order that property be transferred from the name of one party to that of another or be sold (Matrimonial Causes Act 1973 - "MCA 1973" - ss.24, 24A). 9.12

Former Position. At one time, a wife who did not work and who had not contributed financially to the value of the property was not entitled as of right to any share in the property when the marriage broke up. She had to rely on common law provisions, if there was any direct financial contribution. She might, of course, have been entitled to maintenance, and there may have been a settlement which took the form of a transfer of ownership of the matrimonial home. Alternatively, property might be transferred into her name, but for the benefit of children of the marriage, in which case she would become the trustee of it herself, but only the trustee. 9.13

Relevant Considerations. Over the years, however, the courts came to recognise that the contribution of the non-earning spouse could not be 9.14

measured purely in terms of direct financial contribution. For a husband's earning power is enhanced by the provision of domestic services by the wife who remains at home, including but not exclusively those involved in care of the children. Similarly, the courts came to recognise that a woman should not live with and be dependent upon her husband for a period of time and suddenly be discarded by him without any further provision for her accommodation or support.

9.15   **Use of Section 24.** Accordingly, section 24 may be used to divide up matrimonial property, including the matrimonial home, in proportions which do not necessarily reflect the limited financial or quasi-financial considerations to which the common law will be limited. These rights, too, however, are mainly of interest only to owner-occupiers, although a court can order the transfer of a tenancy under these provisions (*Hale* v. *Hale*, 1975) regardless of whether the tenancy is protected or not. But it seems likely that this will only be possible if there is no provision in the tenancy agreement prohibiting assignment. The powers could not be used in connection with a licence, however, as a licence does not constitute the sort of property which the court can transfer: a licence is a personal right, while tenancy is a form of property.

3. *Domestic Violence and Matrimonial Proceedings Act 1976*

9.16   **Limited Options.** Until the Domestic Violence Act came into force on June 1, 1977, the choices open to a woman being battered by a man with whom she was living were comparatively few. A married woman could commence divorce proceedings, in the course of which she could obtain an injunction compelling her husband to leave the matrimonial home, whether or not it was in his name alone, or in their joint names. But divorce proceedings are complex and awkward to launch, and cannot be brought in every civil court (9.29). Furthermore, many women did not actually want a divorce, despite violence, but sought only the immediate protection of the law. It was considered inappropriate that a woman should be confronted with the limited choices of either a full divorce, or no protection at all.

9.17   **Cohabitation.** Cohabiting women were in a different position. They could not, of course, sue for divorce. They could make a claim for assault, in the county court, but to do this they would need to attach a claim for damages in order to bring the matter within the county court jurisdiction. Furthermore, this could not be used as a way of getting a man out of the home, if the home was in the man's name, or even in the couple's joint names. In that situation, the woman herself would have to leave, possibly to be confronted with homelessness and an unsympathetic local authority (9.30-9.31).

Range of Orders.   The Domestic Violence Act confers on the court   9.18
power to make an order preventing one person molesting another, or molesting children living with that other, or ordering one partner to leave the domestic home, or ordering a person to readmit an excluded partner into the domestic home. An application to the court for one or more of these orders may be made by a spouse, or anyone who has been living together with the person from whom protection is sought as man and wife. Cohabiting couples can, therefore, use the Act.

Power of Arrest.   The court has an additional power, to ''back'' the   9.19
injunction for arrest. This means that a police officer can arrest without warrant any person whom he suspects is in breach of an order under the Act. The person must be brought back before the judge within 24 hours. This power can, however, only be used where there has been actual violence or the threat of violence.

Application of Powers The right to exclude one partner from the do-   9.20
mestic home exists even if he is the owner-occupier, tenant or contractual licensee. The provisions do not assist trespassers or bare licensees, although in the latter case, the same effect - exclusion from the home - could be achieved at the instigation of the person the couple are living with.

Short Term Remedy. For some time it was thought that the provisions   9.21
would not apply if, for example, the man was either the owner-occupier or the tenant, or even if he was a joint owner or joint tenant. In *Johnson* v. *Davies* (1978), however, it was held by the House of Lords that the spirit and intention of the Act was to ensure that a battered woman could both remain in the domestic home and exclude the violent male, regardless of his property interests in the home. It is available, therefore, to a cohabitant with no legal interests in the property at all, against the owner- or tenant-partner. The injunction is, however, a short-term remedy and will not create an indefinite right of occupation, nor can it be used to alter basic property rights.

4.   *Domestic Proceedings and Magistrates' Courts Act 1978*

Power of Magistrates' Court. A similar power to exclude a party to a   9.22

marriage, confined however to cases where there has been actual or threatened violence, is conferred on magistrates' courts, by section 16 of the Domestic Proceedings and Magistrates' Courts Act 1978.

5. *Matrimonial Homes Act 1983*

9.23   **No Exclusion without Court Order.** Regardless of whether occupation is owner-occupation, tenancy or contractual licence, one party to a marriage cannot exclude another from occupation of the matrimonial home without an order of the court (Matrimonial Homes Act 1983 - "MHA 1983" - s.1(1)). This order will normally be made in the course of matrimonial proceedings dealing with a number of considerations, but it could be made on application under this Act alone. The court also has power to make an order permitting a spouse who has been wrongfully evicted or excluded from the matrimonial home to re-enter. The court can make the order in respect of part only of the premises, *e.g.* excluding a husband from the residential part of the premises but allowing him to carry on his business in another part.

9.24   **Acceptance of Payments.** When someone who is not the owner-occupier, tenant or contractual licensee takes over mortgage or rent payments under these provisions, the landlord or mortgage company is obliged to accept them as though they were made by the owner-occupier, tenant or licensee (MHA 1983, s.1(5)). The court will exercise its powers to order one party to leave the matrimonial home whenever it is "fair, just and reasonable" to do so (*Walker* v. *Walker,* 1977) and will bear in mind the conduct of the parties generally, their respective needs and financial resources, the needs of any children of the marriage (*Samson* v. *Samson,* 1960) and all the circumstances of the case.

9.25   **Registrable Right of Occupation.** A spouse who is not named on the deeds of a house or flat has a right of occupation under these provisions which she is entitled to register with the Land Charges Registry (MHA 1983, s.2). The effect of this is that if the house is sold, the purchaser buys it subject to her right of occupation and is deemed to have known that she was and can remain in occupation. This is to prevent, for example, a husband selling the home over the head of a wife, before a court has an opportunity to make any order for transfer.

9.26   **Transfer of Tenancy.** The court also has power to order the transfer of a Rent Act protected tenancy, whether contractual or statutory, from the name of one spouse into the name of another (MHA 1983, s.7 and Sched. 1). Where the tenancy is contractual, the power may be exercised at any time up to the remarriage of the non-tenant spouse remaining in occupation. The law is however, unclear as to whether a transfer order can effectively be made after decree absolute if the tenancy is statutory and the tenant-spouse is no longer in occupation. From the one case which has touched upon this point (*Lewis* v. *Lewis*, 1985), it would seem that it cannot. For this reason it is essential to seek the order before decree absolute. The same powers apply to Housing Act secure and Housing Act assured tenancies, but there are similar difficulties if a divorce is already final. Note, also, that the power exists only where the property has been used as the matrimonial home, so that it did not apply where the husband rented a property for his spouse, after their separation, in which they never lived together (*Hall* v. *King*, 1987).

6. *Matrimonial and Family Proceedings Act 1984*

Relationship to Foreign Orders. This Act is intended to deal with divorce or legal separation in another country, but which is entitled to be recognised as valid in this, where one of the parties is domiciled or has been habitually resident in this, or either or both of the parties had at the date of application under the Act an interest in a dwelling-house in this country which has at some time during the marriage been a matrimonial home (ss.12, 15). The Act permits applications for financial relief, of various kinds, including (s.17) a property adjustment order under section 24 of the 1973 Act (9.12), sale under section 24A of that Act, and (s.22) transfer of tenancy under the 1983 Act (9.26).   9.27

7. *Children Act 1989*

New Concepts. The Children Act 1989 introduces a number of new concepts - "contact order" - "prohibited steps order" - "residence order" - "specific issue order" - being orders of a class which may be sought in proceedings under any of the above Acts, or under the inherent jurisdiction of the High Court in relation to children, some of which orders (*e.g.* "an order settling the arrangements to be made as to the person with whom a child is to live," *i.e.* a residence order) will concern housing. If such an order is sought, therefore, during proceedings under these Acts, the general principles of the Children Act 1989, s.11, will be applied, and ancillary powers will be available (*e.g.* a family assistance order under s.16). In general terms, the Act does not substantively alter the description in the foregoing paragraphs of this chapter, nor is it   9.28

possible here to describe its terms in any detail.

8. *Further Considerations*

(i) *Which court?*

9.29   **Accredited Courts.** All matrimonial proceedings have to be brought in a properly accredited court. The High Court has power to conduct matrimonial proceedings which means that, in London, the Family Division of the High Court will hear the case, and in other cities where the High Court sits, the case will be brought in the Divorce Registry. However, some county courts also have power to hear matrimonial disputes, provided that they have been listed as a divorce county court. Domestic Violence Act proceedings can be brought in any county court or in the High Court, either as the sole basis for an action, or in conjunction with matrimonial proceedings. In addition, the magistrates' court has the limited power referred to above (9.22).

(ii) *Rehousing*

9.30   **Homelessness.** A woman who leaves the domestic home because of violence or the fear of violence is considered to be homeless for the purposes of Part III of the Housing Act 1985 (see Chapter 10). Many authorities will, however, take the view that if there are proceedings available of the order considered in this chapter, which the woman does not use, she has become homeless intentionally (10.15-10.30). They cannot do this if the woman was ignorant of available domestic proceedings, or if there were none available or if it would be wholly unreasonable in all the circumstances.

9.31   **Discrimination.** A woman who is not rehoused by the local authority will have difficulties finding anywhere else to live. She should bear in mind the provisions of the Sex Discrimination Act 1975 which make it unlawful for anyone concerned in the management, sale or rental of property to treat a woman any the less favourably than they would treat a man, for example, by refusing to grant a mortgage to a woman, or adding some term such as a demand for a guarantor for rent or mortgage payments. This Act does not apply to resident landlords or buildings so small that they are either subdivided into no more than three separate units of accommodation or can only accommodate a maximum of six people within them. A housing association set up to cater for the needs of one sex only, *e.g.* single mothers, female ex-prisoners, male ex-mental patients, etc., is also exempt from the Act. Unlawful discrimination can be the subject of a normal county court action.

10 Homelessness

10.01   **Homeless Persons Act 1977.** Since 1977, local authorities have been under a duty to secure that accommodation is made available for many of those who are homeless: the provisions, first contained in the Housing (Homeless Persons) Act 1977, are now to be found in Part III of the Housing Act 1985 ("1985"; references to Part III in this chapter should be read as referring to the earlier legislation where appropriate). The 1977 Act placed the duty on housing authorities to provide for the homeless: district councils, the London borough councils and the Common Council of the City of London.

10.02   **Limited Entitlements.** It would be wrong, however, to assume that all the homeless are entitled to substantive assistance: the duty to ensure that accommodation is made available (10.46) for an indefinite period, or in practice to provide permanent housing, only arises when the local authority are satisfied that an applicant for assistance under the Act is: (*a*) homeless; (*b*) in priority need of accommodation; and (*c*) did not become homeless intentionally (1985, s.65(2)). Others may be entitled to "advice and assistance," which means no more than such advice and assistance as the authority consider appropriate (1985, ss. 65(4), 66(3)), *e.g.* the homeless not in priority need, or the homeless in priority need who have become homeless intentionally. Some may be entitled to no more than temporary accommodation, *e.g.* those whom the authority have reason to believe may be homeless and in priority need, but in relation to whom investigations and enquiries are continuing (1985, s.63), or those who are homeless and in priority need but who have become homeless intentionally (1985, s.65(3)).

10.03   **Key Concepts.** It will already be apparent that the key definitions are of: (*a*) homelessness; (*b*) priority need; and (*c*) intentional homelessness. In addition, under the local connection provisions of Part III, one authority may be able to shift responsibility for a homeless person on to another authority (1985, s.67). Local connection, too, must therefore be defined. The duties imposed on local authorities are only comprehensible once these terms have been understood. In this chapter, we shall consider:

1. *Homelessness;*
2. *Priority need;*
3. *Intentional homelessness;*
4. *Local connection;*
5. *Local authority duties;* and,
6. *Enforcement of duties.*

1. *Homelessness*

No Rights in Accommodation. A person is homeless for the purposes 10.04
of Part III if he has no accommodation in England, Wales or Scotland,
and a person is deemed to lack accommodation if there is no
accommodation: (*a*) which he is entitled to occupy by virtue of an
interest in it, (*e.g.* ownership, tenancy); or (*b*) which he is entitled to
occupy by virtue of an order of a court, (*e.g.* in the course of domestic
proceedings, see Chapter 9); or (*c*) which he has an express or implied
licence to occupy, (*e.g.* service occupants, members of the family or (*d*)
which he is occupying as a residence by virtue of any enactment or rule
of law giving him the right to remain in occupation or restricting the
right of any other person to recover possession of it (1985, s. 58(2)).

Accommodation Reasonable to Continue to Occupy. The last part 10.05
of the definition is a cross-reference to the terminology of the Protection
from Eviction Act 1977, s.1 (8.05), intended to cover not only, *e.g.*
statutory tenants, but anyone whom it would be illegal to evict other
than by way of court proceedings (8.07-8.13). In every case, the
applicant is to be treated as homeless if the accommodation in question
is not available for himself, and also for any member of his family who
normally resides with him, or for any other person who normally resides
with him in circumstances in which it is reasonable for that other person
to do so. Furthermore, the applicant is to be treated as homeless if any
accommodation is so bad that he could not reasonably be expected to
continue to reside in it; however, for this purpose, the local authority are
entitled to have regard to the general housing conditions in their area,
and as they normally will be, and always will be said to be, "very bad",
this does not add much in most cases. The meaning of the term
"reasonable to continue to occupy" is considered below, in relation to
intentional homelessness (10.15-10.30), as the purpose of this part of the
definition is to declare that if an applicant could quit accommodation
without being considered homeless intentionally, he ought to be treated
as, in effect, already homeless.

10.06   **Additional Categories of Homeless.** A person is *also* homeless for
the purposes of Part III if: (*a*) he has accommodation but cannot secure
entry to it (*e.g.* the peremptorily evicted tenant); or (*b*) it is probable that
occupation of the accommodation will lead to violence from some other
person residing in the accommodation, or to threats of violence from
some other person residing in the accommodation who is likely to carry
out those threats (*i.e.* domestic violence); or (*c*) the accommodation
consists of a movable structure, vehicle or vessel designed or adapted
for human habitation, and there is no place where he is entitled or
permitted both to put it and to live in it (*i.e.* mobile homes, houseboats)
(1985, s.58(3)). The fact that violence or threats of violence are being
made by someone who does not reside in the property, does not mean
that the violence or threat of it is not relevant to the question whether it
is reasonable for the applicant to continue to occupy the property
(*Hammell* v. *Royal Borough of Kensington & Chelsea*, 1988; *R.* v.
Broxbourne B.C., ex p. Willmoth, 1989).

10.07   **Threatened with Homelessness.** A person is threatened with
homelessness when it is likely that he will become homeless within 28
days (1985, s.58(4)).

10.08   **Homelessness and Temporary Accommodation.** What constitutes
homelessness under section 58 has been considered in a number of
cases. In *R.* v. *Ealing London Borough Council, ex p. Sidhu* (1982), the
local authority held that a woman temporarily housed in a women's
refuge was not homeless, because she had a licence to occupy a room in
the hostel: the court roundly rejected this argument. Similarly, the court
would not uphold an argument that a man who usually slept in a night
shelter, on a day-to-day basis, but who could be turned away if the
shelter was full at the time of his arrival, was not homeless: *R.* v.
Waveney District Council, ex p. Bowers (1982). These were temporary
arrangements, and it was quite ludicrous to suggest that the people were
not homeless. In *Din* v. *London Borough of Wandsworth* (1981), Lord
Lowry commented: "... to be homeless and to have found some
temporary accommodation are not mutually inconsistent concepts. Nor
does a person cease to be homeless merely by having a roof over his
head or a lodging, however precarious." Those in purely temporary,
emergency accommodation, *e.g.* with friends or family, should,
therefore, be considered homeless.

2. *Priority Need*

Statutory Definition. A person has a priority need for accommodation   10.09
under Part III if: (*a*) he has dependent children who are residing with
him, or who might reasonably be expected to reside with him; or (*b*) he
is homeless or threatened with homelessness as a result of an emergency
such as flood, fire or other disaster; or (*c*) he, or anyone who resides or
might reasonably be expected to reside with him, is vulnerable as a
result of old age, mental illness or handicap or physical disability or
other special reason; or (*d*) she is a pregnant woman, or the applicant
resides or might reasonably be expected to reside with a pregnant
woman (1985, s.59).

Code of Guidance. Some of these expressions are subject to elabora-   10.10
tion in the Code of Guidance issued under the Act by the Secretary of
State for the Environment, and to which authorities are bound to have
regard in the discharge of their duties (1985, s.71), which is not the same
as saying that they are bound to comply with its contents in the same
way as they are bound to comply with Part III itself (*De Falco* v.
Crawley Borough Council, 1979).

Dependent Children. Dependent children are usually treated as those   10.11
still in full-time education or training, or otherwise up to the age of 16.
In *Sidhu* (10.08), the authority argued that until the applicant had what
they called a "final" or "full" custody order, in the course of pending
divorce proceedings, they need not consider her as in priority need. The
court held that custody was irrelevant to priority need, for a custody
order can be varied at any time until the child reaches 18, or one parent
may have custody, while another has care and control. The issue is
solely one of fact: are dependent children residing, or are there
dependent children who ought reasonably to be expected to reside, with
the applicant? In *R.* v. *Hillingdon London Borough Council, ex p. Islam*
(1981), in the High Court, the authority suggested that priority need only
arose if children both are residing, and might reasonably be expected to
reside, with the applicant. But, as the court held, Part III says "or."
Indeed, authorities should make every effort to avoid splitting families
even for short periods because of the personal hardship, the risk of long-
term damage to the children and social cost (Code of Guidance, para.
6.5).

Partial Dependency. It is not a requirement that the child is wholly   10.12
dependent on or wholly and exclusively residing with the applicant, so

in a genuine case where custody is split an applicant may be in priority need even although the child is with him only for part of the week: *R. v. London Borough of Lambeth, ex p. Vagliviello* (1990). However, in *R. v. Port Talbot B.C., ex p. McCarthy* (1990), it was held that where a father was granted staying access to his children, under an order of joint custody, but the mother had care and control of the children, this did not amount to the children residing with their father.

10.13 **Children in Priority Need.** A child is entitled to apply under the Act in his own right, and may be in priority need because of his vulnerability (see next para.; see also *Kelly* v. *Monklands District Council*, 1985, where it was held that a 16 year old girl was at risk and therefore vulnerable for "other special reason"), or because he lives with someone who is, or she is, pregnant or has a child, or because of an emergency: *R. v. Bexley L.B.C., ex p. B, R. v. Oldham M.B.C., ex p. G*, 1992. (But see below, para. 10.22, for the limitations on this).

10.14 **Vulnerability.** Vulnerability on account of age necessitates not just looking at the age of the applicant but whether it has made it hard for them to fend for themselves, but all applications from people over 60 should be considered carefully, although a lesser age may be one factor in a number which make up vulnerability as a result of special reason (*R. v. Waveney District Council, ex p. Bowers*, 1982). For these purposes "vulnerable" means "less able to fend for oneself so that injury or detriment will result when a less vulnerable man will be able to cope without harmful effects" (*Bowers*, above), or "vulnerability in housing terms or the context of housing" (*R. v. Bath City Council, ex p. Sangermano*, 1984), or less able both to find and to keep accommodation (*R. v. Lambeth London Borough Council, ex p. Carroll*, 1987). A distinction must be drawn between mental illness (*i.e.* psychotic) and "mere" mental handicap, although subnormality will not necessarily amount to vulnerability in every case (*Sangermano*). Not every case of epilepsy will render a person vulnerable (*R. v. Reigate and Banstead B.C., ex p. Di Domenico*, 1987). The authority must reach their own decision, and not merely "rubber-stamp" a medical opinion, unless that is decisive on the only relevant issues (*Carroll*, above and *R. v. Wandsworth L.B.C., ex p. Banbury*, 1986).

3. *Intentional Homelessness*

10.15 **Act or Omission.** A person becomes homeless intentionally if he deliberately does anything or fails to do anything in consequence of which he ceases to occupy accommodation which is available for his occupation and which it would have been reasonable for him to continue to occupy (1985, s.60(1)). Becoming threatened with homelessness intentionally is similarly defined (1985, s.60(2)), and there is no distinction in principle between the two concepts (*Dyson* v. *Kerrier District Council*, 1980). (All future references to intentional homelessness may, accordingly, and save where an express distinction is drawn, be taken to refer also to becoming threatened with homelessness intentionally.)

Good Faith. An act or omission in good faith, on the part of a person unaware of a relevant fact, *e.g.* invalidity of notice to quit (1.45-1.50), security of tenure (Chapters 3-6), financial assistance (3.77), with rent or mortgage, is not to be treated as deliberate for these purposes (1985, s.60(3)). Good faith in these circumstances can encompass honest blundering and carelessness (*e.g.* in a business deal) and should be contrasted with dishonesty where there can be no question of good faith: *R.* v. *Hammersmith & Fulham L.B.C., ex p. Lusi* (1991). 10.16

Reasonable to Continue to Occupy. Finally, when considering whether or not it was reasonable for the applicant to remain in occupation of his former accommodation, the authority are entitled to have regard to the general circumstances prevailing in relation to housing in their own area (1985, s.60(4)), *i.e.* they may consider whether there are others putting up with worse conditions. This permits authorities to claim that applicants should have remained in what may objectively be considered appalling conditions, and means that people can rarely if ever safely quit without a real likelihood of a finding of intentionality, merely on account of the physical condition of their current accommodation. 10.17

Available Accommodation. This concept of intentionality has given rise to considerable litigation. Before an authority can properly hold that a person has become homeless intentionally, it must be possible to say that each limb of the definition has been fulfilled: something must have been done or omitted deliberately; the act or omission must have caused the homelessness; the lost accommodation must have been available for the applicant's accommodation; and, it must have been reasonable for the applicant to remain in occupation. Accommodation is only available for a person's accommodation if it is available for himself *and* for anyone with whom he might reasonably be expected to reside (1985, s.75). 10.18

10.19   **The Islam Case.** The most important case under these provisions was the Islam case (10.11). Mr Islam was in occupation of a shared room in Uxbridge, and had lived and worked in Uxbridge since his arrival in this country 16 years before his application under the Act to the London Borough of Hillingdon. He had returned to Bangladesh on five occasions: on the first, he had married; on the subsequent occasions, his wife had conceived children. She and, as they were born, their children, lived at Mr. Islam's parents' house in Bangladesh. They applied for entry clearance to join Mr. Islam here, but had to wait six years before it was granted: once granted, it had to be used within six months, or they would have to reapply. Accordingly, they immediately came to this country, notwithstanding Mr. Islam's lack of available accommodation for them. Although they were put up for a short time by Mr Islam's landlord, they were all eventually evicted and it could not be disputed that Mr. Islam had lost his shared room on account of the arrival of his family. However, by no stretch of the imagination could that shared room be considered "available" accommodation in the statutory sense, (*i.e.* for himself and for his family, who might reasonably be expected to reside with him), and on that ground it was not open to the authority to hold that he had become homeless intentionally when he lost that room. The only thing that might seem to make it unreasonable for the family to be expected to live together was the want of accommodation, but as that was the very problem Part III was designed to solve, it could not be taken into account.

10.20   **The Applicant's Conduct.** Furthermore, it is the *applicant* who must have become homeless intentionally. Thus, in *R.* v. *North Devon District Council, ex p. Lewis* (1980), a woman lived with a man by whom she had a child, but to whom she was not married. He quit his job and in consequence lost his tied accommodation. When he applied under Part III, he was held to have become homeless intentionally. The woman then applied in her own right. The authority said two things: (*a*) they did not have to consider her application, because she was governed by the decision on his application; and (*b*) she had in any event acquiesced in his decision to quit his job, so that she, by association, had done an act of intentionality in her own right. The court rejected the authority's first argument, but upheld their decision on the second point, in this particular case. It would not have been appropriate to deem her to have so acquiesced if she had done all she could to prevent him, but he had gone ahead notwithstanding, just as it will not be appropriate to treat as intentionally homeless a woman who had done all she can to prevent her husband spending the rent money on drink, or otherwise.

***Lewis* Applied.** In *R.* v. *West Dorset District Council, ex p. Phillips* 10.21
(1984), *Lewis* was applied so as to compel an authority to house a
woman who turned on her husband during their homelessness interview
and attacked him for spending money on drink, but in other cases (*R.* v.
Swansea City Council, ex p. Thomas, 1983) attempts to apply the *Lewis*
principle have failed. In *R.* v. *Mole Valley District Council, ex p. Burton*
(1988), the attempt was successful, when the authority failed to consider
that a wife had acted in good faith when she had believed her husband's
assurances that they would be rehoused if he quit his job and
accordingly lost his tied accommodation. In *R.* v. *East
Northamptonshire District Council, ex p. Spruce* (1988), it was said that
a spouse's mere knowledge of, *e.g.* rent or mortgages arrears would not
be enough to amount to acquiescence, or he or she might have learned
so late that the arrears were too big to do anything about.

Children and Intentionality. In *R.* v. *Bexley L.B.C., ex p. B, R.* v. 10.22
Oldham M.B.C., ex p. G, 1992, an attempt was made to carry *Lewis* to
applications by children who could not, generally and in those cases
(where the children were four years old), be considered to have
acquiesced in the conduct of parents which had given rise to a finding
of intentionality. The court held that while an application could be made
by a minor, even one of four years, notwithstanding the absence of
mental capacity to understand and appreciate the significance of the
application, a dependent child was not for that reason alone in priority
need, *i.e.* unless some other basis could be established for priority need
(above, para. 10.13), he would not be in priority need; accordingly, there
would be no entitlement to housing (below, para. 10.43) and thus the
parents' intentionality could not be circumvented.

Loss of Tied Accommodation. It will not always be appropriate to 10.23
treat someone who has quit or been dismissed from his job and thus lost
tied accommodation, as intentionally homeless. There must be a
sufficient link, or proximity, between the act which caused the loss of
job, and the loss of accommodation (*R.* v. *Thanet District Council, ex
p. Reeve,* 1981). Thus, a direct act, *e.g.* theft from an employer, which
could reasonably be foreseen to lead to loss of job and accommodation,
may amount to intentional homelessness; however, loss of job through,
e.g. a period of incompetence, should not. Nor does the fact that
someone appears voluntarily to have quit employment necessarily mean
that he has become homeless intentionally: he may have been forced
into it, so that his resignation was a constructive dismissal (*R.* v.
Thurrock Borough Council, ex p. Williams, 1982).

10.24   **Burden in Intentionality.** If there is any doubt over whether or not someone has done a sufficiently direct act to qualify as intentionally homelessness it should be resolved in the applicant's favour (*Williams*). In every case, it should be noted that it is for the authority to satisfy themselves that a person became homeless intentionally, not for an applicant to satisfy the authority that he did not (*Lewis, Williams*).

10.25   **Grounds for Possession.** Rent arrears, non-payment of mortgage instalments, and nuisance and annoyance causing eviction (3.33-3.35, 4.43-4.44, 5.78-5.79), can qualify as acts of intentional homelessness, though in each case, again, there must be sufficient proximity, or foreseeability, between act and loss of home. In each case, too, ignorance of ways of avoiding loss of home will be a defence. In *R*. v. *L.B. Hillingdon, ex p. Tinn* (1988), which only secondarily concerned this issue, it was said by the court that by definition it could not be reasonable to continue to occupy accommodation if the applicants could not pay the rent or mortgage without depriving themselves of the ordinary necessities of life, such as food, clothing, heat and transport. However, this did not mean that the authority could be forced to buy back the home from the applicant (which had been purchased on shared-ownership under the "right-to-buy" :3.55), or that the court would make a declaration of unintentional homelessness prior to homelessness itself occurring. In *R*. v. *Leeds C.C., ex p. Adamiec*, 1991, however, a sale before the commencement of possession proceedings by the building society was upheld as intentional, even though it was likely that in the long run the applicant would not have been able to afford to continue living in the house.

10.26   **Relevant Considerations.** In *R*. v. *Hammersmith and Fulham London Borough, ex p. Duro Rama* (1983), it was said that "reasonable to continue to occupy" involves a range of questions, not confined to the condition of the housing formerly occupied, and in *R*. v. *L.B. Tower Hamlets, ex p. Monaf* (1988), that it calls for a "balancing exercise" between reasons for departure and coming to the area where application has been made, and housing conditions in that area. In *R*. v. *L.B. Hillingdon, ex p. H* (1988), political and racial harassment was considered relevant to the question of reasonable to continue to occupy. In the context of homelessness (10.05), harassment from former husbands or cohabitees has been considered relevant (*Hammell* v. *Royal Borough of Kensington & Chelsea*, 1988; *R*. v. *Broxbourne B.C., ex p. Willmoth*, 1989).

Intervening Accommodation. How far back can an authority look? 10.27
Can present homelessness be deemed intentional on account of the loss
of accommodation in the past, if there has been some intervening
accommodation? This question was decisively answered in *Dyson* v.
Kerrier District Council (1980). In this case, a woman took a winter let
in the private sector on a fixed-term lease for eight months (5.75),
before surrendering her local authority accommodation. Had she not
quit, then by the time the winter let came to an end, she would still have
been in occupation of the local authority letting. On a cause-and-effect
test, her subsequent homelessness was attributable to the voluntary
surrender of the earlier accommodation. In *Lambert* v. *Ealing London
Borough* (1982), similarly, a family who quit accommodation in France,
at a time when they could have remained in occupation, were held to be
intentionally homeless notwithstanding two intervening holiday lettings
in England. The same result followed in *De Falco* v. *Crawley Borough
Council* (1979), in which an Italian family were held intentionally
homeless on account of their departure from accommodation in Naples,
notwithstanding intervening accommodation with friends here.

Accommodation Abroad. *De Falco* and *Lambert* are also authority for 10.28
the proposition that even if accommodation abroad does not count for
the purposes of section 58 (10.04), departure from accommodation
abroad can constitute an act of intentional homelessness.

Premature Departure. *De Falco* was expressly approved by the House 10.29
of Lords in *Din* v. *Wandsworth London Borough Council* (1983). In that
case a different question was raised. A family had, contrary to the advice
of the local authority, quit accommodation at a time when they could
have remained, albeit only until a court order was made against them.
At that time, they were, therefore, homeless intentionally. They did not
apply to the authority until much later, when the authority agreed that
they would have become homeless in any event, and not intentionally
so. None the less, the authority took the view that as their homelessness
was intentional at its start, and there had been no intervening period of
settled residence anywhere else (the family having stayed with friends
in the meantime), their intentional homelessness had not "been
broken." This view was upheld by the House of Lords and it is,
accordingly, now clear that a person must find and occupy some
accommodation which may be described as "settled residence" before
he will have "purged" his earlier intentional homelessness.

Settled Accommodation. There is no judicial or other definition of 10.30

settled residence, but accommodation which is indefinite at its outset should qualify, although an intention that it is indefinite will not always be sufficient, where the accommodation is of a precarious nature (*R.* v. *London Borough of Merton, ex p. Ruffle*, 1988). In relation to assured shorthold agreements (Chapter 6), the Code suggests (para.7.8) that whether such accommodation is settled should be assessed in the light of the expectation of the tenant at the outset, *i.e.* did they expect that they would be able to remain after the expiry of the original term.

4. *Local Connection*

10.31   **Statutory Definition.** A person has a local connection with an area: (*a*) because he is, or in the past was, normally resident in it and that residence was of choice; or (*b*) because he was employed in it; or (*c*) because of family associations; or (*d*) for any special circumstance (1985, s.61(1)). Residence is not ''of choice'' if: (i) it is in consequence of service in the armed forces; or (ii) it is in consequence of detention under an Act of Parliament (*e.g.* imprisonment, compulsory in-patient), (1985, s.60(2), (3)). Employment does not count if it is employment in the armed forces (1985, s.60(3)). Note, however, that the overriding term is ''local connection,'' which must be attributable to one of the specified ''grounds''; merely demonstrating that there is, *e.g.* employment, or family connection, without the authority finding it sufficient to amount to a ''local connection'' will not be enough (*Re Betts*, 1983).

10.32   **Conditions.** The local connection provisions only serve to permit one authority to transfer to another the full, or permanent, housing duty which arises under section 65(2) (10.46). They are irrelevant to all other duties, including the duty to make enquiries into such questions as homelessness, priority need and intentionality (10.40). The provisions will only apply if: (*a*) *neither* the applicant *nor* any person who might reasonably be expected to reside with him has a local connection within the area to whom he has applied; *and* (*b*) *either* the applicant, *or* a person who might reasonably be expected to reside with him, *does* have a local connection with the area of another authority; *and* (*c*) *neither* the applicant, *nor* any person who might reasonably be expected to reside with him runs the risk of domestic violence in that other authority's area (1985, s.67).

10.33   **No Local Connection.** If an applicant has no local connection with anywhere in England, Scotland or Wales, the local connection provisions do not apply, and the burden of housing will remain with the authority to which application is made, as in *R.* v. *Hillingdon London Borough Council, ex p. Streeting* (1980), a case concerning a refugee from Ethiopia.

Disputes between Authorities. These provisions are a breeding ground for argument between authorities. Pending resolution of a dispute between authorities, the authority to which application has been made must provide temporary housing (1985, s.68(1)). It is also the authority to which application is made which must decide whether the applicant is homeless, in priority need, and intentionally homeless. This is so, even if the authority suspect that the local connection provisions will apply and that they will be referring the applicant on to another authority.

10.34

Merry-Go-Round. The decisions on these points of the authority to which the application has been made are binding on an authority to whom they subsequently refer the application. This remains true even if the applicant has formerly applied to one authority, been found homeless intentionally, and moved on to apply to another authority: the second authority can still reach a decision, different from that of the first authority, that the applicant did not become homeless intentionally, and then invoke the local connection provisions to refer the applicant back (*R.* v. *Slough Borough Council, ex p. Ealing London Borough Council,* 1980). This produces a "merry-go-round," for the first authority will still be bound by the decision of the second, even in this case where it conflicts with their own, earlier decision. The proposition illustrates how views may differ as to whether or not someone has become homeless intentionally. There is nothing to stop an applicant applying to authority after authority in the hope of a favourable decision.

10.35

Enquiries by Second Authority. In such a case, where there has been no intervening change of circumstances, the authority to which a subsequent application has been made must treat the application carefully, and give the authority to which the applicant will be returned, and which earlier found him to be homeless intentionally, an opportunity of discussing the case and, above all, of discussing any discrepancies in the explanations offered for the homelessness by the applicant (*R.* v. *L.B. Tower Hamlets, ex p. L.B. Camden,* 1988) Futher, before deciding to refer the second authroity must take into account the general housing circumstances in the area to which they are referring (*R.* v. *London Borough of Newham, ex p. London Borough of Tower Hamlets,* 1990).

10.36

10.37   **No Change of Mind.** An authority who find that an applicant is
unintentionally homeless and then refer the applicant to another
authority cannot change their mind on intentionality simply because the
referral is unsuccessful and the applicant comes back to them (*R.* v.
Beverley District Council, ex p. McPhee, 1978).

10.38   **Local Authority Agreement.** As a first stage, authorities will try to
reach agreement as to who should house the applicant, (1985, s.67(4)).
To assist in reaching agreement, associations of local authorities have
agreed amongst themselves criteria to be applied to questions of what
constitutes local connection: the Local Authority Agreement. The terms
of this document do not bind anyone, not even an authority which is
party to it: it is a voluntary guideline, for administrative purposes only,
and if an authority choose to depart from it in a particular case, they are
free to do so; indeed, it will be irrelevant to any court or arbitration
proceedings (*R.* v. *Mr. Referee McCall, ex p. Eastbourne Borough
Council*, 1981).

10.39   **Arbitration.** As a second stage, assuming no agreement, the matter is
to be referred to arbitration (1985, s.67(4)). Detailed provisions
governing arbitration have been made by statutory instrument. From the
point of view of the homeless person, it is important to note that
although not a party to the arbitration, he will be entitled to give
evidence to it, and where there is an issue as to which other authority he
may be referred to, his own wishes may be taken into account (provided
all other considerations are equally balanced, *McCall*).

5. *Local Authority Duties*

10.40   **Enquiries.** If a person applies to a local authority, and the authority
have reason to believe that he may be homeless or threatened with
homelessness, the authority are under a duty to make appropriate
enquiries (1985, s.62(1)). Applications do not have to be made in any
specific way (*R.* v. *Chiltern District Council, ex p. Roberts*, 1990), and
can be made by anybody, whatever their immigration status (*R.* v.
*Secretary of State for the Environment, ex p. London Borough of Tower
Hamlets*, 1992). It has been noted above (paras. 10.13, 10.22) that
applications can even be made by children: *R.* v. *Bexley L.B.C., ex p.
B, R.* v. *Oldham M.B.C., ex p. G*, 1992. Authorities must enquire
whether or not the applicant is homeless, and whether or not he has a
priority need and has become homeless intentionally (1985, s.62(2)).
They may also enquire into whether or not he has a local connection

with the area of another authority (1985, s.62(2)).

Accommodation Pending Enquiries. As these enquiries may take 10.41
some time, if the authority have reason to believe that the applicant may
be already homeless, and in priority need, they must secure that suitable
accommodation is made available for his occupation pending their
decision (1985, s.63). These duties are immediate: the authority cannot
avoid them by keeping their offices shut for prolonged periods; in the
cities, they are expected to maintain a 24-hour service, *i.e.* an
emergency, out-of-hours service as well as a normal office service (*R.*
v. *L.B. Camden, ex p. Gillan,* 1988).

Available Accommodation. Two further observations on this early, 10.42
temporary duty will apply throughout the housing duties to be
considered below, whether temporary or permanent. First of all, the duty
to secure that suitable accommodation is made available for a person's
occupation is a duty to secure that such accommodation is made
available not only for the applicant, but also for any person with whom
he might reasonably be expected to reside (1985, s.75). Secondly, the
authority are not under any duty to provide their own accommodation:
they may do so, of course, but they may also discharge the duty by
securing that suitable accommodation is provided by some other person,
e.g. a housing association, hostel, private landlord, or by giving such
advice and assistance as secures that suitable accommodation is
provided by some other person, *e.g.* a travel warrant to the area of
another authority, where suitable accommodation within that authority
is appropriate (10.49; 1985, s.69).

Advice and Assistance. If the authority are satisfied that an applicant 10.43
is homeless or threatened with homelessness, then they will have further
duties towards him (1985, ss.65, 66). If they are satisfied that the
applicant is homeless or threatened with homelessness, but not that he
is in priority need, their duty is to provide no more than advice and
appropriate assistance (1985, ss.65(4), 66(3)), which rarely amounts to
more than a list of local housing associations or accommodation
agencies. It may be noted that, even although children will not be in
priority need merely because their parents have been held homeless
intentionally (*R.* v. *Bexley L.B.C., ex p. B, R.* v. *Oldham M.B.C., ex p.
G,* 1992 - above, paras. 10.13, 10.22), they are entitled to make an
application and are therefore entitled to advice and assistance.

10.44   **Temporary Accommodation for the Intentionally Homeless.**
          Authorities are under the same duty to provide advice and appropriate
          assistance if they are satisfied that the applicant is homeless and in
          priority need, but they are also satisfied that he has become homeless
          intentionally (1985, s.65(3)). In this latter case, however, they are also
          obliged to secure that suitable accommodation is made available for the
          applicant's occupation for such period as they consider will provide him
          with a reasonable opportunity to find somewhere for himself (1985,
          s.65(3)). This should not be a fixed period for all applicants, *e.g.* four
          weeks, but a period determined individually in every case, having regard
          to the applicant's circumstances, and local housing availability (*Lally* v.
          Royal Borough of Kensington and Chelsea, 1980). The provision of
          temporary accommodation under this duty does not amount to a settled
          residence (10.30) so as to break the intentionality (*Delahaye* v. *Oswestry
          Borough Council*, 1980).

10.45   **Accommodation and Threatened with Homelessness.** If the
          authority are satisfied that the applicant is threatened with homelessness,
          and is in priority need, and are not satisfied that he became threatened
          with homelessness intentionally, their duty is to ensure that
          accommodation does not cease to be available for his occupation (1985,
          s.66(2)). In effect, this means that they must make arrangements so as
          to secure accommodation from when homelessness actually occurs: this
          duty cannot, however, be used as a defence to an action for possession
          by the authority themselves, *i.e.* of their own property (1985, s.66(4)).

10.46   **Permanent Housing Duty.** If the authority are satisfied that the
          applicant is already homeless, and in priority need, and they are not
          satisfied that he became homeless intentionally, then they are under
          what has been described as the permanent housing obligation (1985,
          s.65(2)). This is, however, subject to the availability to the authority of
          referring the case to another authority under the local connection
          provisions (10.31-10.39).

10.47   **Reasonable Preference.** It has already been noted that even this
          permanent housing duty is not a duty to provide accommodation from
          the authority's own stock (10.42). However, in the selection of their own
          tenants, the authority are bound to give a reasonable preference to those
          towards whom they owe duties under sections 65 and 66, including
          those towards whom the permanent duty is owed, and those towards
          whom are owed the duties described in the last two paragraphs, *i.e.* even
          the intentionally homeless (1985, s.22). The phrase ''reasonable

preference" is extremely vague, and for this reason cannot be described as giving rise to a positive, enforceable entitlement on the part of any individual.

Permanent but Temporary. The authority are not bound to provide permanent accommodation immediately: they must do the best they can, even if this means temporary accommodation, or even a series of, *e.g.* short-life lettings, until an adequate final offer can be made (*R.* v. *Bristol Corporation, ex p. Hendy*, 1973) Note that misconduct causing the loss of a "stage" in the provision of permanent accommodation, (*e.g.* a room in a hostel pending permanent allocation) can constitute intentional homelessness (10.15-10.30; *R.* v. *East Hertfordshire District Council, ex p. Hunt*, 1985).

10.48

Suitable Accommodation. When the authority offer accommodation, whether of their own stock, or through some other landlord, the accommodation must be suitable. They must, when deciding suitability, have regard to the provisions of the Housing Acts governing fitness (Chapter 12), overcrowding and houses in multiple occupation (Chapter 14). The authority must also take into account the particular circumstances of the applicant and his family, *e.g.* medical evidence (*R.* v. *London Borough of Brent, ex p. Omar*, 1991). It must be adequate as regards size for the family's needs, and also as to such other factors as nature of area and employment prospects (*R.* v. *Wyre Borough Council, ex p. Parr*, 1982). A vague offer of unidentified accommodation cannot be a proper discharge of the duty.

10.49

Accommodation and Area. The accommodation need not be in the authority's own area, but that is not to say that the applicant can be housed anywhere at all. Thus, an offer which means that a person has to give up his job, which may be the very factor providing him with a local connection with the authority's area, would clearly not be an appropriate or adequate offer. Nor should a person be sent to an area with which he has no connections, against his wishes. In *R.* v. *Bristol City Council, ex p. Browne* (1979), a woman who applied to Bristol, with whom she had no local connections, was rehoused by arrangement with her home town in Eire. This was a proper discharge through "some other person" (10.42). (The local connection provisions were themselves unavailable because Eire is outside the jurisdiction of Part III.) It should be noted, however, that it was only an acceptable discharge because Bristol first checked that the woman ran no further risk of domestic violence in her home town, which was the original reason she left: discharge through

10.50

some other person could not be used as a way of getting around the provisos to the local connection qualification (10.31).

10.51   **Indefinite Accommodation.** The accommodation offered must be indefinitely available, as opposed to available for a fixed period only, even where what has been left was only available for a limited period (*R.* v. *Camden London Borough, ex p. Wait,* 1986).

10.52   **Alternative Accommodation Arrangements.** Not only are the authority entitled to discharge the accommodation duty through housing owned by someone else, they are not obliged to offer their own, normal, Part II housing stock: in an appropriate case, they may also arrange such accommodation as old people's accommodation under the National Assistance Act 1948, Part III, or else, in the case of a minor, they could use their powers under the Children Act 1989.

10.53   **Part III, Children Act 1989.** Section 20 of the Children Act 1989 provides:
> "(1) Every local authority shall provide accommodation for any child in need within their area who appears to them to require accommodation as a result of -...
> (c)...the person who has been caring for him being prevented (whether or not permanently, and for whatever reason) from providing him with suitable accommodation or care...
> (3) Every local authority shall provide accommodation for any child in need within their area who has reached the age of sixteen and whose welfare the authority consider is likely to be seriously prejudiced if they do not provide him with accommodation..."

Section 17 provides:
> "(1) It shall be the general duty of every local authority...
> (a) to safeguard and promote the welfare of children within their area who are in need; and
> (b) so far as is consistent with that duty, to promote the upbringing of such children by their families
> by providing a range and level of services appropriate to those children's needs..."

10.54   **Part III v. Part III.** Duties under the Children Act 1989 are imposed on social service authorities. These are the same as local housing authorities in London, and in the metropolitan counties. In the non-metropolitan counties, however, housing is discharged by district councils and social services by county councils. In *R. v. L.B. Tower*

Hamlets, ex. p. Monaf (1988), where what was in issue was "assistance" under the Children and Young Persons Act 1980 (now s.17(6) of the 1989 Act: "(6) The services provided by a local authority...may include giving assistance in kind or, in exceptional circumstances, in cash..."), it was said that while the housing priority of children is governed by the Housing Act, where necessary the children retained the right to receive assistance under the Children Act. The relationship between Part III of the Housing Act 1985 and Part III of the Children Act 1989, however, is more complex, as the 1989 includes the more extensive, and specific, accommodation provisions that are set out in the last paragraph. Commonly, a child who is vulnerable (above, para. 10.13) will also be a child "in need" under the 1989 Act. It would seem that, where an authority have both classes of duty, they should consider applying either or both Acts. The Code of Guidance (para. 6.16) stresses the need to avoid any possibility of children or young people being sent to and fro between departments or authorities, and suggests a clear corporate policy and departmental procedure should be adopted to ensure co-operation.

Decisions in Writing. In addition to the housing duties, the authority must always notify an applicant of their decision, in writing, and of the reasons for their decision if the decision is anything other than that they accept the duties under section 65(2) or section 66(2) (10.45-10.46; 1985, s.64). Thus, if they form the view that the applicant is homeless intentionally, or not in priority need, or not homeless, or if they form the view that they may refer the application to another authority, they must tell the applicant so, and explain the basis for their decision.   10.55

No Delay in Decisions. Although Part III does not spell out the duty to take a decision, it is clearly implied, and the structure of Part III is such that authorities are not entitled to defer a decision in the hope or expectation that circumstances may change in such a way as to reduce their obligations, *e.g.* because children may grow up and cease to be dependant (*R.* v. *London Borough of Ealing, ex p. Sidhu,* 1982). If circumstances do change, the authority may still, if appropriate, be able to evict, for the applicant will not become a secure tenant, even in their own stock, for a period of one year from when housing commences (1985, s.79 and Sched. 1, para. 4; 3.14(*e*)), nor if they have arranged accommodation through another landlord will the tenant become assured for the same period (1988, s.1; 4.10). (In each case, however, this presumes that the housing provided started before the decision was made and notified.)   10.56

10.57   **Protection of Property.** In connection with the duties described thus far, the local authority have power to take steps to protect the property of someone who has applied to them for assistance (1985, s.70). In some cases, there is a positive duty to do so, where there is a danger of loss or damage to property because of the applicant's inability to protect or deal with it himself. The duty arises if accommodation is being provided pending the outcome of enquiries (10.41), or for a period to permit someone who became intentionally homeless but who has a priority need to find somewhere else to live (10.44), or to provide accommodation pending a decision over local connection (10.34), or where the full housing duties exist (10.46). In other cases, even if the authority are not obliged to take such steps to protect property, they have power to do so. In relation to both duty and power, the authority have powers of entry into premises to deal with an applicant's property, *e.g.* premises from which a person has been evicted, or from which a woman has fled on account of domestic violence.

10.58   **Charges.** The authority may charge for accommodation provided by them, or may charge for accommodation provided by another for which they are paying, *e.g.* bed-and-breakfast. They may also make charges for storing property taken into their care under the last paragraph.

10.59   **Offences.** In addition to these powers, there are provisions to deal with applicants who make false statements to the authority in order to get rehousing under the Act (1985, s.74). A person commits an offence if he, with the intention to making an authority believe that someone who has applied for rehousing under Part III is either homeless or threatened with homelessness, or has a priority need, or did not become homeless or threatened with homelessness intentionally: (*a*) knowingly or recklessly lies in a material particular to the authority; or (*b*) withholds information reasonably required by the authority in connection with an application. It is also an offence for an applicant to fail to notify an authority of any change of facts material to the application, which occurs before the applicant receives notification of the authority's decision (10.55). The authority, however, have to explain the duty to inform them of material change in clear and ordinary language, and must also explain the possibility of criminal penalties. It is a defence to this charge to show that the warning was not given, or that although it was given, the applicant has a good excuse for failing to conform.

6. *Enforcement of Duties*

Challenge. Challenge to a decision of an authority is no easy matter. 10.60
Each of the duties under Part III is prefaced with the formula "if the
authority have reason to believe," "if the authority are of the opinion,"
or, most commonly, "if the authority are satisfied," that a certain state
of affairs exists, the duty shall arise.

Principles of Administrative Law. One might think that this would 10.61
make it impossible to challenge a decision, for if the authority declare
that they are not satisfied as to a relevant fact, how can one gainsay
them? The answer lies in what are sometimes called the principles of
administrative law. This means that while there is no direct appeal to the
courts on a question of fact, the courts can be asked judicially to review
the decision of the authority, to see if they have approached it correctly.
For example, the authority must act in good faith, they must not take
into account something irrelevant, or disregard relevant factors, they
must correctly interpret the law, if individual decisions are called for -
as they are called for under Part III - they must approach each decision
individually, and not by way of a fixed policy (*Att.-Gen., ex rel. Tilley*
v. *London Borough of Wandsworth*, 1980), there must be a factual
foundation for the decision (*Secretary of State for Education and
Science*v. *Metropolitan Borough of Tameside*, 1976), and they must not
reach a decision so absurd that no reasonable authority could have
reached it, they must act in accordance with the requirement of fair
administration.

Fairness. Thus, the authority should usually provide the applicant with 10.62
an opportunity to comment on a prospective decision on intentionality.
They must have regard to the Code of Guidance. They must make
adequate enquiries, although they are not obliged to go in for "CID-type
enquiries" (*Lally*v. *Royal Borough of Kensington and Chelsea*, 1980).
If the applicant indicates that a particular enquiry may assist his case, it
would be quite wrong for the authority to turn a blind eye to the
information (*Krishnan* v. *London Borough of Hillingdon*, 1981; *R.* v.
West Dorset District Council, ex p. Phillips, 1984), although the
authority are free to draw proper inferences from what the applicant tells
them (*De Falco* v. *Crawley Borough Council*, 1979). If the applicant
wishes to rely on some special feature of his case, he is bound to put the
authority on notice of it (*R.* v. *Wandsworth London Borough, ex p.
Henderson*, 1986). But in the final analysis, provided the authority
approach the matter fairly, with an open mind, and correctly apply the

law, decisions are for them, not for the courts.

10.63   **Judicial Review.** An applicant dissatisfied with the decision of the
authority must apply for judicial review in the High Court (*Cocks* v.
Thanet District Council, 1982). This includes any challenge as to the
suitability of the accommodation which is being offered in discharge of
a rehousing duty (10.49; *London Borough of Tower Hamlets* v. *Ali*,
1992). There must be no delay seeking relief (*R.* v. *Hillingdon London
Borough, ex p. Thomas*, 1987). The courts are extremely reluctant to
grant leave to challenge an authority's decision: Parliament had
entrusted the decision-making power to the authority, and the courts
should only intervene, if at all, on the limited grounds described in this
and the last paragraph (*R.* v. *Hillingdon London Borough Council, ex
p. Puhlhofer*, 1986).

10.64   **Discharge.** An authority will be under no duty whatsoever, however,
if they can claim already to have discharged their duty, *i.e.* to have made
an adequate (10.49) offer, which the applicant has turned down (*R.* v.
Westminster City Council, ex p. Chambers, 1982), the applicant can
only re-apply if there has been a material change in his circumstances
(*R.* v. *L.B. Ealing, ex p. McBain*, 1985). This means a change which
would have affected the accommodation he was offered on the earlier
application, *e.g.* because there are now more children of the family.
When deciding whether or not different, *e.g.* larger, accommodation
would have been offered, the authority can take into account the housing
conditions in their area (10.17), which means that applicants should be
extremely cautious about refusing an offer, for the circumstances which
will qualify as a material change may be fewer than they would
anticipate, *i.e.* authorities may say that the change has made no
difference.

11 Disrepair – The Occupier's Remedies

Civil Proceedings. In this chapter we shall consider the remedies open   11.01
to an occupier who suffers from the effects of disrepair, by means of
civil proceedings. We shall not consider redress by way of complaint to
a justice of the peace under section 606 of the Housing Act 1985, that
a house (or an area of housing) is unfit for human habitation
(12.12-12.14). Nor shall we consider proceedings by way of a summons
for statutory nuisance, under section 82 of the Environmental Protection
Act 1990 (13.06-13.14). It should be remembered that these other
proceedings remain available, however, and that they, and the other
remedies considered in the following three chapters, are additional to
those considered in this.

Contract and Tort. In this chapter we are concerned with remedies in   11.02
both contract and tort. Contract may assist when there is a specific
agreement, whether express or implied; tort is the body of law governing
relations between individuals where there is no contractual relationship,
or where the contractual relationship does not itself cover the harm
alleged to have been suffered by one at the fault of another. In the main,
we are concerned with tenants and other occupiers: owners, whether
under freehold or leasehold, normally have no one upon whom they can
impose the burden of disrepair, although leaseholders of flats will
usually have to pay the freeholder for works to a block, or building, and
may have to use the law in order to compel the leaseholder to carry out
works, or to agree the amount the leaseholder seeks to recover by way
of "service charges." These provisions are considered briefly in this
chapter (11.43-11.44). But remedies in tort may assist even an
owner-occupier of a house.

1. *Contract*

Contractual and Statutory Provisions. The starting-point will always   11.03
be what is set out in any written agreement that may exist. It is, of
course, impossible to analyse all the combinations which may be found
in practice: they are as unlimited as human imagination. In the main,

though, it is landlords who draw up letting agreements, and consequently the object of the agreement will be to impose upon the tenant the most extensive obligations that the law permits. In a number of cases, however, the law will intervene: these circumstances are considered in context, but it should be noted that in short leases, and periodic tenancies, any such attempts by a landlord are likely to contravene the provisions of section 11 of the Landlord and Tenant Act 1985 (11.21-11.33), that other leases, at low rents, may have to comply with the provisions of section 8 of the Landlord and Tenant Act 1985 (11.18-11.20), that relief may be obtainable under the provisions of the Unfair Contract Terms Act 1977 (11.40-11.42), and that remedies in tort may be available where there are none in contract.

11.04   **Notice of Disrepair.** There is one principle that is common to almost all of the provisions to be considered under this heading. That is, that a landlord's obligation to repair does not arise until he has had actual notice of conditions such as to put him, if not on actual notice of what is in disrepair, then at least on sufficient notice to cause him to inspect and find out. The only exception to this is the case of an express repairing covenant which does not itself say that the tenant has to give notice (*Minchburn* v. *Peck*, 1987).

11.05   **Illustration by Cases.** The leading cases on the need for notice usefully illustrate its operation. In *O'Brien* v. *Robinson* (1973), works had been executed to a ceiling, several years before it fell down. There had been no further complaint or warning, by tenant or otherwise, to the landlord before it in fact fell down. The landlord was not, accordingly, in breach of the obligation to repair. In *Sheldon* v. *West Bromwich Corporation* (1973), however, a plumber employed by the defendant corporation inspected a water tank. The tank was corroded, but it was not yet weeping. Subsequently, it burst. It was held that the condition of the water tank at the time of the inspection, even without the weeping - which would be sure and final sign of corrosion calling for repair - was sufficient to put the corporation on notice that something needed to be done.

11.06   **Recent Cases.** In *McGreal* v. *Wake*, 1984, a repairs notice was served on the landlord by the local authority. When the landlord did not carry out the works, the local authority carried them out in default (see Chapter 12). For the period from after the landlord had a reasonable opportunity to comply with the notice, until the authority completed the works, the landlord was held to be in breach of his obligation to repair.

From these and other cases (see also *Dinefwr B.C.* v. *Jones,* 1987, *Hall* v. *Howard,* 1988) emerge the following propositions: (*a*) that notice need not be *from* the tenant, so long as the landlord has actually had notice, *e.g.* by way of a notice under one of the many provisions considered in the next three chapters, or perhaps by way of notice from or to his employee; and, (*b*) that although the notice must be sufficient to warn him that he ought to inspect, it is not necessary for the tenant actually to identify causes, or to specify defects in such detail that it could, *e.g.* serve as a schedule of (necessary) works. But the notice must be unequivocal: where a tenant gave notice of disrepair, saying that he would subsequently give the landlord the details, the landlord was entitled to await the further information (*Al-Hassani* v. *Merrigan,* 1987).

Classes of Term. In the following paragraphs we shall consider: 11.07

(i) terms implied by law, which may be additional to those expressed in an agreement, or may provide a basic and minimum indication of liabilities when there is neither written nor verbal agreement between the parties;

(ii) terms implied by statute, which again may well override what has expressly been agreed, or may operate where nothing express has been agreed, and will accordingly include the provisions of the Unfair Contract Terms Act 1977; and,

(iii) remedies for breach of obligation (whether express, implied by law or implied by statute).

(i) *Terms implied by law*

Fitness for Human Habitation. There is no general term implied into   11.08
the contract for the letting of residential accommodation, either that the dwelling is fit for human habitation, at the start of the tenancy, or that it will be so kept by the landlord during, the tenancy (*Hart* v. *Windsor,* 1844). The only term which is implied as to the condition of the property at the commencement of the tenancy is one which is implied only into *furnished* lettings, that it is at the start of the tenancy fit for human habitation (*Smith* v. *Marrable,* 1843). Fitness for these purposes is fitness at common law, not fitness for human habitation as defined for the purposes of the Housing Acts (12.12-12.14). What is meant by fitness, therefore, must be considered as a matter of common law, though statute may be a helpful guide to contemporary standards, for it is clear that what one generation means by fitness is not the same as another generation.

11.09   **Remedies for Unfitness.** It is well established that if premises are not so fit, the tenant can quit, and will not be liable for the rent. Unfortunately, that is rarely an option available in the current climate of housing shortage, especially since a person quitting could not be sure that he would not be found to be homeless intentionally under Part III of the Housing Act 1985 (10.15-10.30). It would seem at the least arguable that if premises are not fit at the commencement of the tenancy, the breach by the landlord should today be treated as the breach of any other repairing obligation, *i.e.* that the tenant can remain in occupation, press for repairs to be executed (11.53) and claim damages (11.47). It would seem that today a similar covenant will be implied into a licence of furnished accommodation (*Smith* v. *Nottinghamshire County Council,* 1981), though it would not be consistent with a licence for short-life user, *i.e.* of property pending demolition or improvement.

11.10   **Weekly Tenancies.** Nor, in the absence of any express agreement as to repair, will the courts invariably assume that under a weekly or monthly periodic tenancy, the landlord will take responsibility for the major repairs, even though the courts readily accept that it is not to be assumed that the tenant will do so instead, for want of any sufficient interest in the property to merit substantial expenditure (*Mint* v. *Good,* 1950; *Sleafer* v. *Lambeth London Borough,* 1959). Under a weekly, or probably other short, periodic tenancy, the landlord will have the right to do repairs, and correspondingly to enter to view the state of the property, but whether or not he is obliged so to do will depend upon whether anything was written or said, or otherwise upon the court's view as to what was intended. Thus, in *Barrett* v. *Lounova* (1988), where the tenant was liable for internal repairs, but nothing was said about structural or external repairs, the court concluded that the landlord must have such liability, in order to give the agreement business efficacy, for otherwise the tenant could not comply with his obligations. In practice, lacunae in responsibility are cured by the provisions of section 11 of the Housing Act 1985, although there remain in existence a number of tenancies which predate its predecessor (Housing Act 1961, s.32), and to which, accordingly, its provisions do not apply, such as in *Barrett.*

11.11   **Licences.** In the case of a licence, other than one expressly granted in consequence of the state of the property, *e.g.* for short-life user, it will not only be the case that the landlord will usually be assumed to undertake liability to keep the property in repair (*Smith* v. *Nottinghamshire County Council,* 1981), but it is considered inconsistent with the nature of licence for the licensee to be under any significant repairing obligation (*Addiscombe Garden Estates* v. *Crabbe*, 1958).

Common Parts. A clear distinction must be drawn between the prem- 11.12
ises the subject of the tenancy, and other parts of a house or building which is not let as a whole. These parts, *e.g.* stairs, roof, halls, corridors, foundations and, in some houses bathrooms and toilets, are parts kept in the landlord's possession and control, and are consequently his responsibility. He is wholly responsible for their upkeep (*Cockburn* v. *Smith*, 1924). He must keep them reasonably safe (*Dunster* v. *Hollis*, 1918). Where they form the means of access to a house, flat or room, in the absence of any express agreement to the contrary, he is to keep them in a reasonable condition (*Liverpool City Council* v. *Irwin*, 1977; *King* v. *South Northamptonshire D.C.*, 1991), perhaps in a condition reasonably approximating that in which they were at the commencement of the letting. It is thought that this obligation is related to, or derived from, that considered in the next paragraph. There is no pre-condition of notice in relation to this covenant (*Melles and Co.* v. *Holme*, 1918).

Non-derogation from Grant. Where the tenant occupies property 11.13
which adjoins that occupied by the landlord (whether actually or as a matter of law, *e.g.* common parts), it is implied that the landlord will not use his retained property so as to "derogate from the grant" of the tenancy, *i.e.* in such a way as to interfere with the tenant's use of the property for the purpose for which it was let.

Quiet Enjoyment. This covenant has been considered above (8.46). It 11.14
is not usually considered in relation to disrepair. However, as the covenant by the landlord that the tenant will be able quietly to enjoy the premises the subject of the tenancy is implied into every letting, it may be a useful "catch all" where, *e.g.* repairs take an undue time to complete, or are executed with such disregard for the tenant's convenience that it may be said unreasonably and unnecessarily to interfere with his use of the premises. There is no reason why disrepair should not also be considered breach of the covenant for quiet enjoyment (*Gordon* v. *Selico Co.*, 1986).

Estoppel and Rent Registration. In some circumstances, even where 11.15
one party has no direct or express legal rights against another, the law will "estop," (*i.e.* stop) the other party denying an absence of legal entitlement. One circumstance related to repairs, and which relies

heavily upon estoppel, is very common indeed. It is noted below (11.21) that the provisions of section 11 of the Landlord and Tenant Act 1985 apply only to tenancies granted after October 24, 1961. Where a tenancy commenced before that date, therefore, there may be no repairing obligations implied into the tenancy at all. However, over time, there may have been applications, more commonly in this situation by landlord than by tenant, for registration of a fair rent (5.93-5.117). Almost invariably, rent officers assume, in the absence of express representations made to them by (again, usually) the landlord, either that section 11 does apply, or that the landlord is - to use a common, rent officer expression - responsible for major and structural repairs, and the tenant for interior decorations. The rent will be assessed on this basis. Of course, the tenant will be paying a higher rent than if he were himself responsible for the major repairs, or than if no one had any such responsibility.

11.16   **Variation of Register.** In such a case, it would be inequitable to permit the landlord both to receive the enhanced rent, and to deny his liability to repair. Accordingly, he will be estopped from denying whatever liability has been set out in the register (*Brikom Investments* v. *Seaford*, 1981). However, he can subsequently apply for a variation in the registration. The estoppel will not, therefore, guarantee future responsibility, but until there is a variation in the registration, liability will have arisen and will remain, and may be sued upon, both for damages and for an injunction in relation to faults arising before variation. In an appropriate case, estoppel may override even the express terms of an agreement.

11.17   **Use in a Tenant-like Manner.** The tenant is under an obligation to use premises in a "tenant-like manner." That is to say, he "must take proper care of the place. He must, if he is going away for the winter, turn off the water and empty the boiler. He must clean the chimneys, when necessary, and also the windows. He must mend the electric light when it fuses. He must unstop the sink when it is blocked by his waste. In short, he must do the little jobs about the place which a reasonable tenant would do. In addition, he must, of course, not damage the house, wilfully or negligently; and he must see that his family and guests do not damage it; if they do, he must repair it. But apart from such things, if the house falls into disrepair through fair wear and tear or lapse of time, or for any reason not caused by him, then the tenant is not liable to repair it." (*Warren* v. *Keen*, 1953, per Denning L.J.).

(ii) *Terms implied by statute*

Landlord and Tenant Act 1985, section 8. Contrary to the normal
rule (11.08) that there is no covenant that premises are fit for human
habitation at the commencement of a tenancy, or that they will so be
kept throughout the tenancy, statute implies such a term into tenancies
at a very low rent (Landlord and Tenant Act 1985, s.8). For these
purposes, fitness bears the same meaning as under the Housing Act 1985
(12.12-12.14). The covenant is, however, implied only into tenancies at
such low rents that the covenant is rarely encountered in practice. In
accordance with the principle discussed above (11.04-11.06), there will
be no obligation until the landlord has had notice of the disrepair
(*Morgan* v. *Liverpool Corporation*, 1927), and the term has no
application where the premises cannot be rendered fit for human
habitation at a reasonable expense (*Buswell* v. *Goodwin*, 1970), an
expression considered in the next chapter (12.41). The term will,
however, carry over into a statutory tenancy (11.34). The term carries
with it a right on the part of the landlord, on not less than 24 hours'
notice in writing, to enter to view the state and condition of the
premises.

11.18

Rent Limits. The rent levels are as follows: where the contract was
made before July 31, 1923, the rent at the beginning of the tenancy must
not have been more than £40 per annum in the administrative county of
London, nor more than £26 per annum in a borough of an urban district
outside London, nor elsewhere more than £16 per annum. In relation to
contracts made on or after that date, but before July 6, 1957, the rent at
the commencement of the tenancy must not have been more than £40
per annum in the administrative county of London, nor more than £26
elsewhere. In relation to contracts made on or after that date, the rent at
the commencement must not have been more than £80 in what was until
April 1, 1965 the administrative county of London and thereafter
Greater London, or £52 per annum elsewhere.

11.19

Short and Long Leases. But the covenant is not only implied into short
lettings: it may also be implied into longer leases, unless it is excluded.
In relation to short lettings, it is now only likely to be found, if at all, in
relation to an elderly tenant, or a statutory successor, and even then such
low levels of rent are uncommon. In relation to a lease for not less than
three years, the covenant will not take effect if the lease contains a term
that the tenant put the property into a condition reasonably fit for human
habitation, and the lease cannot be brought to an end by the landlord or

11.20

by the tenant, other perhaps than by forfeiture (1.42-1.44), within the first three years.

11.21   **Landlord and Tenant Act 1985, section 11.** This is the main repairing covenant now implied into most lettings of residential accommodation. It does not apply if the letting is for a term of seven years or more (Landlord and Tenant Act 1985, s.12), which will be dated from the commencement of occupation, either under the tenancy or under a binding agreement for a tenancy (*Brikom Investments* v. *Seaford,* 1981). A periodic tenancy is not for seven years or more, even though it may last or have lasted that long or longer. The Act contains power for the parties to apply to the county court for an order excluding or modifying the operation of section 11, but in the absence of any such order the Act overrides the express terms of any agreement, and any contract purporting to exclude the provisions of section 11 -- or to penalise the tenant because the landlord has to comply with them -- is void, and of no effect. The section applies only to tenancies granted after commencement of the Housing Act 1961, when the provision was introduced (October 24, 1961).

11.22   **The Implied Covenant.** The term is of such importance that it should be set out in full:
"In any lease of a dwelling-house, being a lease to which this section applies, there shall be implied a covenant by the lessor -
(*a*) to keep in repair the structure and exterior of the dwelling-house (including drains, gutters and external pipes); and
(*b*) to keep in repair and proper working order the installations in the dwelling-house
(i)   for the supply of water, gas and electricity, and for sanitation (including basins, sinks, baths and sanitary conveniences but not, except as aforesaid, fixtures, fittings and appliances for making use of the supply of water, gas or electricity), and
(ii) for space heating or heating water ... "

11.23   **Part of House or Building.** The provision applies as much to part of a house or building as to a house (Landlord and Tenant Act 1985, s.16). Where only a part of house or building is involved, then the covenant extends to an obligation to keep the structure and exterior of the house or building in repair, and to keep in repair and proper working order an installation (for the same purposes) which serves the part of the house the subject of the tenancy, provided it forms part of a building in which the landlord has an interest, or the installation itself is owned by the landlord or is under his control (Landlord and Tenant Act 1985, s.11(1A), added by Housing Act 1988, s.116). This is not so, however, unless the disrepair actually affects the tenant's enjoyment of his property, or of the common parts (Landlord and Tenant Act 1985, s.11(1B)). The provisions extending s.11 beyond the premises the subject of the tenancy relate only to tenancies granted on or after November 15, 1988 (unless pursuant to a contract for a tenancy which predates November 15, 1988).

Limits of Covenant. The provisions do not, however, go so far as to require the landlord to do works for which the tenant is liable under the duty to use premises in a tenant-like manner (11.17), or to rebuild or reinstate the premises in the case of destruction or damage by fire, or by tempest, flood or other inevitable accident, or to keep in repair or maintain such of the tenant's own belongings as he is entitled to remove from the property (Landlord and Tenant Act 1985, s.11(2)). It is a defence to an action based on failure to repair a building in which the premises are situated, or installations outside the premises but which service them, that the landlord was unable to obtain sufficient rights to do the works (Landlord and Tenant Act 1985, s.11(3A)). There will only be a breach of the covenant if the landlord has had notice of disrepair (11.04-11.06), but the covenant will carry over into any statutory tenancy (11.34). The covenant carries with it a right on the part of the landlord, on giving not less than 24 hours' notice in writing, to enter to view the state of the premises (Landlord and Tenant Act 1985, s.11(6)). 11.24

Standard of Repair. The problems arising under this provision relate to what standards it imposes. The Act itself provides that regard shall be had to the age, character and prospective life of the property, and the locality in which it is situated (Landlord and Tenant Act 1985, s.11(3)). It is no defence to an allegation that installations are not in proper working order to show that they suffer from a design defect (*Liverpool City Council* v. *Irwin*, 1976). Indeed, although the covenant requires only that the landlord keep the premises in repair to the extent set out, the law interprets this as meaning that the landlord must also put them in repair, for that which is not in repair at the commencement of the tenancy can hardly be kept in repair (*Saner* v. *Bilton*, 1878). The obligation extends to essential means of access to the premises (*Brown* v. *Liverpool Corporation*, 1969). 11.25

Exterior. A dividing wall between two terraced houses will be part of the exterior of each (*Green* v. *Eales*, 1841), and the walls of a flat - 11.26

whether to the outside, or to the inside of the building, - and the ceiling and floor, will all be exterior (*Campden Hill Towers* v. *Gardner*, 1976). Windows are part of the exterior (*Quick* v. *Taff Ely Borough Council*, 1985; *Ball* v. *Plummer*, 1979; *Boswell* v. *Crucible Steel*, 1925; *Irvine* v. *Moran*, 1990). That is not to say that the landlord is liable for a breakage by the tenant, for that would be the tenant's responsibility as part of his duty to use the premises in a tenant-like manner (11.17).

11.27   **Structure.** Structure is perhaps more difficult. A house is a complex whole, and anything which touches upon that complex unit may properly be deemed to be part of the structure (*Pearlman* v. *Keepers and Governors of Harrow School*, 1978). The roof of a block of flats or a house converted into flats may be part of the structure of the top floor flat, but then again it may not, depending on, *e.g.* whether there is a roof space or an attic (*Douglas-Scott* v. *Scorgie*, 1984).

11.28   **Dampness and Plaster.** Disrepair must be *to* the structure or exterior, not merely *resulting from it*; thus, dampness caused by a leak or defective brickwork will mean that structure or exterior is in disrepair, but where the mere construction of the structure and exterior result in dampness from ordinary use of the premises (*i.e.* "condensation dampness"), *without* actual disrepair, this will not class as disrepair within this implied covenant (*Quick* v. *Taff Ely Borough Council*, 1985). Thus, in *Stent* v. *Monmouth D.C.* (1987), it was held that if a door "merely" fails to keep out water, there will not be disrepair to the structure, but if the water ingress damages the door itself, there will be. In *Staves* v. *Leeds City Council* (1990) because of condensation dampness the physical condition of the plaster was such that it required renewal. Given a concession that the plaster was part of the structure it followed that there was disrepair. In *Irvine* v. *Moran* (1990), however, it was held that internal wall plaster was not part of the structure of a dwelling-house since it was more in the nature of a decorative finish than an essential material element of the house.

11.29   **Repair.** The final issue turns on the word "repair." For many years, it had been thought that the proper way of defining repair was by distinguishing it from such terms as "improvement," or "renewal." It was also commonly thought that an inherent defect could not be cured within a repairing obligation. The key test was - and to this extent remains - whether the works executed would result in the delivery up of something different in quality to that which was originally let. Thus, for example, it was thought that a repairing obligation could not be used to require a landlord to introduce a damp-proof course (*Pembery* v. *Lamdin*, 1940), or to provide underpinning (*Sotheby* v. *Grundy*, 1947).

Extent of Works. It has recently been held, however, that these older   11.30
cases turned on the extent or degree of works called for, *i.e.* they turned
on their own facts rather than setting precedents as to what works are or
are not within a covenant to repair: *Ravenseft Properties Ltd.* v.
Davstone (Holdings) Ltd. (1978), a case involving the same block of
flats as the subject of the action in *Campden Hill Towers* v. *Gardner*
(1976). In that case, when the block was constructed, no expansion
joints were included to retain a stone cladding against the concrete
frame when natural movement ("settling") commenced. Accordingly,
the stone cladding threatened to fall away. But the only proper way any
competent engineer would permit rectification would be by the
introduction of the missing expansion joints. It was argued that such
works to the structure, involving the introduction of a new method of
construction, and the curing of a construction defect, could not be within
the covenant to repair. Having regard to the sort of works involved,
which were not, in comparison to the whole block, that extensive, to the
necessity for the joints, and also to the cost of the works compared to the
value of the block as a whole, it was held that these works could be
compelled within the repairing obligation.

Contemplation of Parties. In another case (*Smedley* v. *Chumley and*   11.31
Hawkes, 1981), a restaurant had been built on a pier, or raft. It was a
recent construction, and there was inadequate underpinning. The
restaurant threatened to sink into the river on which it had been built.
The court asked what was in the contemplation of the parties, and was
strongly influenced by the fact that these were modern premises, not an
old and deteriorating property: it was held that underpinning could be
compelled within a covenant to repair.

Principles in Practice. How do these principles work in housing? In   11.32
Wainwright v. *Leeds City Council* (1984) it was considered that the
older authorities prevailed. But in *Elmcroft Developments Ltd.* v.
Tankersley-Sawyer (1984), and most recently in *Quick* v. *Taff Ely
Borough Council* (1985), the Court of Appeal has upheld *Ravenseft* and
it would seem: (*a*) that where a modern property is in issue, works can
be ordered, even within section 11 of the Landlord and Tenant Act 1985,
which comprise works to cure an inherent or constructional defect and
which involve the introduction of a new construction method; and, (*b*)
that where an older house is in issue, having regard both to

contemporary values, and to the comparatively small cost of such works as damp-proof coursing, and perhaps influenced by the modern emphasis on retention in use of older housing stock, the courts may now be prepared to order whatever works are necessary to keep a house in a reasonable condition, provided those works are not so extensive or expensive as to involve virtual reconstruction or overall improvement such as will turn the old house into a new dwelling. In *Murray* v. *Birmingham C.C.* (1987), it was held that the covenant *could* extend to the provision of a new roof, although in that case such extensive works were not considered necessary.

11.33   **Three Tests.** In *McDougall* v. *Easington D.C.* (1989) the Court of Appeal considered whether a major rehabilitation programme requiring over £10,000 worth of works to each property but only increasing the value of the properties from £10,000 to £18,000 amounted to a repair of the properties. The Court held that there were three tests which could be applied separately or concurrently to decide whether works amounted to a repair within section 11 of the Landlord and Tenant Act 1985:

(*a*) **Whole or Subsidiary Structure.** Whether the alterations went to the whole or substantially the whole of the structure or only to a subsidiary part;

(*b*) **Character.** Whether the effect of the alterations was to produce a building of a wholly different character than that which had been let;

(*c*) **Cost.** The cost of the works in relation to the previous value of the building and their effect on the value and life span of the building.

11.34   **Rent Act 1977; Housing Act 1988.** Though the Rent Act 1977 and the Housing Act 1988 do not concern themselves directly with repairs, they contain a number of provisions affecting this subject:

(*a*) **Continuation of Covenants.** Both a Rent Act statutory tenancy (5.12) and a Housing Act assured statutory periodic tenancy (4.25) are on the same terms as the preceding contractual tenancy (1977, s.3(1); 1988, s.5), from which it follows that any express or implied repairing obligations will be continued (*McCarrick* v. *Liverpool Corporation*, 1947).

(*b*) **Access.** It is an implied term of all Rent Act protected tenancies (whether contractual or statutory, see Chapter 5) and of all Housing Act assured tenancies (Chapter 4) that the tenant will afford the landlord all reasonable facilities for access and the execution of any repairs which the landlord is entitled to carry out (1977, ss.3(2), 148; 1988, s.16).

(*c*) **Grant-Aided Works and Court Order.** Where a landlord wishes to carry out works which qualify for a renovation (12.64), a common parts (12.65), a disabled facilities (12.66), or an HMO (12.68) grant under the Local Government and Housing Act 1989, and a Rent Act protected tenant will not consent to the execution of such works, the landlord may apply to the court for an order compelling the tenant's consent, which may be subject to terms such as those relating to the housing of the tenant during the works, and which will be granted or refused bearing in mind such alternative accommodation, the age and health of the tenant, and any disadvantages that might be expected to result to the tenant from such works (1977, s.116). There is no equivalent provision under the Housing Act 1988, although extensive works may constitute a ground for possession (4.35).

Landlord and Tenant Act 1954. On the termination of a long lease, a tenant at a low rent may yet become a statutory tenant under the Rent Act 1977 (2.02-2.07). Under the long lease, the tenant will usually have been responsible for repairs; it would be inconsistent with the nature of statutory tenancies for the tenant to retain such an obligation, but on the other hand it might be considered unfair to the landlord were he suddenly to find himself in the position of having to rectify breaches of the tenant's covenant, *i.e.* the tenant's failure to repair during the lease. To this end, amongst the provisions governing "conversion" of the long leaseholder to the status of statutory tenant, is to be found provision for the execution of "initial repairs" (Landlord and Tenant Act 1954, s.7). The notice proposing the statutory tenancy (2.05) must itself propose: (*a*) what initial repairs are to be carried out; and (*b*) what balance of repairing obligation is to pertain during the statutory tenancy. 11.35

Initial Repairs. These matters are to be agreed between landlord and tenant at least two months before the statutory tenancy comes into existence, or otherwise application must be made to the county court for a determination (Landlord and Tenant Act 1954, s.7). The purpose of the provision is to ensure that the property is in an acceptable state for the commencement of the statutory tenancy, for which purpose it is assumed that the state will be such as if the tenant had fulfilled all his contractual obligations; the burden of initial repairs will, then, commonly fall on the tenant. However, a court cannot order the tenant to execute the initial repairs: it can only order the tenant to pay for them, unless the tenant says that he is willing to have them carried out himself. Rather, the court must order the landlord to execute the works, to a maximum standard of "good repair," or such higher standard of works as the landlord indicates he is willing to attain (Landlord and Tenant Act 1954, s.9). The court may order payment for the initial repairs in 11.36

instalments, or in a lump sum (Landlord and Tenant Act 1954, s.8).

11.37 **Continuing Repairs.** The court can also determine the balance of obligations which will follow the initial repairs, but it cannot order the landlord to maintain the premises at a higher standard than at the completion of the initial repairs or, if there are no initial repairs, than the state of the premises at the date of the court's hearing (Landlord and Tenant Act 1954, s.9). The court is under no obligation to make any order governing continuing repairing obligations (Landlord and Tenant Act 1954, s.8). It is common to order or agree that the balance will be as under the Landlord and Tenant Act 1985, section 11 (11.21-11.33). (Note, there are no equivalent provisions where the termination of the long tenancy falls to be dealt with under the Local Government and Housing Act 1989, Sched. 10 (2.08-2.10).)

11.38 **Leasehold Reform Act 1967.** On the extension of a lease under this Act (2.11-2.14) there is a general power for variation by consent or by court order of the repairing terms of the original lease (Leasehold Reform Act 1967, s.15).

11.39 **Housing Act 1980; Housing Act 1985.** Under these Acts, certain Rent Act protected tenants, Rent Act statutory tenants and Housing Act secure tenants, enjoy a qualified "right to improve" their homes. It is a term of all such tenancies that the tenant will not make any improvement, without the written consent of the landlord, which consent is not unreasonably to be withheld (1980, s.81; 1985, ss.79-99). Although cast in a negative frame, the term substantively confers a positive entitlement to improve, where consent has been grated. A refusal of consent can be challenged in the county court (1980, s.82; 1985, s.110). The term does not apply, however, in the case of a shorthold tenant (Chapter 6), or one to whom notice has been given under the mandatory grounds for possession in the Rent Act 1977 (5.69-5.76). For these purposes, improvement includes addition or alteration to a dwelling, and external decorations (1980, s.81(5); 1985, s.97). If the landlord does refuse consent, he is obliged to provide a written statement of reasons, and in the course of any subsequent challenge by the tenant, the burden lies on the landlord to show that the refusal was reasonable, which he may do, amongst other ways, by showing that the imnprovement would make the dwelling, or neighbouring premises, less safe, or that it would cause him to incur additional expenditure, or that it would reduce the value of the house either for the purposes of sale or rental (1980, s.82; 1985, s.98). Again, there is no equivalent inclusion of Housing Act assured tenants under the Housing Act 1988 (see Chapter 4).

Unfair Contract Terms Act 1977. Although this Act does not apply to the creation or termination of an interest in land (Unfair Contract Terms Act 1977, s.1 and Sched. 1), it may apply to other terms in a tenancy, and applies generally to licences. It follows that it may affect an express repairing obligation, imposed on an occupier, and not excluded by another statutory provision, *e.g.* Landlord and Tenant Act 1985, s.11. The Act only applies to "consumers" dealing with a person, on his written standard terms of business (Unfair Contract Terms Act 1977, s.3), and so is unlikely to apply, *e.g.* in the case of a resident landlord (4.20-4.23, 5.28-5.34).   11.40

Requirements. Under the provisions of this Act, a landlord may neither limit his own liability for breach of the contract, nor claim to be entitled to offer no service at all, or a service substantially different from that which might reasonably be expected of him, save to the extent that is reasonable (Unfair Contract Terms Act 1977, s.3). In this context, no service, or a substantially different service than that expected, may be the provisions most relevant to repairing obligation, *i.e.* if the landlord takes no such responsibility, or seeks to limit his responsibility unreasonably.   11.41

Reasonableness. For these purposes, reasonableness means that the term in question is or is not fair and reasonable to include in the contract having regard to the actual circumstances known to the parties when the contract was made, or which ought to have been so known, and in particular having regard to the relative bargaining positions of the parties, alternative possibilities, (*i.e.* here, accommodation) open to the consumer, and trade or custom (Unfair Contract Terms Act 1977, s.11).   11.42

Landlord and Tenant Act 1985, sections 18-30. Leaseholders of flats will normally, and leaseholders of houses may sometimes, have to pay a "service charge," *i.e.* a contribution towards the freeholder's costs (or those of someone with a superior leasehold interest to that of an individual flat leaseholder) of management, maintenance, insurance and repair of the property as a whole, or on an estate. In recent times, these provisions have become extremely contentious and occupiers often claim (*a*) that the landlord is not executing the works, and/or (*b*) that the landlord is demanding substantially more money than accurately represents the works he is carrying out (if any).   11.43

11.44   **Reasonable Amounts, Reasonable Standard.** Under the service charge provisions of the Landlord and Tenant Act 1985, as amended by the Landlord and Tenant Act 1987, a landlord can claim no more than a reasonable amount, in respect of works to a reasonable standard. In some cases, the landlord is obliged to obtain prior estimates for the works, and to consult with the leaseholders, or a recognised tenants' association (Landlord and Tenant Act 1985, s.20), and there are provisions enabling leaseholders, or a recognised association, to obtain documentary evidence of what has been spent. Disputes may be taken to the county court, regardless of amount involved, and whether by way of resisting a claim for a service charge, seeking reimbursement, or for a declaration as to whether or not the charge is recoverable or works are to a reasonable standard.

11.45   **Housing Act 1985, section 96.** In Chapter 3, reference was made to the "right to repair" which secure tenants enjoy, in effect instead of the landlord (3.63). In the event that a secure tenant does exercise this right, it will follow that for a period of time the landlord's repairing obligations - under section 11 of the Landlord and Tenant Act 1985 or otherwise - have been suspended, so far as they concern the item of repair which the tenant seeks to carry out on his own behalf; this is therefore confined to the operation of obligations on the tenant's own premises, and does not affect their operation on common parts or the building in which a flat is situated (11.23-11.24).

(iii) *Remedies*

11.46   **Classes of Remedy.** Both landlord and tenant may wish to seek remedies against the other for breach of a repairing obligation. If the tenant breaks his obligations, the landlord may seek possession of the premises, by way of an action for forfeiture and under the Rent Act 1977, the Housing Act 1985 and the Housing Act 1988. He may also seek damages. More commonly, it is the tenant who will be seeking redress against the landlord: here, possession will not be in issue, but the tenant will want an order for works to be executed, and may also require compensation for the period of disrepair. The remedies which fall to be considered are:
    (a) *damages for breach by landlord;*
    (b) *damages for breach by tenant;*
    (c) *set-off and counterclaim by tenant;*
    (d) *specific performance/injunctions;*
    (e) *receiving orders;*

(*f*) *forfeiture*;
(*g*) *possession*.

Damages for Breach by Landlord. When a landlord allows premises   11.47
to fall into disrepair, the first measure of the damages to which the
tenant will be entitled is the amount that represents the difference in
value to the tenant of the premises in their repaired state and their
unrepaired state (*Pembery* v. *Lamdin*, 1940). If the state of repair is such
that the tenant has to move out for a period, the tenant will be entitled
to the cost of alternative accommodation (*Calabar Properties Ltd.* v.
Stitcher, 1983). In addition, the tenant is entitled to any consequential
loss, *e.g.* clothing or other property destroyed or harmed by damp,
personal injuries, suffered not only by the tenant but also by anyone for
whose benefit the tenancy was taken, *e.g.* family or friends (*Jackson* v.
Horizon Holidays, 1975). The tenant is also entitled to damages for
inconvenience, unfulfilled expectations, disappointment, distress or loss
of enjoyment (*Jarvis* v. *Swans Tours*, 1973; *Personal Representatives of
Chiodi* v. *De Marney*, 1988), or ill-health (*Calabar*). The fact that there
may be a rent registered which has taken into account the want of repair
(3.94) does not mean that the tenant cannot also have damages, for the
rent officer will be bound to have presumed that the landlord would yet
comply with his obligations, *i.e.* the repairing covenant itself has a value
(*Sturolson & Co.* v. *Mauroux*, 1988). There is no one set of rules as to
how damages should be calculated: the purpose is to put the tenant in the
same position as if the breach had not occurred (*Calabar, McGreal*).

Reinstatement of Premises. Finally, the tenant is entitled to require   11.48
the premises to be reinstated, including by way of internal redecorating
necessitated by the landlord's works, and in the absence of such
reinstatement or redecoration will be entitled to damages for having to
do them himself (*McGreal* v. *Wake*, 1984; *Bradley* v. *Chorley B.C.*,
1985).

Damages for Breach by Tenant. The principles governing a breach of   11.49
an obligation to repair on the part of a tenant are different. The amount
which the landlord can recover is the amount by which his reversionary
interest in the premises, (*i.e.* the interest which he enjoys on account of
his future repossession of the premises), has been depreciated (*Smith* v.
Peat, 1853; *Drummond* v. *S. & U. Stores*, 1980). If the landlord has
already repossessed the premises, the damages represent the
depreciation in the value of what he has recovered possession of,
compared to what he ought to have got back (*Hanson* v. *Newman*,

1934). If the tenant is to remain in occupation, *e.g.* as a statutory tenant on account of the Landlord and Tenant Act 1954 (2.02-2.07), then it would seem that unless "initial repairs" (11.35-11.36) serve to eliminate any deterioration in the value of the landlord's reversion, the valuations of repaired and unrepaired property are based on the fact that a sitting tenant is, and will remain, in occupation (*Jeffs* v. *West London Property Corporation*, 1954).

11.50   **Set-off and Counterclaim by Tenant.** One of the most common responses by tenants to repairs inactivity by the landlord is to withhold the rent. For a long time, it had been thought that this was an improper response. In recent years, however, it has come to be seen that in certain circumstances it is not improper, but indeed a legal entitlement on the part of the tenant. However, at the outset of this discussion, it should be said that although a court is unlikely to find it reasonable to make an order for possession if the reason that rent has been withheld is on account of a dispute over repairs (*Lal* v. *Nakum*, 1982, but *cf. London Borough of Haringey* v. *Stewart*, 1991), even if in the event the tenant fails to prove his case, a tenant is always well-advised either to pay rent, or to save the rent, although it may be believed that these principles are applicable. Housing Act assured tenants may find that they are subject to a *mandatory* ground for possession if they withhold rent and their right to set-off is not later upheld (4.38).

11.51   **What Set-off Covers.** "Set-off" is the main principle with which we are concerned. It is now well-established that breach of a repairing covenant is so closely related to the obligation to pay rent that it is appropriate for a tenant to set-off his damages (11.49) against the rent. In the earlier stages of its recent development, this privilege extended only to money actually expended by the tenant on arranging for his landlord's obligations to be executed in default and was not technically a set-off, but an ancient common law entitlement achieving the same effect (*Lee-Parker* v. *Izzet*, 1971). Initially, it was thought this could only be done when the landlord had been given a warning, an opportunity to review estimates, and the money was to be taken out of future rent. Subsequently, it was held that the same principle could apply in relation to past rent withheld, *i.e.* rent arrears (*Asco Developments Ltd.* v. *Lowes*, 1978). In the most recent development, it was held that not only could the tenant withhold money so expended, but he could also set-off his general damages, *i.e.* reduction in value of premises, loss of enjoyment, or his special damages, *e.g.* destroyed property (*British Anzani (Felixstowe)* v. *International Marine*

Management (U.K.), 1978; *Televantos* v. *McCulloch*, 1990).

Caution. Nonetheless, a tenant should, if possible, withstand the temp- 11.52
tation to resort to this way of trying to force the landlord to carry out
repairs. It is better to pay the rent, and then to claim, in the course of
proceedings, for his damages, which will of course be calculated as
described above (11.49). There are only two circumstances in which
set-off can safely be used: (*a*) when there is a clear breach, and the
tenant, after giving his landlord ample warning of his intentions, causes
the work to be carried out in default; and (*b*) when arrears have already
accrued by the time an adviser is in a position to assist. In the first
circumstance, there is still a danger that the tenant will be incorrect in
his view that the obligation is that of the landlord; in the second, if it is
possible to pay any amount off that withheld or unpaid, a court will look
with more respect upon a tenant who has honoured his obligations, in
the face of default by the landlord, than on one who has, as it were,
taken the law into his own hands. Unless the amount claimed by way of
set-off is clearly substantially less than the amount owing to the landlord
in rent, a counterclaim should in any event be added, with which to
recoup the excess of damages over rent unpaid.

Specific Performance and Injunctions.   An order for specific per- 11.53
formance is an order of the court requiring someone to fulfill a
contractual obligation; an injunction is an order to do something, which
may or may not arise under contract, (*e.g.* it may be used in relation to
tort, 11.60). Although there has been contention in the past as to whether
the county court has had power to grant an order for specific
performance, there is now no practical difference between the two
remedies: either may be sought in the county court (Landlord and
Tenant Act 1985, s.17, governing specific performance; County Courts
Act 1984, s.22, governing injunctions), unless the claim is attached to
a claim for damages which exceeds the level of the county court
jurisdiction, which given the recent increase to £50,000 is unlikely.
Neither class of order may be made against a tenant (*Hill* v. *Barclay*,
1811; *Regional Properties* v. *City of London Real Property*, 1980) but
a landlord's want of financial ability to comply with an order is no
defence to such an order at all (*Francis* v. *Cowcliffe*, 1976).

Receiving Orders. Where a landlord fails to carry out his obligations, 11.54
the High Court has power (Supreme Court Act 1981, s.37) to appoint a
receiver to take over the whole or part of the management of a property,
including the receipt of rents and/or the execution of works, where it

considers it just and convenient to do so. However, the courts will not appoint a receiver under this power where the landlord is the local authority carrying out its statutory housing duties, *i.e.* to provide and manage housing, because to do so would usurp Parliament's express conferral of those powers on the authority (*Parker* v. *Camden London Borough Council*, 1985).

11.55   **Landlord and Tenant Act 1987, Part II.** These powers have recently been codified into Part II, Landlord and Tenant Act 1987 and, where Part II applies, it replaces the earlier powers. Part II applies, however, only to a building where there are two or more flats, where at least 50 per cent. of the floor area of the building (excluding its common parts) is occupied for residential purposes, and the landlord is neither a resident landlord (defined in similar terms as under the Housing Act 1988; see 4.20), nor an "exempt landlord," defined to include local authorities and a number of other public bodies (Landlord and Tenant Act 1987, s.21). Action under Part II requires a prior notice fulfilling the requirements of section 22 of the Act, followed by application under section 23 for the appointment of a manager, if the landlord does not comply with the notice.

11.56   **Forfeiture.** Forfeiture is one of the means of bringing a tenancy to an end (1.42-1.44). There is no right to forfeit a tenancy unless such a right is expressly reserved in the agreement. The right is, however, commonly reserved in most written tenancy agreements, and is commonly drafted in such terms as to apply on breach of a tenant's repairing obligation. Where a landlord has known of a breach by the tenant, but has so conducted himself as to be deemed to have waived the breach (*cf.* waiver of illegal sub-letting; 1.71), then the landlord will also have waived his right to forfeit the tenancy (*Doe d. Morecraft* v. *Meux*, 1825), although if the obligation imposed on the tenant is not only to put but also to keep the property in repair, the breach continues so long as the tenant fails to repair and there is, accordingly, no waiver (*Doe d. Hemmings* v. *Durnford*, 1832).

11.57   **Relief from Forfeiture.** Where a landlord seeks to forfeit a tenancy, the tenant can usually apply to the court for relief from forfeiture, which will, however, almost invariably be on conditions, requiring the tenant to rectify his breach, although not if the court considers that the extent of the obligation is unreasonable (Law of Property Act 1925, s.147): there is doubt whether a Housing Act assured tenant (Chapter 4) can apply for relief (4.25). Before seeking to forfeit, the landlord must serve notice specifying the breach which is the subject of his complaint, if the breach is remediable, requiring remedy, and demanding compensation (Law of Property Act 1925, s.146). The landlord must also allow sufficient time for remedy of a repairing breach.

Leasehold Property (Repairs) Act 1938. In relation to long leases, of which at least three years remain unexpired, the section 146 notice must also advise the tenant of his right to claim by way of counter-notice the protection of the Leasehold Property (Repairs) Act 1938, under the terms of which the landlord cannot proceed with an action for forfeiture other than with the leave of the court. The court will not grant leave unless an immediate remedy is needed to prevent a substantial reduction in the value of the landlord's interest, or where remedy would now be cheap compared to remedy later, or in order to comply with any statute, or where the tenant is not in occupation and repair is needed for the protection of other occupiers, or where in all the circumstances the court considers it just and equitable to grant leave.   11.58

Possession. Even if a tenancy is determined by forfeiture, it will still be necessary to prove that it is reasonable to make an order for possession against either a Rent Act protected or statutory (Rent Act 1977; see Chapter 5) tenant, or a Housing Act secure (Housing Act 1985; see Chapter 3 above) or Housing Act assured (Housing Act 1988; see Chapter 4) tenant.   11.59

2. *Tort*

Classes of Tort. In this section, we shall briefly consider remedies for disrepair, or other unacceptable housing conditions, which arise independently of contract. They may be available to those with a contract, or those without; and to owner-occupiers. The headings of tort with which we are here concerned are: 11.60
   (i) *negligence*;
   (ii) *breach of the Building Regulations*;
   (iii) *defective premises*;
   (iv) *occupier's liability*;
   (v) *nuisance*; and,
   (vi) *waste, a tort peculiar to the relationship of landlord and tenant.*
In addition, we are, of course, concerned with:
   (vii) *remedies.*

(i) *Negligence*

11.61   **Duty of Care.** Although negligence is what might be described as a common sense or moral obligation to have regard to those who might be harmed by one's actions, it must be considered slightly more technically in law, though one should not lose sight of that fundamental proposition. Action in negligence only arises when there is a legal duty of care. This means "you must take reasonable care to avoid acts or omissions which you can reasonably foresee would be likely to injure your neighbour. Who, then, in law is my neighbour? The answer seems to be: persons who are so closely and directly affected by my act that I ought reasonably to have them in contemplation as being so affected when I am directing my mind to the acts or omissions which are called into question" (*Donoghue* v. *Stevenson*, 1932, per Lord Atkin).

11.62   **Duty to Tenants and Visitors.** Illustrations will assist. Thus, in addition to the landlord's contractual duty to make sure that common parts are kept reasonably safe (11.12), he also owes a duty of care to tenants or others who may visit premises to ensure that they are safeguarded against damage from any danger of which he knows, or ought to have known (*Cunard* v. *Antifyre Ltd.*, 1933).

11.63   **Duty of Builders.** Anyone carrying out work on premises is under a general duty to use reasonable care for the safety of those whom he knows or ought to know might be affected by those works, or who are lawfully in the vicinity of those works (*A.C. Billings & Son* v. *Riden*, 1958). A builder of a house, whether or not he is also the landlord, owes a duty of care in the construction of the building, to potential occupiers of it, but the liability only extends to personal injury and not to economic loss because *e.g.* it is worth less than was paid for it (*Murphy* v. *Brentwood D.C.*, 1990).

11.64   **Developers.** Developers, whether also the landowner, or not, of, *e.g.* housing for sale, owe a duty of care to purchasers (*Sutherland* v. *Maton (C.R.) & Son*, 1976; *Batty* v. *Metropolitan Property Realisations*, *Rimmer* v. *Liverpool City Council*, 1985; *Targett* v. *Torfaen Borough Council*, 1991). Architects, engineers, surveyors, and others involved in the construction of a dwelling owe a similar duty to future occupiers to take reasonable care in the execution of their functions (*Cedar Transport Group* v. *First Wyvern Property Trustees Co.*, 1980). In the light of *Murphy* any such liability will be limited to damages for personal injury and not economic losses. A landlord may also be responsible in negligence for other works, *e.g.* for the manner of carrying out his repairing obligations (*Sharpe* v. *Manchester M.D.C.*, 1977) or for the quality of works done prior to the commencement of a letting. There is no negligence, however, in *failing* to carry out works before a letting (*Arden* v. *Pullen*, 1842; 11.08).

Home Purchase. A further, and important, illustration of negligence arises in the course of home purchase. Many people buying their own homes will take advice from professionals such as a surveyor, and a solicitor. The surveyor will report on the condition of the house: if he does so negligently, he will be liable for the effects of his default. A solicitor will have a number of legal functions to carry out, including finding out information about the purchaser's title, and whether the local authority have any plans, *e.g.* for clearance (12.44-12.49) which may adversely affect the purchaser's intended occupation. He, too, may be liable in negligence.

11.65

Report to Building Society. Where a purchaser failed to have his own survey carried out, but instead relied upon the fact that a building society was willing to advance the mortgage, knowing that the building society had themselves sought a survey, the surveyor was held liable to the purchaser, even though the purchaser never saw his report to the building society (*Yianni* v. *Evans (Edwin) & Sons*, 1981; see also *Smith* v. *Bush*, 1987; *Harris* v. *Wyre Forest D.C.*, 1987; *Davies* v. *Idris Parry*, 1988). The principle is that the surveyor is deemed to know that the consequences of his negligence would not only affect the building society's decision on mortgage, but also the purchaser's decision as to whether or not to buy. In practice today many building societies release such reports to their members.

11.66

Local Authorities. It should also be remembered that local authorities may commit negligence, in the execution of their functions, Alternatively, they may be liable for breach of statutory duty, which is technically a separate tort, for failing properly to carry out their obligations under an Act of Parliament. Thus, where an authority were obliged to inspect property in the course of construction, to see whether there had been compliance with Building Regulations, (see also 11.69) and were alleged to have done so negligently, action was available at the instigation of later occupiers (*Anns* v. *Merton L.B.C.*, 1977). This will only apply where there is a personal injury suffered, not where the loss is purely economic, because *e.g.* the house is worth less because of defective foundations (*Murphy* v. *Brentwood D.C.*, 1990).

11.67

11.68 **Causation and Consequence.** The fact that there is a defect, however, is not enough: that defect must be caused by an act which a reasonable man would not have done or an omission to do something which a reasonable man would have made sure was done (*Bolton* v. *Stone*, 1951). Further, the act or omission must cause the harm (or the likelihood of harm, see 11.70). There must be a line of causation between act or omission and harm, so that the latter is not too remote a consequence of the former. Another way of putting the same proposition is that it must have been reasonably foreseeable (which is not to say reasonably foreseen) that harm of the order which has resulted would result.

(ii) *Breach of the Building Regulations*

11.69 **Health and Safety at Work Act 1974, section 71.** In a large number of cases where housing is constructed, or improved or altered, or its use changed, it will be obligatory to comply with the Building Regulations. It is now provided that anyone who is obliged to comply with the Regulations and fails to do so will, save where the Regulations themselves otherwise specify, be liable to an action in tort at the instance of a person harmed by his failure (Health and Safety at Work Act 1974, s.71).

(iii) *Defective premises*

11.70 **Defective Premises Act 1972, section 3.** Anyone who carries out work of construction, repair, maintenance or demolition, or any other work in relation to premises owes a duty of care to persons who might reasonably be expected to be affected by resulting defects in the state of the premises (Defective Premises Act 1972, s.3). The duty of care persists through any subsequent sale or letting of the premises, and is co-extensive with the duty of care in negligence (11.68). It does not, however, apply to omissions to repair or execute other works which may be needed. It applies only in relation to works carried out prior to a sale or letting which itself followed the commencement of the Act (January 1, 1974).

11.71 **Defective Premises Act 1972, section 1.** The same Act imposed a duty of care on anyone doing any work, for or in connection with the provision of a dwelling, by erection, conversion or enlargement (Defective Premises Act 1972, s.1). The duty of care is to see that work is done in a workmanlike manner or - if the person involved is a professional, *e.g.*architect, engineer-in a professional manner, and with proper materials, so as to ensure that the dwelling will be fit for habitation when completed. The duty is owed to, among others, purchasers and tenants. The duty is also additional to the duty of care in negligence (11.68) but again applies only to work following the commencement of the Act (January 1, 1974).

(iv) *Occupier's liability*

Occupier's Liability Act 1957, section 2. The occupier of premises 11.72
is the person in possession and control of them. Thus, a tenant is an occupier, but only of the premises the subject of the letting. In a block of flats, the landlord is the occupier of the block, just as in a house let out in bedsitting-rooms or flats the landlord retains possession and control of the house itself. An occupier owes a common duty to take such care as is reasonable in all the circumstances of the case to see that "visitors" to the premises will be reasonably safe in using the premises for the purposes for which he was allowed in (Occupier's Liability Act 1957, s.2). The term "visitors" will include those on the premises with the express or implied permission of the occupier, *e.g.* a tenant or licensee of some part, or the tenant's or licensee's own visitors. The extent of the duty may vary with circumstances, including factors affecting the class of visitor: *e.g.* the elderly, children. In some circumstances, there is even a duty of care to those not lawfully on the premises, *i.e.* trespassers: see Occupier's Liability Act 1984.

Defective Premises Act 1972, section 4. Further, whenever a land- 11.73
lord is under an obligation to repair (howsoever this may arise, *i.e.* implied by law (11.08-11.12); implied by statute (11.18-11.33); or express, he owes "to all persons who might reasonably be expected to be affected by defects in the state of the premises a duty to take such care as is reasonable in all the circumstances to see that they are reasonably safe from personal injury or from damage to their property ... ": Defective Premises Act 1972, s.4. The duty arises whenever the landlord knows of the defect, or ought to have known of it, so that this duty may be an appropriate cause of action if, for want of notice (11.05-11.06) action cannot be taken under a contractual obligation. The duty is owed both to tenants, and to the tenant's visitors.

Relevant Defects. The duty only arises, however, in relation to "rel- 11.74
evant defects." A relevant defect is one arising from or continuing because of an act or omission by the landlord which actually constitutes

a breach of his repairing obligation, or which would have constituted a breach of his repairing obligation if he had had notice of it. In substance, this means any defect which is within the obligation to repair, of which the landlord knew, or ought to have known. But even if the repairing obligations are obscure, if the landlord has a *right* to repair (as distinct from a duty), he is treated for these purposes as being under a repairing obligation, (Defective Premises Act 1972, s.4(4), and see *McCauley* v. *Bristol City Council*, 1991) so that in weekly tenancies (11.09) Rent Act protected and statutory, and Housing Act assured, tenancies (11.34), and those to which the Landlord and Tenant Act 1985, sections 8 (11.18) and 11 (11.21) apply, there will be an obligation for the purposes of this provision, in relation to any class of works which the right of entry is designed to permit the landlord to execute. The Act does not apply, however, to defects which arose before the commencement of the 1972 Act (January 1, 1974) and which no longer existed at that date. The Act does not create any obligation wider than the landlord's repairing obligation (*McNerney* v. *L.B. Lambeth*, 1988).

(v) *Nuisance*

11.75   **Act or State of Affairs.** The meaning of nuisance is considered above (8.55). It is mentioned here because, like breach of covenant for quiet enjoyment (11.14), in appropriate circumstances a landlord's control of neighbouring property may be such that it interferes with the tenant's reasonable use of the premises let. To constitute a nuisance, there must be some act or state of affairs in one set of premises, which adversely affect use and enjoyment of another. Only someone with a right to occupy the premises suffering the nuisance can sue (*Read* v. *Lyons & Co.*, 1946), not a mere visitor.

(vi) *Waste*

11.76   **Alteration of Nature of Premises.** Waste is a tort peculiar to the law of landlord and tenant. In some ways, it may be considered the equivalent in tort of action for breach of the tenant's duty to use premises in a tenant-like manner (11.17). An act of waste is an act by the tenant which alters the nature of the premises let. Normally, this will be an act of deterioration of the premises, *e.g.* cutting down a tree or knocking down an outhouse, or any other act of damage, including to the premises themselves. Technically, it can also be something which might otherwise be regarded as an improvement, *e.g.* an alteration. There will be no waste, however, if the landlord's consent to the act in question has been secured, and an act of waste will only give rise to a claim for possession (3.37, 4.44, 5.80) if it is also an act of deterioration.

(vii) *Remedies*

Classes of Damages. If one person commits a tort which causes harm to another, that other is to be put in the position he would have enjoyed had the tort not occurred. Thus, damages will be available on this principle, whether the claim is against landlord or tenant, for such harm as has ensued. "Special damages" are those which are identifiable, such as loss of earnings, loss of property, including clothing, medical expenses, alternative accommodation, travelling expenses. In addition, there are "general damages," for pain and suffering, personal injury, and nervous shock, though not, as a general rule, for inconvenience or discomfort (*cf.* 11.47).   11.77

Two Points to Note.   Two points on damages are of importance to occupiers of housing. First, there is no reduction in a claim for damages because the claim is against a public body, engaged in a socially useful task, such as the discharge of their housing functions (*Taylor* v. *Liverpool Corporation*, 1939). Secondly, where the claim is in relation to damage to a house, *e.g.* by an owner-occupier suing someone who has negligently advised in the purchase, of a house (11.65), damages will be the cost of repairs, assessed as at the date when, having regard to all the circumstances, the repairs could reasonably have been undertaken, rather than when the harm occurred: the financial ability or inability of the person suing may be a factor in requiring the deferral (and so the increased cost) of repairs (*Perry* v. *Sidney Phillips & Son*, 1982). In some cases, however, any claim will be limited to damages for personal injury, and will not cover any loss of value in the house or cost of repairs (11.63, *Murphy* v. *Brentwood D.C.*, 1990).   11.78

Injunction. In addition, and in principle, there is no reason why an injunction should not be sought, either to prevent harm arising from a tort, or to rectify it. Although the prospect of damage should not be too remote, it is not necessary to wait until a building is about to collapse, and assistance may be secured by way of injunction as soon as it is clear that if something is not done, the harm feared will indeed occur (*Anns* v. *Merton L.B.C.*, 1977; *Crump* v. *Torfaen Borough Council*, 1982).   11.79

Access to Neighbouring Land Act, 1992. Where works are required to neighbouring land to preserve the condition of the adjacent land, it   11.80

may possible to obtain an order for access to the neighbouring land to carry out the required works: Access to Neighbouring Land Act 1992, although not yet in force as at June 1, 1992).

3. *Limitation*

11.81 **Six Years or Three Years.** As a general rule, actions both in tort or contract must be brought within six years of the date on which the cause of action accrued, *i.e.* when the right to sue arose (Limitation Act 1980, ss.2,5.). However, if the claim is for personal injuries, it must be brought within three years (Limitation Act 1980, s.11). The three years run from when the person injured knew of the injury, knew that it was serious enough to merit action, knew that it was attributable to the landlord's default, and knew who the landlord was (Limitation Act 1980, s.14). Where the claim arises out of a breach of repairing obligation, then whether or not for personal injuries, a breach of a repairing obligation is a continuing breach, not a breach only at its outset, time can run from any point until the landlord rectifies the defect.

11.82 **Latent Damage.** More problematic is an action in tort where a defect is not obvious, perhaps for many years. In such a case, the limitation period will be the longer of the usual six-year period, accruing from the date when the damage came into existence, or three years from the date when the complainant discovers (or could have discovered) the damage (Limitation Act 1980, s.24A, added by Latent Damage Act 1986). An overriding time-limit (or "long-stop") of 15 years is applied, during which the complainant must bring the action (Limitation Act 1980, s.24B, added by Latent Damage Act 1986). A successor in title, who buys in ignorance of the damage, may also benefit from the extended time-limits (Latent Damage Act 1986, s.3).

12 Disrepair Under the Housing Act 1985

Purpose of Legislation. One of the principal purposes of the Housing   12.01
Act 1985 ("1985") is to ensure that buildings used for housing are only
so used if they reach acceptable standards. Those standards are as
defined in the 1985 Act. There are several standards applicable to the
general subject of disrepair, and the main standard, that of fitness for
human habitation, was substantially revised by the Local Government
and Housing Act 1989 ("1989").

Housing and Environmental Health. The 1985 Act may be disting-   12.02
uished from the Environmental Protection Act 1990, considered in the
next chapter, which has as its principal objective the remedying of
conditions which are so bad as to put in jeopardy the health of
occupants. The provisions of the Housing Act and of the Environmental
Protection Act are cumulative, not mutually exclusive: *Salford City
Council* v. *McNally* (1975). In the main, the Housing Act sets a higher
standard than will be reached by Environmental Protection Act action
and save in those exceptional circumstances when Environmental
Protection Act action encompasses all that which ought to have been
taken under the Housing Acts, or, less exceptionally, vice versa; action
under one body of law is no substitute for action under the other
(*McNally, R.* v. *Kerrier District Council, ex p. Guppy's (Bridport) Ltd.,*
1985). Nor does action under the provisions to be considered in the
present chapter exclude action by the occupier (Chapter 11), or action
under the provisions specifically directed towards overcrowding,
multiple occupation and common lodging houses (Chapter 14).

Repair or Closure. The main thrust of the 1985 Act is to ensure that   12.03
houses which are unfit for human habitation are either repaired or closed
to domestic use (1985, Part VI and IX). Onto the framework designed
to deal with unfitness in individual houses (Part VI) have been grafted:
(*a*) provisions designed to prevent housing which is in serious disrepair
from deteriorating further into a state of unfitness for human habitation;
(*b*) provisions permitting local authorities to take action to remedy
conditions which are such as materially to interfere with the personal

comfort of an occupying tenant; and (*c*) provisions to deal with blocks of flats or houses converted into flats or let in rooms.

12.04 **Slum Clearance.** Part IX of the 1985 Act concerns slum clearance. It involves individual housing which cannot be dealt with by way of repair or remedy under Part VI. It also concerns unfitness not in individual houses, but in whole areas of housing, which are best dealt with by way of clearance. Part IX also contains provisions to deal with obstructive buildings, and to exempt from some of the unfitness procedures houses which are subject to improvement or redevelopment schemes by their owners.

12.05 **Improvement.** Demolition, closure or clearance were, until 1969, the main means of dealing with unfitness. Since then, there has been a shift in emphasis towards improvement. The Housing Act 1974 introduced new provisions for improving inadequate housing: (*a*) by way of improvement grants for individual houses, which can sometimes lead to compulsory improvement notices; and, (*b*) by way of the declaration of improvement areas. The 1989 Act sought to move back slightly from the emphasis on improvement: it brought in a new test to decide between repair, demolition or closure; the provisions for compulsory improvement notices were repealed; a new set of grants were introduced together with new provisions for area improvement.

12.06 **Displacement of Occupiers.** These provisions can lead to the displacement of occupiers, permanently or temporarily. In the case of permanent displacement, occupiers will enjoy rights to rehousing and also to compensation, both for tenants and for owner-occupiers. These provisions, too, will be considered in this chapter.

12.07 In this chapter, therefore, we shall consider:
1. *Unfitness;*
2. *Serious disrepair,*
3. *Interference with personal comfort;*
4. *Redevelopment and improvement by owners;*
5. *Clearance areas;*
6. *Obstructive buildings;*
7. *Grants and group repair schemes;*
8. *Renewal areas;*
9. *Rehousing and compensation;* and
10. *Occupier's action.*

Preliminary Points. Before turning to these different topics, however, there are two points of general application which must be mentioned: (*a*) which are the local authorities for the purposes of these provisions?; and (*b*) inspection duties. It may also be germane to observe that although there are circumstances, noted below (12.112-12.114) in which an occupier may be able to initiate these procedures, they are essentially procedures designed to be operated by local authorities and, to this extent, the tenor of the text must necessarily shift from law governing the relationship between individuals, to that governing the conduct of public bodies.

12.08

Local Authorities. For the purposes of these provisions, local authorities are: (i) district councils; (ii) London Borough Councils; and (iii) the Common Council of the City of London (1985, s.1), save that in the area of a Housing Action Trust (3.78) these powers may be transferred to the Trust, additionally to or instead of the local authority (Housing Act 1988 - "1988"- s.65). Although county councils have some reserve powers in relation to housing, they are powers to provide housing, not to take action under these provisions (1985, s.28).

12.09

Inspection Duties. Under section 605 of the 1985 Act, the authorities mentioned above (12.09), are obliged at least once a year to consider the housing conditions in their district, with a view to deciding what action they ought to take under the provisions to be considered in this chapter, and in Chapter 14. The Secretary of State for the Environment is entitled to give the authority directions as to exercise of this duty, with which directions the authority are obliged to comply.

12.10

1. *Unfitness*

Premises. The most common object of action under these provisions is the terraced house. The provisions apply however, to dwelling-houses, houses in multiple occupation and buildings containing flats. A dwelling-house includes both houses, properly so-called and flats (1985, ss.207, 183). "House in multiple occupation" is defined in the same way as for the provisions which deal specifically with such houses (14.12). A building not constructed as a house but used as such will qualify (*Ashbridge Investments* v. *Minister of Housing and Local Government*, 1965).

12.11

Principal Definition. The principal definition of unfitness for the purpose of these provisions is to be found in section 604 of the 1985 Act.

12.12

Under section 604 of the 1985 Act, a dwelling-house is fit for human habitation unless it fails to meet one or more of the specified requirements and by reason of that failure it is not reasonably suitable for occupation in that condition. The requirements are: it is structurally stable; it is free from serious disrepair; it is free from damp prejudicial to health; it has adequate provision for lighting, heating and ventilation; it has an adequate supply of wholesome water; there are satisfactory facilities for the preparation and cooking of food (including a sink with hot and cold water); it has a suitably located water-closet; there are suitably located fixed baths or showers and wash-hand basins with hot and cold water; and, it has an effective system for the draining of foul, waste and surface water.

12.13   **Condition.** In addition, where a flat is concerned, unfitness may be found by reference to the condition of the building in which it is situated (1985, s.604(2)), if the building or part of it fails to meet one of the specified requirements and by reason of that failure the flat is not reasonably suitable for occupation. The requirements are: that the building or part is structurally stable; it is free from serious disrepair; it is free from dampness; it has adequate provision for ventilation; and, it has an effective system for the draining of foul, waste and surface water.

12.14   **Ordinary Use.** In one case, the only window in one of the bedrooms of a house had a broken sash-cord. It could only be opened at risk of injury, and the house was small enough that it could no longer be said to be properly ventilated. "If the state of repair of a house is such that by ordinary use damage may naturally be caused to the occupier, either in respect of personal injury to life or limb, or injury to health, then the house is not in all respects reasonably fit for human habitation." This proposition was first expounded by Atkin L.J. in his minority judgment in *Morgan* v. *Liverpool Corporation* (1927). He later adopted the passage as part of the majority in *Summers* v. *Salford Corporation* (1943), upholding the local authority's finding of unfitness in the case of the broken sash-cord.

12.15   **Unfitness in Outline.** If a dwelling-house or house in multiple occupation is unfit for human habitation, then the burden of action falls on the local authority. Once satisfied of the unfitness, the authority are bound to adopt one of three courses of action: they must either adopt the repairs procedure to ensure that the premises are rendered fit again, or serve a demolition or closing order (*R.* v. *Kerrier District Council, ex p. Guppy's (Bridport)*, 1985). The only exception to this is where the authority are proposing to implement a group repair scheme (12.85), in which case the requirement to serve a repairs notice, in relation to works included in the scheme, is lifted while the scheme is carried out (1985, s.109A).

Most Satisfactory Course. In deciding whether to serve a repairs notice, a demolition order or a closing order the authority must choose which is the most satisfactory course of action. This new test was introduced by the 1989 Act and replaced the predominantly economic test of whether the property was repairable at reasonable expense. Authorities are to make the choice taking into account the Guidance issued by the Secretary of State for the Environment under s.604A of the Housing Act 1985. This Guidance is to be found in D.O.E. Circular 6/90, Annex F, and suggests that the individual unfit property should be looked at in the broader context of its surroundings, and that as well as economic factors, social and environmental ones should also be incorporated into the assessment.

12.16

(i) *Repairs notices*

On Whom Served. The notice is served on the person having control of the premises (1985, s.189) or, in the case of a flat found to be unfit because of the condition of the building in which it is situated, on the person having control of that part of the building which requires repair. Where a house in multiple occupation is unfit the notice can, alternatively, be served on the person managing the house (14.33). It must, additionally, be served on others with an interest in the premises.

12.17

Person Having Control. The person having control is defined in relation to a dwelling-house or house in multiple occupation as the person in receipt of the rack-rent, whether on his own account or as agent or trustee for another, or who would be in receipt of the rack-rent were the premises let (1985, s.207). "Rack-rent" means a rent of at least two-thirds of the rateable value of the premises. If the landlord cannot be found, the notice may be served on an agent. Where action is being taken with regard to a building (12.13) the person having control is the owner who, in the opinion of the authority ought to execute the works specified in the notice. Owner means the freeholder or someone holding a lease of three years or more (1985, s.207). The premises need not be tenanted: the provisions could be though rarely are, used against owner-occupiers. The authority may also, but are not obliged to, serve a copy of the notice on anyone else they know to have an interest in the

12.18

house, such as a freeholder or mortgagee. Where there is a long lease of a dwelling-house, the person having control will usually be the leaseholder, rather than the freeholder.

12.19   **Service on Local Authorities.** Where the authority obliged to serve the notice are themselves the person having control, the repairs notice procedure is inapplicable (*R.* v. *Cardiff City Council, ex p. Cross,* 1983). This is because the law considers that Parliament cannot have intended authorities to serve notices on themselves, at least where there is no one else to be served with a copy of the notice. The exemption does not stem from the authority's status as a public body. Thus, if one authority has property in the area of another authority, it is the second authority who will be obliged to serve notice under section 189, and they are free to serve such a notice on the first authority. Similarly, if the authority serving the notice happen to be the freeholders but a private landlord or housing association is the long leaseholder, the notice should still be served. But if the authority have the leasehold, then even though there may be a private freeholder, the provisions will not apply.

12.20   **Contents of Repairs Notice.** The notice must specify what works are, in the opinion of the authority, necessary to render the premises fit, and must state the opinion of the authority that once the works are carried out they will be fit (1985, s.189). The works must be specified with enough precision to enable a reasonable builder to provide an estimate (*Church of Our Lady of Hal* v. *Camden L.B.,* 1980). The notice must give the person served a minimum of 28 days within which to commence the works and a reasonable period in which to complete them.

12.21   **Effect of Repairs Notice.** The service of a repairs notice gives the person served, if a landlord, an absolute entitlement to receive from the local authority any grant to comply with the works (1989, s.114). Where an owner-occupier or tenant applies for a renovation grant it will be mandatory if the premises are unfit, whether or not a notice has been served. As to amount of grant, see 12.62.

12.22   **Ancillary Provisions.** Unless there is an appeal (12.23) the notice will become operative 21 days from service (1985, s.189). If the person served neither appeals nor complies with the notice in the time permitted by the notice, the local authority may themselves go in and do the work in default (1985, s.193). There are ancillary provisions for the authority to recover their expenenses. It is a criminal offence to fail to comply with the notice (1985, s.198A). Non-compliance means not commencing and completing within the time allowed (unless there is an appeal: 12.23) or not making reasonable progress with works, in which latter case, however, it is a defence to both a criminal offence and a claim for recovery of works in default that in fact reasonable progress was being made. Once the authority have served notice of their intention to execute works in default, a criminal offence may be committed by any subsequent attempt to do the works, by the person served, unless he can show that it was necessary in order to obviate danger towards the occupiers.

Appeal against Repairs Notice. Appeal lies, at the instigation of the person served with, or anyone aggrieved by the service of the notice, to the county court (1985, s.191). The appeal must be lodged within 21 days of service. Once the appeal has been lodged, then the notice does not become operative until the time allowed on the final determination of the appeal or 21 days after the withdrawal of an appeal (1985, s.193). The county court has power to confirm the notice, to quash it or to vary it, *e.g.* by the addition or deletion of works. There is a specific ground of appeal applicable to repair of parts of a building containing flats which are outside the flat itself, that some other person ought to do or pay (in whole or part) for the cost of the works, and of course providing for notice to be served on that other person, in which case the court can also vary the notice to achieve this effect, or make such a cost-allocation order (1985, s.191(3A)). It is also a specific ground of appeal that a demolition order or closing order would have been a more satisfactory course of action. If the judge decides to allow the appeal on this basis, then the authority may ask him to include in his judgment a specific finding as to the most satisfactory course of action, and the judge is bound to comply with this request. 12.23

(ii) *Closing and Demolition orders*

Closing Orders. A closing order may be made where an authority are of the opinion that this is the most satisfactory course of action (12.16) for an unfit dwelling-house, house in multiple occupation or building (1985, s.264). The order is to be served on any owner of the premises (12.18) and every mortgagee whom it is reasonably practical to ascertain (1985, s.268). 12.24

Effect of Closing Order. The order prohibits the use of the premises for any purpose other than a purpose approved (12.27) by the local 12.25

authority (1985, s.267), and by necessary construction of the provisions this cannot, of course, include use for human habitation. The order will become operative 21 days after service, unless there is an appeal (12.37), in which case the order will become operative on the final determination of the appeal (1985, s.268). Use of the premises in contravention of the closing order may constitute a criminal offence (1985, s.277).

12.26   **Protection, Rehousing and Compensation.** Tenants in premises the subject of a closing order will lose their Housing Act 1988 and Rent Act 1977 protection (1985, s.276), but they, and any owner-occupier, will gain rights to rehousing (12.100-12.104) and to compensation (12.105-12.112). The fact that statutory protection has been lifted does not mean that the landlord can recover possession without terminating the contractual tenancy (1.39-1.50; *Aslan* v. *Murphy* (1989).

12.27   **Non-Residential Use and Revocation.** No express provision is made for seeking the approval of the local authority to use the premises for a particular (non-residential) purpose (12.25): such approval may be granted on the issue of the closing order, or may be granted later. The authority are not unreasonably to withhold consent to a particular use (1985, s.267), and a person aggrieved by the withholding of such a consent may appeal to the county court against the refusal within 21 days of the refusal (1985, s.267). Application may also be made for revocation of the closing order, in whole or in part, on the ground that the premises have again been rendered wholly or partially fit for human habitation (1985, s.278(1)). Refusal of such revocation may also be appealed (1985, s.278(2)), though not by anyone still in occupation under a tenancy of which there is less than three years to run (1985, s.278(3)), which will include a periodic tenant, such as a weekly or monthly tenant.

12.28   **Substitution of Demolition Order.** At any time after a closing order has been made on a house (but not a flat), the authority may revoke it and substitute a demolition order: this might occur if houses in a terrace have been closed individually, but not demolished because of the support they provide to houses not yet closed, and the last house has itself now been closed or ordered to be demolished, so that the need for support has gone (1985, s.279). If the authority do substitute a demolition order for a closing order, then the same consequences follow as if they had imposed a demolition order in the first place (12.29-12.32), although time for appeal (12.37) will run from the date of substitution a demolition order, not from the original imposition of the closing order.

Demolition Orders. As with a closing order, a demolition order may be made where an authority or of the opinion that this is the most satisfactory course of action (12.16) for an unfit dwelling-house, house in multiple occupation or building (1985, s.265). The order is to be served on any owner of the premises (12.18) and every mortgagee whom it is reasonably practical to ascertain (1985, s.268).   12.29

Effect of Demolition Order. Unless there is an appeal against a demolition order (12.37), the order becomes operative 21 days after service (1985, s.268). However, the order itself will specify a time within which the building is to be vacated, which is to be not less than 28 days after the order becomes operative, and a time within which it is to be demolished, which is to be within six weeks of the premises being vacated, or such longer period as the authority may specify (1985, s.267). Once the order has become operative, the authority are bound to serve on any occupier in the premises a notice which states the effect of the order, specifies the date by which the building is to be vacated, and requires the occupier to quit within 28 days of service of this notice (1985, s.270).   12.30

Protection, Rehousing and Compensation. Once a tenant is obliged to quit, he loses his Housing Act 1988 and Rent Act protection (1985, s.270), although he, and any owner-occupier, will, again, be entitled to rehousing (12.100-12.104) and to compensation (12.105-12.112). Entry into occupation of the premises after the order has become operative is a criminal offence (1985, s.270).   12.31

Ancillary Provisions. Not only can the landlord seek possession of the premises from an occupier, but so also can the local authority (1985, s.270). The authority have power to cleanse the building of vermin before demolition, should it appear to be necessary (1985, s.273). If the owner does not proceed to demolish the building, the authority may themselves do so in default (1985, s.271), and recover their costs of so doing.   12.32

Substitution of Closing Order and Revocation. If, after a demolition order has become operative, but before the house is demolished, the house becomes a listed building under the Planning (Listed Buildings and Conservation Areas) Act 1990, s.1, the authority are to substitute a   12.33

closing order (1985, s.304). An owner, or anyone else who appears to the authority to be in a position to put such a proposal into practice, may also cause demolition to be deferred, to provide an opportunity for the premises to be reconstructed, enlarged or improved in such a way as to provide one or more houses fit for human habitation (1985, s.274). If the works are completed to the authority's satisfaction, the demolition order is then determined.

12.34   **Purchase Notice.** In place of either demolition or closing order, the authority may serve a purchase notice, if it appears to them that the premises are, or can be, rendered capable of providing accommodation which is adequate for the time being (1985, s.300). They cannot purchase premises which are a listed building (1985, s.300(5), see also 12.33). These provisions cannot be used when the premises are a flat, although the authority may purchase a whole building containing flats, if an order has been made on the building.

12.35   **Effect of Purchase Notice.** The purchase notice becomes operative 21 days after service, unless there is an appeal (12.37), in which case it will become operative on the final determination of the appeal (1985, s.300(2)). If the owner will not agree to sell the house to the authority, it may, with government consent, compulsorily purchase it (1985, s.300(3)). Compensation will be available to owner-occupiers, tenants or other occupiers when they are actually moved (12.103-12.111, but see 1973, s.41), at which point they will also acquire rights to rehousing (12.100-12.104). During the intervening period, Housing Act protection is lost (1988, s.1 and Sched. 1, para. 12) and so is Rent Act protection (Rent Act 1977, ss.14, 19), but it would seem that occupiers do not become secure tenants (1985, s.79 and Sched. 1, para. 3: 3.14(*d*)).

12.36   **Use for Time Being.** It is implicit in the provisions that the standard to which the property is to be maintained for the time being is lower than that of fitness for human habitation, and the provisions of section 8 of the Landlord and Tenant Act 1985 (11.18-11.20) are expressly stated not to apply (1985, s.302). The purpose of the power is to do no more than provide temporary accommodation: the power cannot be used to add to the authority's permanent housing stock (*Victoria Square Property Co. Ltd.* v. *Southwark L.B.C.*, 1977). An authority might wish to use this power in order to turn the house over for a period to one of the number of short-life housing associations or organisations whose specific purpose is the retention in use of housing eventually to be demolished or improved until it actually is to be demolished or

improved. The provisons of the Environmental Protection Act (Chapter
13) will, however continue to apply, and the authority must prevent the
property from becoming a statutory nuisance as long as it remains in use
(*Salford City Council* v. *McNally*, 1975).

Appeals. A demolition order, closing order, or purchase notice can be   12.37
appealed. The appeal must be lodged within 21 days of service of the
appropriate notice, and pending the appeal, the authority are to carry out
no action in relation to the notice (1985, s.269). A tenant may not appeal
if he is in occupation under a lease with less than three years to run, *e.g.*
a periodic tenant (1985, s.269(2)), although in the rare circumstances
when a challenge can be made on principles of administrative law
(10.61), such a tenant may seek a judicial review of the authority's
decision (*R.* v. *Maldon D.C., ex p. Fisher*, 1986). An appeal lies to the
county court, which has power to confirm, quash, or vary the notice or
order (1985, s.269(3)). It is a specific ground of appeal that an
alternative course of action, *i.e.* repair or demolition in the case of a
closing order, and repair or closure in the case of a demolition order,
would have been a more satisfactory course of action (12.16). If the
judge decides to allow the appeal on this basis, then the authority may
ask him to include in his judgment a specific finding as to the most
satisfactory course of action, and the judge is bound to comply with this
request.

(iii) *Ancillary provisions*

Powers of Entry, Offences and Other Orders. The Act contains fur-   12.38
ther, related powers: (*a*) permitting authorities to enter premises (s.319);
(*b*) creating additional offences of obstruction of authorities or, in some
circumstances, persons served with notice requiring works (ss.315, 320);
and (*c*) granting the county court power to make orders affecting or
altering the rights of persons affected, or who may be affected, by local
authority action under the Act (ss.317-318).

2. *Serious Disrepair*

Prevention of Unfitness. Where an authority are satisfied that, al-   12.39
though a dwelling-house or house in multiple occupation are not unfit
for human habitation, substantial repairs are required to bring them up
to a reasonable standard, they may also serve a repairs notice (1985,
s.190(1)). They may also serve a notice in relation to a building
containing a flat where works are necessary to a part of the building

outside the flat where they are satisfied that the works are necessary to bring the flat up to a reasonable standard (1985, s.190(1A)). The purpose of this provision is to prevent housing becoming unfit (*Hillbank Properties Ltd.* v. *Hackney L.B.C.*, 1978). Such a notice cannot be served, except on a house in multiple occupation, unless there is an "occupying tenant," *i.e.* someone who is not an owner-occupier who is a tenant, a statutory tenant (5.12), a restricted contract occupier (6.04) or an agricultural occupier (4.06, 5.24) (1985, s.207) or the premises are in a renewal area (12.91).

12.40   **Notice.** The notice is served upon the person having control of the premises, or alternatively in the case of a house in multiple occupation the manager, and others with a relevant interest in them (12.18). It must allow a minimum of 28 days for commencement of the works and a reasonable time for completion. It must specify the works required, but those works cannot include works of internal decorative repair. In all other respects, the provisions governing the service of such a notice are the same as those governing an unfitness repairs notice, including the power of the local authority to execute works in default and the offence of non-compliance (12.22).

12.41   **Reasonable Expense?** Although not specified in the legislation it has been held that such a notice should only be served if the works could be executed at a reasonable expense (*Hillbank Properties Ltd.* v. *Hackney L.B.C.*, 1978). In this latter respect, however, it would seem that a county court on appeal can take a much broader, social view of what constitutes reasonable expense (*Kenny* v. *Kingston-upon-Thames Royal L.B.C.*, 1985), and given the repeal of this requirement in relation to unfit premises (12.16) it remains to be seen whether the courts adopt instead the broader requirements set out in the Secretary of State's Guidance.

3. *Interference with Personal Comfort*

12.42   **Complaint of Occupying Tenant.** Where an authority are satisfied that premises are in such a state of disrepair that, although they are not unfit, the condition is such as materially to interfere with the comfort of an "occupying tenant," (12.39) they may also serve a repairs notice (1985, s.191). All of the remarks made in the last paragraph apply in relation to a notice under this provision. Such a notice can either be served on the authority's own initiative or on the complaint to the authority of an "occupying tenant." It is also limited in the same way, to dwelling-houses and flats where there is an occupying tenant or to a renewal area.

4. *Redevelopment and Improvement by Owners*

Proposals by Owners. The Act also contains provisions permitting the submission of proposals: (*a*) for the redevelopment of property; or (*b*) for the improvement of property (1985, ss.308,310). If accepted by the authority, a redevelopment scheme prevents any action under the provisions considered thus far, or under the clearance area provisions considered below. If accepted by the authority, an improvement scheme prevents action to under the procedures to close, demolish or purchase the premises considered above (12.24-12.38), or the clearance area provisions considered below. Neither set of provisions is available when a demolition order has already become operative (12.30), or if the property is in a clearance area in respect of which there is already a confirmed compulsory purchase order (12.47, (1985, s.310). Note, however, the alternative provisions in the case of an operative demolition order (12.33).   12.43

5. *Clearance Areas*

Decline of Use. Clearance areas were once the principal means of dealing with large sections of unfit housing. Today, improvement is more probable, and, although no longer described as a "last resort" (D.O.E. Circular No. 13/75), clearance is unlikely to be the most viable option in many cases. In outline, the clearance area provisions operate by: (*a*) declaration of clearance area; (*b*) compulsory purchase proceedings to enable the local authority to acquire property not already in their ownership; (*c*) demolition. Provisions is also made for temporary user pending demolition (12.49).   12.44

Pre-Conditions. The preconditions for declaration of a clearance area are: 12.45
  (*a*) Unfitness. The authority are satisfied that "residential buildings," *i.e.* dwelling-houses, houses in multiple occupation and buildings containing one or more flats in the area are unfit for human habitation; or
  (*b*) Bad Arrangement. The authority are satisfied that residential buildings in the area are dangerous or injurious to the health of inhabitants, by reason of their bad arrangement, or the narrowness or bad arrangement of the streets; and

(*c*) **Non-Residential Buildings.** The authority are satisfied that any other buildings in the area are also dangerous or injurious to the health of inhabitants, for the same reasons; and

(*d*) **Demolition the Most Satisfactory Course.** The authority are satisfied that the most satisfactory course of action having regard to the Secretary of State's Code of Guidance (see 12.16) is demolition of all the buildings in the area; and

(*e*) **Representations.** The authority have considered the representations made to them following the consultation they are required to carry out with those with an interest in the buildings and the occupiers of any residential buildings; and

(*f*) **Alternative Accommodation.** The authority are satisfied that they can provide or secure alternative accommodation for those displaced prior to demolition; and

(*g*) **Resources.** The authority are satisfied that they have enough resources to carry out the clearance programme (1985, s.289).

12.46   **Compulsory Purchase.** The principal stage in the clearance procedure is compulsory purchase (1985, s.290). The authority are entitled not only to seek to purchase the houses and other buildings in the area, but also any land (including houses and other buildings) surrounded by the area, or adjoining the area, which is necessary in order to acquire a cleared area of convenient shape, or in order satisfactorily to develop the area (1985, s.290(2)). They may include in the proposals any land which they already themselves own, which qualifies either under the last paragraph, or under this (1985, s.293).

12.47   **Need for Confirmation.** In normal circumstances, there will need to be government approval for the compulsory purchase, and this will mean that an inquiry will be held into the proposals. At any time before the compulsory purchase order is confirmed, application can be made for the exclusion of land from the order on the ground that the owner will himself execute the demolition, and the authority do not, in those circumstances, actually need the land for the purpose of redevelopment of the area (1985, s.292).

12.48   **Protection, Rehousing and Compensation.** Tenants and owner-occupiers who are displaced by the programme will be entitled to rehousing (12.100-12.104) and to compensation (12.105-12.112). Tenants will lose the status of assured tenant under the 1988 Act (1988, s.1 and Sched. 1, para. 12) once the authority become their landlord, and their Rent Act protection, (1977, ss.14, 19) but, it would seem, will not become secure tenants (3.14(*d*) and 1985, s.79 and Sched. 1, para. 3).

Demolition. Once the order has been confirmed, the authority's main   12.49
obligation is to demolish all the buildings on the land, and either sell or
let the land for redevelopment or themselves redevelop the land (1985,
s.291). But demolition only follows "as soon as may be," an extremely
vague phrase: commonly, clearance area land is left untreated for many
years. The authority may postpone demolition and retain the housing in
use, if satisfied that the houses are, or can be rendered, capable of
providing accommodation "at a standard which is adequate for the time
being" (*cf.* 12.34; 1985, s.301). This is implicitly a standard that is
lower than that of fitness for human habitation, and section 8 of the
Landlord and Tenant Act 1985 (11.18-11.20) is expressly excluded.
However, the provisions of the Environmental Protection Act will
continue to apply (Chapter 13), so that the authority must prevent the
property from becoming a statutory nuisance so long as it remains in use
(*Salford City Council* v. *McNally*, 1975).

6. *Obstructive Buildings*

Dangerous or Injurious to Health. The local authority also enjoy   12.50
powers in relation to "obstructive buildings," defined as a building
which "by reason only of its contact with, or proximity to, other
buildings, is dangerous or injurious to health" (1985, s.283). Note that
this power extends beyond houses to any building, of course including
houses, and that the criterion is danger of injury to health (13.07). The
procedure is very similar to that which used to lead to a demolition
order. Thus the system of a time-and-place notice at which all the owner
of the building is entitled to be heard is retained. Not until this has taken
place can the authority proceed to a demolition order, with right of
appeal. (1985, ss.284, 285). However, the proceedings cannot be used
against the property of statutory undertakers (*e.g.* gas, electricity or
water suppliers), nor can it be used against the property of any local
authority (1985, s.283).

Ancillary Provisions. Tenants lose their Housing Act 1988 and Rent   12.51
Act security (1985, s.286), but they and owner-occupiers will acquire
rights to rehousing (12.100-12.104) and to compensation (12.105-
12.112). In addition, an owner can serve on the authority a purchase
notice, so that the authorty buy the property and carry out the demolition
themselves as owners, instead of by way of requiring the owner to
demolish, and this works in default (1985, s.287). A criminal offence

may be committed by entry into occupation after the demolition order
has become operative (1985, s.286).

7. *Grants and Group Repair Schemes*

12.52   **Need to Check Current Regulations.** The 1989 Act, Part VIII
introduced a new scheme of grants for improvement and repair of
dwellings. Two of the main innovations of the Act were the inclusion of
means-testing for eligibility for grant aid and the new group repair
scheme (12.85). The question of improvements will be considered in
less detail, with the intention of outlining what is available, and to
whom, under Part VIII of the 1989 Act. The provisions are of
considerable technicality, which is exacerbated by regular revision of
financial matters. It is, therefore, a subject in relation to which the reader
is reminded of the need to check current regulations at time of
application.

12.53   **Constraints on Commencement of Works.** "Improvements," or
other works to a house, may involve application for permission under
the Town and Country Planning Act 1990, or may have to comply with
the Building Regulations under the Building Act 1984 (in London, with
the London Building Acts). Further, when the occupier is a leaseholder
or tenant, the permission of the landlord may be necessary; and even a
freeholder, or a leaseholder or tenant, may find that those in possession
of neighbouring land enjoy the benefit of covenants restricting what the
person wishing to carry out the improvements may do, *e.g.* if the
improvement were to interfere with a right of way, or of light, or of
support. As a general proposition, works for which it is intended to
apply for a grant under the 1989 Act should not have been started before
approval of application, unless there is good reason, or the grant is a
mandatory one because the property is unfit and a repairs notice has
been served (12.69) (1989, s.108).

(i) *Grants available*

12.54   **Range of Grants.** There are four main types of grants available:
   (*a*) **Renovation.** The "renovation grant" for the improvement of
repair of a dwelling or the provision of dwellings by the conversion of
a house or other building;
   (*b*) **Common Parts.** The "common parts grant" for the improvement
or repair for the common parts of a building;
   (*c*) **Disabled Facilities.** The "disabled facilities grant" for the

provision of facilities for a disabled person in a dwelling or in common parts of a building;

(*d*) H.M.O.s. The "H.M.O. grant" for the improvement or repair of a house in multiple occupation or the provision of a house in multiple occupation by conversion (see 14.12, for the definition of a house in multiple occupation, although for these purposes any part occupied as a separate dwelling is excluded: 1989, s.138) (1989, s.101).

(ii) *Applications and requirements*

Pre-Conditions. All applications for grants must be made on the pre-scribed form, and include details of the works and at least two estimates for the costs of carrying out the works (1989, s.102). Except in the case of a disabled facilities grant the application cannot be accepted unless the premises are at least ten years old (1989, s.103). 12.55

Required Interest. The applicant must also have the requisite inter-est in the property (1989, s.104). For all grants, save the common parts grant, he must either be an owner, *i.e.* be the freeholder or have a leasehold interest of at least five years, or be a tenant. A tenant cannot, however, apply for an H.M.O. grant, nor a renovation grant for the conversion of premises, and must either be required to carry out the works under the terms of his tenancy or be seeking a disabled facilities grant. For an application for a common parts grant to proceed the applicant must show that at least 75 per cent of the flats in the building are occupied by tenants (whether on long or short leases) and the application must be made either by the freeholder of the building or by 75 per cent of those tenants who have a duty to carry out, or contribute towards the costs of the works (1989, s.105). 12.56

Future Use. All applications must be accompanied by the appropriate certificate of intention as to future and/or current occupation (1989, s.106). In the case of a renovation grant or disabled facilities grant the application must be accompanied by an owner-occupation certificate, a tenant's certificate, a certificate of intended letting, or a special certificate, to cover classes to be designated by the Secretary of State. An HMO grant must be accompanied by a certificate stating that the applicant has an owner's interest and intends or has already let or licensed the dwelling for a period of not less than five years, on a tenancy which is not a long tenancy to someone other than a member of the family. An application for a common parts grant must be accompanied by a certificate which sets out the interest of the applicant 12.57

or applicants and certifies that the required proportion is occupied by occupying tenants.

12.58 **Owner-Occupation Certificate.** This certifies that the applicant has an owner's interest and that he or a member of his family intends to occupy the dwelling or flat as their main or only dwelling (*cf.* 3.13) for at least twelve months from the completion of the works (1989, s.106(2)).

12.59 **Tenant's Certificate.** This certifies that the applicant is a tenant and that he or a member of his family intend to live in the dwelling as their only or main residence (1989, s.106(3)). A tenant must also present a certificate of intended letting from his landlord, unless the authority consider is unreasonable to require one (1989, s.106(6)).

12.60 **Certificate of Intended Letting.** This certifies that the applicant has an owner's interest and intends or already has let the dwelling as a residence for a period of five years from completion of the works, on a tenancy which is not a long tenancy, to someone other than a member of his family (1989, s.106(4).

(iii) *Approval, refusal and amount of grant*

12.61 **Terms of Approval.** Authorities must, by notice in writing, approve or refuse a grant application as soon as reasonably practicable, and no later than six months after it has been made (1989, s.116). An approval must include a statement of the works eligible for grant and the amount of grant. The amount will be the costs which is the authority's opinion are properly incurred on the eligible works, together with any preliminary or ancillary services or charges (*e.g.* the cost of having plans drawn up) less any amounts deducted by the means-testing process. The Secretary of State has power to set maximum grants (1989, s.116(5)). The amount of grant may be increased in the event of either a new estimate having to be obtained or unforseen works coming to light (1989, s.116(4).

12.62 **Means-Testing.** Where the application is accompanied by an owner-occupation certificate, a tenant's certificate or a special certificate, the amount of grant is reduced in accordance with regulations which are very similar to those applied to housing benefit calculations, and which ascertain an amount which the applicant could himself finance, and by which the grant is accordingly reduced (1989, s.109). The details of the scheme are too complex and subject to change to be included here. Where the application is for a tenant's common-parts grant (12.56) special provisions apply to ascertain the proportion for which each individual tenant is liable (1989, s.111).

Amount of Grant. The means-testing provisions applicable where the application is by a landlord, are less proscribed. In deciding the amount of grant the authority should have regard to: the cost of the works; where the property is currently let, any increase in income which might be expected following the works; and if not let the expected open market rent if the property is let under a Housing Act assured tenancy (see Chapter 4); and other matters as the Secretary of State may direct (1989, s.110). The Secretary of State's directions are to be found in D.O.E. Circular No. 12/90, Annex B. The basic effect of the matters required to be taken into account is to reduce the amount of grant relative to any increased rental income. 12.63

Renovation Grants. Approval of an application for a renovation grant by an owner-occupier or tenant is *mandatory* where the dwelling is not fit for human habitation (12.12) and the relevant works, being the most satisfactory course of action, will make the dwelling fit (1989, s.112). Where the application is by a landlord the approval is mandatory where completion of the relevant works is required to comply with a repairs notice under 1985, ss.198 or 190 (12.17, 12.39). Mandatory approval is also extended to owner-occupier's applications where a section 190 notice has been served. If the works go beyond that which is required to make the premises fit or are other than those that will make it fit the authority *may* approve them if they are for one of the following purposes: 12.64

(*a*) to put the dwelling in reasonable repair;

(*b*) to provide the dwelling by the conversion of a house or other building;

(*c*) to provide adequate thermal insulation;

(*d*) to provide adequate facilities for space heating;

(*e*) to provide satisfactory internal arrangements;

(*f*) to ensure the building complies with requirements as to construction and physical condition specified by the Secretary of State;

(*g*) to ensure there is compliance with any requirements specified as to the provision and condition or services and amenities. In deciding whether to approve the grant the authority must have regard to the expected life of the building. Additionally, in the case of a landlord's application, if the works are for the purpose of rendering the premises fit for human habitation (1989, s.115).

12.65   **Common Parts Grant.** An application for a common parts grant by a landlord will be *mandatory* if it is made in order to comply with a notice served under section 198 or 190 of the 1985 Act (12.17, 12.39) (1989, s.113). In addition a landlord's or tenant's application may be approved if it is for any of the purposes (*a*) and (*c*) to (*g*) set above in relation to renovation grants or it is to meet any of the requirements for fitness of a building set out in section 604 of the 1985 Act (12.13) (1989, s.115).

12.66   **Disabled Facilities Grant.** A disabled facilities grant may not be approved unless the authority are satisfied that the works are necessary and appropriate to meet the needs of the disabled occupant; and that it is reasonable and practicable to carry out the works having regard to the age of the condition or building (1989, s.114(1)). Applications should be assessed in conjuction with the social services authority. Applications are *mandatory* if they are for one or more of the following purposes:
   (*a*) facilitating access by the disabled occupant to and from the premises;
   (*b*) facilitating access by the disabled occupant to a room used or usable as the principal family room;
   (*c*) facilitating access to, or providing, a room used or usable for sleeping;
   (*d*) facilitating access to, or providing, a room in which there is a lavatory, bath, shower or wash-hand basin, or facilitating the use of such a facility;
   (*e*) facilitating the preparation and cooking of food;
   (*f*) improving any heating system in the dwelling to meet the needs of the disabled occupant, or, if there is no existing heating system or it is unsuitable, providing a suitable system;
   (*g*) facilitating the use by the disabled occupant of a source of power, light or heat, by altering the position of access and control or providing additional means of control; and,
   (*h*) facilitating access and movement by the disabled occupant around the dwelling in order to enable him to care for a person who is normally resident in the dwelling and is in need of such care (1989, s.114(3)).

12.67   **Discretionary Grant.** Where the works do not fall within any of the above criteria, a discretionary grant may be paid where the works are required in order to make the dwelling suitable for the accommodation, welfare or employment of the disabled occupant (1989, s.114(4)).

12.68   **H.M.O. Grant.** Approval of an H.M.O. grant is *mandatory* where the application is by the landlord and the works are necessary to comply with a notice under section 189 or 190 of the 1985 Act (12.17, 12.39) or under section 352 of the 1985 Act (14.24) (1989, s.113). Approval is discretionary in the same circumstances as a renovation grant (12.64) and additionally, where the works are required in order to enable the house to meet one of the requirements set out in section 352 of the 1985 Act (14.25) (1985, s.115).

Refusal of Grant. Unless mandatory because of service of a notice, or in the case of a renovation grant mandatory under section 112 (12.64) and a repairs notice has been served, authorities must refuse applications in the following circumstances:　12.69

(*a*) where the application relates to a dwelling or house which is not fit for human habitation (12.12), and the authority are of the view that the works will not make the dwelling or house fit;

(*b*) where the works have already been completed prior to service of the notice of refusal by the authority;

(*c*) where the authority intend to serve a closing order (12.24) or demolition order (12.29) on the property within three months of the notice of refusal;

(*d*) where the authority intend to declare a clearance area, (12.44) including the property within a period of 12 months from the notice of refusal;

(*e*) if the property is of a system-built type which has been designated under Part XVI of the Housing Act 1985, and the applicant is eligible for assistance under that Act, and the relevant grant works would reinstate the property (these provisions are not considered in this book);

(*f*) where the application is for a common parts grant, if the authority are of the view that the works will not be sufficient to bring the building up to the fitness standard (12.13) (1989, s.107).

Further Grounds for Refusal. The approval of an application for grant is also prohibited in the following circumstances:　12.70

(*g*) where the works are those which will be carried out under an approved group repair scheme (12.85);

(*h*) where works fall within directions made by the Secretary of State;

(*i*) where an H.M.O. grant relates to means of escape from fire or other fire precautions, which are required to be carried out by statute (1989, s.107).

Payment of Grant. Once approved, an authority may only refuse to pay the grant in six circumstances: where the applicant ceases to be a person entitled to grant; where the applicant fails to complete the works　12.71

satisfactorily within the time allowed (12.74); where the cost of the eligible works and costs incurred on preliminary or ancillary service is less than the estimated expense; where the authority ascertain that without their knowledge the works were started before the application was approved (1989, ss.133, 134); where the works are not carried out to the satisfaction of the authority; and, where the applicant fails to provide an acceptable invoice, demand or receipt for payment for the works or for the preliminary or ancillary services and charges (1989, s.117). In such circumstances there are provisions, where appropriate, for the recovery of grant already paid (1989, s.134).

12.72   **Stage Payments.** The authority may make the payment in whole after completion of the works. Alternatively, they may make stage payments, as the work progresses, provided that no more than nine-tenths of the grant is paid before completion (1989, s.117).

(iv) *Grant conditions*

12.73   **Permitted Conditions.** Authorities may not impose any conditions on the approval or making of a grant, except those required or permitted by the statute, or those for which the Secretary of State's consent has been obtained (1989, s.116).

12.74   **Conditions as to Completion of Works.** The authority may make it a condition of the grant that the works are carried out in accordance with their specifications, *e.g.* as to materials to be used. It is a mandatory condition of all grants that the works are finished within 12 months of approval, although the authority may extend this time at their discretion (1989, s.118).

12.75   **Condition as to Availability for Letting.** Where an application for a renovation grant or a disabled facilities grant was accompanied by a certificate of intended letting it is a condition of the grant that the dwelling is either to be let or available for letting as a residence (not for a holiday, *cf.* 4.17), on a tenancy which is not a long tenancy by the owner to a person who is not connected with him or, will be occupied or available for occupation by an agricultural worker pursuance to a contract or service (disregarding any period in which neither condition is fulfilled, but the dwelling is occupied by a protected occupier under Rent (Agriculture) Act 1976 or under an assured agricultural occupancy under Housing Act 1988, Part I) (1989, s.119).

Period of Condition. The condition lasts for five years from the completion of the works. In order to ensure that the condition is fulfilled, the owner of the dwelling is liable to be served with a notice by the authority requiring him to provide a certificate of compliance. The landlord has 21 days in which to reply. In addition, any tenant must furnish the owner with such information as the owner requires to enable him to comply with the authority's noticeThe condition will cease if the grant is repaid on breach of condition, or is repaid voluntarily. So long as it is in force, it binds any owner for the time being, other than a local housing authority or a registered housing association.

12.76

Repayment on Disposal - 1. Landlords. Where a renovation grant was accompanied by a certificate of intended letting (12.60), it is a condition of the grant that if the owner makes a disposal, with vacant possession within five years from the date of completion of the works, he must repay the whole grant on demand (1989, s.120). If the sale is not with vacant possession, repayment is reduced by one-fifth for each complete year. The condition applies not only to the initial recipient of the grant but to subsequent owners. In most cases, however, subsequent owners will not be bound by the condition, since the condition ceases to have force once any demand for repayment is satisfied or the grant is repaid voluntarily. The condition only applies to disposals of the freehold or on a long lease and certain disposals, *e.g.* to members of the family, and under the Matrimonial Causes Act 1973 (9.12) are exempt.

12.77

Repayment on Disposal - 2. Owner-Occupiers. Where an application for a renovation grant was accompanied by a certificate of owner-occupation (12.58); it is a condition of the grant that the owner must repay the grant if there is a disposal of the dwelling by the owner, within three years of completion of the works (1989, s.121). The condition applies not only to the original recipient but to subsequent ownersThe condition remains in force for the three years, unless repaid to satisfy the condition or repaid voluntarily. As with landlords, the disposal must be of the freehold or on a long lease, and certain disposals are exempt. On an exempt disposal the condition will lapse. The authority may also waive the demand for repayment where there is a relevant disposal by an elderly or infirm owner who is moving into sheltered accommodation or a residential care home.

12.78

Conditions On H.M.O. Grant. Three conditions are imposed on H.M.O. grants:
(i) That throughout the five-year period from completion of the works

12.79

the house will be residentially occupied or available for occupation under tenancies or licences by persons who are not connected with the owner.

(ii) A condition requiring the provision of information, when demanded, similar to that for availability for letting (12.76).

(iii) That if the owner makes a disposal, which is not exempt, within five years from the date of completion of the works he shall repay the grant on demand (1989, s.122).

12.80   **Condition for Repayment of Landlord's Common Parts Grant.** Where the applicant for a landlord's common parts grant, or any successor, disposes of the freehold or on a long lease of the building within five years, it is a condition that he repays the grant on demand to the authority. Certain disposals are exempt. The condition will be discharged by repayment under this section or by voluntary repayment (1989, s.123).

12.81   **Voluntary Repayment.** An owner or mortgagee entitled to exercise the power of sale can voluntarily repay the grant. On such a repayment all grant conditions cease to have effect (1989, s.125).

12.82   **Repayment for Breach.** For each condition there is provision for the repayment of the grant, with interest, on breach. There is generally no reduction for "years of compliance."

(v) *Minor works assistance*

12.83   **Meaning of Minor Works.** In addition to the principal grants there is a wholly discrete "grant" for "minor works" (1989, s.131). Assistance may be granted for five types of work:

(*a*) the provision or improvement of thermal insulation;

(*b*) the carrying out of works or repair to a dwelling in a clearance area (12.44) or which the authority intend to include in a clearance area within the next twelve months;

(*c*) the carrying out of repair, improvement or adaptation for an elderly tenant or owner;

(*d*) the carrying out of adaptation works for an elderly person who is to be resident in a dwelling but is not the owner or tenant;

(*e*) any other purpose specified by the Secretary of State.

12.84   **Assistance.** Assistance may be by way of grant or by provision of materials. The amount of assistance is cash limited to £1,000. This limit cannot be circumvented by several applications, as there is an overall limit of £3,000 in three years for one dwelling. If the works are already included in those for which a main grant or group repair (12.85) has already been approved, they cannot be included for minor works assistance. Applications must be in writing and contain certain prescribed information. Eligibility is governed by the Secretary of State, he has used this power to limit availability to applicants who (S.I. 1990 No. 338):

(*a*) are wholly or mainly resident in the dwelling; and,

(*b*) have a sole or joint owner's interest in, or are a sole or joint tenant of, the dwelling; and

(*c*) are (or whose spouse, or person they live with as husband and wife, is) in receipt of Income Support, Housing Benefit, Community Charge Benefit or Family Credit; and,

(*d*) if the works are for the improvement, adaptation, or repair of the home of an elderly owner or tenant, are 60 years old or more.

(vi) *Group Repair Schemes*

"Enveloping." Under the 1985 Act where a local authority had declared a housing action area, one of the possible courses of action open to them was the use of what was known as "enveloping." This type of action, where external works are carried out to a linked group of houses, has now been extended and codified in the 1989 Act. It is included in the provisions relating to grants, since unlike under the 1985 Act, participants will generally have to pay for works under the scheme, unless eligible for financial assistance. As defined by the 1989 Act a group repair scheme is one drawn up by the local housing authority, that has the approval of the Secretary of State, under which the authority obtain the consent of the participants to carry out external works (*i.e.* those to parts of the building open to the elements and to *e.g.* boundary walls; 1989, s.128(6)) to qualifying buildings which will bring the exterior of the building into reasonable repair (1989, s.127(1)).   12.85

Criteria and Pre-Conditions. The Secretary of State may approve specific schemes or generally. The criteria for general approvals are set out in D.O.E. Circular 12/90, Annex B, Section 5. Participants in group repair schemes are divided into two groups (1989, s.127(3), (4)): assisted and unassisted participants. Assisted participants are all those who have an owner's interest (12.56) in a dwelling or other premises comprised in a building within the scheme, who are not a "public sector landlords." Such public sector landlords may participate as unassisted   12.86

participants. In addition, assisted participants must fulfil three further requirements (1989, s.127(5)):

(*a*) in relation to the dwelling or other premises, they must be able to give possession of the part of the building to which it is proposed to carry out the works, and they must have the consent of the occupier of that part of the building to the carrying out of the works;

(*b*) if their interest is in a dwelling they must provide either an owner-occupier's certificate (12.58) or a certificate of intended letting (12.60);

(*c*) if their interest is in an H.M.O., and the owner is not a charity, then an H.M.O. certificate must be provided (12.57).

12.87   **Qualifying Buildings.** A group repair scheme only applies to qualifying buildings. To constitute a qualifying building the whole or part of the exterior of the building must be out of reasonable repair, and the lack of reasonable repair must affect at least 75 per cent of the building (1989, s.128(1)). One of the qualifying buildings within each scheme must be a "primary building," *i.e.* one comprising four or more separate houses. All other qualifying buildings must comprise at least one house and be contiguous or adjacent to the primary building. Other qualifying buildings must also have an exterior which is not in reasonable repair and is in need of works similar to those required to the exterior of the primary building. Carrying out the works to the building and the primary building at the same time must also be the most effective way of securing the repair of each of them (1989, s.128). There are complex provisions relating to the definition of building and house, the effect of which is to exclude purpose-built blocks of flats from group repair schemes (1989, s.128). Unless the exterior of a building is substantially free from rising or penetrating damp it is not to be regarded as in reasonable repair (1989, s.128(8)), but reasonable repair is not otherwise defined.

12.88   **Liability for Costs and Contributions.** Once a participant has signalled his consent to the works in the scheme, he becomes liable to contribute towards the costs of the works to the property in which he has an interest. Where the property is a house which has subsequently been divided into flats, so that there is more than one person with an owner's interest in it, then the cost of the works is to be apportioned between them as the owners decide, or in default of agreement, between them equally. Unassisted participants are to contribute 100 per cent of the costs. An assisted participant, whose interest is not in a house or flat, must contribute 25 per cent of the cost if the building is in a renewal area (12.91) and otherwise 50 per cent. Where the assisted participant has an owner's interest in a house or flat, the contribution is to be between 0 and 25 percent of the cost if the premises are in a renewal area (12.91), and otherwise between 0 and 50 per cent. In determining the exact level of contribution the authority must have regard to how the means and income testing provisions would have applied if the participant has been seeking a renovation or HMO grant (12.62), and to guidance given by the Secretary of State (1989, s. 129).

Prohibition on Works. Unless there is someone who has given their 12.89 consent to the scheme in relation to any house, flat, or other premises within a building, and is therefore liable to make a contribution, no works can be carried out to that part of the building (1989, s.129(7). This prohibition is, however, lifted:
 (*a*) if the works are to a part of a building for which there is no person eligible to participate, or that person cannot be ascertained or,
 (*b*) if the works are to a part of the building, and the owner, while consenting to the works, refuses to consent to the scheme, and thereby become liable for the costs *and,* the works are required in order satisfactorily to complete the works to another part of the building for which there is a person liable to contribute (1989, s.129(9)).

Condition of Repayment on Disposal. For a period of three years 12.90 from completion of the works, each assisted participant is subject to a condition of repayment of the balance of the costs of the works, if he makes a disposal, which operates similarly to conditions for other grants (12.77; 1989, s.130). It does not, however, bind subsequent owners and the authority may demand a reduced repayment subject to a minimum of one-third.

8. *Renewal Areas*

Area Action. There is now only one class of area in which an authority 12.91 may take action for improvement: the renewal area. The provisions governing the declaration of and powers and duties in renewal areas are to be found in Local Government and Housing Act 1989, Part VII.

Declaration. The starting-point for the declaration of a renewal area is 12.92 a "report" requested by the local housing authority (1989, s.89). The report may include any matters which the authority consider relevant and in particular must include particulars of the following matters:
 (*a*) Living Conditions. The living conditions in the area concerned;
 (*b*) Improvement. The ways in which conditions may be improved

(whether by the declaration of a renewal area or otherwise);

(*c*) **Powers.** The powers available to the authority if the area is declared;

(*d*) **Proposals.** The authority's detailed proposals for the exercise of those powers during the period that the area will be a renewal area;

(*e*) **Costs.** The costs of the proposals;

(*f*) **Resources.** The financial resources available, or likely to be available, to the authority for implementing the proposal.

The report must contain a reasoned recommendation as to whether a renewal area should be declared.

12.93 **Guidance.** A renewal area may be declared if the authority are satisfied, on the basis of the report, that the living conditions in an area within their district, which consists primarily of housing accommodation, are unsatisfactory and can most effectively be dealt with by declaring a renewal area (1989, s.89(1)). In reaching this decision the authority must have regard to the guidance issued by the Secretary of State, which is to be found in D.O.E. Circular 6/90, Annex B. The guidance recommends a method known as Neighbourhood Renewal Assessment which "provides a thorough and systematic appraisal technique for considering alternative courses of action." It involves both an economic and a socio-environmental assessment of different options.

12.94 **Prior Publicity.** Prior to declaration the authority must also publicise any proposed declaration, in newspapers, by notices displayed in the area, and notification to each address in the area, and consider any representations made to them, providing a written explanation to the person who made the representation where it is not proposed to accept the point.

12.95 **Pre-Conditions.** A renewal area must also comply with the following conditions (1989, s.90 and D.O.E. Circular 6/90, Annex E):

(*a*) it must have a minimum of 300 dwellings;

(*b*) 75 per cent of those dwellings must be privately owned;

(*c*) the physical condition of the dwellings in the area must be such that 75 per cent are unfit (12.12) or would qualify for grant approval (12.64);

(*d*) the financial circumstances of those living in the area must be such that at least 30 per cent appear to the authority to be dependant to a significant extent on one or more of the following benefits: Housing Benefit, Unemployment Benefit, Family Credit, Income Support, or Community Charge Benefit.

Duration and Termination. The renewal area will last for 10 years   12.96
(1989, s.89(6)). It may, however, be brought to an end at an earlier date,
or have land excluded from it, by a resolution (1989, s.95). Prior and
subsequent to making such a resolution the authority must fulfil certain
requirements as to publicity, consideration of representations and
notification of the Secretary of State.

Duties and Powers. As soon as possible after making the declaration of   12.97
the renewal area the authority must publicise the declaration, set up an
advice an information service for those living and owning property in
the area who wish to carry out works to housing accommodation, and
send information regarding the declaration to the Secretary of State
(1991, s.91). As well as the duty to publicise the declaration, the
authority are under a continuing duty to bring to the attention of
residents and property-owners information about the proposed and
existing action in the area and assistance available for the carrying out
of works (1989, s.92).

Compulsory Purchase Powers. Local housing authorities may by ag-   12.98
reement or, with the consent of the Secretary of State, compulsorily
acquire land in a renewal area, which comprises premises consisting of
or including housing accomodation. The purchase must be for one of the
following objectives (1989, s.93):

(*a*) improvement or repair of premises, either by the authority or by
someone (*e.g.* a housing association) to whom they propose to dispose
of them;

(*b*) proper and effective management and use of housing
accommodation, again either by the authority themselves or by another;

(*c*) the well-being of residents in the area.

They may also compulsorily acquire any land in the area in order to
improve the amenities in the area, whether they intend to effect the
improvement themselves or dispose of the land to someone else
intending to do so (1989, s.93(4)).

Works. The authority have power to carry out works on any land they   12.99
own in the area (whether acquired under their powers of acquisition
outlined above, or not) (1989, s.93(5)). They may also assist in the
carrying out or works on any land in the area they do not own. This
assistance may take the form of grants, loans or guarantees, the
incurring expenditure for the benefit of the person assisted, the
executing the works themselves or the provision of materials (1989,
s.93(5)). No such assistance may be given, however, if grant (12.54),

group repair (12.83) or minor works assistance (12.85) is being or has been provided. The power to provide such assistance may be delegated to a housing association or other person. There are also special powers relating to extinguishing rights of ways over highways (1989, s.94) and powers of entry, together with correlative offences of obstruction, in order to survey and inspect (1989, s.97).

9. *Rehousing and Compensation*

(i) *Rehousing*

12.100　**Relationship to Homelessness.** The rights to be considered under this heading are entirely separate from , and additional to, those provided under Part III of the Housing Act 1985 (Chapter 10). Thus, for example, it is not necessary for a displaced occupant qualifying under these provisions to show also that he has a priority need for accommodation (10.09-10.14).

12.101　**Duty to Rehouse.** Unless suitable alternative residential accommodation is otherwise available, on reasonable terms, a person displaced from land in consequence of a series of public actions will be entitled to rehousing from, or arranged by, usually, the local authority (in some cases, from another public body such as a Housing Action Trust, new town corporation or the Development Board for Rural Wales) (Land Compensation Act 1973 - "1973" - s.39). The entitlement is not, however, to immediate permanent rehousing: the authority have do no more than their best, and if this means that the displaced occupant is provided with a series of short-life dwellings pending permanent rehousing, the authority will properly have discharged their duty (*R.* v. *Bristol Corporation, ex p. Hendy,* 1973).

12.102　**Pre-Conditions.** The circumstances are:
　　(*a*) displacement in consequence of compulsory purchase;
　　(*b*) displacement in consequence of a housing order or undertaking, *i.e.* a demolition order under Part IX of the Act (12.29-12.33), or a closing order under Part IX (12.24-12.28) or section 368 (14.30).
　　(*c*) displacement by an authority who have previously acquired the land, and who now decide to redevelop or improve it.

12.103　**Additional Conditions.** Displacement in consequence of improvement must be permanent displacement in order for an occupier to qualify (1973, s.39(6A)). So also must be displacement in consequence of an undertaking. An occupier claiming rehousing under (*b*) in the last paragraph must have been in occupation at the time the relevant order was made, undertaking accepted or notice served (1973, s.39(6)). An occupier claiming to be rehoused under (*a*) or (*c*) above, will not qualify unless he was in occupation when proceedings to purchase the land were commenced (1973, s.39(6)). Only a person in lawful occupation will qualify, not a trespasser, nor someone to whom permission has been given to use the property pending demolition or improvement, *i.e.* short-life user (1973, s.39(3)). The 1973 Act contains provisions enabling the local authority to advance money to a displaced owner-occupier (1973, s.41), and an owner-occupier who avails himself of this power, cannot also claim the right to rehousing (1973, s.39(4)).

Caravan Dwellers, Local Authority Tenants. Analogous rehousing provision is made for caravan dwellers displaced by the same public activities (1973, s.40). Local authority tenants may qualify under (*a*) or (*c*), but as authorities will not usually be obliged to serve a demolition or closing order on themselves (12.19), they will not normally enjoy rights to rehousing under this provision (*R.* v. *Cardiff City Council, ex p. Cross*, 1983). However, the authority will usually be obliged to offer alternative accommodation under 1985, s.84 and Sched. 3, Ground 10 (3.45), and duties under 1985, Part III will still apply (Chapter 10).

12.104

(ii) *Home loss payment*

Availability. Home loss payments will be available in the same circumstances set out in paragraph 12.102, and also in the event of permanent displacement of a housing association tenant on the carrying out of improvement to the dwelling or redevelopment of the land by the association and to those evicted following an order under Ground 10 or 10A of the Housing Act 1985 (3.45) (1973, s.29(1)). While this payment will in the circumstances set out in paragraph 12.102 normally be paid by the local authority (even where one of the other public bodies has the rehousing obligation), displacement by a housing association under this additional ground results in payment from the association. Local authority tenants will have difficulty qualifying under 12.102(b) but ought to qualify instead under 12.102(c) (*R.* v. *Corby District Council, ex p. McLean*, 1975).

12.105

Pre-Conditions. Home loss entitlement is limited to those with a legal interest in the dwelling, (*i.e.* freeholders, leaseholders, tenants), statutory tenants, those with a restricted contract, and those with a right to occupy

12.106

the dwelling under a contract of employment (1973, s.29(4)). The main limitation is that the claimant must have been in occupation of the dwelling for a minimum of one year, ending with the date of displacement (not purchase proceedings or other action, *cf.* 12.103), and that occupation was: (*a*) as or with a tenant or other person entitled to payment; (*b*) as an only or main residence; and (*c*) of the whole dwelling or a substantial part of it (1973, ss.29(2), 32(3)).

12.107   **Additional Conditions.** Where the claimant has been in occupation of different rooms in the same building, *e.g.* a series of bedsitting-rooms, he is entitled to be treated as if he had remained in one room (1973, s.32(5)). Where there are two or more persons equally entitled, *e.g.* joint tenants (1.84-1.95), they each get one equal share (1973, s.32(6)). In the case of paragraph 12.102(*a*), the claimant does not have to remain in occupation until required to leave by the authority: provided his qualifying period is fulfilled, he may leave at any time after the date when the authority were given consent to make the compulsory purchase, although not before (1973, s.29(3)). A spouse with occupancy rights in the matrimonial home under the Matrimonial Homes Act 1983 (9.23) may also claim (1973, s.29A).

12.108   **Amount.** The amount of the home loss payment, which must be claimed within six years of displacement (1973, s.32(7A)), is, in the case of an owner 10 per cent. of the market value of the interest, up to a maximum of £15000. In all other cases the amount in £1500.

(iii) *Disturbance payment*

12.109   **Availability.** This payment is available in the same circumstances as a home loss payment, set out at paragraph 12.102. It is available from the same body (12.105) (1973, s.37(1)). The claimant must have been in lawful possession of the land: in a case within 12.102(*a*) at the date when notice was first published of the intention compulsorily to purchase; within 12.102(*c*) when proceedings towards the purchase were begun; or within 12.102(*b*) at the date when the order was made, notice was served, or undertaking accepted (1973, s.37(3)). No payment is made if the claimant is entitled to compensation for the making of a closing or demolition order (12.111). Displacement in consequence of an undertaking, or the carrying out of improvement, must be permanent (1973, s.37(3A)). Where there is no absolute entitlement under these provisions, and no compensation under any other enactment, the local authority have a discretion to make a disturbance payment in any event

(1973, s.37(5)).

Amount. The amount of the disturbance payment is "the reasonable   12.110
expenses of the person entitled to the payment in removing from the
land from which he is displaced" (1973, s.38(1)). These words mean
more than mere removal costs, but include the costs of setting up in the
new home. Many local authorities purport to fix amounts for disturbance
payments, by scale, by maxima, or by limiting the matters for which
payment will be made. There is no legal authority for such an approach:
the amount may be small, or it may be large, and each case is to be
judged on its facts. A dispute may be referred to the Lands Tribunal
(1973, s. 38(4)), which is one of the few tribunals for which legal aid is
available.

(iv) *Compensation for closing and demolition orders*

Availability and Amount. Where a closing (12.24) or demolition order   12.111
(12.29) is made every owner of the premises is entitled to compensation
(1989, s.584A). The amount of compensation is determined on the day
the order is made and is the diminution in the compulsory purchase
value of the owner's interest as a result of the order being made. If a
demolition order is subsequently substituted for the closing order, then
the compensation already paid is to be deducted from that paid for the
demolition order. Where the demolition order is revoked to permit
reconstruction of the premises (12.33) or a closing order determined
because the premises are rendered fit (12.27), the recipient must, on
demand, repay the compensation to the authority (1989, s.584B). Where
the closing order is determined in relation to part only of the premises,
provision is made for the amount repayable to be apportioned.

10. *Occupier's Action*

Taking the Initiative. An occupier can specifically initiate action   12.112
where there is interference with personal comfort (12.42). Of course,
there is nothing to stop an occupier complaining about other conditions,
or seeking other classes of action from the authority. Indeed, authorities
are usually obliged to act wheresoever their information comes from,
and an authority which declined to hear or act on information, without
cause, could be compelled to take action by the courts. It is not possible
in this work to specify the circumstances in which an authority can be
so compelled by the courts, but it should be noted that public bodies
must act within the ambit of legislation, and that the courts will

intervene (using their powers of judicial review), if such authorities misunderstand or misapply the law, act in bad faith or otherwise fail to take relevant matters into account or disregard the irrelevant, or fail to take decisions in individual cases where they were obliged to do so. It is sometimes said that in such cases the authority act *ultra vires,* (outside their powers), or that they act unreasonably.

12.113   **Limits of Judicial Review.** It is imperative to bear in mind that a court (other than a court given express powers on appeal), reviewing the conduct of a public body, does not intervene because it dislikes or disagrees with a decision entrusted by Parliament to that authority, nor because its (or the applicant's) view of what is reasonable is different from that of the authority, but because the authority have acted so unreasonably that no reasonable authority, properly approaching the matter, could have acted as they have done (see also 10.61-10.63).

12.114   **Complaint to J.P.** The 1985 Act, however, does provide the occupier with one, express and additional recourse. He may complain to a justice of the peace (magistrate) either that an individual dwelling-house or house in multiple occupation or that a whole area is unfit for human habitation (1985, s.606). If the magistrate is satisfied that the complaint is correct, perhaps following a visit to the premises or area, he will in turn complain to the local authority's Medical Officer of Health or, if they have none, the proper officer of the authority. It is this officer's duty then to inspect house or area, and report to his authority (or appropriate committee). That is as far as the obligation goes. There is no sanction. The officer or committee are free to disagree with the magistrate. But the procedure is a useful way of making the authority inspect, and if the inspection satisfies them of the unfitness they will, of course, be bound to take action.

13 Disrepair Under Environmental Law

Scope. In this chapter, we are concerned with a series of powers which 13.01
are now to be found principally in the Environmental Protection Act
1990 ("1990"), which consolidated much of the law formerly contained
in the Public Health Act 1936 ("1936") and the Public Health
(Recurring Nuisances) Act 1969. We will also briefly consider some
related powers to be found in the Building Act 1984 ("1984") and in
various Public Health Acts. It should be appreciated that in relation to
housing the Environmental Protection Act does not amount to a
comprehensive or cohesive programme or policy. The provisions are not
aimed exclusively at housing. The approach of this chapter is,
accordingly, necessarily selective.

Local Authorities. Like the last chapter, and the next, we are here 13.02
concerned primarily with duties imposed on local authorities, rather than
rights as between individuals. Local authorities for these purposes are
the same authorities who have duties under the Housing Acts (12.09),
save that in the area of a Housing Action Trust (3.78) some of these
powers may be transferred to the Trust, additional to or instead of the
local authority (Housing Act 1988, s.68). Where duties arise under the
1990 Act, the Secretary of State for the Environment has power to
declare that an authority are in default of their duties, and may direct
them to carry out actions to remedy their default, or even take upon
himself their obligations (1990, Sched. 3).

Inspection. Authorities do not have a general inspection duty, as they 13.03
have under the Housing Acts (12.10), although they are specifically
obliged to inspect their districts with an eye to the performance of their
duties in relation to statutory nuisances, the main class of action with
which we shall be concerned in the present chapter (1990, s.79).
However, if the need for action is observed during the course of a
Housing Act inspection, an authority will still be obliged to take action
under the Environmental Protection Act, where appropriate. Action
under the Housing Acts and under the Environmental Protection Act is
not mutually exclusive: thus, for example, statutory nuisance procedure

is no substitute for procedure under Parts VI or IX, Housing Act 1985 (12.11-12.50; *R.* v. *Kerrier District Council, ex p. Guppy's (Bridport)*, 1985) and even though an area may be declared a clearance area (12.44-12.49), under the Housing Act 1985, Part IX, the authority will still be bound to take action under the 1936 Act if such action is called for (*Salford City Council* v. *McNally*, 1975).

13.04   **Powers of Entry, Obstruction.** Whether the purpose of the entry is in order to inspect premises, or in order to carry out works where they are entitled to do so, local authorities have a general power of entry into premises, which may be exercised at any reasonable hour (1990, Sched. 3, para. 2). At least 24 hours' notice must be given to the occupier of residential premises under this general power, although there is an additional power to apply to the magistrate's court for a warrant authorising entry, if necessary by force, which can be issued not only when entry has been sought and refused under the general power, but also when warning of a visit would defeat the purpose of the visit (1990, Sched. 3, para. 2(3), (4)). A criminal offence may be committed by the obstruction of an officer of the authority executing duties under the Acts (1990, Sched. 3, para. 3). Authorities have power to enter *unoccupied* premises, in order to prevent them being or becoming a danger to public health (Local Government (Miscellaneous Provisions) Act 1982, s.29), although they are obliged to give an owner of the premises 48 hours' notice of intention of so doing.

13.05   **Outline.** The matters with which we shall be concerned in this chapter are:

1. *Statutory nuisance*;
2. *Dangerous buildings*;
3. *Dilapidated buildings*;
4. *Fire Precautions*;
5. *Sanitary accommodation*;
6. *Drains and sewers*;
7. *Food storage*;
8. *Vermin*; and
9. *Disease*.

1. *Statutory Nuisance*

13.06   **Definition.** For the purposes of this work, a statutory nuisance means "any premises in such a state as to be prejudicial to health or a nuisance" (1990, s.79(1)). The limbs are alternative, so that statutory nuisance may be established by way of prejudice to health or nuisance.

Prejudicial to Health. Prejudicial to health is, in turn, defined as meaning "injurious or likely to cause injury to health" (1990, s.79(7)). This phrase has not been much considered by the courts, though it is clear that the most common complaint - dampness, including condensation dampness - is recognised as being capable of causing injury to health (*G.L.C.* v. *Tower Hamlets London Borough*, 1983; *Dover D.C.* v. *Farrar & Others*, 1979). The persons best equipped to determine prejudiciality to health are doctors and environmental health officers. Whether or not premises are injurious to health, although a question of fact, may be to an extent a technical question, so that magistrates cannot substitute their own opinions for those of a qualified person, unless, of course, they have cause to disbelieve their evidence (*Patel* v. *Mehtab*, 1981). There can be a statutory nuisance even although the landlord is not in breach (see Chapter 11) of any repairing obligation (*Birmingham City District Council* v. *Kelly*, 1985). 13.07

Nuisance. To qualify as a nuisance within the definition it must be shown that there is what is recognisable as a nuisance at common law (*National Coal Board* v. *Thorne*, 1976). It follows (see also 8.55) that the nuisance must emanate from one set of premises, and create an effect in another. Thus, a leaking roof may be a nuisance to the occupier of the house, but unless it is injurious to his health, it will not be a statutory nuisance. However, if the effect of the leak spreads to the next-door property, there will be a nuisance, and as such a statutory nuisance, in the leaking premises, actionable in relation to the next door house. In this connection, it should be noted that where what is occupied is a flat or a room, or anything less than a whole building, the common parts of the building will remain in the landlord's possession, and for these purposes will constitute another set of premises, *e.g.* roof, halls, stairs, corridors. To this extent, the occupier of less than a whole house is in a better position to cause action to be taken than the occupier of a whole house. It is important to define the premises which suffer the nuisance: where there was condensation throughout a block of flats, it was none the less each flat which suffered the nuisance, not the block as a whole (*Birmingham District Council* v. *McMahon*, 1987). 13.08

(i) *Abatement proceedings by authority*

Whose Responsibility? Once an authority are satisfied that there is a 13.09

statutory nuisance, or a nuisance that is likely to recur, they are obliged to take action (1990, s.80). They must serve an abatement notice on the "person responsible" for the nuisance. This is the person "by whose act, default or sufferance" the nuisance is attributable (1990, s.79(7)). If that person cannot be found, then the authority may serve the notice on either owner or occupier. However, if the abatement notice requires structural works, they can only serve the notice on the owner; and, if it is clear that there is no fault on the part of either owner or occupier, and they cannot find the person responsible to serve an abatement notice on him, they may, instead of serving an abatement notice, carry out such works themselves as they consider necessary to abate the nuisance and to prevent its recurrence.

13.10   **Owners.** Owner is not defined in the 1990 Act, although under the Public Health Act 1936, it was defined in similar terms to the person having control under the Housing Acts (12.18). It is clear that in many cases this will be the authority themselves. In such a case, they cannot serve a notice on themselves (*R*. v. *Cardiff City Council, ex p. Cross,* 1983: 12.19), although the occupier will still be able to take his own proceedings against them (13.15-13.21).

13.11   **Abatement Notice.** If the abatement can be effected without works, *e.g.* by the removal of some object causing the nuisance, the authority need do no more than require abatement of the nuisance; if works are needed, however, then the authority must specify what works they require (1990, s.80; *Millard* v. *Wastall,* 1898). The authority should allow a reasonable time for abatement, which they should state in the notice.

13.12   **Appeal Against Abatement Notice.** A person who is served with an abatement notice may appeal it to a magistrates' court within 21 days of service (1990, s.80(3)). Appeal is by way of complaint and there is a further right of appeal to the Crown Court (1990, Sched. 3). The grounds of appeal are set out in S.I. 1990 No. 2276, and include that the notice was not justified, that it should have been served on another person and that the time given to comply was not long enough. On hearing the complaint the magistrates' court may: (*a*) quash the notice; or, (*b*) vary it in favour of the appellant; or, (*c*) dismiss the appeal (S.I. 1990 No. 2276, para. 5).

13.13   **Prosecution for Non-Compliance.** If, without reasonable excuse, the abatement notice is not complied with, and any appeal is unsuccessful, the recipient may be prosecuted. If found guilty he may be fined up to level 5 on the standard scale, and one tenth of that amount for each day the the offence continues after conviction (1990, s.80(40, (5)). A nuisance is not abated just because the premises have been vacated (*Lambeth London Borough Council* v. *Stubbs*, 1980). Prosecution is a criminal proceeding, and does not lie within the residual civil jurisdiction of the magistrates' court: it should, accordingly, be commenced by information and summons, rather than by complaint (*R.* v. *Newham East Justices, ex p. Hunt*, 1976).

Works in Default. Where an abatement notice has not been complied with, the authority may, either additionally or instead of prosection, abate the nuisance themselves and carry out any necessary works (1990, s.81(3)). Any expenses incurred may be recovered from the person by whose act or default the nuisance was caused (1990, s.81(4)).   13.14

(ii) *Proceedings by occupier*

Person Aggrieved. There is a special procedure which can be used by a private individual (1990, s.82). The individual must be a "person aggrieved" by the nuisance, *i.e.* someone suffering its effects, not - as it were - a mere busybody. A person cannot be aggrieved in relation to a whole block of flats, only in relation to the flat he occupies (*Birmingham District Council* v. *McMahon*, 1987). Legal aid is not available for the prosecution of criminal offences, and is, accordingly, not available to an occupier seeking to use this provision, although limited legal advice may be available in the preparation of the case under the Legal Advice and Assistance Scheme (also known as the "Green Form Scheme") (Legal Aid Act 1974). If the person responsible appeals against any order to the Crown Court the person aggrieved will be entitled to legal aid (*R.* v. *Inner London Crown Court, ex p. Bentham*, 1988).   13.15

Local Authority Landlords. There are two circumstances in which an occupier is likely to want to use section 82: when the authority will not take action against a private landlord: and, more commonly, when the landlord is the authority themselves. It is well-established that section 82 permits proceedings against a local authority, even the authority who would otherwise be responsible for taking action (*R.* v. *Epping (Waltham Abbey) Justices, ex p. Burlinson*, 1948). Action is to be taken against the person responsible or the owner in the same way as with an abatement notice (13.09; 1990, s.82(4)).   13.16

13.17   Powers of Court. Prior to taking any proceedings under this section the occupier must give 21 days notice in writing to the proposed defendant (1990, s.82(6), (7)). Having heard the complaint the magistrates' court may do one or more of the following:

(*a*) Nuisance Order. Make a nuisance order requiring the defendant to abate the nuisance and/or execute works to prevent its recurrance (1990, s.82(2);

(*b*) Fine. Impose a fine not exceeding level five on the standard scale (1990, s.82(2));

(*c*) Prohibition of Use. If the nuisance renders the premises unfit for human habitation, prohibit the use of the premises for that purpose (1990, s.82(3));

(*d*) Works in Default. Where neither the person responsible for the nuisance, not the owner or occupier can be found, direct the local authority to do anything which the court would have ordered that person to do (1990, s.82(13)).

If without reasonable excuse, the nuisance order is not complied with further proceedings may be taken against the defaulter and he may be fined, the fine continuing on a daily basis (1990, s.82(8)).

13.18   Types of Work. It is, of course, quite clear that the works included in a nuisance order can include structural works (13.09). There is, indeed, no express limitation on what works can be ordered, and cases under the Public Health Act 1936 will be relevant in this regard. In one case (*Dover District Council* v. *Farrar and Others*, 1980), a magistrates' court ordered the installation of gas heating in place of electric heating, in premises suffering severely from condensation-dampness. The Divisional Court quashed this order, for the reason the electric heating was not being used was not that it did not work, but that the tenants could not afford to use it. It is quite clear from the case, though, that had the electric heating not worked, or had it been wholly unsuitable to eliminate such dampness even if fully and properly used by the tenants, that the order could have been regarded as a proper order, within the power of the magistrates.

13.19   Division of Responsibility - Landlord and Tenant. In another case (*G.L.C.* v. *Tower Hamlets London Borough*, 1983), the G.L.C. owned a corner flat on the ground floor of a block, but at a raised level, with three sides and the whole of its underneath open to the air, so that an exceptionally large part of the flat was exposed to the elements. Originally, the flat had an open solid fuel fire, but subsequently this was blocked up and replaced with an electric heater, itself later removed.

The flat suffered from severe condensation dampness. It was held that the flat was prejudicial to the health of the occupants, because of the dampness caused by the failure of the landlord to take necessary precautions, either by way of ventilation or insulation, or by providing any special form of heating, for a propery wholly exceptionally vulnerable to condensation. A landlord has to apply his mind to the need for ventilation, and, if need be, to insulation and heating, and must provide a combination of these factors to make a house habitable for the tenant. Once the landlord has done so, it is the tenant's responsibility to use the facilities and if the cause of continuing condensation is the tenant's unwillingness to do so, then the landlord cannot be held responsible.

Contents of Order. An order should be as detailed and as specific as possible (*Salford City Council* v. *McNally*, 1975). The court has a relatively generous discretion as regards time. Thus, although the fact that Housing Act action is to be taken, *e.g.* by way of clearance (12.44-12.48), does not exclude the court's duty to make a nuisance order (13.17), it may influence the time allowed for compliance (*Nottingham Corporation* v. *Newton*, 1974). There is also a discretion as to extent of works: if the premises are shortly to be demolished, they may order less works than otherwise, provided what they order is sufficient to abate the nuisance for the period for which the property is likely to remain in use (*Lambeth London Borough Council* v. *Stubbs*, 1980; *Coventry City Council* v. *Doyle*, 1981). However, the fact that the premises are to be vacated does not mean that the nuisance will be abated, for in the absence of an order under the next paragraph, the premises might yet be used again (*Lambeth London Borough Council* v. *Stubbs*, 1980).

13.20

Expenses. The court has a discretion (1990, s.92(12)) to order a defendant to pay the person bringing the proceedings an amount it considers reasonably sufficient to compensate him, for any expenses (including legal expenses) properly incurred in the proceedings, but only if the alleged nuisance existed at the date of making the complaint.

13.21

(iii) *Urgent statutory nuisances*

Unreasonable Delay. In view of the length of time which normal court proceedings can take, the local authority also have power to use a special, speedy procedure, when it appears to them that premises are in such a defective state as to be a statutory nuisance, and that there would

13.22

be unreasonable delay were the abatement procedure to be used (1984, s.76). In one case (*Celcrest Properties Ltd.* v. *Hastings B.C.*, 1979), the difference between four weeks under one of the Public Health Acts, and 11-12 weeks under normal abatement procedure, was upheld as an unreasonable delay, justifying use of the speedy procedure.

13.23   **Notice and Counter-Notice.** The procedure commences with a notice of intent served by the authority on the same person as would an abatement notice be served (13.09). The notice has to state what works the authority intend to execute. The notice must be served at least nine days before commencement of works. During the seven days following service, the person served is entitled to serve on the authority a counter-notice, stating that he intends himself to remedy the defects which have been specified by the authority. The authority are then debarred from using this speedy procedure, unless the person who has served the counter-notice does not commence or progress with the works within what seems to the authority to be a reasonable time.

13.24   **Claim by Authority.** The owner's remedy against use of this procedure is to do nothing: after the works have been completed, the authority will issue civil proceedings (generally in the county court), to recover their expenses; it is a defence to such a claim to show that no unreasonable delay would have flowed from use of the abatement procedure, and if this defence is upheld, the authority recover none of their expenditure, even although the owner will have benefitted to the extent of the works executed. This proves a powerful disincentive to use of this procedure by authorities. The owner may also defend a claim for the authority's expenses if he served a counter-notice (13.23), but the authority entered to do works on the ground of unreasonable time, by proving to the court that the time taken to start or complete the works was not unreasonable.

13.25   **Building Preservation Order.** The 1984 Act procedure is not available if the works would contravene a building preservation order under the Planning (Listed Buildings and Conservation Areas) Act 1990 designed for the protection of buildings of special historic or architectural interest. But the 1984 Act procedure can be used, even although the works to be carried out could have been ordered by way of repairs notice under section 189 of the Housing Act 1985 (12.17-12.23).

(iv) *Appeals*

13.26   **Courts.** Appeal lies from the magistrates' court to the Crown Court, although in certain circumstances it is possible for the appeal (on a point of jurisdiction) to lie by way of proceedings in the Divisional Court. Appeal lies from both a county court and the High Court to the Court of Appeal.

2. *Dangerous Buildings*

Two Procedures. A dangerous building is a building which is in such a condition, or is used to carry such a load, that is dangerous (1984, s.77). Authorities have two means of dealing with dangerous buildings: by normal procedure, and by urgent procedure. 13.27

Normal Procedure. The normal procedure is by way of application by the authority to the magistrates' court, for an order requiring the owner (13.10), at his own election, either to carry out works to obviate the danger, or to demolish the building or the dangerous part of the building (1984, s.77). Works to obviate the danger means something in the nature of a permanent or semi-permanent remedy, rather than shoring it up (*London County Council* v. *Jones*, 1912), or securing the doors against entry and excluding the tenants (*Holme* v. *Crosby Corporation*, 1949). Though the magistrates does not have to specify the exact works needed, he will need to specify a time for compliance, for no offence of non-compliance will arise until the time allowed has elapsed, nor will the authority acquire their rights to carry out the works in default (1984, s.77). No provision is made for the removal, rehousing or compensating of tenants. 13.28

Urgent Procedure. The urgent procedure is similar to that available in relation to urgent statutory nuisances (13.22-13.25). However, there is no provision for counter-notice (13.23), and the authority need only serve notice of intention if it is reasonably practicable to do so (1984, s.78). It is a defence to the authority's proceedings to recover their costs, to show that the normal procedure (13.28) could reasonably have been used, and if this defence is successful, then again (*cf.* 13.24) the authority recover no part of their costs. There is no provision for removal, rehousing or compensation of tenants. 13.29

3. *Dilapidated Buildings*

Procedure. For these purposes, a dilapidated building is one which is seriously detrimental to the amenities of the neighbourhood, (*e.g.* unsightly, health hazard), by reason of its ruinous or dilapidated 3.30

condition (1984, s.79). Procedure is by way of notice requiring the owner (13.10) either to carry out works of repair or restoration or, at his own election, to demolish the building or a part of it. This procedure is subject to special appeals and enforcement provisions contained in 1984, Part IV, which will permit the owner to challenge the notice by way of appeal on specified grounds, will give the authority power to do works in default of compliance with the notice, and creates offences of non-compliance. No provision is made for removing, rehousing or compensating tenants.

4. *Fire Precautions*

13.31   **Fire Precautions Act 1971.** Apart from the provisions governing fire precautions in houses in multiple occupation, and common lodging houses, which are considered in the next chapter (14.29-14.32, 14.46), there is not much legislation in force governing fire precautions in housing. The principal enactment is the Fire Precautions Act 1971. Save in relation to a house which is used as a single dwelling, a fire certificate could be required by the fire authority, but section 3 of the Fire Precaution Act 1971 which would give them this power has still not been brought into force. Some part of the Act is in force, however: section 1 makes a fire certificate mandatory for premises subject to a designated use, but the only designated use relevant to housing is use for providing sleeping accommodation, for staff or guests, in connection with the carrying on of a business as a hotel or a boarding house (S.I. 1972 No. 238).

13.32   **Building Act 1984.** Local authorities enjoy a residual power to require fire precautions, but only in buildings which exceed two storeys in height and in which the floor of any upper storey is or will be 20 feet above the surface of the street or ground at any point around the building (1984, s.72). The building must, additionally, be one which is let in flats or tenements, or is used as an inn, hotel, boarding-house, hospital, nursing home, boarding school, children's home or similar institution, or is used as a restaurant, shop, store or warehouse and has sleeping accommodation for employees on the upper floor.

13.33   **Procedure.** The authority may serve notice on the owner of the building, requiring the execution of such works or the provision of such other facilities as may be necessary to provide the building with such means of escape from fire as the authority consider necessary in respect of each of the storeys of the building above the 20-foot limit specified

(1984, s.72). Owner is defined for these purposes (1984, s.126, *cf.* 13.10), again in terms similar to the Housing Act 1985 as the person for the time being receiving the rack-rent, including an agent or trustee, or the person who would receive it if the premises were let at a rack-rent. The provisions are subject to the special appeals and enforcement procedures contained in Part IV of the 1984 Act (13.30).

5. *Sanitary Accommodation*

Powers. Local authorities have a duty to serve notice on an owner (13.10) of premises, requiring the provision of closets, when a building has insufficient sanitary accommodation, or when any part of the building occupied as a separate dwelling has insufficient sanitary accommodation (1984, s.64, as amended). They also have a duty to serve a similar notice if they are satisfied that such sanitary accommodation as exists is in such a state as to be prejudicial to health or a nuisance (13.07-13.08) and cannot be rendered satisfactory without reconstruction (1984, s.64). For the purposes of this latter provision, local authorities not only enjoy their usual powers of entry (13.04), but are also entitled to apply tests or otherwise examine the closet's condition (1936, s.48).

13.34

Procedures. If, on examination, the authority come to the conclusion that the closet can be rendered satisfactory without reconstruction, they shall serve notice requiring the execution of such works as may be necessary (1936, s.45). Such a notice may, however, be served on the owner or occupier. Finally, the authority have power to require the replacement of earth or other (non-water) closets with water closets, even if the existing closets are in all other respects satisfactory (1936, s.47). This power can, however, only be used if there is a sufficient supply of water and sewer available. In the case of one such "substitution" order, the authority must pay half the costs of the installation; but the authority have a choice between ordering the owner to execute the works and recovering half the costs from them, and doing the work themselves and recovering half the costs from the owner (1984, s.66).

13.35

Appeals, Works in Default and Offences. These provisions are subject to the appeals procedure contained in 1984, Part IV (13.30), which will entitle the person served to challange a notice, by way of appeal, but which also entitle the authority to carry out works in default, and create offences of non-compliance. In addition, there are three further offences

13.36

related to sanitary accommodation:

(*a*) **Flushing or Deodorising.** Failure to keep the convenience supplied with water for flushing, or in the case of an earth closet with dry earth or other suitable deodorising material (1936, s.51);

(*b*) **Injury, Fouling and Obstruction.** When a convenience is used by more than one family, anyone who injures or improperly fouls the convenience, or anything used in connection with the convenience, or who wilfully or negligently obstructs the drain leading from the convenience, commits an offence (1936, s.52); and

(*c*) **Insanitary State.** When a convenience is used by more than one family, leaving the convenience or the approach to the convenience in an insanitary state, for want of cleaning or attention, is also an offence (1936, s.52.).

6. *Drains and Sewers*

13.37   **Powers and Procedure.** Local authorities enjoy generous powers to require owners (13.10) to make satisfactory provision for drainage and sewage, *e.g.* if a drain or sewer admits subsoil water, or is prejudicial to health or is a nuisance (1984, ss.21, 59). In some circumstances, they may require remedial action by an occupier as well as, or instead of, by an owner: *e.g.* in the case of a blockage (Public Health Act 1961, s.17). In this last case, the authority can require removal of a blockage within 48 hours, in default of compliance with which they may themselves enter and carry out the works in default, recovering their expenses of so doing. An authority may also secure repair of a drain or sewer, if they conclude: (*a*) that it is not sufficiently maintained and kept in good repair; and (*b*) that it could be repaired at a cost of less than £250 (Public Health Act 1961, s.17). This power proceeds by way of notice of intention to carry out the works themselves, and recover the costs of so doing. There is no appeal against either of the last two classes of notice, but in each case the authority's decision can be challenged by way of defence to the claim for recovery of expenses. Local authorities have additional discretionary powers to cleanse drains, at the request and cost of an owner or occupier (Public Health Act 1961, s.22).

7. *Food Storage*

13.38   **Powers and Procedure.** Local authorities have power to require the provision of sufficient and suitable accommodation for the storage of food in houses, or in parts of a building occupied as separate dwellings (1984, s.70). The power proceeds by way of notice on the owner

(13.10), who may challenge the notice under Part IV, 1984 Act (13.30), which also gives the authority power to execute works in default, and recover the costs of so doing.

8. *Vermin*

Powers. Vermin are harboured by filth. It follows that, not uncommonly, the property most in need of repair will be verminous, for everyday experience shows how impossible it is as a matter of practice for those living in shoddy property to keep the premises clean, and how little incentive there is constantly to clean up, when the more serious problems of disrepair are never remedied. If the local authority are satisfied that premises are so filthy, or in such an unwholesome condition, as to be prejudicial to health (13.07) or verminous, they are bound to take action (1936, s.83, as amended).   13.39

Procedure. Action is by way of notice served on either the owner (13.09) or the occupier. The notice may require such steps as may be necessary for preventing the prejudiciality to health, or removing and destroying the vermin, which steps can include, if necessary, the removal of wallpaper and other wall-coverings, papering or repapering, painting and distempering, at the option of the person served (1936, s.83, as amended). In the event of non-compliance, the authority may execute works in default, and seek to recover their costs from the person served, though it will be a defence to such an action to show either: (*a*) that the notice was not necessary; or (*b*) that as between owner and occupier, it is the other who should have been served (1936, s.83).   13.40

Gas Attack. In some cases, the premises may be in such a condition that a gas attack is called for. A gas attack is carried out by, and at the cost of, the authority, who must give notice to both owner and occupier of their intention to proceed. They may require the premises to be vacated, and may even require neighbouring premises to be vacated, during the attack, in which cases they must provide alternative temporary accommodation, free of charge (1936, s.83; Public Health Act 1961, s.36). A notice requiring the premises to be vacated may be appealed, but subject to the right of appeal it is an offence not to comply with it (1936, s.83).   13.41

9. *Disease*

Classes of Disease. These provisions govern notifiable diseases, and   13.42

infectious diseases. A notifiable disease means cholera, plague, relapsing fever, smallpox, typhus or any other disease specified by the Secretary of State in regulations (Public Health (Control of Disease) Act 1984, ss.10, 13).

(i) *Notifiable diseases*

13.43   Classes of Offences concerning Notifiable Disease. There are three classes of offence related to notifiable diseases:
(*a*) Enquiries by New Occupier. If a person seeking to rent premises asks whether there is, or during the preceding six weeks has been, anyone in the house suffering from a notifiable disease, it is a criminal offence, committed by anyone involved in letting the house, or showing the house with a view to its being let, or who has recently ceased to occupy the house, to give an answer known to be false (Public Health (Control of Disease) Act 1984, s.29).
(*b*) Clearance Certificates. A person letting premises in which someone has suffered from a notifiable disease, without first securing a clearance certificate from the local authority or a registered G.P., commits an offence (Public Health (Control of Disease) Act 1984, s.29).
(*c*) Departing Occupiers. If notice has been given both to the owner (13.10) and to an occupier, by the local authority informing them of their obligations in relation to notifiable diseases, anyone who ceases to occupy premises in which, to his knowledge, anyone has, within the six weeks prior to his departure, suffered from a notifiable disease, may commit one of three, further offences: (i) failing to have the house and any articles within it liable to retain infection, disinfected and certifed as such by authority or registered G.P.; (ii) failing to give the owner of the premises notice of the existence of the disease; (iii) giving a false answer to an owner who expressly asks whether anyone has been suffering from a notifiable disease during the six weeks before departure (Public Health (Control of Disease) Act 1984, s.30).

(ii) *Infectious diseases*

13.44   Cleansing of Premises and Property. If the Medical Officer of Health, or proper officer of the authority, certifies that premises need cleansing of infectious disease (which includes, but is not limited to the specified notifiable diseases, *cf.* 13.42), or articles in the premises likely to retain infection require cleansing or destruction, the local authority must give notice to the occupier that they intend to enter and cleanse or destroy, unless within 24 hours the occupier notifies them that he will himself execute all works as are specified in the notice, within a time to be stated for this purpose in the body of the notice (Public Health (Control of Disease) Act 1984, s.31). If there is no counter-notice, or if the occupier fails to comply with his counter-notice, the authority may carry out the works in default of compliance and recover their costs. If the authority form the view that the occupier would in any event be unable to comply, they may dispense with the notice, and proceed directly to the works, but must then bear the cost themselves.

Removal and Vacating. The authority enjoy additional power to re-   13.45
move persons fom the premises, with consent or on an order of a justice of the peace, but only if the Medical Officer of Health or proper officer has certified that this is necessary (Public Health (Control of Disease) Act 1984, s.32). The authority may also order the house to be vacated for the purpose of disinfecting it. In either event, the authority may provide, free of charge, alternative, temporary accommodation.

14 Overcrowding, Multiple Occupation and Common Lodging Houses

14.01   **Governing Legislation.** Overcrowding is dealt with in Part X of the Housing Act 1985, save to the extent that it concerns houses in multiple occupation, in which case the provisions are to be found in Part XI of the 1985 Act. The overcrowding provisions in houses in multiple occupation (H.M.O.s) will be discussed under the latter heading. H.M.O.s are dealt with in Part XI of the Housing Act 1985. Common lodging houses are governed by Part XII of the 1985 Act. These subjects are treated together in one chapter because in practice the problems tend to overlap.

14.02   **Local Authorities.** The authorities who have responsibility for all of these provisions are the same as those who have general responsibility under the 1985 Act (12.09), save that in the area of a Housing Action Trust (3.78) these powers may be transferred to the Trust, additional to or instead of the local authority (Housing Act 1988, s.65).

14.03   **Inspection.** The Housing Act duties to be considered in the present chapter are amongst those for the purposes of which the authority are bound to consider housing conditions in their districts on an annual basis (12.10; 1985, s.605). In addition, whenever it appears to an authority that occasion has arisen for a report on overcrowding in their district, they must inspect and prepare such a report for submission to the Secretary of State, including in the report their proposals for dealing with the problem by way of providing new accommodation (1985, s.334). The Secretary of State has power to require them to carry out such an inspection.

14.04   **Powers of Entry.** The authority enjoy the powers of entry referred to in connection with the unfitness provisions (12.38). In addition, there are further powers to enable the authority to obtain a warrant of entry for the purpose of examining premises to decide whether powers under Part

XI (14.12-14.43), should be exercised (1985, s.397).

1. *Overcrowding*

(i) *Definition*

Use As A Separate Dwelling. The overcrowding provisions apply to 14.05
premises used or suitable for use as a separate dwelling (1985, s.343).
It is clear that as much as a house could be overcrowded, or as little as
a single room.

Alternative Tests. There are alternative tests of overcrowding. If either 14.06
is offended, the premises are overcrowded in law:
(*a*) **Room standard.** There is overcrowding whenever there are so
many people in a house that any two or more of those persons, being ten
or more years old, and of opposite sexes, not being persons living
together as husband and wife, have to sleep in the same room (1985,
s.325). For these purposes, children under ten may be disregarded. A
room, however, means any room normally used in the locality as either
a bedroom *or* a living room (1985, s.325). This is important because a
kitchen is usually considered to be a living room, and may so be held in
this connection, provided at least that it is big enough to accommodate
a bed (*Zaitzeff* v. *Olmi*, 1952). The final point to note, which reduces
the impact of this test, is that there is overcrowding not when two or
more people actually do sleep in the same room, as prescribed, but when
they must do so. Thus, a couple, with two children, of opposite sexes
and ten years old or more, with two living rooms, are not overcrowded,
because the couple could occupy separate rooms, with one each of the
children (of the appropriate sex).
(*b*) **Space Standard.** This standard works by the calculation of a
permitted number for the dwelling, in one of two ways, and the lower
number thus calculated is the permitted number for the dwelling (1985,
s.326). One test is based on the number of living rooms in the dwelling
(disregarding a room of less than 50 square feet): one room, two
persons; two rooms, three persons; three rooms, five persons; four
rooms, seven and a half persons; five rooms or more, ten persons plus
two for each room in excess of five rooms. The reference to a "half
person" is because, for these purposes, a child below the age of one
counts not at all, and a child from one year old but who has not yet
reached ten counts as a half. The other test is based on floor areas of
each room size: less than 50 square feet, no-one; 50 to less than 70
square feet, half a person; 70 to less than 90 square feet, one person; 90

to less than 110 square feet, one and a half persons; 110 square feet or larger, two persons.

(ii) *Permissible overcrowding*

14.07   **Categories.** There are four circumstances in which overcrowding, though it offends the definitions set out above, is still permissible:

(*a*) **Licensed overcrowding.** On the application of an occupier, or an intending occupier, of a dwelling (but not on the application of the landlord, or of the local authority), a licence may be issued, in prescribed form, and which lasts for no more than one year at a time (1985, s.330). The licence is issued by the local authority, having regard to exceptional circumstances, expedience and, where appropriate, seasonal increases in population. The licence must state how many people are to be permitted, a copy must be served on the landlord, and it may be revoked at any time, by one month's notice.

(*b*) **Temporary overcrowding.** There is no overcrowding if the additional people are members of the occupier's family, staying with him temporarily (1985, s.329). A child away at boarding school is considered to be in permanent rather than temporary residence (*Zaitzeff* v. *Olmi*, 1952).

(*c*) **Natural growth.** Natural growth occurs when a child achieves one of the relevant ages (14.06). If the occupier applies to the local authority for alternative accommodation, either before the child reaches the relevant age, or else before any prosecution is instigated (or possession proceedings, *cf.* 14.11), there will be no illegal overcrowding until *either* there is an offer of suitable alternative accommodation (14.08) by the authority, which the occupier fails to accept, or the opportunity arises, after the child reaches the relevant age, of asking someone else living in the house, who is not a member of the occupier's family, to leave, which opportunity the occupier fails to take (1985, s.328). An occupier need only ask someone else to leave if it is reasonably practicable for that person to leave, which is to be considered in all the circumstances, including whether or not there was suitable alternative accommodation available to him. The exemption also only continues to apply provided all the people sleeping in the house are those who were sleeping there at the date on which the child reached the relevant age, or are children of such people.

(*d*) **Original overcrowding.** This refers to premises overcrowded when the overcrowding provisions themselves first applied to the house (Housing (Consequential Provisions) Act 1985, Sched. 4). As the provisions have applied throughout the country since at least 1935, this exemption is unlikely to be of much relevance today.

Suitable Alternative Accommodation. Although the same phrase is 14.08
used in the Rent Act 1977 (5.91) and the Housing Acts 1985 (3.42) and
1988 (4.40-4.42), the term has its own meaning in the context of
overcrowding (14.07, (*c*), (*d*)). Alternative accommodation is only
suitable for these purposes if the occupier and family can live in the
house without overcrowding, the authority certify it as suitable to his
needs and the needs of his family as regards security of tenure,
proximity to work, means, and otherwise, and, if the house belongs to
the authority, they can certify it as being suitable to his needs as regards
extent of accommodation (1985, s.342). This last they may only do if
they provide a house with two bedrooms (*not* living rooms), for four
people, three bedrooms for five, and four bedrooms for seven. It is,
accordingly, a higher standard than that set by the overcrowding limits.

(iii) *Offences*

Categories of Offence. There are three sets of offences created by the 14.09
overcrowding provisions:
(*a*) **Rent Book Offences.** Every rent book or similar document must
contain: (i) a summary of the overcrowding offences; (ii) a statement of
the power of the authority to licence overcrowding (14.07, (*a*)); and (iii)
a statement of the permitted number of occupants (14.06, (*b*)), (1985,
s.332). Either the occupier or the landlord can ask the authority for a
written statement of permitted number at any time. The authority can
require the occupier to produce his rent book for inspection, and it is an
offence to fail to comply with this request provided the occupier has it
(1985, s.336). It is also an offence to fail to provide the prescribed
information, although it is a defence to a charge based on the insertion
of an incorrect permitted number, that the number has been provided by
the authority (1985, 332).
(*b*) **Landlord's Offences.** A landlord who causes or permits a
dwelling to be overcrowded commits an offence (1985, s.331). This may
occur when the landlord has reasonable cause to believe there might be
illegal overcrowding, or by failing to make enquiries as to the number
which it is intended shall occupy a dwelling, or, if the authority serve
notice on the landlord that there is illegal overcrowding, by failing to
take possession proceedings (14.11; 1985, s.331). Finally, unless the
authority already know of the overcrowding, the landlord is obliged to
notify the authority once he learns of it (1985, s.333).
(*c*) **Occupier's Offences.** The occupier commits an offence when he

causes or permits premises to be illegally overcrowded (1985, s.327). The authority have power to seek information as to numbers in a dwelling, from the occupier, and failing to comply with this demand, or providing an answer which the occupier knows to be false in a material particular, is also an offence (1985, s.335).

14.10 **Prosecution of Offences.** It is clear that the local authority may themselves commit an offence under these provisions. No one but a local authority may prosecute an overcrowding offence committed by a private individual, but a private individual may prosecute an authority, with the consent of the Attorney-General (1985, s.339). The Attorney-General's consent will not easily be forthcoming.

(iv) *Possession proceedings*

14.11 **Protection.** Rent Act protection is lost to occupiers whose premises are illegally overcrowded (Rent Act 1977, s.101). However, only illegal overcrowding removes Rent Act protection, so that permissible overcrowding will allow the occupier to remain in the premises. The landlord must still determine a tenancy at common law (1.39-1.50). In addition, the authority may themselves bring proceedings for possession of premises illegally overcrowded, and recover their costs from the landlord (1985, s.338). The authority must serve prior notice on the occupier, which gives the occupier 14 days within which to abate the overcrowding. There is no equivalent lifting of Housing Act 1988 security for Housing Act assured tenants.

2. *Houses in Multiple Occupation*

14.12 **Single Household.** A house in multiple occupation (H.M.O.) is a house occupied by persons who do not form a single household (1985, s.345). This definition was extended by the Local Government and Housing Act 1989 to include parts of buildings, *i.e.* flats in multiple occupation (1985, s.345(2)). Occupation for these purposes includes any class of occupation (Chapter 1), not just tenants, so that a former tenant occupying pending the expiry of a suspended possession order was held still to be in occupation under these provisions (*Minford Properties* v. *Hammersmith London Borough Council*, 1978). The key question is whether the occupants form a single household. There are no certain criteria for this (*Simmons* v. *Pizzey*, 1977). One definition offered is occupation by ''a number of persons where the relationships between the various individuals resident at any one time are so tenuous as to support the view that they can neither singly nor collectively be regarded as forming a single household" (Ministry of Housing and Local Government Circular 67/69, repeated in D.o.E. Circular 12/86).

Hostels. A house used as a hostel for women, including alcoholics and the mentally disturbed, who stayed for different lengths of time and lived in dormitories has been held to be an H.M.O. (*Silbers* v. *Southwark London Borough Council*, 1977). Similarly, a Women's Aid Refuge, in which 75 people were living temporarily, was held to be an H.M.O. even though no-one had any particular part of the house to themselves, and the business of the house (eating, cooking, cleaning), was organised collectively (*Simmons* v. *Pizzey*, 1977). People living in single rooms but sharing a kitchen could still be held to constitute a legal household (*Hackney London Borough Council* v. *Ezedinma*, 1981). A bed-and-breakfast hotel used to accommodate the homeless can be an H.M.O. (*R.* v. *Hackney London Borough Council, ex p. Thrasyvoulou*, 1986; *R.* v. *Hackney London Borough Council, ex p. Evenbray*, 1987). 14.13

Classes of Action. There are five classes of action which an authority may take in relation to an H.M.O., in addition to the availability of the HMO grant for owners wishing, or compelled, to improve (12.54). They are: 14.14
   (i) *overcrowding controls*;
   (ii) *registration schemes*;
   (iii) *execution of works*;
   (iv) *management regulations*; and
   (v) *control orders*.
These powers are additional to those considered in the last two chapters.

(i) *Overcrowding controls*

Overcrowding Notice. Under 1985, s.358, a local authority may serve notice in respect of an H.M.O. which appears to them to accommodate, or to be likely to accommodate, an excessive number of persons, specifying the maximum number who are to sleep in each room in the house. The notice may also state that some rooms are unsuitable for sleeping. The maximum stated may be age-related. The notice is to be served on the occupier of the house, or on any person having control and management of the house. The notice must additionally contain one of two further classes of prohibition: 14.15
   (*a*) **Reduction of Existing Occupation.** The person served must not:
(i) knowingly permit a room to be occupied other than in accordance

with the notice; and (ii) allow so many people to live in the house that it is impossible for them to occupy without offending the notice, or without sleeping in parts of the house which are not rooms, or without two persons of the opposite sex and over the age of 12 (*cf.* 14.06(*b*)), not living together as man and wife, being obliged to sleep in the same room;

(*b*) **Natural Wastage.** The person served must not: (i) knowingly permit a room to be occupied by a new resident, other than in accordance with the notice; and (ii) knowingly permit a new resident to occupy any part of the premises if it is not possible so to do without offending the notice, or without sleeping in parts of the house which are not rooms, or without two persons of the opposite sex and over the age of 12, not living together as man and wife, being obliged to sleep in the same room.

14.16   Procedures. Breach of either class of notice is a criminal offence. The authority must provide seven days' notice of intention before serving the overcrowding notice itself, to permit appeal, the effect of which will be to defer the operative date of the notice until the final determination of the appeal. The notice may be revoked or varied by the authority at any time, on application by someone with an estate of interest in the house, and a refusal to revoke or vary may also be appealed. If the authority have served notice of class (*b*), above, they may revoke it and substitute a notice of class (*a*) at any time.

14.17   Overcrowding Directions. Under 1985, s.354, the authority have additional power to serve directions to reduce overcrowding, by fixing a limit to the number of persons, or households, or both, who may occupy the house, in order either to remedy, or to prevent the occurrence of, a state of affairs calling for a works notice (14.24-14.28). Though the house must be in multiple occupation at the time of service of the directions, the number stated may be a larger number than is currently in occupation, so that, to this extent, it is not exclusively a direction to *reduce* (*Simmons* v. *Pizzey,* 1977). Directions do not require the owner or occupier of the house to reduce to the number set, by eviction: if there are already more people in the house than the authority have specified, his duty is not to permit the number to increase further, and not to replace departing occupants. If the number set is higher than the number in the house for the time being, the duty is not to pass the number set.

14.18   Procedure. The authority must again give seven days' notice of intention to issue directions, and must post a copy of this notice and, when they issue, the directions, in some part of the house where it is accessible to those living there (*e.g.* entrance hall). There is no direct right to appeal the directions themselves, but the persons served may make representations to the authority between notice of intention and issue of directions, and may apply for variation or revocation of directions, on refusal of which application an appeal may be made to the county court. It is an offence to fail to comply with the duties imposed by the directions.

Directions and Works Notice. Finally, an authority may, when issuing a "works notice" (14.24-14.28), instead of specifying such works as are necessary for the people presently in occupation, specify lesser works for a smaller number, and contemporaneously issue a direction under the last paragraph (1985, s.352).   14.19

Additional Powers. When an overcrowding notice or directions has or have been issued, the authority enjoy additional powers to require of any occupier information that enables them to supervise continued occupation of the premises. It is a criminal offence to fail to comply with such a request, or to reply with information known to be false in a material particular (1985, s.356).   14.20

(ii) *Registration scheme*

Power and Procedure. Local authorities enjoy power to introduce registration schemes, for all H.M.O.s, or for all H.M.O.s within a specified description, or area, which have no greater purpose in themselves than to record information about H.M.O.s in their districts (1985, s.346). The scheme must be approved by the Secretary of State for the Environment. A scheme may also be revoked at any time, with such approval. The authority must publicise the scheme, and any steps which the scheme requires people to take, such as the provision to the authority of particulars of occupancy, and subsequent changes in such particulars. Authorities may charge for notification under the scheme (S.I. 1991 No. 982). The authority obtain additional powers to require information from persons with an interest, or living, in an H.M.O. within a scheme, failure to comply with which request, or compliance with which contains what is known to be a mis-statement, constituting a criminal offence.   14.21

Control Provisions. Onto a registration scheme, the authority may graft "control provisions" (not to be confused with control orders: 14.22

14.36-14.43)(1985, s.347). Such provisions cannot affect occupation at the time they are imposed, nor can they affect occupation in a house which contains no more than two households, or one household plus four other persons.

14.23   **Scope of Provisions.** The provisions may prevent occupation of a house which is not registered under the scheme, or prevent occupation in numbers greater than those for which the house is so registered. Control provisions may empower the authority to decline registration, on the grounds of unsuitability of premises, or that the person to have control of the house is not a fit and proper person to do so. They may also empower the authority to impose a precondition to registration, by way of requiring works to make the premises suitable for the extent of use for which registration is sought. The authority are bound to give written reasons for refusal of registration. There is power to apply to the authority for variation of the terms of a registration, and refusal of both application for variation and original registration may be appealed. Breach of any requirement of the scheme, including occupation of an unregistered house, or occupation by a number in excess of those for which the house is registered, is a criminal offence.

(iii) *Execution of works*

14.24   **Works Notices.** Authorities can require works to be carried out to houses in multiple occupation. Although the general powers now encompass works relating to means of escape from fire it is still necessary to consider separately the additional powers, and duties, in relation to the latter. It should be noted that these powers are additional to those considered in the last two chapters, and that grant-aid will be available for an owner or other person served with a notice under these provisions (12.68). Authorities must keep a register of any works notices (1985, s.352).

14.25   **General Works.** Under 1985, s.352, an authority may serve notice requiring the execution of those works it considers necessary where the premises fails to meet one or more of the requirements set out and because of the failure the premises are not reasonably suitable for occupation by the number of people or households for the time being accommodated on the premises. Alternatively, the notice may specify a lesser schedule of works, and be accompanied by overcrowding directions (14.17). The requirements are (*cf.* 12.12):
    (*a*) satisfactory facilities for the storage and preparation and cooking

of food including an adequate number of sinks with a satisfactory supply of hot and cold water (although note that in *R.* v. *Hackney L.B.C., ex p. Evanbray* (1987), it was held that no reasonable local authority could require the provision of cooking facilities in a hotel where food was available);

(*b*) an adequate number of suitably located water closets for the exclusive use of the occupants;

(*c*) an adequate number of suitably located fixed baths or showers and wash-hand basins each of which has an satisfactory supply of hot and cold water for the exclusive use of occupiers;

(*d*) an adequate means of escape from fire; and

(*e*) adequate other fire precautions.

Service of Notice. The notice is to be served on the person having control of the house (12.18), or on anyone to whom the house (*i.e.* the whole house, not just a part of the house), is let, or on anyone who, as agent or trustee of the person to whom the house is let, receives rent or other payments from tenants or lodgers in the house (1985, s.352). The authority must also serve a copy of the notice on anyone else they know to have an interest in the house. If the authority are themselves the landlords, then it would appear that an authority could only serve a notice on themselves if someone else had one such interest (*cf.* 12.19), but as the power is discretionary, it is unlikely that any authority would wish to engage in the exercise where they themselves have control of the house. 14.26

Compliance. The authority have power to withdraw the notice if, after service, they are satisfied that the numbers in the house have been reduced to such an extent that the works are no longer necessary (1985, s.352). In the absence of withdrawal, even if there is an appeal, the works must be executed within such time as the authority specify in the notice, which must be not less than 21 days after service, or such longer time as the authority may subsequently permit: an authority will normally permit a longer time if there is an appeal (14.28), though they are not bound to do so. However, appeal defers any criminal offence: it is an offence to fail to comply with the notice within the time specified, or allowed, or within such longer time as the court may allow of the final determination of an appeal (1985, s.376). Once there has been criminal non-compliance, or if the authority are of the opinion that reasonable progress towards compliance is not being made, the authority have power, on giving seven days' notice, to execute the works in default, and to recover their costs of so doing (1985, s.375). 14.27

14.28   **Appeal.** Appeal lies to the county court, and must be issued within 21 days of service of notice (1985, s.353). The court has limited powers, and there are limited grounds on which an appeal may be pursued. These include: that the notice was not justified having regard to conditions in the house, and number of occupants; that the authority have unreasonably refused to agree an alternative schedule of works; that the works required are unreasonable in extent or character, or are unnecessary; and, that the time allowed is insufficient. If the court is satisfied that since service the numbers in the house have been reduced, it may revoke the order, or vary the schedule of works, provided that it is also satisfied that adequate steps have been taken, (*e.g.* by the issue of directions: 14.17), to keep the numbers down. The reference to an alternative schedule of works underlies the essentially administrative nature of these provisions. However, there will invariably have been prior consultation between authority and person served, and even after service the authority may decline to take further action, or postpone the time for compliance with the notice, to enable the person served to execute such alternative works.

14.29   **Means of Escape from Fire.** While the provisions governing means of escape from fire, which are now contained alongside those governing general works in 1985, s.352 (14.24) are on their face discretionary, in the case of any house within a class designated by the Secretary of State for the Environment, the powers become mandatory, *i.e.* the authority are bound to use them (1985, s.365). The Secretary of State has used this designation power to make mandatory application of the provisions to houses which comprise at least three storeys (excluding a storey lying wholly or mainly below the floor level of the principal entrance to the house), and of which the combined floor area (including the area of any staircase) of all storeys (therefore now including basements and semi-basements) exceeds 500 square metres (S.I. 1981 No. 1576).

14.30   **Partial Closure.** In addition to the power under section 352 to order works, if the authority conclude that existing means of escape would be adequate, were part of the H.M.O. not used for human habitation, they may make a closing order on that part (1985, s.368). Alternatively, they may accept an undertaking that part is not used for human habitation. In either event, the same provisions as in relation to unfitness (12.24-12.28) apply, including as to rehousing and compensation (12.100-12.110), save that the only ground on which the authority may subsequently determine the order is that there has been such a change of circumstances that the means of escape from fire would then be adequate, even if the formerly closed part were again to be used.

Scope of Notice. Before serving a notice, the authority are bound to   14.31
consult with the fire authority (1985, s.365). The extent of precautions
required can include smoke screens at the top of a flight of stairs
(*Horgan* v. *Birmingham Corporation*, 1964), and the authority can have
regard to the age, character, or other requirements of the particular
occupants, including whether or not there is any supervision, *e.g.* by
way of a housekeeper, in the house (*Kingston-Upon-Hull County
Council* v. *University of Hull*, 1979). The notice must specify a time for
completion of the works, although the authority may subsequently
extend this time, and if the notice is not complied with not only may a
criminal offence be committed, but the authority also acquire power to
execute the works in default, and recover their costs of so doing (14.27).

Cumulative Provisions. These provisions are additional to those con-   14.32
sidered in the last chapter: 13.31-13.33.

(iv) *Management Regulations*

Proper Standards of Management. Under 1985, s.369 the Secretary of   14.33
State may issue regulations ("Management Regulations") for ensuring
that the person managing a house in multiple occupation observes
proper standards of management (1985, s.369). The manager of the
house is defined for the purposes of the regulations as an owner or
lessee who, directly or indirectly, receives rent or other payments from
tenants or lodgers; if the rents are received through an agent or trustee,
the agent or trustee is the manager (1985, s.398). The current
Management Regulations prescribed by the Secretary of State are to be
found in S.I. 1990 No. 830. The regulations require the manager of the
house to ensure the repair, maintenance, cleansing or, as necessary the
good order of -
   (*a*) all means of water supply and drainage in the house;
   (*b*) parts of the house and installations in common use;
   (*c*) living accommodation;
   (*d*) windows and other means of ventilation;
   (*e*) means of escape from fire, apparatus, systems, and other things
provided by way of fire precautions;
   (*f*) outbuildings, yards etc in common use.
The manager must also:
   (*g*) make satisfactory arrangements for the disposal of refuse and litter
from the house;

(*h*) ensure the taking of reasonable precautions for the general safety of residents;

(*i*) display in the house a notice of the name and address and telephone number, if any, of the manager;

(*j*) provide specified information to the local authority about the occupancy of the house where the authority give him written notice to that effect.

Note: Those living in the house have duties imposed upon them to ensure that the manager can effectively carry out these requirements. Failure to comply with the regulations is a criminal offence.

14.34   **Execution of Works.** If the authority are of the opinion that the condition of the premises is defective because of a failure to comply with the management regulations, they may in addition order the execution of works (1985, s.372). Notice is served on the manager of the house (14.33). Notice must specify not only the works to be carried out, but a a time of not less than 21 days for commencement and a reasonable time for completion. If there is an appeal, the notice does not take effect until such time as the court may allow from the final determination of the appeal (14.35). Once the notice takes effect, however, the authority acquire the right to carry out works in default and recover their expenses of so doing, in the same way as failure to comply with a works notice under 1985, section 352 (14.27). It is a criminal offence to fail to comply with a notice.

14.35   **Appeal.** An appeal against a works notice under these provisions is on similar grounds to those available against a work notice under section 352 (14.28).

(v) *Control order*

14.36   **Vesting Control in Authority.** This has been described as the most draconian measure which a local authority can apply to an H.M.O. Substantively, it involves vesting in the authority themselves "control," by which is meant management and possession, of the premises.

14.37   **Conditions.** The power to make a control order arises if either: (*a*) a notice has been served or directions given under sections 372 (14.34), 352 (14.24-14.28), or 354 (14.17) of the 1985 Act; or (*b*) it appears to the authority that action might be taken under any of these provisions (1985, s.379). Further, it must appear to the authority that living conditions in the house are such that, for the protection or the safety, welfare or health of people living in the house, it is necessary to make the order. The inclusion of welfare would seem to enable the authority to take into account factors which would not necessarily qualify under any of the specified provisions, *e.g.* smells, noise, anti-social behaviour. The threat of eviction has been held a proper welfare consideration (*R. v. Southwark London Borough, ex p. Lewis Levy,* 1983).

Procedure. The control order comes into force as soon as it is made (1985, s.379). It is deliberately peremptory, to prevent action against occupiers in retaliation for, or to remove conditions calling for, the order. As soon as practicable after making the order, the authority enter into possession of the premises and take such steps as appear to them necessary to protect the safety, welfare or health of residents. The authority must also post a copy of the order, and a notice setting out the effect of the order, in some place in the house where it is accessible to those living in it (*cf.* 14.18), and serve a copy of the order and notice on anyone the authority know to have been the manager of the premises (14.33), and anyone else with an interest in it. Existing orders under the provisions considered hitherto come to an end on the commencement of the control order (1985, s.381).   14.38

Rights of Occupation. The authority may, but need not, exclude from the effect of the order a part of the premises occupied by someone having an interest in the house, though not someone without such an interest who merely qualifies as the manager of the house (1985, s.380). In relation to existing tenancies, Rent Act and Housing Act 1988 security will continue notwithstanding the control order (1985, s.382), although any new tenancies which the authority may create will not be protected by the Rent Acts or the Housing Act 1988 (1985, s.381), but would seem to be secure tenancies, under the Housing Act 1985, at least until there is a determination of the control order, at which time they will become protected or assured. The authority have power to grant new tenancies or other rights of occupation (*i.e.* licences), though they cannot grant a fixed-term entitlement for a period in excess of one month, or a periodic right which requires more than four weeks' notice (1985, s.381).   14.39

Life of Order. Unless previously determined by revocation on the authority's own motion, or on application (1985, s.392), or on appeal against imposition of the order or refusal to revoke (14.43), or by compulsory purchase by the authority, the control order lasts exactly five years from the date when it was made (1985, s.392). The authority   14.40

enjoy power to purchase, compulsorily if needs be, a house made the subject of a control order, in which case they are exempt from the obligation to draw up a management scheme (1985, s.394 and Sched. 13), for the improvement of the house, provided the compulsory purchase order is made within 28 days of the control order (14.48).

14.41　　**Powers.** Once the control order is in operation (14.38), the authority have power to do anything which anyone else in possession of the premises could do. They must exercise this power so as to maintain proper standards of management in the house (*cf.* the Management Regulations, 14.33), and are otherwise to take such steps as, had the control order not been imposed, they would have considered necessary by way of notice or directions (1985, s.381). The authority may also take over responsibility for any furniture in the house which has been provided to residents (1985, s.383). The owner of any such furniture may, however, ask the authority to renounce this right, if they think fit. The authority acquire rights to enter the house and any part of it, for the purposes of survey, examination or the execution of works, and if anyone obstructs them in the exercise of this power, they may apply to the magistrates' court for an order to permit such exercise, breach of which is a criminal offence (1985, s.397).

14.42　　**Management Scheme.** In addition, and subject to the exercise of the compulsory purchase power (14.41), the authority must draw up a "management scheme" for the house, within eight weeks of making the order (1985, s.386). If the authority do seek to use their compulsory purchase powers, within 28 days of the control order, this obligation is deferred until eight weeks after the Secretary of State's final decision on the purchase (1985, Sched. 13). The scheme is a plan for the improvement of the house, by way of a statement of what works the authority would have considered necessary under the powers considered in paragraphs (14.24-14.35), above, or under any public health legislation (Chapter 13). The scheme must specify a maximum number of occupants, and must estimate the cost of the works to be executed. A copy of the scheme must be served on anyone known to the authority to have an interest in the house, and anyone else on whom the control order was served (14.38), primarily for the purposes of appeal (14.43). Provision is made for detailed accounts to be drawn up and maintained by the authority (1985, s.390), and for the payment of compensation, on a scale related to market rents, to the dispossessed proprietor (1985, s.389).

Appeal. There are three classes of appeal: 14.43

(*a*) **Against Control Order.** This lies to the county court, and must be made within six weeks of the date a copy of the management scheme is served (1985, s.384). The grounds include: that it was not necessary to make the order to protect the safety, welfare or health of residents; that conditions in the house do not call for a control order; and, that a part of the premises occupied by a dispossessed proprietor ought to have been excluded. If, on an appeal, the court is minded to revoke the order, it may authorise the authority to create longer residential interests than it could otherwise have created (14.39), although only interests which will determine within six months of the proposed date for termination of the order (1985, Sched. 13). The purpose of this power is to protect the occupants when the dispossessed proprietor resumes control.

(*b*) **Against Management Scheme.** An appeal against a management scheme also lies to the county court, and must be brought within six weeks of service of a copy of the scheme: if there is an appeal against the order as well as the scheme, the two appeals should be heard together if possible (1985, Sched. 13). The grounds include: that the works proposed are unreasonable in character and extent; that the number of individuals specified for the house is unreasonably low; and, that the appellant does not accept financial factors in the scheme. The court has power to vary or revoke the scheme, though if it decides to revoke the order itself it need not trouble with the appeal against the scheme.

(*c*) **Against Refusal to Revoke.** This also lies to the county court, and no special grounds are set out, though if the court dismisses an appeal against refusal to revoke, the appellant cannot appeal against a further refusal to revoke for another six months (1985, s.393).

3. *Common Lodging Houses*

Common Rooms. A common lodging house is a house provided for the 14.44 purpose of accommodating by night poor people, who are not members of the same family, and who are allowed to occupy one common room for the purpose of sleeping or eating (1985, s.401). Part only of a house so used can be treated separately as a common lodging house. The essence of the definition is that there should be a common room: whether that common room is one used for eating, or whether it is one used for sleeping. A room will remain a common room even although it is divided up into cubicles.

Registered Keepers. No one may keep a common lodging house unless 14.45

he is registered under the 1985 Act (1985, s.402). The only exceptions to this are persons registered under corresponding local enactments prior to the introduction of these provisions, in the Public Health Act 1936 (now unlikely, but not impossible), and the widow or other member of the family or a registered lodging-house keeper, for a period of four weeks or such longer period as the local authority may allow after his death. The authority are bound to keep a register of common lodging house keepers, and of their deputies, detailing their names and addresses, the location of the common lodging house, and the number who may be accommodated in each (1985, s.403). In the absence of specified grounds for refusal, the authority must register an applicant, though such registration must follow inspection by an officer of the authority. A certificate of registration lasts for the period stated in it, to a maximum of 13 months.

14.46   Refusal of Registration. The grounds for refusal are: (*a*) the proposed keeper, or any deputy employed or to be employed by him, is not a fit person to keep or to be employed in a common lodging house; (*b*) the premises are not suitable or suitably equipped for use as a common lodging house, as regards sanitation, water supply, means of escape from fire, and otherwise; and (*c*) use of the premises as a common lodging house is likely to cause inconvenience or annoyance to other residents of the neighbourhood (1985, s.404). An applicant who has been refused is entitled to demand a statement of grounds for refusal, and the refusal may be appealed to the magistrates' court (1985, ss.404, 405).

14.47   Duties of Keepers. Local authorities enjoy power to make by-laws governing common lodging houses, and the Secretary of State is entitled to require them to use this power (1985, s.406). The by-laws may govern numbers who may be taken in; separation of sexes; cleanliness and ventilation; washing of walls and ceilings; precautions when disease occurs; and, regulations for the general well-ordering of the house. In addition, registered keepers may be required to fix to the outside of the house, a legible and conspicuous notice that the house is a registered common lodging house (1985, s.407). Both keeper and deputy are bound to manage the house and supervise people using it, and one or other of them must be constantly on the premises between nine in the evening and six each morning. They must allow an official of the authority to have free access to all parts of the house, for the purposes of inspection. The authority are entitled to require keepers of houses used by "beggars and vagrants," to provide them with a daily report as to who has used the house during the preceding day and night, but if they exercise this power they must provide proformas for the keeper's use.

Diseases. The keeper is bound to report immediately to the authority 14.48 when someone in the house is found to be suffering from an infectious disease; if the authority have reasonable grounds for believing that someone in a common lodging house is suffering, or has recently suffered, from a notifiable disease (13.42), they may obtain from a justice of the peace a warrant entitling them to enter the common lodging house and examine anyone found there (Public Health (Control of Diseases) Act 1984, s.40). If the authority are satisfied that an occupant of a common lodging house is suffering from a notifiable disease, and that there is a risk of infection to others, they can order him to be removed to any hospital which has room for him and which has agreed to receive him (Public Health (Control of Diseases) Act 1984, s.41) and the magistrates' court may, on application by the authority, order a common lodging house closed on account of the existence or recent existence of notifiable disease within it (Public Health (Control of Diseases) Act 1984, s.42).

Offences and Disqualification. It is an offence to contravene any of 14.49 the provisions governing common lodging houses, including the provisions of a temporary closing order (14.48), or failing to keep premises suitably equipped for use as a common lodging house, or applying while disqualified from registration for registration as a keeper, or making a statement known to be false in an application for registration or renewal of registration (1985, s.408). Disqualification from registration, and cancellation of registration, may occur in the course of prosecution for an offence (1985, s.409).

Index

Accommodation Agencies, 4.58-4.59

Agricultural Workers, 1.67, 4.06, 5.24, 7.18

Armed Forces, 5.71

Assignment, 1.100-1.101
long-lease of, 1.07
protected shorthold tenancy of, 6.41
secure tenancy of, 3.20

Assured Shorthold Tenancy, 6.03, 6.51 *et seq.*
ground for possession, 6.52
prescribed notice, 6.51
rent, 6.53 *et seq.*

Assured Tenancies, 4.01 *et seq.*, 5.03
1980 Housing Act under, 4.02-4.03
assignment of, 4.56
demolition of, 4.35
exceptions to, 4.09-4.23
exempt landlords, 4.19
fixed-term, 4.25
forfeiture of, 4.45
grounds for possession, 4.28 *et seq*
misrepresentation of, 4.46

Assured Tenancies *cont'd.*
homeless persons and, 4.10
implied terms of, 4.55-4.56
qualifying conditions, 4.08-4.09
rent, 4.47-4.54
high, 4.12
low or none, 4.13
statutory periodic, 4.25
subletting of, 4.56
succession to, 4.05
termination of, 4.24-4.25, 4.29

Attendances, 5.43-5.44, 6.08

Bankruptcy, 1.03

Bed-sitting room, 1.22

Block of Flats
acquisition order, 2.22-2.24
right of first refusal, 2.15 *et seq.*

Board, 5.46

Business Lettings, 3.14, 4.15, 5.23

Children
homeless, 10.11 *et seq.*, 10.22, 10.53 *et seq.*

Clearance Areas, 12.44 *et seq.*